Within the Confines

Within the Confines

Women and the Law in Canada

EDITED BY
JENNIFER M. KILTY

Women's Press
Toronto

Within the Confines: Women and the Law in Canada

Edited by Jennifer M. Kilty

First published in 2014 by

Women's Press, an imprint of Canadian Scholars' Press Inc.

425 Adelaide Street West, Suite 200

Toronto, Ontario

M5V 3C1

www.cspi.org

Canadian Scholars' Press Inc./Women's Press gratefully acknowledges financial support for our publishing activities from the Government of Canada through the Canada Book Fund (CBF).

Library and Archives Canada Cataloguing in Publication

Within the confines : women and the law in Canada / edited by Jennifer M. Kilty.

Includes bibliographical references and index. Issued in print and electronic formats.

ISBN 978-0-88961-516-8 (pbk.).—ISBN 978-0-88961-517-5 (pdf).—ISBN 978-0-88961-518-2 (epub)

1. Feminist jurisprudence—Canada. 2. Women—Legal status, laws, etc.—Canada.

3. Women—Canada—Social conditions. 4. Sex discrimination against women—Canada.

I. Kilty, Jennifer M., 1978-, editor

KE509.W57 2014 342.7108'78 C2014-904470-4 KF478.W57 2014 C2014-904471-2

14 15 16 17 18 5 4 3 2 1

Text and cover design by Peggy & Co. Design

Printed and bound in Canada by Webcom.

Contents

Acknowledgements

Editing this wonderful collection of essays by Canadian feminist socio-legal scholars was a privilege. I want to express my thanks and gratitude to the individual authors for their willingness to participate and to contribute their work to this volume. Thank you for producing such interesting and thoughtful chapters, for your careful reflection and consideration of my comments and suggestions, for keeping to such a strict schedule, and for your ongoing support of this project. Working with you has been a pleasure.

Evaluating scholarly texts is a time-consuming and oftentimes thankless job. I would like to express my gratitude to the two anonymous evaluators who provided such thorough and supportive comments. Your careful review of the manuscript greatly enhanced the quality of the book. I would also like to thank the team at the Canadian Scholars' Press/Women's Press, especially Lily Bergh for her initial interest in having me produce an edited volume, and Nancy Reilly, Daniella Balabuk, Caley Clements, and Emma Johnson for their hard work throughout the editorial and production processes. To the production department, thank you for your careful review and assemblage of the manuscript.

Finally, I would like to acknowledge the hard work and dedication of an amazing doctoral candidate and bright young scholar, Erin Dej. Thank you Erin, for your time, effort, and ongoing support. In this project—as in many others—I could not have done it without you.

This book was published with the help of a grant from the University of Ottawa's Publication Assistance Program.

Jennifer M. Kilty

Introduction

Jennifer M. Kilty

What Does It Mean to Take a Critical Perspective?

Knowledge development is a process of moving toward an understanding of the world and of the knowledge that structures our perceptions of that world. Critical social research is thus an analysis of social processes, delving beneath ostensive and dominant conceptual frames to reveal the underlying practices, their historical specificity, and structural manifestations (Harvey, 1990: 3–4).

Given the title of this edited collection, it seems important to initiate a discussion of what it means to take a critical perspective in academic research, particularly that which examines law as a social process, the gendered nature of the law, and thus how law affects women in Canada. In its broadest sense, the notion of a critical perspective or paradigm may best be considered as an umbrella term that houses several "alternative" or radical theoretical and methodological approaches that includes, but is certainly not limited to, feminism, Marxism, and materialism (Guba & Lincoln, 2004; Harvey, 1990). While scholars often debate what it means to adopt a critical perspective in their research (Hammersley, 2005), this book takes up Harvey's (1990) position that to do critical research requires questioning dominant conceptual frames and social processes such that the investigator may come to understand the socio-political and historically situated structural relations of power that shape the world.

Accordingly, taking a critical perspective in academic research requires examining how an individual's or group's lived experiences or material realities are shaped over time by a constellation of social, political, cultural, economic, racial/ethnic/Indigenous, gender, and sexuality factors that become "crystallized (reified) into a series of structures that are now (inappropriately) taken as 'real,' that is, natural and immutable" (Guba & Lincoln,

2004: 26). Moreover, critical scholars tend to place a much greater value on the issues of voice and hegemony than do positivist/post-positivist researchers, which corresponds to the greater volume of critical scholars conducting qualitative and theoretical research. Given that taking a critical perspective often means valuing "voice," the researcher may be required to act as either the "transformative intellectual as advocate and activist" or the "passionate participant as facilitator of multi-voice reconstruction" (Guba & Lincoln, 2004: 29). This point is frequently demonstrated in critical research that claims to offer a prioritized space for those subjugated knowledge(s) and voices from below (Alcoff, 2009; Harding, 2004; Harvey, 1990). Rather than positioning the researcher as expert, adopting a critical perspective can entail listening to and engaging with those voices from below, even facilitating some degree of collaboration with participants, and thus decentring the researcher as expert. In this sense, a critical perspective accepts the value of embedded, embodied, experiential, and material knowledge that may only be accessed by listening to voice rather than speaking for others (Alcoff, 2009).

The goal and aim of critical inquiry, then, is to interpret and provide analytic understanding of the beliefs and discourses that individuals and institutions advance. In so doing, over time we may develop more informed analyses that facilitate our ability to critique and transform the social, political, cultural, economic, colonial, racial/ethnic, and gendered structures that confine, exploit, and disadvantage different groups (Guba & Lincoln, 2004: 30). The critical inquirer is thus also often an advocate or activist who seeks emancipation, social change, and transformation (Adamson, Briskin, & McPhail, 1988; Chunn & Lacombe, 2000; Guba & Lincoln, 2004; Harding, 2004; Harvey, 1990; Kilty, 2014). Unfortunately, research as praxis via advocacy and activism remains a marginalized practice in the sphere of academe, which traditionally prides itself on its objectivism—a point that many critical and feminist scholars reject as impossible and undesirable in lieu of acknowledging the ways in which research is always already subjective. In this sense, a critical perspective often entails examining the situated, processural, and dynamic nature of knowledge production (Harvey, 1990).

Generating critique is essential to taking a critical perspective and it is foundational for engaging socio-political change and transformation. It is upon this premise that feminists have historically engaged with the law in their efforts to garner both formal and substantive equality for women (Adamson et al., 1988; Chunn & Lacombe, 2000). As Harvey writes: "Critical social research is underpinned by a critical-dialectical perspective which attempts to dig beneath the surface of historically specific, oppressive social structures" (1990: 1). If we accept that "knowledge is structured by existing sets of social relations" (Harvey, 1990: 2), then adopting a critical perspective demands that the inquirer examine how social structures produce knowledge that hierarchizes social relations in patterns that maintain power in the hands of the few; namely, in the hands of the White, the wealthy, the heterosexual, and the male.

In this way, critical social research not only engages with the oppressive structures and institutions that it seeks to examine, but it also questions normative knowledge and what Guba and Lincoln (2004) describe as the "received view" (positivism) in research. The goal is to draw attention to the processes and institutions that legitimate and thus also de-legitimate different knowledge sets and approaches to generating knowledge in ways that sustain the normative (and thus gendered, racialized, classed, and heterosexist) social order (Guba & Lincoln, 2004; Harvey, 1990: 6).

Taking a Critical Perspective Specific to Women and the Law

Harvey (1990) and countless others (Adamson et al., 1988; Chunn & Lacombe, 2000; Comack & Balfour, 2004; Guba & Lincoln, 2004; Harding, 1987, 2004; Kilty, 2014; Smith, 1987, 1990) identify feminist work as one of the primary sites of contemporary critical social research. Generally speaking, feminism is considered to be an inherently critical perspective that involves the privileging of women's voices and material experiences in order to examine the structural and embodied ways in which women experience disadvantage, prejudice, discrimination, sexism, and misogyny (Chunn & Lacombe, 2000; Comack & Balfour, 2004; Harding, 1987, 2004; Harvey, 1990; Kilty, 2014; Smith, 1987, 1990). There are a number of internal debates within, and tensions between, the multiple and varied interpretations and applications of feminism. Clearly, different strands of feminist thought reflect varying degrees of criticality. Some maintain a more radical stance, while others advance a more conservative one that may be criticized for upholding normative ideals typically reflective of the status quo (Adamson et al., 1988; Chunn & Lacombe, 2000; Comack & Balfour, 2004; Harding, 2004; Kilty, 2014). While this edited volume is not meant as an attempt to reconcile the larger internal debates within feminist thought and praxis, on the whole it works collectively to showcase the continued need to examine the ways in which variable categories of analysis, such as gender, race, ethnicity, indigeneity, class, and sexuality coalesce within the confines of the law so as to produce effects that disadvantage, marginalize, and even discriminate against women in Canada.

Critical feminist academics are increasingly taking up what Crenshaw (1991) first conceptualized as an intersectional approach to studying the interactional nature of multiple systems of oppression and discrimination. Intersectionality emerged as a challenge to earlier feminist claims that gender was the primary factor affecting women's socio-economic and political status, equality, and broader social advancement. By considering the relationships between different oppressions, intersectional research seeks to examine how various biological, social, and cultural categories (e.g., sex, gender, race, ethnicity, indigeneity, sexual orientation, class, and ability) and other aspects of identity contribute to structural and systematic injustices and social inequalities. The fundamental premise of intersectionality is that these forms of oppression do not act independently of one another; rather, they intersect and work together to create a complex system of oppression that Hill-Collins (2000) refers to as an "interlocking matrix of domination."

While a number of the chapters in this book consider the intersection of different oppressions in the Canadian context, it is especially important to acknowledge and consider the devastating and long-lasting effects of White settler colonialism that disproportionately harms Indigenous women.[1] For example, Aboriginal women have poorer overall health than non-Aboriginal women and remain more likely to be victims of poverty, exploitation, isolation, and violence. At the same time, and despite pressure from the United Nations, the Government of Canada continues to refuse to conduct an inquiry into the missing and murdered Aboriginal women, numbered at near six hundred known cases by the Native Women's Association of Canada (2010). In terms of Indigenous women's involvement with the criminal law more specifically, we must recognize that part of the destructive legacy of colonialism is the deeply entrenched nature of systematic prejudice, discrimination, and racism that, similar to the experiences of Black and Latina women in the United States (Sudbury, 2005), sees First Nations, Inuit, and Metis women[2] vastly overrepresented at every level of the criminal justice and carceral control systems in Canada (Balfour & Comack, 2006; Comack & Balfour, 2004).

Feminist and other critical scholars have long identified the ways in which legal processes and social institutions legitimate knowledge(s) and practice(s) that sustain power relations in favour of White men, as well as the ways in which women have worked to challenge and change law so as to reduce or minimize its gendered and racialized prejudicial and discriminatory effects. That the law functions as both a process and as a historically situated institution that legitimates (and thus also de-legitimates) particular interpretations is clear (Chunn & Lacombe, 2000). Therefore, in order to better situate the critical and feminist approaches taken to examine the diverse substantive topics addressed in this edited volume, we may consider Chunn and Lacombe's (2000) important work in their book *Law as a Gendering Practice*. In many ways, *Within the Confines* builds on Chunn and Lacombe's work, which they identify as advancing Carol Smart's central point that law is a social process that develops unevenly, and often through a long series of case law ("law-as-practice") and legislative changes and amendments ("law-as-legislation"). As Chunn and Lacombe write:

> While a focus on law-as-legislation highlights the political gains achieved by feminist campaigns for change, a focus on law-as-practice often reveals the means by which a repressive social order is reproduced.... In these more complicated formulations, law becomes an ensemble of practices and discourses, or resources, that people can mobilize to reproduce or transform the conditions under which they live. In other words, law becomes a site of struggles. In contrast, as a reified concept, law becomes a homogenous entity disconnected from people's activities. It exists "out there" according to its own independent logic, producing predetermined effects. Consequently, law can be only a liberator or an oppressor. (2000: 11, 12)

To address this dual formulation of law-as-practice/law-as-legislation, Chunn and Lacombe adopt a more dynamic method that considers the "mutually generative relationship" (2000: 13) between social agents and the power relations that form the social world. This approach is akin to Dorothy Smith's conceptualization and examination of what she terms the "relations of ruling" (Smith, 1987, 1990). The contributing authors have embraced this undertaking to analyze how law constitutes and is constituted by these relations of ruling by accounting for the effects of the intersection of different categories of characterization, such as gender, race/ethnicity, indigeneity, class, and sexuality. Because law is one of the defining features and main governing institutions of contemporary Western societies, individual citizens are in one sense made up or constituted in and through law (via regulation and discipline). Yet, at the same time, they are also able to discursively and non-discursively challenge and potentially alter, shift, or transform law.

Law is most certainly a hegemonic process, and there are a number of different social agents that draw on their respective resources and knowledge(s) (both material and empirical) to enter that "site of struggle" and to mobilize change—substantively, processurally, and within the institutional arrangements that affix things "as they are." This book not only examines the divergent and at times contradictory ways that the law constructs and acts to constrain women, but it also looks at how the law enables women to be able to participate in the processes that question and aim to reform its meanings, interpretations, applications, and uses.

Accepting Chunn and Lacombe's (2000: 17) position, that law is both an institutional and a cultural strategy that is active in the constitution of the category "woman" as the starting point of our analytic inquiry, allows us to pose three broad and important questions that were used as the foundational structure for this book. First, what are the gendered effects of law-as-practice and/or law-as-legislation? Second, how do different institutional sites (e.g., law, media, policy, medicine, family) intersect to produce gendered, racialized, classed, and heteronormative effects? And finally, how have women worked to form and transform law (and/or other institutional sites) in ways that seek to eliminate, minimize, or reform some of these gendered, racialized, classed, and heteronormative effects? These are decidedly broad questions that the contributors attempt to answer through their analyses of a number of different and, at times, controversial topics.

Key Contributions of the Book

This edited volume highlights emerging and ongoing feminist critiques of the practices and effects of the law as they relate to women and as they appear and operate in the Canadian context. Read collectively, the chapters in this book identify a number of ways in which key institutional sites—namely, the media, social policy, the law, the courts, and the criminal justice system as a whole—produce effects that marginalize or discriminate against women. To varying degrees, these chapters examine the intersection of gender, race, ethnicity, indigeneity, class, and sexuality in social, media, policy, and legal discourses. A number of the contributing authors note the effects of neoliberal[3] and neoconservative[4] laws and policies on women's experiences of in/justice and prejudice, and situate these discussions historically to highlight the continuity and resonance of legal and moral discourses over time.

While it is beyond the scope of this introduction to discuss the innumerable ways that neoliberal and neoconservative political rationalities have come to affect women within the context of the law, it is worth noting that the mid to late 1970s marked a distinct shift away from postwar welfarist policies toward political agendas that sought economic expansion through free-market solutions to social issues that have been largely characterized by deregulation, privatization, individualism, and doctrines of self-responsibilization. Wendy Brown (2006: 690) argues that these two "political rationalities work symbiotically to produce a subject relatively indifferent to veracity and accountability in government and to political freedom and equality among the citizenry." For women and other marginalized groups, the emblematic result has been a lack of social support and resources that has marked a growing division between the wealthy and the poor and the general erosion of the middle class. In the context of the criminal justice system, albeit on a smaller scale than that witnessed in the United States, neoliberal and neoconservative policies and laws have been linked to increasing rates of imprisonment and the unprecedented and rapid growth of the carceral state (Balfour & Comack, 2006; Comack & Balfour, 2004; Sudbury, 2005).

Ultimately, the book identifies how contemporary legal, media, and socio-political narratives often fail to acknowledge the extensive evidence confirming that neither women nor racialized minorities have achieved fundamental social transformation in liberal democracies since the 1960s. In fact, the gap between the privileged and the disadvantaged has increasingly widened since the dismantling of the Keynesian state and the ascendancy of neoliberal and neoconservative political agendas (Chunn & Lacombe, 2000; Comack & Balfour, 2004). The feminist counter-narratives offered here explain that substantive equality is still far from a reality for many women in Canada. In all Western democracies, formal engagement with the law has long been a key strategy used by social justice movement advocates, such as feminists, and their allies in their efforts to organize for change (Adamson et al., 1988). Starting from this premise, then, the authors interrogate a number of the different ways that Canadian law and policy shape women's experiences of gendered in/justice. Most notably, Sheryl C. Fabian (Chapter 7), Kirsten Kramar (Chapter 9), Emma Cunliffe (Chapter 10), Angela Cameron (Chapter 11), Camilla A. Sears (Chapter 13), and Stacey Hannem and Chris Bruckert (Chapter 14) contextualize and discuss the evolution of particular laws, and the gendered effects these laws have had on women, and on vulnerable, marginalized, victimized, and criminalized women in particular.

The book's contributions are wide-ranging. Notably, they bring together diverse pieces of original research by emerging and established Canadian feminist academics that, when read together, offer a systematic and comprehensive overview of the relationship that different groups of Canadian women have with the law. Moreover, many of the contributing authors examine issues that are currently before the courts and thus offer innovative discussions and analyses of notable and timely socio-legal concerns and questions. Although the objective of the collection is to deepen an understanding of the ways in which key institutional sites (namely, law, policy, and media) are gendered and produce gendered effects, several of the contributors pursue that task at a more macro level by analyzing the broader and often historical trajectory of feminist struggles for legal change with respect to a variety of different substantive topics, such as women's reproductive rights (see the chapter by Cameron), criminal harassment (Fabian), infanticide (Kramar, and Cunliffe), obscenity (Sears), and sex work (Hannem and Bruckert). Other contributors do so at the micro level by examining individual cases, such as Jennifer M. Kilty (Chapter 12), Mythili Rajiva and Amar Khoday (Chapter 8), and Colleen Cardinal and Kristen Gilchrist (Chapter 2).

In addition to the socio-legal histories and case studies offered by these contributors, a number of the chapters also provide more empirical analyses of some of the most important and distressing issues that continue to affect women, including: domestic or intimate partner violence (see Chapter 6 by Holly Johnson and Ashley McConnell, and Chapter 7 by Fabian); the criminal-sentencing patterns of Aboriginal women (Chapter 5 by Gillian Balfour); and women's material experiences of homelessness (Chapter 3 by Emily K. Paradis). It is of note that the contributors draw on both qualitative and quantitative methodological approaches to conduct their empirical work. The two remaining chapters are distinct in that one is highly descriptive of women's patterns of drug use (Chapter 4 by Rebecca Jesseman and Florence Kellner), while the other offers a theoretical examination of women's rights claims with respect to carceral punishment (Chapter 1 by Vicki Chartrand).

Other strengths of the book are its Canadian content and the interdisciplinary perspectives brought to the fore by many of the contributors. In combination, these features result in a book that is both integrated and coherent, notwithstanding the fact that the contributors investigate diverse institutional sites, examine different types of laws and policies, and address issues ranging from sexualized violence to reproductive rights, to sentencing disparities, to culturally saturated media constructions of gender-based violence and victimization, among other substantial topics.[5]

The Structure and Organization of the Book

The book is organized into three parts, each of which reflects a broad area of ongoing feminist inquiry and critique. Within this three-part structure, the contributing authors were able to examine a diverse set of salient subject matter that showcases women's material experiences with the law. In the first section of the book, entitled "Institutional and Intersectional Oppressions," the contributing authors examine a number of different ways in which women in Canada are subject to varying degrees of oppression that are very clearly aggravated by the intersection of gender, race, ethnicity, indigeneity, class, and sexuality. The topics examined include poverty and homelessness (see Paradis's chapter), the racialization of crime and sentencing (see Balfour's chapter), and women's experiences of drug use (see Jesseman and Kellner's chapter). A number of the contributing authors in this section situate their arguments in rights-based discourse and most work to prioritize discussions of Aboriginal women's particularly situated experiences of historic and ongoing colonial violence (in particular, see the chapters by Cardinal and Gilchrist, Balfour, and Chartrand). Given the vast overrepresentation of Aboriginal and First Nations women in Canadian prisons and jails (Comack & Balfour, 2004), and the fact that racially minoritized women remain the fastest growing component of the prison population worldwide (Sudbury, 2005), these discussions prove especially significant in the current conservative socio-political climate. Of note, the chapter by Cardinal and Gilchrist is a collaborative storytelling piece, rather than a traditional research text, that reflects the importance of slowly building trust and rapport with Aboriginal communities working to overcome their legacies of colonial violence through grassroots and community-based efforts that recentre the subjugated voices and lived experiences of Indigenous peoples.

The second section of the book, entitled "Facets of Families, Motherhood, and Violence," explores the relations of power that complicate women's experiences of motherhood and gender-based familial violence. More specifically, the authors included in this section tackle the important topics of gender-based violence (see the chapters by Johnson and McConnell, and Rajiva and Khoday), criminal harassment (see Fabian's chapter), and infanticide (see the chapters by Cunliffe and Kramar). Together, these five chapters provide a feminist reading of the role and the construction of women's agency and responsibility in relation to these forms of violence and victimization as they play out in legal and media discourses. It is of note that a number of the chapters in this section provide discursive readings of the related case law on the varying subject matters so as to situate their discussion within women's material experiences of law and legal renderings (in particular, see the chapters by Fabian, Johnson and McConnell, Cunliffe, and Kramar).

The third and final section of this book, entitled "Sex and the Social Context," contains four chapters that examine how laws related to women's reproductive autonomy and legal parenthood, obscenity, prostitution, and the criminalization of HIV nondisclosure are distinctly gendered in ways that disadvantage women. The first chapter in this section, by Angela Cameron, examines women's reproductive rights as they operate in same-sex relationships and among women-led families. In particular, she shows how hetero- and nuclear-normative ideals of family structure continue to affect interpretations of legal parenthood in ways that disadvantage the non-biological female parent. In this section, we also explore how legal and media discourses construct HIV-positive women as vectors of disease and thus as threats to public health, similar to the ways in which sex workers or "loose" women were historically constructed in and through the application of early twentieth-century contagious diseases act legislations. Kilty's chapter examines two cases of women who were found guilty of sexual assault for failing to disclose their HIV-positive status and the lingering effects of "whore stigma" that had international-level implications. This discussion leads into the following two chapters, which examine the evolution of obscenity (see Sears' chapter) and prostitution (see Hannem and Bruckert's chapter) laws in Canada as they relate to women's agency, labour rights, and autonomy of the body. Of note, Hannem and Bruckert work to problematize the divisive nature of different feminist interpretations of sex work in order to decentre the legal moralism that typically encircles the prostitution debate.

Although their substantive exemplars are many and varied, the contributing authors collectively address similar questions about how legal and policy changes, or proposed changes, have been perceived and (re)presented over time in a number of institutional sites, including the courts, legislatures, the mainstream media, and the academy. The contributors' respective examinations of competing conceptions and perceptions of feminism, law, and social change held by feminists/women and their critics lend thematic unity to the book. What emerges from the book's various research studies is a collective picture of critical socio-legal commentary on women's material experiences with the law that is complex and at times even contradictory. By critically examining law and its gendered effects, the authors identify diverse ways in which law may be interpreted, yet they also demarcate women's potential for mobilizing shifts in law's normative institutional arrangements that marginalize, oppress, and discriminate against women.

Notes

1 For a more detailed discussion of the effects of Canadian law on Indigenous women, see Patricia Monture's (1999) chapter, "Standing Against Canadian Law: Naming Omissions of Race, Culture, and Gender," in E. Comack (ed.), *Locating Law: Race/Class/Gender Connections.* Halifax: Fernwood Publishing.

2 While the focus of this book centres on women's experiences with the law, it is important to acknowledge that Aboriginal men are similarly overrepresented in the criminal justice and carceral control systems in Canada, although women constitute the fastest growing segment of carceral populations worldwide (Sudbury, 2005).

3 While subject to much discussion and debate, the late modern or contemporary use of the term "neoliberalism" is most often employed to describe social, political, and legislative initiatives that push for free trade, deregulation, enhanced privatization, and an overall reduction in state control of the economy in favour of free-market governance strategies.

4 Like neoliberalism, neoconservatism is a political rationality that similarly devalues political liberty, equality, substantive citizenship, and the rule of law in favour of free-market governance strategies. It also valorizes state power to govern according to putatively moral ends. The effects of neoconservative political agendas have been criticized for undermining both the culture and institutions of constitutional democracy (Brown, 2006).

5 A number of the chapters in this book acknowledge that women's engagement with the law, including but not limited to that resulting from their criminality, may often be situated along a kind of "victimization-criminalization continuum" (Balfour & Comack, 2006). This notion of a continuum locates women's law-breaking and broader political engagement with the law as resulting from their material experiences of victimization and/or oppression, which include marginalizing social, political, and economic hardships in addition to emotional, psychological, physical, and sexual forms of exploitation and abuse.

References

Adamson, N., Briskin, L., & McPhail, M. (1988). *Feminist Organizing for Change: The Contemporary Women's Movement in Canada.* Toronto: Oxford University Press.

Alcoff, L.M. (2009). "The problem of speaking for others." In A.Y. Jackson & L.A. Mazzei, eds., *Voice in Qualitative Inquiry: Challenging Conventional, Interpretive, and Critical Conceptions in Qualitative Research* (pp. 117–138). New York: Routledge.

Balfour, G., & Comack, E. (2006). *Criminalizing Women.* Halifax, NS: Fernwood Publishing.

Brown, W. (2006). "American nightmare: Neoliberalism, neoconservatism, and de-democratization." *Political Theory*, 34(6): 690–714.

Chunn, D., & Lacombe, D. (2000). *Law as a Gendering Practice.* Don Mills, ON: Oxford University Press Canada.

Comack, E., & Balfour, G. (2004). *The Power to Criminalize.* Halifax, NS: Fernwood Publishing.

Crenshaw, K. (1991). "Mapping the margins: Intersectionality, identity politics, and violence against women of color." *Stanford Law Review*, 43(6): 1241–1299.

Guba, E.G., & Lincoln, Y.S. (2004). "Competing paradigms in qualitative research." In S. Hesse-Biber & P. Leavy, eds., *Approaches to Qualitative Research: A Reader on Theory and Practice* (pp. 17–38). New York: Oxford University Press.

Hammersley, M. (2005). "Should social science be critical?" *Philosophy of the Social Sciences*, 25(2): 175–195.

Harding, S. (1987). *The Science Question in Feminism.* Ithaca, NY: Cornell University Press.

Harding, S. (2004). "Introduction: Standpoint theory as a site of political, philosophic, and scientific debate." In S. Harding, ed., *The Feminist Standpoint Theory Reader: Intellectual & Political Controversies* (pp. 1–16). New York: Routledge.

Harvey, L. (1990). *Critical Social Research.* London: Unwin Hyman Ltd.

Hill-Collins, P. (2000). *Black Feminist Thought.* New York: Routledge.

Kilty, J.M. (2014). "The evolution of feminist research in the criminological enterprise: The Canadian experience." In J.M. Kilty, M. Felices-Luna, & S.C. Fabian, eds., *Demarginalizing Voices: Commitment, Emotion, and Action in Qualitative Research.* Vancouver: UBC Press.

Native Women's Association of Canada. (2010). *Sisters in Spirit.* Ottawa: Government of Canada.

Smith, D. (1987). *The Everyday World as Problematic: A Feminist Sociology.* Toronto: University of Toronto Press.

Smith, D. (1990). *Conceptual Practices of Power: A Feminist Sociology of Knowledge.* Boston: Northeastern University Press.

Sudbury, J. (2005). *Global Lockdown: Race, Gender and the Prison Industrial Complex.* New York: Routledge.

Part 1

Institutional and Intersectional Oppressions

Chapter 1

Inalienable, Universal, and the Right to Punish: Women, Prison, and Practices of Freedom

Vicki Chartrand

While there is a lower class I am in it, while there is a criminal element I am of it, while there is a soul in prison I am not free.
—Eugene Victor Debs

We escape then a domination of truth, not by playing a game that was a complete stranger to the game of truth, but in playing otherwise or in playing another game.
—Michel Foucault

Today, women are identified as the fastest growing prison population worldwide (Bastick, 2005) and as a distinct socially and economically disadvantaged and vulnerable group (e.g., Gelsthorpe & Morris, 2002; O'Brien & Harm, 2002). It is further reported that women are incarcerated for less serious and violent offences and present the least amount of risk to society (Belknap, 2000; Parkes & Pate, 2006). It is widely argued that the trend has been to criminalize and punish women's survival and social disadvantage. Women's poor or unequal social, economic, and political standing is recognized internationally and has been referred to as the feminization and criminalization of poverty.[1] State practices are criticized for criminalizing and often imprisoning women for poverty-related practices, such as drug muling, sexual exchanges, shoplifting, and fraud. Criminal punishment is subsequently criticized as an excessive, intrusive, and counterproductive response. Rather, there is a need to ensure women can access essential entitlements and supports such as employment, education, health care, childcare, housing, and financial aid. If women were to obtain better provisional entitlements and safeguards, then more equitable choices and opportunities to live, work, and prosper in larger society would also be available and the circumstances for which women are criminalized would be reduced. State governments are thus made responsible for failing to provide for women's social and economic needs.

Activists, academics, advocates, and feminists, drawing on national and international conventions and agreements, are increasingly using human rights discourses as a strategy and tool to challenge the criminalization and punishment of women and the state's failure to provide women with basic social and economic entitlements and safeguards.[2] Within countries such as Australia, Canada, Ireland, and elsewhere, several human rights complaints have been launched to have state oversight bodies investigate human rights allegations of women in prison. In New South Wales (NSW), Australia, members of the Beyond Bars Alliance group appealed to the NSW Anti-Discrimination Board for an investigation into the NSW Department of Corrective Services's systemic discrimination of women in prison based on sex, race, and disability (Armstrong, Baldry, & Chartrand, 2005, 2007).[3] The complaint documents how the criminal justice system increasingly and disproportionately impacts poor and racialized women and women with mental or cognitive health concerns. For example, the report demonstrates how women who are released from prison are not afforded the essential services needed to live and remain law-abiding in the community or how women with mental health concerns are disproportionately paternalized and penalized for their behaviour within a prison environment. The complaint thus argues that criminal justice practices systemically discriminate against women.

The predecessor to the NSW complaint was originally lodged in Canada by the Canadian Association of Elizabeth Fry Societies (2003) with the Canadian Human Rights Commission (2003), who carried out an investigation of the said discrimination and released a report entitled *Protecting Their Rights: A Systemic Review of Human Rights in Correctional Services for Federally Sentenced Women*. Complaints were also lodged in other Australian states, such as Queensland (Sisters Inside, 2004) and Victoria (Federation of Community Legal Centres, 2005), that appealed to state anti-discrimination commissions to investigate similar systemic discrimination. Where in NSW and Victoria human rights investigations were not carried out, the Anti-Discrimination Commission Queensland (2006) released a report entitled *Women in Prison: A Report by the Anti-Discrimination Commission Queensland*. Another complaint on rights violations of women prisoners was filed in Northern Ireland (Scraton & Moore, 2005), with an investigation carried out by the Northern Ireland Human Rights Commission (2005).

Generally, the complaints and investigations highlight women's histories of poverty, abuse, and neglect, the punitive and brutalizing nature of penal practices, that exacerbate and worsen conditions for women, the discriminatory nature of risk assessments that convert women's social and economic needs into risks and to increased security classifications, and the failure to provide women with social and economic entitlements, such as health care and protections and safeguards from violence, and for their general well-being. The complaints and investigations also document the failure of the system to ensure correctional accountability and oversight and the penal system's limits to observe, accommodate, or support the needs of women and particularly Aboriginal women, women with mental health concerns, women with lifestyles of substance use, and culturally and linguistically diverse women. Finally, they outline the failures of quasi-oversight bodies and internal grievance procedures to adequately arbitrate penal practices.[4] Criticism of the penal system's lack of external accountability, limits of the women's access to redress mechanisms, and the neglect of women's social and economic disadvantages are advanced as significant failures of the penal system and the state. With criticisms of the arbitrary, restrictive, and intrusive practices of a penal system, challenges are mounted against state governments for failing to provide women with basic rights, entitlements, and safeguards. Focusing on both national and international covenants and obligations, there is a call for state governments to remedy the compounding and overlapping forms of penal repression and social disadvantage experienced by women.[5]

A human rights approach to address social disadvantage and the criminalization of women is a useful strategy to draw attention to the broader social arenas of women's lives and to move attention away from individual women and onto state practices. The above-noted human rights complaints and investigations did not necessarily carry the political sway as per their original intent and, in some ways, even had unintended consequences. For example, the Correctional Service of Canada (2006), in their response to the Canadian Human Rights Commission, argue that they continue to improve their capacity to promote and maintain rights as legislated by the *Corrections and Conditional Release Act* (1992). The response has generally been to ensure that the penal system remains the arbitrator of what is normal and necessary for the management of rights and women in the system. Where it has its advantages in raising awareness of systemic concern and institutional practices, a rights-based approach also remains consistent with liberal modes of reasoning that legitimate a penal necessity. The political processes and legal mechanisms used to promote and defend rights are limited in their ability to shape an articulation and exercise of rights outside of the very institution responsible for the violations.

Human rights, as enshrined in national and international conventions and obligations, emerge within legal and political frameworks that shape and define the character of rights and, ultimately, how freedom is understood and articulated. Rights, as the product of an historical ethos, are realized through a series of ideas, techniques, and strategies that govern the way they are conceived and advanced. Articulated as inalienable and universal, human rights expressions give an appearance of an unfettered approach to freedom, while in practice they collude and collide within a legal and penal system that creates other problem sites and localities for control, and limits a concept of freedom within codified norms. It is important to explore the context of how rights are shaped and limited to better understand how their expression and exercise limit a concept of freedom, particularly as something that is tenable through a human rights approach. In looking at this context, a concept of freedom can also then be conceptualized otherwise; as something that is dynamic, diverse, and open to multiple understandings, possibilities, and tensions. Rather than abandon a rights approach, particularly given that it is one of the few mechanisms for those who live within states of repression and domination, it is important to (re)consider how anti-punitive strategies and tactics can be reconceived to avoid some of the traps of the law and penality and to support ongoing struggles and expressions of freedom as a critical and tactical strategy to advance women's rights and other social justice concerns.

A Brief Context and History of Rights

Human rights were first articulated as the natural civil rights of individual citizens in the seventeenth and eighteenth centuries, and were endorsed in various national bodies as legal obligations after the French and American revolutions (Hughes, 1999: 48). Rights were given universal and inalienable applicability through the development of the *Charter of the United Nations* of 1945 and the *Universal Declaration of Human Rights* of 1948 that conferred humans with an inherent dignity and equality. The United Nations, as an oversight body with a mandate to see that international obligations are observed, was established to "protect and promote freedom, equality, dignity and human rights."[6] Generally, human rights reflect four basic pillars and generations of thought and practice. The first pillar, with its roots in rationalist Enlightenment commitments (e.g., Magna Carta, 1215), reflect a basic human dignity bestowed to all despite religion, creed, ethnicity, religion, or sex. Second pillar and first-generation rights emerged in the eighteenth century through the *Bill of Rights* in the United States and France's *Declaration of the Rights of Man* and are enshrined in the 1948 *Universal Declaration of Human Rights* and the 1966 *International Covenant on Civil and Political Liberties.* Second pillar rights reflect a "freedom from" repression and unnecessary restraints or restrictions, and largely reflect a liberal politics that promotes individuality opportunity and less government interference. Third pillar and second-generation rights reflect a "freedom to" with equal access to social, economic, and cultural entitlements, such as in the 1966 *International Covenant on Economic, Social and Cultural Rights* as well as the 1948 *Universal Declaration of Human Rights.* This ideal was advanced with the Industrial Revolution and the promotion of an economy of private capital and monetary realism.

Fourth pillar and third-generation rights support group and collective rights through development, human security, peace, and self-determination, and later developed a recognition of Indigenous rights and a need to support life-sustaining environments (De Baets, 2001: 7014–7015; Ishay, 2004: 359).

It is often evidenced that rights were given significant widespread consideration in response to growing concerns after the events of the Second World War (see Johnson, 1998; Rodley, 1999). Given their historical context, Foucault (2007) alternatively argues that rights emerged with liberal politics as a mechanism to align individuals toward existing political, social, and economic objectives of the state, so as to become healthy and productive liberal subjects. Despite inalienable and universal affixes, human rights have a fragmented history and emerged with different contexts to advance specific political and economic goals, particularly those of a liberal character.

Punitive Rights and Protections

Despite being universal and inalienable, human rights are entrenched in legal discourses that require a productive social and civic participation (Cruikshank, 1999). Given this, a rights discourse does not result in the absence of punitive or repressive interventions, but rather conditions other legal interventions and mechanisms of control that advance a self-sustaining liberal subject and participation. As Wendy Brown (2002: 422) points out, "[A right] may entail some protection from the most immobilizing features and designations, [but] it reinscribes other designations as it protects us, and thus enables further regulation through that designation." Criminalized women, constituted as disadvantaged, require other forms of protections and interventions, often punitive and corrective, to bring them back into line with a liberal subject—one that is law-abiding, pro-social, right-thinking, and the like.

Given that civil and human rights were developed in tandem with liberal rationalities, the same mechanisms used to protect individual rights are also codified in legal norms that legitimate punitive practices to protect social interests. This idea is reflected in the following quote adopted by the UN's Economic and Social Council: "Effective criminal justice systems can only be developed based on the rule of law and the rule of law itself requires the protection of effective criminal justice measures."[7] Rights are circulated within specified legal and political fields that are central in administering not only individual protections, but also societal ones. UN treaties, for example, maintain that prisoners should retain all rights that non-incarcerated persons enjoy, except for those rights that must be forfeited or limited to administer the penal sanction (Bouloukos & Dammann, 2001: 757). This is one of the main non-derogable rights under article 4 of the *International Covenant of Civil and Political Liberties* that "every person has a right to be recognized as a person *before the law*" (emphasis added). As Caleb Smith (2009: 23) states, "Prisoners are not beyond the embrace of law; they are mortified by it." In this way, tensions that exist between human rights and penal practices are reconciled within legal discourses that operate alongside security practices. These practices continue to legitimate penal norms as a way to advance societal protections and interests, with penality deciding what is necessary and normal for civil society.

Identified as sharing common points of disadvantage, women in the system are considered to be acting against social conventions in order to cope, adapt, or survive their living circumstances. While a rights discourse advances an understanding of women's criminalization as the result of social and economic discrimination, the penal system becomes the panacea for addressing social and economic disparities. For instance, the Canadian Human Rights Commission (2004: 14) outlines the need to promote strong correctional principles in women's prisons:

> The challenge is to give effect to the principles that guide the correctional system, including human rights and public safety, while resolving the inevitable tension between those principles in the correctional context. This conflict also gives rise to an opportunity to create an organizational structure, a culture and practices that are consistent with human rights principles and that enhance safe and secure operational effectiveness.

Addressing criminalized women's social disadvantage is understood as a common good, and socio-economic concerns are thus combined with individual and social protection. This results in other regulatory and punitive responses, such as mandatory treatments and programs, low-wage labour schemes, compulsory urinalysis testing, regular community surveillance and interventions, and parole conditions and electronic monitoring—the very types of invasive interventions that continue to prioritize societal protections and civic participation.

Given that a rights discourse is rationalized within the same traditions that promote social protections and civil obligations, the penal system is positioned to identify and remedy women's social disadvantage, with a focus on women's civic/liberal participation. In this way, the state can meet its rights obligations while divesting itself of the responsibility of adding additional resources elsewhere (see also Drabsch, 2006). Punitive and penal thought and practice are further legitimated through a rights discourse that weighs a perceived common good against an individual good. The penal apparatus thus continues to be legally reasoned as essential to administer what is just and necessary for the protection of civil society and what is now necessary for addressing the rights of women caught in the system.

With women's social disadvantage linked to the penal apparatus, human rights appeals are used to further intertwine penal and corrective mechanisms in the lives of women. This is reflected in the variety of international research programs, conferences, and assemblies on penal and correctional management that promote practices for correctional management with a focus on poverty, education, homelessness, mental health, and, more recently, even human rights.[8] As Wendy Brown (2002: 422) further comments, "[R]ights that entail some specification of our suffering, injury, or inequality lock us into the identity defined by our subordination." For instance, in the Australian Capital Territory, the Alexander Maconochie, a minimum-to-maximum penal centre for women and men that opened in 2008, is said to be the first prison in Australia to operate under human rights principles. A rights discourse is used to support and legitimate the use of a penal system—a system from which disadvantaged groups are supposed to be protected. Within a rights discourse, the penal apparatus is strategically placed to identify and remedy women's criminalization, disadvantage, and discrimination.

With penality positioned to rectify rights violations and provide effective protections, it is more difficult to make visible and challenge its punitive practices, particularly when a rights discourse is made part of its exercise. Security, discipline, and good order are priorities routinely invoked by prison service managers. A rights discourse, as articulated within the original pillars and generations of liberal thought, does not necessarily subvert corrective or punitive tendencies, but rather creates new conditions of penal practice and other legal restrictions—under a pretense of being natural and equitable. While a rights approach in its articulation was developed to act as a mechanism to arbitrate power and to counter repressive regimes, it remains embedded in systems of thought and practice consistent with those mechanisms that also promote penal norms and processes, and simply shifts the modalities by which they are legally, administratively, and morally prescribed. Whether presented as rational actors, pathologically determined, or socially disadvantaged, women are thus invested in other punitive and restrictive vestiges of control and sites of subjugation. In addition to this, legal modes of reasoning are used to reduce any of the conceptual tensions that might exist between women's rights and the use of a penal system by advancing concerns for both individual and social protection. A conception of freedom within a rights discourse, without a clear articulation of how it remains embedded in the practices and discourses it seeks to challenge, can result in the recycling of restrictive and corrective measures to other domains and locales. This invariably ties women to the normalizing discourses deemed necessary for social protection and civil society and in the promotion of a liberal subject.

A Disciplinary Maintenance of Rights

Rights, as a legal strategy, define a norm, a way of being, and establish what is acceptable, desirable, and reasonable within certain social, political, and economic currencies. Linked to legal processes, penal knowledge and practices continue to inform a rights project and also shape a norm by which women in the system are understood. A strategy to responsibilize state governments for the discriminatory treatment of women in the system invokes a legal framing of the issue that is central in the dispersion of punitive and corrective strategies to new areas, different problems, and various populations. A rights and freedom framework has been significant in shaping and determining conformity, compliance, and classifications, and in developing new sites and new categories for legal determination and review. According to Rose (1985: 204), "[I]t is precisely the inability of persons to conform to or support this conception of free, rational, consistent, unified, choosing individual that is frequently the ground for making [a legal] ascription." Identified within criminal justice processes as owing specific rights, women are also thought of in terms of their own responsibilities based on a liberal subject—one that participates in those practices considered necessary for civic participation. Where the penal system is invested in normalizing practices by defining and promoting acceptable modes of life, the law is invested in regulation to ensure acceptable modes of life can occur (Rose & Valverde, 1998: 543). According to Gruber (1989: 619),

> The profound rights for individuals which were secured by great political documents and legal traditions were made insignificant by the complacent dependence of these formal institutions and processes on the expertise of the human sciences that legitimize the disciplines. This is most apparent in the decisions of a judicial system, which although formally radically insistent on the rights of the juridical individual, completely relies on, and defers to, the judgments made about individuals who have previously been made in the disciplinary archipelago.

Whether women are understood through labels of criminality, pathology, or disadvantage, the law assists in establishing and promoting this norm. As Valverde (1996) argues, individuals are subject to legal controls and regulations to ensure that a normalizing process takes place. With crime now linked to their social and economic disadvantages, women are made responsible for making better life choices with social disadvantage as the focal point for regulation, modification, and normalization (see also Carlen & Tombs, 2006; Carlen & Worrall, 2004; Fox, 1999; Hannah-Moffat, 2002; Kendall, 2002; McCorkel, 2003, 2004; Moore & Hannah-Moffat, 2005). Women must align themselves with those discourses and programs mapped out through specific corrective projects, language, strategies, and programs designed to normalize them: "[It is] the process through which women gain insight into their situation, identify their strengths and are supported and challenged to take positive action to gain greater control of their lives" (Hart, 2000: 4; Lynch, 2000). Services for women are designed around areas of relationships and living skills, problem-solving abilities, alcohol and drug issues, health, education, vocational training, offence-specific programs, and recreational activities, along with women-equitable provisions. Rights and entitlements are only conferred when individuals avail themselves of the necessary resources and practices for a certain type of civil participation. The penal institution determines the context of disadvantage and offending, and offers programs and modifications to prepare women to take advantage of their newfound rights and personal responsibility.

Linked to normalizing strategies, the penal apparatus decides what is reasonable, necessary, and normal for civil society. A woman's failure to adequately avail herself of her corrective management plan suggests an individual inability or unwillingness to attain current liberal standards and norms. Within such liberal discourses, those whose rights are violated are also targeted as somehow lacking in their ability to properly confer themselves with rights. The penal system is therefore germane to the process of locating and isolating groups that fail to live as rights-imbued liberal subjects and promote a particular social and economic existence. Those institutions designed to control, regulate, and monitor modes of life are also used to ensure that one's rights are being exercised, such as was done in Australia by constructing a human-rights prison in the Australian Capital Territory, as noted above. This is also reflected with the Anti-Discrimination Commission Queensland (2006: 5), who were interested in ensuring the penal system became better managers of rights: "Since the Anti-Discrimination Commission Queensland (ADCQ) began this review, the Queensland Department of Corrective Services (DCS) has implemented significant improvements in a number of policies and procedures affecting women prisoners" (2006: 13). A rights discourse legitimates normalizing strategies of the prison to ensure social participation, under the umbrella of what is just in promoting rights to social and economic entitlements.

Despite claims of consistency, fairness, impartiality, universality, and so forth, the law is combined with other systems, discourses, and mechanisms to promote a norm. With the law deployed to support and authorize the power of the norm (Rose & Valverde, 1998: 548), it is positioned to arbitrate and regulate rights. The rule of law, in its far-reaching potential to inscribe any and all, is used to locate and isolate individuals and groups for the administering of normalizing processes, punitive or otherwise, within formal and codified arrangements. Through notions such as equality, justice, rights, and freedom, it advertises as owning a capacity for objective or blind justice and equal application, while reproducing strategies of correction and domination.

Legal Limits of Rights

In addition to penal logics mediating rights, the more technical, procedural, administrative, and bureaucratic translations of rights and legal processes tend to further remove a rights discourse from its initial project of freedom. A rights process takes place in a complicated arena of legal doctrines, political systems, and institutions that create and shape the way rights can be understood and exercised. Within legal processes, the ability to articulate a certain right must be sufficiently substantiated in facts, evidence, and argument. Woodiwess (2002: 145) argues that "politically inspired arguments can now only hope to make a difference if they use legal terms or, minimally, do not challenge legal norms or procedures." Responsibility is placed on individuals or groups to demonstrate the entitlements, deservedness, or violation of rights, relative to various legal discourses. As a specialized knowledge, those who are privy to and disciplined within legal modes of thought and language can navigate legal systems and procedures in the presentation of argument and proof. By operating through specialized thought and formal procedures, rights and freedom are dependent upon those who have considerable access to, are the most invested in the processes of, and are the least hindered by legal discourses and repressive systems or socio-economic arrangements (see also Christie, 1986).

Legal rights and entitlements, as determined by those who are the least restricted and yet most implicated in its doctrine, also reproduce what is considered reasonable, normal, and necessary. Arguments and claims must be consistent with both legal rules and liberal norms to gain legitimacy. With a normalizing function and erudite knowledge, access to rights is limited from those who are socially disadvantaged and who fail in life, labour, and health, but who need them the most and are furthest removed from the benefits of its exercise. According to Anleu (1999: 200), "While all individuals may have formal rights, the vast differences between those who have access to resources to be able to exercise their rights and seek remedies for their abrogation, and those who do not, undermine the reality of formal rights." Embedded in legal doctrine, a rights approach can further promote or reaffirm their inaccessibility. Collective resistances and political actions are made administrative, technical, and mechanical through the letter of the law. A rights discourse is thus limited through legal administrative processes that undermine a more complex and anti-liberal engagement.

Legal processes often depoliticize or remove social justice initiatives away from political and collective energies and visions, and invest them in administrative and bureaucratic sites. Where the Queensland Human Rights Commission took on such an investigation, the NSW Anti-Discrimination Board cited a lack of resources to even respond to the anti-discrimination complaint submitted by the Beyond Bars Alliance group (Armstrong, Baldry, & Chartrand, 2007). Within this administrative detail, collective action loses its momentum as it is blended within bureaucratic schemes that detract from its grassroots and social justice origins. The possibility of resistance is narrowed or minimized within the more technical and procedural arrangements that become another part of the problem for the struggle.

Pickett (1996: 404) argues that rights are often diluted by the disciplines, networks, and projects also involved in systems of penality and other power dynamics and programs. Using the law and penal logics and practices, it becomes increasingly difficult to argue and reveal the way these systems stray or detract from the original rights project. As Rose (1985: 202) asks, "[We] lack the means to conceptualize the nature, objectives and consequences of different mechanisms of control—who seeks to regulate what, by what means, in relation to what problems, in pursuit of what objectives, according to what distributions of power?" Within the legal system, new bureaucratic controls and necessities define and shape rights and a criteria of freedom, always with a danger of creating new forms of penality, discipline, obedience, correction, punishment, regulation, scrutiny, and so on and that do not act in accordance with an initial rights strategy or project of freedom.

Agonism and Practices of Freedom

By shifting focus to how the system criminalizes and penalizes women's social disadvantage, a rights approach seeks to draw attention to state practices that must provide its citizens with basic provisions and maximize protections from unnecessary restraint. In advancing women's liberties in this way, however, appeals are made within legal, political, and administrative frameworks that are historically consistent with the same mode of thinking and practices that continue to legitimate a penal exercise. With freedom invariably fixed to some form of constraint and normalizing practices, it is perhaps not a question of how to obtain a freedom "from" or "to," but rather to consider how a conception of freedom is currently shaped and ask how a notion of freedom can be differentially understood and exercised.

Rights, as articulated in covenants and protocols, are understood as inalienable and universal—that is, rights confer a "freedom from" repression and discrimination along with a "freedom to" equal social, political, and economical entitlements to any and all. As discussed, this conceptualizing of rights fails to consider the inherently normative, restrictive, and problematic nature of the legal and penal fields involved in the articulation and exercising of rights—let alone the shaping and limiting of to whom rights are conferred. The institutions and practices involved in the production of rights are grounded within schemes that also shape and determine the articulation and administration of a conception of freedom—one that is implicated in and disguises practices of control and discipline. An ongoing reliance upon legal frameworks to determine and shape a concept of freedom minimizes the possibilities of moving away from the very apparatuses that produce and reproduce systems of control, subordination, and so forth. A rights-based approach is a useful tactical strategy that reveals and challenges how women are socially, economically, and punitively managed. It is also useful in redirecting thought from an individualized focus on women to a problematization of state and penal practices (see also Allspach, 2010). It is also, however, within the pillars and generations of rights that a concept of freedom is conceived in the image of a liberal subject, while notions such as "inalienable" and "universal" give the illusion that one's freedom is boundless. As Foucault (1988a: 14–15) states, "[I]t presents a certain form of our ethics as a universal model for any kind of freedom. I think that there are more secrets, more possible freedoms, and more inventions in our future than what we can imagine in humanism."

Freedom, particularly as it is advanced within modern civil rights and liberties, is more commonly understood as existing in some inherent attainable form, as existing outside of mechanisms of oppression. This conception of freedom remains consistent with liberal rationalist thought that gives an appearance of liberty and choice while creating norms for acceptable conduct, survival, standards of living, and the like in order to attain or be conferred such a freedom—a reasoning that gives rise to what is or can be considered oppressive or discriminatory when the acceptable participation is not attained, whether it is a result of disadvantage or otherwise.

> [S]uch freedoms are suffused with disciplines and at once pose limits for the very thematic interests they would advance. If the individual obtains rights in that tradition, this would be another way in which identity has been problematized and certain liberties set up within constraints. (Aladjem, 1991: 287)

To consider freedom as having an essential or attainable form overlooks how a rights discourse itself is born out of and reproduces modes of reasoning inscribed in a norm that has been long associated with legal and penal systems.[9] Freedom is part of the very logics and practices that make it difficult to reason possibilities for women outside of a penal system and what is established as free and un-free, rational and irrational, or desirable and undesirable.

Freedom does not exist outside of power. Nor does freedom exist in some essential, absolute, or liberating form. It is the ontological condition of the political, economic, and legal mechanisms that shape its articulation and exercise. If a specific freedom is sought through a rights discourse, the diverse modes of reasoning, processes, and practices to which a notion of freedom is bound ought also be considered. According to Ivison (1998: 142), "All rights talk, whether singular or natural, is to some extent tactical, for it is always a case of using it to pre-empt and/or facilitate a possible action or range of actions." Freedom, then, is tactical; a strategy that reshapes or reproduces legal configurations of the subject, and that can reaffirm or reinvent normalizing practices.

> The system of right, the domain of law, are permanent agents of these relations of domination, these polymorphous techniques of subjugation. Right should be viewed, I believe, not in terms of a legitimacy to be established, but in terms of the methods of subjugation that it instigates. (Foucault, 1980: 96)

Considering how a rights discourse implicates and constrains our understanding of freedom, we also reconsider social justice politics and modes of resistance within the ensemble of practices, institutions, and languages in which they are tied. Widder (2004: 415) argues that "power continues to hide itself while we retain the comforts of an idea of resistance—and political resistance in particular—as being opposed to power." Rather than opposing power, resistance too is embedded in its operation, and any conception of freedom will invariably implicate and subsume liberating practices, political action, or resistances into other projects and domains of production, coercion, and restriction. As Widder (2004: 66–67) further points out, "Resistances take various roles as adversary, target, support, or handle in power relations while being the odd term in relations of power." As power transforms, divides, retreats, or multiplies, so do the conditions of freedom that make such power possible.[10] Freedom, then, does not exist outside of power but as a condition of its exercise.

A conception of resistance would benefit from a consideration of the ways in which it not only acts against or fragments the field, but also how it reaffirms its exercise; how it can repurpose, negate, subsume, or advance penal operations. Freedom, as a condition of the exercise of resistance and power, ought to be understood as both enabling and constraining in order to be able to consider other passages and other possibilities, and creating other spaces to do otherwise.

> Liberty is a practice. So there may, in fact, always be a certain number of projects whose aim is to modify some constraints, to loosen, or even to break them, but none of these projects can, simply by its nature, assure that people will have liberty automatically, that it will be established by the project itself. (Foucault, 1999: 135)

All resistances hold multiple potentials. Freedom, or other projects of resistance, would be better understood in terms of their relationship "to" and not "against" existing arrangements. In this way, it becomes more of a question of approaches, tactics, and understandings rather than overarching equalities, impartial justices, or blanket protections. For example, a critical knowledge of rights must not privilege one approach or strategy over another, but can serve to reshape ways of thinking about practices of freedom as an ongoing project and how it can be contemplated, strategized, and renegotiated within the power matrices of the legal and penal systems, particularly as discussed above.

One way to advance a conception of freedom in this way is by considering resistance as a form of agonism—a permanent provocation of power (Foucault, 1982: 790). Agonisms are those practices that provoke, prompt, and destabilize particular forces of power and question or alter the direction or focus of its exercise—not something that eliminates or acts outside of power and repressive practices, but that shifts its exercise. A careful and ongoing analysis is needed to look at the agonism of particular strategies and tactics and their ability to pull, disrupt, fragment, or reaffirm problematic fields. We therefore look for hidden agonisms that not only expose and challenge forms of authority or repression, but that are also inconsistent with its rules and games. It is not a matter of finding a new order, but to play the game differently, to disrupt and displace what exists through what Derrida (1982: 18) refers to as an approach of *différance*: "the active moving discord of different forces, and of differences of forces ... against the entire system." Such an approach has no fixed identity and recognizes no permanent authority—nor does it privilege its own approach, or existing ones. Similarly, this approach does not suggest acquiescence to current practices or suggest inaction. It acts as a contingency—continually rethought and recreated through relations of support and agonisms that contemplate and contradict institutional arrangements, discourses of language and knowledge, and authority and relations of power: "on the one hand, it is an outside that threatens the inside; on the other hand, it is an outside that is formulated from the inside" (Newman, 2001: 12). Although forms or conditions for resistance are not offered here, the above suggestion is meant to reflect some of the possibilities that a shift in analysis can achieve in its relationship with existing arrangements, and assist in dislocating and disrupting various practices, structures, and regimes of truth, including our own.

Conclusion

Anti-discrimination and human rights complaints and investigations offer many possibilities for struggle. They are particularly directive by shifting attention from women as criminal to the processes and practices of criminalization. With a rights discourse owning its own political and historical ethos and current political and legal arrangements, rights are also inscribed in both old and new sites of penality and correction. Bevir (1999: 69) states, "The liberal view of freedom evokes areas of life, often defined by rights, where the individual should not be subject to any social constraint ... [but also] enshrines a faith in an autonomous subject who can avoid local prejudices and who can be freed." With the penal system responsible for providing individual and social protection, combined with the promotion of a liberal subject who must qualify for rights and freedoms, penality individualizes collective concerns and localizes resistance to sites of correction. Given the illusion of an unrestrained freedom, without a consideration of how rights themselves are also invested in power, there is a danger of reconstituting and reaffirming the very forces that rights seek to challenge.

A rights and freedom discourse, as something that is very much a part of a landscape of power with its own prescriptions and boundaries, opens up new relationships, new struggles, and new strategies that must be considered and recognized with its own arrangements, investments, and implications in the production of truth.

> The thought that there could be a state of communication which would be such that the games of truth could circulate freely, without obstacles, without constraint and without coercive effects, seems to me to be Utopian. (Foucault, 1985: 18)

An investigation of rights and freedom in this way does not discourage its application, but directs attention to how rights operate through a legal and penal field that reinforces or produces repressive sites of control. Resistance must seek to dislocate authority and hegemony, liberate spaces for new ways of thinking, challenge the matrices, networks, and frameworks of power, including those within which freedom itself is articulated—it is to reinvest resistances to other arenas and games of truth. In concerning ourselves with the historical and political ethos and rationalities of certain domains such as rights, and by framing our understandings of freedom as something that is not tenable outside of power, resistances become an articulation, negotiation, and struggle within specific locales, at particular times, and in relation to particular modes of reasoning.

Rather than offer an alternative conception of how a rights discourse approach might be advanced, I have attempted to highlight some of the more subtle or hidden dangers in privileging an approach that is contemplated as inalienable and universal, and have offered an alternative framework for thought and action. Without providing a definitive framework or criteria for a project of resistance, I offer insight into how women in the penal system can be enlisted into dominant corrective frameworks through a project of resistance, specific to rights and freedom. Without insisting on an abandonment of rights, I suggest how a rights discourse might be considered otherwise and as part of a strategy in the games and mechanisms of truth.

Notes

1 See, for example, United Nations Population Fund (2000), *Review and Appraisal of the Implementation of the Beijing Platform for Action: Report of the Secretary-General*. United Nations, Department of Public Information.

2 The two main treaties referred to in the context of prisons are the *International Covenant on Civil and Political Rights* (*ICCPR*) 16 December 1966, supplemented by the *Optional Protocol to the ICCPR* (*ICCPR-OP1*) 16 December 1966, and the *Second Optional Protocol to the ICCPR, aiming at the abolition of the death penalty* (*ICCPR-OP2*) 15 December 1989; and the *Convention Against Torture and Other Cruel, Inhuman or Degrading Treatment or Punishment* (*CAT*) 10 December 1984, supplemented by the *Optional Protocol to the CAT* (*OP-CAT*) 18 December 2002. For a rights framework specific to women, appeals are made to the *Convention on the Elimination of All Forms of Discrimination Against Women (CEDAW)* 18 December 1979 and the *CEDAW Optional Protocol* (*CEDAW-OP)* 10 December 2000. There are also UN declarations of international standards that include the Standard Minimum Rule for the Treatment of Prisoners, 1957, and the *Body of Principles for the Protection of All Persons under Any Form of Detention*, 1988.

3 The NSW Beyond Bars Alliance is a coalition of community and church organizations, activist groups, academics, and individuals with an interest in social justice.

4 For instance, the position of the NSW Inspector General of Corrective Services, established in 1997 with a mandate to oversee the penal service's performance and operations, was abolished in 2003. The NSW Department of Corrective Services's Women Services Unit, established with a mandate to inform policy on woman's issues, was disbanded in May 2005. Although the Women's Action Committee established by the department still exists, in 2006 the committee's only former women prisoner member was dismissed.

5 These failures and inadequacies of penal management and practice are raised in relation to both international covenants and treaties as well as national rights obligations, such as the equality provision of section 15 in the *Canadian Charter of Rights and Freedoms* or articles 2 and 3 of the *European Convention on Human Rights*, which protect the right to life and the right to be free from torture, inhumane and degrading treatment, respectively. It is noteworthy that Australia carries no such binding domestic rights document, although it observes the *Minimum Standard Guidelines for the Treatment of Prisoners*, 1984, and the *Anti-Discrimination Act 1977*.

6 *Universal Declaration of Human Rights*, adopted and proclaimed by General Assembly resolution 217 A (III) 10 Dec 1948.

7 Resolution of the Commission on Crime Prevention and Criminal Justice, strengthening the technical co-operation capacity of the United Nations Crime Prevention and Criminal Justice Programme in the area of the rule of law and criminal justice reform, Vienna, May 2005.

8 See, for example, "What Works with Women Offenders: Challenging Stereotypes and Achieving Change" Conference, Prato, Tuscany, September 2007.

9 Take, for example, the Aboriginal deaths in custody, such as the death of Mulrunji Doomadgee, or the various inquests that fail to find fault with police practices, such as the T.J. Hickey inquest (see the Indigenous Social Justice Association), or the long-standing and ongoing neglect of investigating the disappearances of Aboriginal and non-Aboriginal women in East Hastings, Vancouver, and elsewhere.

10 For instance, collectively, NSW has seen the development of groups such as Women's Ex-Inmate Support Service, Women and Girls in Custody Group, Justice Action, NSW Women Behind Bars, Civil Liberties Prisoners' Action Group, Beyond Bars Alliance group, and the Penal Reform Association to challenge penal thought and practice through avenues such as media campaigns, public demonstrations, and political lobbying among others (see also Baldry & Vincson, 1991: 91–104).

References

Aladjem, T.K. (1991). "The philosopher's prism: Foucault, feminism, and critique." *Political Theory*, 19(2): 277–291.

Allspach, A. (2010). "Landscapes of (neo-)liberal control: The transcarceral spaces of federally sentenced women in Canada." *Gender, Place & Culture*, 17(6): 705–723.

Anleu, S.R. (1999). "Sociologists confront human rights: The problem of universalism." *Journal of Sociology*, 35(2): 198–212.

Anti-Discrimination Commission Queensland. (2006). *Women in Prison: A Report by the Anti-Discrimination Commission Queensland*. Brisbane: Anti-Discrimination Commission Queensland.

Armstrong, K., Baldry, E., & Chartrand, V. (2005). *Submission to the NSW Antidiscrimination Commissioner for an Inquiry into the Discrimination Experienced by Women Within the Criminal Justice System in New South Wales*. Sydney: Beyond Bars Alliance.

Armstrong, K., Baldry, E., & Chartrand, V. (2007). "Human rights abuses and discrimination against women in the criminal justice system in New South Wales." *Australian Journal of Human Rights*, 12(2): 203–227.

Baldry, E., & Vinson, T. (1991). *Actions Speak: Strategies and Lessons from Australian Social Action*. Melbourne: Longman Cheshire.

Bastick, M. (2005). *Women in Prison: A Commentary on the Standard Minimum Rules for the Treatment of Prisoners: Discussion Draft*. Geneva: Quaker United Nations Office.

Belknap, J. (2000). *The Invisible Woman: Gender, Crime, and Justice* (2nd ed.). Belmont, California: Wadsworth.

Bouloukos, A.C., & Dammann, B. (2001). "The United Nations and the promotion of prison standards." In D. Van Zyl Smit & F. Dunkel, eds., *Imprisonment Today and Tomorrow: International Perspectives on Prisoners' Rights and Prison Conditions* (2nd ed., pp. 756–774). The Hague, Netherlands: Kluwer Law International.

Brown, W. (2002). "Suffering the paradoxes of rights." In W. Brown & J. Halley, eds., *Left Legalism/Left Critique* (pp. 420–434). Durham & London: Duke University Press.

Canadian Association of Elizabeth Fry Societies. (2003). *Submission of the Canadian Association of Elizabeth Fry Societies (CAEFS) to the Canadian Human Rights Commission for the Special Report on the Discrimination on the Basis of Sex, Race and Disability Faced by Federally Sentenced Women.* Ottawa: Canadian Association of Elizabeth Fry Societies.

Canadian Human Rights Commission. (2004). *Protecting Their Rights: A Systemic Review of Human Rights in Correctional Services for Federally Sentenced Women.* Ottawa: Canadian Human Rights Commission.

Carlen, P., & Tombs, J. (2006). "Reconfigurations of penality: The ongoing case of the women's imprisonment and reintegration industries." *Theoretical Criminology*, 10(3): 337–360.

Carlen, P., & Worrall, A. (2004). *Analysing Women's Imprisonment.* Cullompton, UK: Willan Publishing.

Christie, N. (1986). "Conflict as property." *British Journal of Criminology*, 17(1): 1–15.

Correctional Service of Canada. (2006). *Ten-Year Status Report on Women's Corrections 1996–2006.* Ottawa: CSC.

Cruikshank, B. (1999). *The Will to Empower: Democratic Citizens and Other Subjects.* Ithaca, NY: Cornell University Press.

De Baets, A. (2001). "Human rights, history of." *Encyclopedia of the Behavioral & Social Sciences* (pp. 7012–7019). Elsevier Science Ltd.

Debs, E.V. (1918). *Statement to the court upon being convicted of violating the sedition act.* Retrieved from www.marxists.org/archive/debs/works/1918/court.htm

Derrida, J. (1982). *Margins of Philosophy.* Brighton: Harvester.

Drabsch, T. (2006). *Reducing the Risk of Recidivism: Briefing Paper No 15.* Sydney: NSW Parliamentary Library Research Service.

Federation of Community Legal Centres. (2005). *Submission to the Anti-Discrimination Commissioner for an Inquiry into the Discrimination Experienced by Women Within the Criminal Justice System in Victoria.* Melbourne: Federation of Community Legal Centres and the Victorian Council of Social Service.

Foucault, M. (1980). *Power/Knowledge: Selected Interviews and Other Writings, 1972–1977* (C. Gordon, L. Marshall, J. Mepham & K. Soper, Trans.). New York: Pantheon Books.

Foucault, M. (1982). "The subject and power." *Critical Inquiry*, 8(4): 777–795.

Foucault, M. (1985). *The Use of Pleasure: The History of Sexuality Volume II* (R. Hurley, Trans., 1992 ed.). London: Penguin Books.

Foucault, M. (1988a). *Politics, Philosophy, Culture: Interviews and Other Writings, 1977–1984.* New York: Routledge.

Foucault, M. (1988b). *Technologies of the Self: A Seminar with Michel Foucault* (L.H. Martin, Trans.). Amherst: The University of Massachusetts Press.

Foucault, M. (1999). "Space, power, and knowledge." In S. During, ed., *The Cultural Studies Reader* (pp. 134–141). London: Routledge.

Foucault, M. (2007). *Security, Territory, Population: Lectures at the Collège de France, 1977–1978* (G. Burchell, Trans.). Hampshire, UK: Palgrave Macmillan.

Fox, K. (1999). "Changing violent minds: Discursive correction and resistance in the cognitive treatment of violent offenders in prison." *Social Problems*, 46(1): 88–43.

Gelsthorpe, L., & Morris, A. (2002). "Women's imprisonment in England and Wales: A penal paradox." *Criminal Justice*, 2(3): 277–301.

Gruber, D.F. (1989). "Foucault's critique of the liberal individual." *Journal of Philosophy*, 86(11): 615–621.

Hannah-Moffat, K. (2002). "Creating choices: Reflecting on choices." In P. Carlen, ed., *Women and Punishment: The Struggle for Justice* (pp. 199–219). Portland, OR: Willan Publishing.

Hart, K. (2000). "The assessment of female offenders." Women in Corrections: Staff and Clients Conference. Australian Institute of Criminology and the Department for Correctional Services South Australia. Adelaide, October 31–November 1.

Hughes, C.L. (1999). "Reconstructing the subject of human rights." *Philosophy & Social Criticism*, 25(2): 47–60.

Ishay, M.R. (2004). "What are human rights? Six historical controversies." *Journal of Human Rights*, 3(3): 359–371.

Ivison, D. (1998). "The disciplinary moment: Foucault, law and the reinscription of rights." In J. Moss, ed., *The Later Foucault: Politics and Philosophy* (pp. 129–148). London: Sage.

Johnson, G.M. (1998). "A Magna Carta for mankind: Writing the universal declaration of human rights." In G.M. Johnson & J. Symonides, eds., *The Universal Declaration of Human Rights: A History of its Creation and Implementation 1948–1998* (pp. 5–16). Paris: UNESCO Publishing.

Kendall, K. (2002). "Time to think about cognitive behaviour programs." In P. Carlen, ed., *Women and Punishment: The Struggle for Justice* (pp. 182–198). Portland, OR: Willan Publishing.

Lynch, M. (2000). "Rehabilitation as rhetoric: The ideal of reformation in contemporary parole discourse and practices." *Punishment & Society*, 2(1): 40–65.

McCorkel, J. (2003). "Embodied surveillance and the gendering of punishment." *Journal of Contemporary Ethnography*, 32(1): 41–76.

McCorkel, J. (2004). "Criminally dependent? Gender, punishment, and the rhetoric of welfare reform." *Social Politics*, 11(3): 386–410.

Moore, D., & Hannah-Moffat, K. (2005). "The liberal veil: Revisiting Canadian penality." In J. Pratt, D. Brown, S. Hallsworth, & W. Morrison, eds., *The New Punitiveness: Trends, Theories, Perspectives* (pp. 85–100). Portland, OR: Willan Publishing.

Newman, S. (2001). "Derrida's deconstruction of authority." *Philosophy & Social Criticism*, 27(3): 1–20.

Northern Ireland Human Rights Commission. (2005). *The Hurt Inside: The Imprisonment of Women and Girls in Northern Ireland*. Belfast: Northern Ireland Human Rights Commission.

NSW Department of Corrective Services. (1994). *Women's Action Plan: A Three-Year Strategy for Female Inmates in NSW Correctional Facilities*. Sydney.

NSW Department of Corrective Services. (2000). *Women's Action Plan 2, 2000–2003*. Sydney.

O'Brien, P., & Harm, N. (2002). "Women's recidivism and reintegration: Two sides of the same coin." In J. Figueira-McDonough & R.C. Sarri, eds., *Women at the Margins: Neglect, Punishment, & Resistance* (pp. 295–318). New York: Haworth Press.

Parkes, D., & Pate, K. (2006). "Time for accountability: Effective oversight of women's prisons." *Canadian Journal of Criminology and Criminal Justice*, 8(2): 251–285.

Pickett, B.L. (1996). "Foucaultian rights?" *Social Science Journal*, 37(3): 403–421.

Rodley, N.S. (1999). *The Treatment of Prisoners Under International Law* (2nd ed.). Oxford; New York: Clarendon Press.

Rose, N. (1985). "Unreasonable rights: Mental illness and the limits of law." *Journal of Law and Society*, 12(2): 199–218.

Rose, N., & Valverde, M. (1998). "Governed by law?" *Social & Legal Studies*, 7(4): 541–551.

Scraton, P., & Moore, L. (2005). "Degradation, harm and survival in a women's prison." *Social Policy & Society*, 5(1): 67–78.

Sisters Inside. (2004). *Submission of Sisters Inside to the Anti Discrimination Commissioner for the Inquiry into the Discrimination on the Basis of Sex, Race and Disability Experienced by Women Prisoners in Queensland, Brisbane*. Brisbane: Sisters Inside Inc.

Smith, Caleb. (2009). *The Prison and the American Imagination*. New Haven, CT: Yale University Press.

Valverde, M. (1996). "'Despotism' and ethical liberal governance." *Economy and Society*, 25(3): 357–372.

Widder, N. (2004). "Foucault and power revisited." *European Journal of Political Theory*, 3(4): 411–432.

Woodiwess, A. (2002). "Human rights and the challenge of cosmopolitanism." *Theory, Culture & Society*, 19(1-2): 139–155.

Legal Cases and Statutes

Anti-Discrimination Act of New South Wales. Act 48. (Sydney: Anti-Discrimination Commission 1977 June 1).

Charter of the United Nations and Statute of the International Court of Justice. (San Francisco: United Nations 1945 October 24).

Declaration of the Rights of Man and of the Citizen. (Paris: National Constituent Assembly 1789 August 26).

International Covenant on Civil and Political Liberties. No. 14668. (General Assembly of the United Nations: New York 1966 December 19).

International Covenant on Economic, Social and Cultural Rights. No. 2200 XXI. (New York: General Assembly of the United Nations 1966 December 16).

United States Bill of Rights. (USA 1791 December 15).

Universal Declaration of Human Rights. (New York: United Nations General Assembly 1948 December 10).

Chapter 2

Resisting Colonial Violence(s) Together: Stories of Loss, Renewal, and Friendship from Algonquin Territory

Colleen Cardinal and Kristen Gilchrist

Introduction(s)

Thank you to Jennifer Kilty for inviting us to contribute to this collection. We'd also like to acknowledge our Indigenous[1] and non-Indigenous readers for taking the time to listen to and hear these words. This chapter is a collaborative effort between two friends: Colleen Cardinal, who is Indigenous, and Kristen Gilchrist, who is White. We both live in Ottawa, Ontario, on unsurrendered Anishinaabe aki (Algonquin land). Over a period of several months, we have worked closely with Families of Sisters in Spirit (FSIS), a local grassroots not-for-profit community organization made up of the families of missing and murdered Indigenous women and girls across these lands.

Our chapter prioritizes first-person voices, especially those of Indigenous women in relation to their lived experiences of colonization and colonialism, and their embodied resistance and resilience in the face of these forces. We have placed storytelling at the centre of our analysis, reflecting Indigenous ways of knowing and being with and in the world (McGuire, 2009; Thomas, 2005). Further, we believe there is nourishment and strength in sharing, telling, and listening to personal testimonies rooted in lived knowledge(s). We both feel that bearing witness to one another's stories represents a crucial starting point for building mutual relationships across our differences and in our personal and collective healing journeys. Before going further, allow us to introduce ourselves.

zhaawanongnoodinkwe mihingan dodem, saddle lake n'doojbah 2013

My name is Colleen Cardinal. I am originally from Saddle Lake, Alberta (near

Edmonton), on Treaty 6 territory. I am a Plains Cree woman, mother, and grandmother to a lively granddaughter named Rosalie. I introduced myself in Anishinabemowin, the Anishinabe language of the peoples upon whose territories I have settled. I enjoy writing and spending time with my friends and chosen family. I am working on a documentary film about Indigenous women's experiences of living under colonialism and colonization.

As a result of generations of colonization and colonialism, the women in my family have endured physical, sexual, emotional, and cultural abuse that has lasted well into the present day. I have lost many loved ones to violence. My sister Gina [Charmaine] Desa was murdered in 1990 when she was 20 years old. My sister-in-law Lynne Jackson was murdered in 2004; the case remains unsolved. An uncle was also murdered, and suicide has touched our family. Even as an adult in charge of my own destiny, I could not escape the grips of violence, which threatened to take my life more than once.

I became involved as a supporter with Families of Sisters in Spirit (FSIS) after I moved to Ottawa in 2011. I attended their annual October 4th Sisters in Spirit vigil held on Parliament Hill. I was there to honour and remember my sisters and all the women and men who have gone missing and been murdered. I was surprised and touched to see Lynne Jackson's photo being displayed so that her case will not be forgotten. In the past year, I have gotten to know and connect with FSIS's co-founders, Kristen Gilchrist and Bridget Tolley. Bridget is an Algonquin kokum (grandmother) whose mother was struck and killed by the Quebec provincial police (SQ) in October 2001.

I'm Kristen. I am a non-Indigenous settler queer-femme born in Ontario, descended from Scottish, French, and Welsh ancestors. On my mother's side, we have a large extended family who are Native.[2] A little over a decade ago, I moved to Ottawa to study criminology and sociology at university. For several years I had no idea I had settled on the traditional and unsurrendered territories of the Algonquin, nor was I aware that the nearest First Nations community was home to the Kitigan Zibi Anishaabe Algonquin Nation located in Maniwaki, Quebec. Like most settler Canadians, my knowledge of colonization and colonialism were almost non-existent.

I am still in university, approaching the end of a doctorate degree in sociology. Although Indigenous peoples were a topic of/for discussion in academic spaces throughout my undergraduate and graduate studies—mostly related to "social issues"—Indigenous peoples themselves were rarely centred, nor were Indigenous worldviews or anti-colonial perspectives brought into the conversations. Even rarer were there critical questions raised about the academy and its role in upholding colonial structures and ideologies. Instead, my "coming into" understandings of colonial power, settler solidarity, and decolonization stem from my engagement with families and communities affected by sexual violence, disappearance, and violent death. For example, I began to volunteer my support (e.g., time, writing skills, and countless other activities that were needed/asked for) to families of missing and murdered Indigenous women several years ago, and later helped to coordinate volunteers for the annual October 4th Sisters in Spirit vigils as a volunteer for Amnesty International Canada's (No More) Stolen Sisters Campaign. I have volunteered full-time for three and a half years for Families of Sisters in Spirit (FSIS).

FSIS was founded in January 2011 after the Government of Canada, under the leadership of Prime Minister Stephen Harper, denied renewed funding to Sisters in Spirit (SIS), a research, education, and policy initiative related to missing and murdered Aboriginal women and girls that was administered by the Native Women's Association of Canada from 2005 to 2010. Not content with seeing the five years of work with families of the missing and murdered end, Bridget Tolley—an Algonquin grandmother and long-time community activist whose own mother was killed by the Quebec provincial police in 2001—asked me to support her efforts to bring FSIS to life. FSIS is led by and for families of missing and murdered Indigenous women and girls, with support from a diversity of friends and allies. FSIS receives no government, agency, or organizational funding. We operate entirely with support from the community, including volunteers, donations, and in-kind support (Tolley, Martin, & Gilchrist, 2012).

My involvement with FSIS and the associated friendships that have been nourished were personally transformative in many ways. They have allowed me to make connections to my own settler ancestral roots, helped to make me feel safe speaking about my personal experiences with sexual violence and mental health struggles, and taught me a considerable amount about the process of learning itself, as well as about humility, courage, and the power of Indigenous women in leading the way forward.

Directions

In this chapter we draw on the writings, stories, experiences, and oral histories of Indigenous women and those who are Two-Spirit—voices that have been systematically silenced—to bear witness to their accounts of colonial violence(s) and pathways of resistance and resurgence.

We contend that colonialism and colonization are themselves structures of violence and that there is a relationship between attacks on sovereign Nations and attacks on Native women's bodies. Indeed, the law and Canadian legal systems have been primary tools of oppression and violence across Indigenous Nations and communities. In addition, we discuss how specific colonial policies and practices encoded in law have created and enabled conditions that increase the vulnerability of Indigenous women, Two-Spirit, and girls to sexual violence, abductions, and homicide. We deconstruct myths embedded in "the Canadian identity" and history, and examine how these reinforce colonial hierarchies and violence(s). Further, we contemplate strategies to address violence(s) that uphold Indigenous self-determination and dignity across various differences of background, experience, and social location(s), which do not rely on and exist outside of colonial institutions.

Before continuing, we wish to acknowledge and give thanks for the powerful work by Indigenous peoples that has been ongoing for generations and centuries in Indigenous Nations across Turtle Island, or North America, as described in Anishinabe and Haudenosaunee languages. In doing so, Indigenous efforts have ensured that cultural traditions, languages, ceremonies, and relationships to Ancestors and Creation were passed on to descendants. Indeed, these efforts have sustained the longest-running social movement across these lands (Ladner & Simpson, 2010).

Colonial Violence(s)

All oppression of Aboriginal Peoples in Canada has operated with the assistance and the formal sanction of law. The legal system is at the heart of what we must reject as Aboriginal nations and as Aboriginal individuals.
—Patricia Monture

Critical dialogue and engagement with the complexities of colonialism and colonization indicate their significant relationships to violence(s) against Indigenous peoples—including sexual violence, forced disappearance, and death by violence. By digging up the roots of violence(s), there can be a deeper and more nuanced understanding of colonial and legal processes as structured forms of violence. We emphasize an expansive definition and thus tend to pluralize the word "violence." This is done to draw attention to a broad spectrum of attitudes and acts (intended or not) that impose and result in domination, coercion, control, overpowering and/or wielding "power over" an/other. The word "violence(s)" is also pluralized as a reminder that such acts and attitudes are not isolated happenings, but instead are deeply interconnected to colonial hierarchies embedded in past and present Canadian society.

The terms "colonization" and "colonialism" are sometimes used interchangeably and are thus presumed to mean the same thing. Although they are mutually reinforcing processes, there are some important distinctions worth noting (see also Kline in Comack, 2008, note 2). Colonization denotes the occupation of a foreign land, in this case, occupation of Turtle Island by a foreign people—namely British and French settlers. In a Canadian context, it entails the wholesale appropriation of the sovereignty and self-determination of Indigenous Nations, theft of land, exploitation of resources, and destruction of traditional ways of living, being, and knowing for the political and economic benefit of settlers (Green, 2007a). Colonization is a concrete and deliberate process intended to control those peoples displaced from their land (Lawrence, 2002: 26), and it is typically encoded in laws, legal systems, policies, education systems, and the popular culture of colonizers (Green, 2007b: 143). A more universal definition used in the life sciences offers much perspective: colonization is the spreading of a new species into a new habitat; the "new species" being White settler men (and later women) and the "new habitat" meaning the ancient inhabited territories of Indigenous communities across Turtle Island.

Colonialism is the broader ideology of White, cis-hetero-patriarchal, Christian, and Anglo-, and Franco-European settler supremacy. Inherent in colonialism is the assumed inferiority and "savagery" of Indigenous populations, which make the acts of colonization not just possible, but also legitimate, normal, and largely untroubling to non-Indigenous settlers. Said another way, the ideology of settler supremacy is the common-sense rationale behind the violent, coercive, and non-consensual acts associated with the ongoing colonization of Indigenous Nations, territories, and bodies. One dominant colonial ideology dictates that, in order to "civilize" so-called "savage" Indians, "half-breeds," and Eskimos, settlers must segregate, assimilate, and dispossess Indigenous peoples of their territories, resources, and sovereignty. This is not understood by settler parties as violent or harmful, but rather as benevolent and well-intentioned (Alfred, 2010; Smith, 2011).

Colonial ideologies continue to shape the identities and experiences of Indigenous and non-Indigenous folk across these lands. Bonita Lawrence (2002) draws attention to the ways in which Canada's origin story and national identity are embedded in colonial ideologies. Specifically, she highlights the mistaken yet widespread notion

> of Canada as a vast northern wilderness; the possession of which makes Canadians unique and "pure" of character. Because of this, and in order for Canada to have a viable national identity, the histories of Indigenous nations, in all their diversity and longevity, must be erased. Furthermore, in order to maintain Canadians' self image as a fundamentally "decent" people innocent of any wrongdoing, the historical record of how the land was acquired—the forcible and relentless dispossession of Indigenous peoples, the theft of their territories, and the implementation of legislation and politics designed to effect their total disappearance as peoples—must also be erased. (23–24)

Prior to contact with Europeans and settlers, the majority of Indigenous Nations and cultures were matriarchal or semi-matriarchal in nature. This was in stark contrast to viciously cis-hetero-patriarchal European traditions, wherein women and children were legislated as the property of their fathers, husbands, or brothers. This disparity in cultural structures led Patricia Monture (2011) to describe the *Indian Act*, the still-existing federal law that governs all "Indians and Indian Lands," as a foreign regime that has rendered First Nations wards of the state and imposed via force destructive ways of relating to each other, the land, and Creation.

Indigenous women and Two-Spirit people played instrumental roles in economic, political, familial, and spiritual aspects of life during the pre-colonial era. Women of all ages were highly respected and valued members of their families and communities, and were part of consensus-building and decision-making in their communities and Nations (LaRocque, 1994; Green 2007a: 22).[3] Across many Indigenous cultures, women were (and are still) viewed as embodying sacred elements of Creation. As the caretakers of the Spirit, keepers of cultural knowledge, and as the "doorway through which all life passes" with the honoured gift of bringing children into the physical world, Indigenous women hold a revered place within their families and Nations (Jacobs, 2011: 11; Monture, 2011; Monture-Angus, 1995).

Two-Spirit folk in particular held ancestral roles as leaders, medicine people, healers, and warriors (Konsmo, in Williams & Konsmo, 2010: 23). The term "Two-Spirit/ed" emerged during the 1990s but is deeply rooted in Indigenous histories and traditions on Turtle Island (Wilson 2008). Cherokee Two-Spirit scholar Qwo-Li Driskill (2010: 72–73) describes Two-Spirit identity as intentionally complex, fluid, falling outside of dominant Eurocentric constructions of gender and sexuality, and inclusive of the Native LGBTQ spectrum. According to Alex Wilson of the Opaskwayak (Swampy) Cree First Nation, Two-Spirit is a self-described identity that honours and integrates sexuality, gender, culture, spirituality, and all other aspects of the person as part of "connect[ing] us to our past and restor[ing] cultural links that have been disturbed or severed by systemic and institutionalized racism, sexism, and homo[queer]phobia" (2008: 44–45). By "coming into" Two-Spirit identity, Two-Spirit people are restoring their place and value in their families, communities, Nations—both past and present (Wilson 2008: 45). Further, "no understanding of sexual and gender constructions on colonized and occupied land can take place without an understanding of the way colonial projects continually police sexual and gender lines" (Driskill, 2010: 73).

It was not by accident that colonial processes cemented the destruction of these traditional roles, as well as the autonomy and authority of Indigenous women and Two-Spirit people in their communities (Driskill, 2010; Jacobs & Williams, 2008; Monture, 2011). For instance, with legal restrictions placed on cultural teachings, the role and value of Elders was similarly negated. In addition, extended kin networks and collective values were "legislated out," and the nuclear family and individualism were seen by colonizers as the yardstick by which Aboriginal families would be measured (Proulx & Perrault, 2000: 16).

Indigenous legal traditions, such as those of the Haudenosaunee (Mohawk) people described by Patricia Monture, are about trying to "live in respect of the laws that the Creator gave ... when she put us here" (1998: 121). Indeed, Indigenous notions of justice and law are about "retaining, teaching and maintaining good relationships," as well as acknowledging our individual and collective responsibilities, "and only then a sense of what is fitting, right or fair" (Monture, 2011: 2).

There are important connections to be made between attacks on the sovereignty of Indigenous Nations; lands; political, social, and legal traditions; and attacks on Indigenous women's bodies. Whether it is in the destruction of a peoples' way of life or the denial of their inherent rights as enshrined in the Treaties and upheld in the *Canadian Charter of Rights and Freedoms*, to be free of settler/state interference, violence(s) against Indigenous women poses a significant threat to Indigenous peoples' safety (Danforth, 2012; Jacobs, 2011; Smith, 2005, 2007). Indeed it is because Indigenous women are the carriers of their nations that they "bare the brunt of colonial anger, racism, and violence" (Da Silva, 2010: 59).

Missing and Murdered Indigenous Women in Context

An unknown number of Indigenous women, girls, and Two-Spirit folk have been murdered or forcibly disappeared in Canada since their first contact with European settlers. Statistics gathered by Sisters in Spirit (2010) indicate that the number is between 500 and 600 women since the 1970s. However, due to limitations in their capacity for data collection,[4] including reliance on secondary data, inconsistent police records and reporting,[5] reliance on media reports, and difficulty in accessing information about historical cases, the estimation of 500 to 600 missing and murdered women may in fact be much higher. Moreover, this number is out of date by three years.[6] We are grateful for SIS's research but wish to highlight that the often cited "500 or 600 missing and murdered Aboriginal women" tells only a fraction of the larger story of violence. Several families linked to FSIS have chosen not to use this figure because it tends to minimize the larger picture of Indigenous violence, and draws attention from their lived realities as experienced on the ground.

This may come as a surprise to non-Indigenous folks, but there are very few First Nations families and communities who have not experienced structural violence in some form or who have not had a relative whose life has been cut short because of violence. As Colleen Cardinal notes, "[O]ur relatives have been raped, molested, beaten by fists and belts, and violently cursed at, belittled, segregated, isolated and dehumanized in the name of 'civilizing' and 'assimilating' our peoples." She adds:

On July 24th, 1990, my sister Gina was murdered in a downtown park in Edmonton, Alberta. She was 20 years old and had two small children. Gina had been killed by an acquaintance who was later charged and convicted of 2nd-degree murder. On the morning of Gina's murder, I happened to catch a glance, and right on the front page of the *Edmonton Sun* newspaper I saw a large picture of the Edmonton police officers wheeling out a stretcher with a black body bag on it. The headline read: "MOTHER OF TWO FOUND DEAD IN A PARK." The article went on to describe the park as being notorious for drug deals, prostitution, and nefarious characters. The media were basically setting the tone that this dead woman must have been up to no good and got herself killed. At the time I did not know that it was my sister. When I did find out, I was too overwhelmed with grief to do anything about it. I was also only 16 years old at the time.

I took a lot of calls from media who were trying to find out the angle of why Gina was in the park: Did she do drugs? Was she a prostitute? They asked questions about her background, and her life leading up to her death. I was young and naive, and talked about Gina's aspirations to do well, be a mother, and have a good life with her family. I shared with them how she had fled our abusive adoptive family for Toronto, and ended up working the streets to get by until she met her husband and came back to Edmonton. I was angry and ashamed when I read the article because my words were being used against Gina to make her look bad. There was no context given whatsoever, so it was as if she had brought this all on herself.

On June 21, 2004, my sister-in-law Lynne Minia Jackson was found murdered in Wetaskiwin, outside Edmonton. Her case is still unsolved. Lynne was a mother, a sister, a dearly loved friend to many. She was an auntie to my boys, Tristan and Sage. She was the youngest of her siblings and left behind children who will never know their mother. A lifetime of battling oppressive colonial policies enforced via laws and systems has left many Indigenous folk with deep and unhealed wounds.

Colonization and colonialism have brought violence to my ancestors' doorsteps in the form of displacement, forced settlement on reserves, institutionalization in residential schools, jails, and prisons, systemic racism, abject poverty, trauma, rape, abductions, and death. But Indigenous

> peoples are still here. Despite living under conditions meant to erase our women, our territories, and our Nations, Indigenous peoples have always been strong and will grow stronger every day.

Testimonies from families of missing and murdered Indigenous women across these lands indicate shared histories of colonial violence and resilience and resistance dating back several generations (Amnesty International Canada, 2004, 2009; Sisters in Spirit, 2010). Below, we discuss a number of specific policies and laws that, while constituting violence(s) against Indigenous women and girls, also shape how Canadian society responds or, rather, does not respond.

Canadian laws and/or legislation, from the *Indian Act* and reaching into the present day, represent direct forms of violence against Indigenous peoples. During the nineteenth century, Indigenous peoples were forcibly segregated and displaced from their lands onto crowded and isolated reserves where families were expected to become peasant farmers (Truth and Reconciliation Commission [TRC], 2012: 28). For those Nations accustomed to a nomadic lifestyle involving hunting, trapping, fishing, and living off the land in order to survive, containment on reserves represented a fate akin to imprisonment (Mercredi, 2006: 136). In addition, parents, grandparents, and the extended family of many missing and murdered Indigenous women and girls were subject to the residential school system; this was the case in Colleen's family. The federal government and officials from Catholic and other Christian churches believed residential schools were necessary to civilize and assimilate Aboriginal peoples into a White, Christian, and capitalist society. Systemic attacks on culture, language, spiritual beliefs, and traditional practices were part and parcel of the residential school experience for Indigenous children and youth across the country.

According to the Truth and Reconciliation Commission's 2012 report, *They Came for the Children*, residential schools were seen as an effective means of separating children from their parents "who were certain to oppose and resist such a radical cultural transformation" (2012: 10). Indeed Canada's first prime minister, Sir John A. Macdonald, who was also Minister of Indian Affairs, warned the House of Commons in 1883 that "when the school is on the reserve, the child lives with his parents who are savages; he is surrounded by savages, and though he may learn to read and write, his habits and training and mode of thought are Indian. He is simply a savage who can read and write" (quoted in TRC, 2012: 6). Seventy-one years later, this remained a prevailing ideology. In 1954, the federal government's Sub-Committee on Eskimo Education concluded that "the residential school is perhaps the most effective way of giving children from primitive environments, experience in education along the lines of civilization leading to vocational training to fit them for occupations in the white man's economy" (quoted in TRC, 2012: 12).

Children from the ages of six to eighteen were mandated to attend residential school, often for more than 10 months each year (Royal Commission on Aboriginal Peoples [RCAP], 1996). From 1920 onward, parents were subject to criminalization if they protested their children's mandatory attendance in residential schools. Criminalization meant risk of arrest, detention, and incarceration (Jacobs & Williams, 2008; see also Mercredi, 2006: 5). Residential schools were chronically underfunded, often overcrowded, lacking in adequate heat and ventilation, reliant on student labour, highly regimented and uniform, punitive, and frequently abusive (TRC, 2012). Many who attended residential school were malnourished, contracted viruses and diseases, and were subjected to ongoing emotional, spiritual, physical, sexual, and cultural abuses (TRC, 2012: 30).

Before residential schools closed their doors,[7] more than 100,000 Aboriginal children and youth had endured the residential school system (McGillivray & Comaskey, 1999). According to the Royal Commission on Aboriginal Peoples (1996), of all colonial practices, residential schools have done the greatest damage to Aboriginal communities, in part because the Aboriginal children and youth attending these schools were aggressively taught to reject their families, communities, cultural values and heritage, and, by extension, their identity and sense of self. The *United Nations Declaration of the Rights of Indigenous Peoples* identifies residential schools as a form of cultural genocide.

The "Sixties Scoop"

As the era of residential schools began to wind down in the 1960s, families and Nations were subject to further assaults on their sovereignty and safety via widespread child apprehension policies. Commonly referred to as the "Sixties Scoop" (although it lasted well into 1980s), this was not a single policy but rather "one segment of a larger period of Aboriginal child welfare history" (Sinclair, 2007: 65). This period was marked by the removal and separation of thousands of Aboriginal children from their birth families and lands and their placement in mostly White families in Canada, the United States, and overseas (Jacobs & Williams, 2008; Sinclair, 2007: 65–67). The policies were such that "governments did not provide any supports to help keep families together: they simply apprehended the children" (TRC, 2012: 19). By 1970, one-third of Indigenous children had been removed from their homes, sometimes without the knowledge or consent of their families or Nations, and with contact between relatives entirely cut off (Sinclair, 2007: 66).

According to "Sixties Scoop" survivor and scholar Raven Sinclair (2007: 67), these policies and practices were highly questionable and resulted in consistently negative outcomes, especially during adolescent years, regardless of the age of apprehension. Here is Colleen's description of her experience of being "scooped":

> In the early 1970s, my two sisters and I were taken away from our biological parents when we were very young and placed in foster homes. We were adopted into a non-Indigenous household in Ontario, three thousand miles away from our homelands, our people, our language, and anything vaguely familiar to our Cree culture. Life was difficult in our new home; we dealt with isolation, racism, and sexual and physical abuse for many years. All three of us had run away by the time we turned 15 years old. Eventually we all found our way back to Alberta.

Upon migrating to towns or urban areas, whether because they are fleeing abuse or are in search of opportunities to become financially independent, oftentimes women and their children are faced with living in neighbourhoods where housing is neither safe nor affordable. Aboriginal and Two-Spirit youth are at a particular disadvantage as they are more likely to be homeless as a result of a lack of secure and appropriate housing (Jacobs & Williams, 2008; Urban Native Youth Association, 2004).

The lack of options for women, youth, and Two-Spirit folk who experience poverty, homelessness, and other violence(s) (especially childhood sexual abuse) often compels them to make decisions that increase their vulnerability to interpersonal violence(s). They experience sexual assault, forced disappearance, and death by violence due to involvement with street economies such as sex work, drug use and dealing, gangs, and theft as a means to "get by" (SIS, 2008; Urban Native Youth Association, 2004). Not surprisingly, involvement in survival and street economies often leads to high rates of violence that are left unreported to the police and/or result in increased conflict with the law, as evidenced by the marked over-incarceration of Aboriginal peoples in jails and prisons across Canada (Monture-Angus, 1995; SIS, 2008). Aboriginal women currently constitute the fastest-growing prison population in Canada, with a 90 percent increase in federally sentenced Aboriginal women in just the past decade. One in three women in prison is Aboriginal (Public Safety Canada, 2012).

Patricia Monture (1998: 77–78) makes deliberate connections between child "welfare" laws and the criminal legal system, noting that both sit on a continuum of state violence against Indigenous peoples. Both institutions remove individuals from their communities through the exercise of state force, punishment, removal, and coercion. The forced removal of Indigenous peoples from their cultural, spiritual, and kin connections can have devastating consequences to individuals and Indigenous Nations. As a result of incarceration, Indigenous women in particular, who were at one time themselves apprehended, are now finding their own children caught up in both child "welfare" and criminal legal systems.

The "Millennium Scoop," as it was dubbed by Lauri Gilchrist, denotes the most recent and ongoing period of apprehension and placement of Aboriginal children and youth. However, rather than being forced into residential schools, they are being placed in long-term foster and institutional care where there is little chance of adoption (in Sinclair, 2007: 65–67). An analysis of cases of First Nations children "in care," a colloquial nicety used to describe the child welfare system, shows that they are no more likely than non-Indigenous children to be apprehended due to abuse. Yet, Indigenous children remain twice as likely to be removed for neglect, which is often associated with structural factors such as poverty and inadequate housing, or due to familial substance misuse (Blackstock, 2009). Nonetheless, "there are more First Nations children in state care today than at any point in history, including during residential school operations" (Blackstock, 2009: 1).

Concluding Thoughts: Telling and Listening as Revolutionary and Healing Acts

There are transformative possibilities for both the Indigenous storytellers and the non-Indigenous listeners/readers when relationships are built and conversations take place with open hearts, spirits, and minds. A commitment to moving forward in these ways upholds self-determination and sovereignty, and supports efforts to reclaim pre-colonial ways of knowing and being. With transformative telling, listening, and sharing, there exist opportunities to foster meaningful, reciprocal, respectful, consensual, and responsible relationships and friendships across our differences. For non-Indigenous folk, this requires acceptance that Indigenous women know how best to define their experiences, are best suited to address problems caused by colonial processes for themselves, their families, and their communities, with the affirmation that this has always been the case. For those who wish to align themselves/act as allies with Indigenous struggles, there must be a willingness to break down deeply held myths that shape Canadian history and identity. This includes comprehending that non-Indigenous folks are the primary beneficiaries of colonialism/colonization and that these processes profoundly altered and had negative consequences for Indigenous peoples' sovereignty and safety—especially including criminal legal systems and the law.

It is impossible for any of us to extricate ourselves fully from colonial patterns because, whether acknowledged or not, they infuse all of our contemporary and historic social relations (D'Archangelis & Huntley, 2012). Failing to recognize our complicity in systems of oppression, such as the criminal legal system, actually functions to mask, replicate, and hold these violent structures in place (Smith, 2011). If we are to envision a future free of violence(s), non-Indigenous folk cannot ignore or discount the privileges they have gained on the backs of Indigenous women, territories, and Nations—all with the full sanction of the law. While this can be a complicated and emotional process, it is imperative that feelings of settler guilt and defensiveness be put aside as they are obstacles to building lasting and meaningful relationships.

Much like our "on the ground" engagement with FSIS, this chapter is part of a broader call to action to disrupt violent colonial processes and ideologies at the roots of systemic dispossession, confinement, and assimilation, as well as sexual violence and the disappearance and death of Indigenous women and Two-Spirit people. We have centred the testimonies and knowledge(s) of Indigenous women, including of co-author Colleen Cardinal, to highlight the connections between colonization and colonialism that enable and generate violence(s) against Indigenous Nations and Indigenous bodies. In order to restore the rightful place of Indigenous women, Elders, youth, and Two-Spirit folk in their communities, Nations, and in wider Canadian society, it is necessary to re-centre and revitalize Indigenous voices and experiences (Jacobs, 2011; Williams & Konsmo, 2010).

In order to address multiple violence(s) and our continued complicity within these systems of oppression, there must be an ongoing commitment to re/building connections between people and groups so as to work past our differences. Moving forward together entails that each of us, regardless of where we are situated, take responsibility for and become accountable to our relations, friends, and allies (Williams & Konsmo, 2010). It is an agreement to meet each other "where we are at" to create nourishing movements rooted in Indigenous values of trust, love, sacredness, friendship, balance, healing, and wholeness as a means of moving toward a peaceful and equitable Canada and Turtle Island. It is the least we can do to honour the generations of missing and murdered Aboriginal women across these lands.

Notes

1 We use the term "Indigenous" to denote the original inhabitants and First Nations of Turtle Island (North America), Metis, and Inuit. The terms "Aboriginal" and "Native" are used throughout as interchangeable with Indigenous. As noted by Patricia Monture and Patricia D. McGuire, "It is always important to remember that the words Aboriginal, Native, Indigenous, or Indian are colonial words imposed upon many diverse nations. They are not our own words for who we are and from this position it does not matter which colonial word you choose to use now.... Generally Aboriginal draws its meaning from Canada's constitution where we are defined as the 'Indian, Inuit, and Métis.' Indian is the correct legal term when used to describe any person registered under the rules found in Canada's *Indian Act*. Often these 'registered' Indians are called 'status' Indians. So those who are not registered under the act do not have status, and frankly we find that reference to others disturbing. All persons have 'status' as a human being and should have equality" (Monture & McGuire, 2009: 1–2).

2 I use the term "Native" because it is how most of my relatives refer to themselves. Some relatives prefer Metis, and less often, Ojibwe is used to self-identify.

3 Although beyond the scope of this paper, we feel it is important to note that Andrea Smith (2006), Jessica (Yee) Danforth (2010), and Krysta Williams & Erin Konsmo (2010) have pointed out that what Western/non-Native feminists have long being trying to achieve—gender equity and self-determination—were being lived and practised for centuries by Indigenous Nations before settler arrival.

4 This should not be interpreted as us saying or believing that the SIS staff is in any way responsible for these limitations. In fact it is the opposite. The staff did the best they could with their resources and mandate, despite many constraints.

5 There is no consistency across Canada in terms of law enforcement keeping racial/ethnic statistics for victims and offenders—and sometimes there has been a reluctance to do so. Many acts of violence against Indigenous women and girls will never come to their attention, and when cases do eventually come to light, there is no longer sufficient evidence to make a determination of "foul play." Recently, Indigenous youth-led organizations have noted that Two-Spirit and trans persons are mis-gendered/misidentified by police (and media), and thus are not being "counted."

6 When Sisters in Spirit came to a close in 2010, so too did the database. There have been no official statistics kept since March 31, 2010.

7 The last residential school, located in the Province of Saskatchewan, closed in 1996. However, residential schools largely fell out of favour in the 1960s (Comack, 2008).

References

Aboriginal Justice Implementation Commission. (1991). *The Justice System and Aboriginal People.* Retrieved from www.ajic.mb.ca/volumel/chapter4.html

Alfred, T. (2010). "Foreword." In P. Regan, *Unsettling the Settler Within: Indian Residential Schools, Truth Telling and Reconciliation in Canada* (pp. ix–xi). Vancouver: UBC Press.

Amnesty International Canada. (2004). *Stolen Sisters: A Human Rights Response to Discrimination and Violence Against Indigenous Women in Canada.* Retrieved from www.amnesty.ca/stolensisters/amr2000304.pdf

Amnesty International Canada. (2009). *No More Stolen Sisters: The Need for a Comprehensive Response to Discrimination and Violence Against Indigenous Women in Canada.* Retrieved from www.amnesty.ca/research/reports/no-more-stolen-sisters-the-need-for-a-comprehensive-response-to-discrimination-and-

Blackstock, C. (2009). "Why addressing the over-representation of First Nations children in care requires new theoretical approaches based on First Nations ontology." *The Journal of Social Work Values and Ethics*, 6(3). Retrieved from www.socialworker.com/jswve/content/view/135/69/

Comack, E. (2008). *Out Here/In Here: Masculinity, Violence and Prisoning*. Halifax: Fernwood Publishing.

Danforth (Yee), J. (2012). *Jessica Danforth: Fucking While Feminist*, Episode 13. Retrieved from www.jaclynfriedman.com/archives/776

D'Archangelis, C., & Huntley, A. (2012). "No more silence: Toward a feminist pedagogy of decolonizing solidarity." In L. Manicom & S. Waters, eds., *Feminist Popular Education in Transnational Debates: Building Pedagogies of Possibility* (pp. 41–58). New York: Palgrave Macmillan.

Da Silva, J. (2010). "Hashinoqwah." In L. Simpson & K.L. Ladner, eds., *This Is an Honour Song: Twenty Years Since the Blockades* (pp. 59–74). Winnipeg: Arbeiter Ring Publishing.

Driskill, Q.L. (2010). "Doubleweaving two-spirit critiques: Building alliances between Native and Queer Studies." *GLQ: A Journal of Lesbian and Gay Studies*, 16(1-2): 69–93.

Green, J. (2007a). "Taking account of Aboriginal feminism." In J. Green, ed., *Making Space for Indigenous Feminism* (pp. 20–32). Halifax: Fernwood Publishing.

Green, J. (2007b). "Balancing strategies: Aboriginal women and constitutional rights in Canada." In J. Green, ed., *Making Space for Indigenous Feminism* (pp. 140–159). Halifax: Fernwood Publishing.

Jacobs, B. (2011). *Restoring the Balance: Aboriginal Women's Issues in Canada*. Vancouver: UBC Critical Issues in Aboriginal Life and Thought Series. Retrieved from www.youtube.com/watch?v=1A6DWgw8_YM

Jacobs, B., & Williams, A. (2008). "Legacy of residential schools: Missing and murdered Aboriginal women." In M.B. Castellano & M. DeGagne, eds., *From Truth to Reconciliation: Transforming the Legacy of Residential Schools* (pp. 119–141). Ottawa: Aboriginal Healing Foundation.

Jiwani, Y. (2006). *Discourses of Denial: Mediations on Race, Gender, and Violence*. Vancouver: University of British Columbia Press.

Ladner, K.L., & Simpson, L. (2010). "This is an honour song." In L. Simpson & K.L. Ladner, eds., *This Is an Honour Song: Twenty Years Since the Blockades* (pp. 1–9). Winnipeg: Arbeiter Ring Publishing.

LaRocque, E. (1994). *Violence in Aboriginal Communities*. Ottawa: National Clearinghouse on Family Violence, Health Canada.

Lawrence, B. (2002). "Rewriting histories of the land: Colonization and Indigenous resistance in Eastern Canada." In S. Razack, ed., *Race, Space, and the Law: Unmapping a White Settler Society* (pp. 21–46). Toronto: Between the Lines.

McGillivray, A., & Comaskey, B. (1999). *Black Eyes All the Time: Intimate Violence, Aboriginal Women, and the Justice System.* Toronto: University of Toronto Press.

McGuire, P.D. (2009). "Wissaakowedikwe Anishinaabekwe Diabaajimotaw Nipigon Zaaga'igan: Lake Nipigon Ojibiway Métis stories about women." In P. Monture & P.D. McGuire, eds., *First Voices: An Aboriginal Women's Reader* (pp. 67–77). Toronto: Inanna Publications and Education Inc.

Mercredi, M. (2006). *Morningstar: A Warrior's Spirit.* Regina: Coteau Books.

Monture-Angus, P. (1995). *Thunder in My Soul: A Mohawk Woman Speaks.* Halifax: Fernwood Publishing.

Monture, P. (1998). *Locating Aboriginal Peoples in Canadian Law: One Aboriginal Woman's Journey through Case Law and the Canadian Constitution.* Master of Laws dissertation, Osgoode Hall Law School, York University, North York, ON.

Monture, P. (2011). "Thinking about Aboriginal justice: Myths and revolutions." *Justice as Healing: A Newsletter on Aboriginal Concepts of Justice*, 16(3): 1–3. Native Law Centre. Retrieved from www.usask.ca/nativelaw//publications/jah/2011/JAH_V16N3_2011_Tree_.pdf

Monture, P., & McGuire, P.D. (2009). "Introduction." In P.A. Monture & P.D. McGuire, eds., *First Voices: An Aboriginal Women's Reader* (pp. 1–5). Toronto: Inanna Publications and Education Inc.

Proulx, J., & Perrault, S. (2000). *No Place for Violence: Canadian Aboriginal Alternatives.* Halifax: Fernwood Publishing.

Public Safety Canada. (2012). *Marginalized: The Aboriginal Women's Experience in Federal Corrections.* Retrieved from www.publicsafety.gc.ca/res/cor/apc/apc-33-eng.aspx

Royal Commission on Aboriginal Peoples. (1996). *The Report from the Royal Commission on Aboriginal Peoples.* Ottawa: Minister of Supply and Services Canada. Retrieved from www.ainc-inac.gc.ca/ap/pubs/rpt/rpt-eng.asp

Sinclair, R. (2007). "Identity lost and found: Lessons from the Sixties Scoop." *First Peoples Child and Family Review*, 3(1): 65–82. Retrieved from www.fncfcs.com/pubs/vol3num1/Sinclair_pp65.pdf

Sisters in Spirit. (2008). *Voices of our Sisters in Spirit: A Research and Policy Report to Families and Communities.* Ottawa: Native Women's Association of Canada.

Sisters in Sprit. (2010). *What Their Stories Tell Us: Research Findings From the Sisters in Spirit Initiative.* Ottawa: Native Women's Association of Canada. Retrieved from www.nwac.ca/sites/default/files/imce/2010_NWAC_SIS_Report_EN_Lite_0.pdf

Smith, A. (2005). *Conquest: Sexual Violence and American Indian Genocide.* Cambridge, MA: South End Press.

Smith, A. (2006). "Native feminism without apology." *New Socialist.* Retrieved from www.whrnet.org/docs/issue-nativefem-0610.html

Smith, A. (2007). "Native American feminism: Sovereignty and social change." In J. Green, ed., *Making Space for Indigenous Feminism* (pp. 93–107). Halifax: Fernwood Publishing.

Smith, A. (2011). "Building unlikely alliances: An interview with Andrea Smith." *Upping the Ante*, 10, in conversation with Sharmeen Khan, David Hugill, and Tyler McCreary. Retrieved from http://uppingtheanti.org/journal/article/10-building-unlikely-alliances-an-interview-with-andrea-smith/

Thomas, R.A. (Qwul'sih'yah'maht). (2005). "Honouring the oral traditions of my ancestors through storytelling." In L. Brown & S. Strega, eds., *Research as Resistance: Critical, Indigenous, and Anti-Oppressive Approaches* (pp. 237–254). Toronto: Canadian Scholars' Press.

Tolley, B., Martin, S., & Gilchrist, K. (2012). "Families of Sisters in Spirit: Solidarity and relationship-building in the family-led movement on behalf of missing and murdered Indigenous women." In B. Depape, ed., *Power of Youth: Youth and Community-Led Activism in Canada* (pp. 133–140). Ottawa: Canadian Centre for Policy Alternatives.

Truth and Reconciliation Commission of Canada. (2012). *They Came for the Children: Canada, Aboriginal Peoples, and Residential Schools.* Winnipeg: Truth and Reconciliation Commission of Canada. Retrieved from www.attendancemarketing.com/~attmk/TRC_jd/ResSchoolHistory_2012_02_24_Webposting.pdf

Urban Native Youth Association. (2004). "Two-spirit youth speak out: Analysis of the Needs Assessment Tool." Vancouver: Urban Native Youth Association. Retrieved from www.unya.bc.ca/downloads/glbtq-twospirit-final-report.pdf

Williams, K., & Konsmo, E. (2010). "Resistance to Indigenous feminism." In J. Yee, ed., *Feminism for REAL: Deconstructing the Academic Industrial Complex* (pp. 21–36). Ottawa: Canadian Centre for Policy Alternatives.

Wilson, A. (2008). "Two-spirit identity: Active resistance to multiple oppressions." *Directions: Research and Policy on Eliminating Racism*, 5(1): 44–45.

Yee, J. (2011). "Introduction." In J. Yee, ed., *Feminism for REAL: Deconstructing the Academic Industrial Complex* (pp. 11–18). Our Schools/Our Selves. Ottawa: Canadian Centre for Policy Alternatives.

Legal Cases and Statutes

Constitution Act, 1982 [en. by the Canada Act 1982 (U.K.), c. 11, s. 1], pt. 1 (Canadian Charter of Rights and Freedoms)

Indian Act, R.S.C., 1985, c. I-5.

Chapter 3

"I Would Like Us to Unite and Fight for Our Rights Together Because We Haven't Been Able to Do It Alone": Women's Homelessness, Disenfranchisement, and Self-Determination

Emily K. Paradis

Introduction

"Homelessness" is widely understood as an individual, material state of being without a place of one's own in which to live.[1] Homelessness, by this common-sense definition, affects many women. Because there is no systematic collection of national data on homelessness in Canada, estimates of the rate of homelessness range broadly, from 150,000 to 300,000 (Echenberg & Jensen, 2008), and a recent survey showed that one in nine Canadians have faced homelessness at some time in their lives (Salvation Army, 2010). Women account for one-quarter to one-third of those enumerated in local street counts (YWCA, 2012). Girls make up an even larger proportion of the population of homeless youth (Novac, Serge, Eberle, & Brown, 2002), and the vast majority of families facing homelessness are headed by women. Women who are Aboriginal, Black, refugee claimants, lone mothers, living with disabilities, and lesbian, bisexual, trans, and Two-Spirit, are overrepresented in shelters for single women, youth, and families. As da Cunha (2005: 163) suggests of incarceration in urban Portugal, the experiences and expectations of impoverished and racialized women in urban Canada increasingly include homelessness "in their horizon." This means that more and more women are exposed to the devastation of their physical health and mental well-being by homelessness (Goodman, Saxe, & Harvey, 1991; Kappel Ramji Consulting Group, 2002; Street

Health Toronto, 2007), leading to a death rate 10 times that of women who are housed (Cheung & Hwang, 2004).

"Homelessness" is also a neologism invented over the past three decades to name a new social phenomenon (Hulchanski, Campsie, Chau, Hwang, & Paradis, 2009: 5). Though Jahiel (1992: 269) proposed "homeless-making" to describe social and economic processes that cause people to become dehoused, there exists no verb form of "homelessness": no word like "psychiatrize" or "criminalize" to describe the complex discursive and material processes by which certain circumstances, certain people, and certain groups come to be constituted as "homeless," and what happens as a result of this categorization.

The continuous escalation of the crisis of homelessness and its brutal effects for women demand an urgent response from researchers, activists, service providers, and policy-makers. At the same time, this response must step back from a definition of "homelessness" as simply an individual material state in order to examine it as a social process whose operations are significant to our understanding of the dominant social and economic order. Women's homelessness in Canada is no accident. Like incarceration and militarism, it is a central feature of the neoliberal security state. Ultimately, it is a project of disenfranchisement: one to exclude from liberal citizenship those who cannot or will not participate in the market. Given this, this chapter poses the question: What constitutes an appropriate response to homelessness? Does a demand for material provision of housing, income, and services adequately address what is at stake?

In her work on the criminalization and imprisonment of women, Sudbury (2005) calls for deep localized descriptions that together yield maps of global processes on which we can chart site-specific paths of resistance. Homelessness, like imprisonment, is a growing phenomenon of great economic, social, and cultural significance in Canada and globally, while its particular meanings and manifestations vary from locality to locality. In order to resist women's homelessness and envision a world without it, we need to understand not only its causes, but also its operations, its functions, and the social and political orders that produce it. We need broad maps that both situate it in relation to the surrounding landscape and provide intricate cartography of its terrain, drawn by the people who have been there and marked with the trails they are blazing through it.

This chapter draws upon critical feminist, decolonizing, and anti-racism literatures, and women's own accounts, to examine homelessness as a social process with discursive and empirical elements, functioning within and for a hegemonic social order. Women's stories and theories of homelessness demonstrate how homeless-making laws and policies are both enacted and resisted in their daily lived experiences. Their negotiations with homelessness suggest that the terrain of struggle is much broader than obtaining the material necessities of life.

A New Genealogy of Homelessness

When situated in historical contexts, homelessness in Canada is often considered in relation to the Great Depression of the 1930s: a modern crisis of capitalism best remedied by state social provision. It takes on a different meaning if we trace its genealogy differently, as a descendant of state and market regimes that have employed the provision or withdrawal of land, housing, and income as tools to control, punish, and erase dominated, colonized, and surplus populations.

Anti-poverty theorist and activist Jean Swanson (2001), for example, traces current Canadian welfare policy to the English Poor Laws. She explains how these laws were imposed in the context of enclosure and privatization of land in order to contain and control the landless population generated by these enclosures. Later, during industrialization, a welfare system was created to control the urban unemployed, defuse uprisings, and maintain a ready pool of labour to fill the most dangerous and menial occupations. In both cases, measures included the confinement of vagrants and unemployed people to poorhouses and workhouses. Significantly, Swanson also suggests that anti-poor beliefs, laws, and policies formed the basis for European racisms.

Homelessness in Canada begins with colonization for at least two reasons. First, European settlers imposed the construct of private property onto this land (Blomley, 2004). It is this colonial construct—bringing with it a whole legal system that establishes ownership of a place and metes out the penalties for being in that place without the owner's permission (Waldron, 1991)—that makes it possible to conceive of any person as not having a home, since any person as an embodied entity must reside some place. Second, Canadian law—mainly through the *Indian Act*, but also through other laws and treaties—has functioned to dispossess Aboriginal peoples of their territories and force them onto reserves. This marks the beginning of the use of the law in the social process of homeless-making in Canada. The high rate of Aboriginal homelessness today is a direct legacy of an ongoing project of colonization and genocide that has included housing-related policies such as the establishment of reserves, the forced relocation of communities (Bussidor & Bilgen-Rienart, 1997), the theft of children by churches and the state, and their confinement in residential schools (Menzies, 2005).[2]

Such laws and policies, of course, had specifically gendered manifestations. The best-known example is the pre-1985 *Indian Act* provision that Aboriginal women registered as "status Indian" would lose their status—and the ability to pass Indian status on to their children—when marrying non-status (or non-Aboriginal) men. Among other impacts, this provision had the effect of suspending women's right to housing in their own communities. However, its reversal through Bill C-31 in 1985 has perpetuated this problem, both through the introduction of a "second-generation cut-off" (meaning reinstated children cannot pass on Indian status) and through the failure of the federal government to increase resources for housing, education, and health services in First Nations communities to accommodate those whose status had been reinstated (Native Women's Association of Canada, 2007).

Razack (2002) describes how the production of Canada as a White settler nation-state relies upon the designation of citizens and non-citizens along racial lines through the organization of spaces. As in the case of Aboriginal peoples, racialized peoples and communities in Canada are often excluded from citizenship through state policies relating to territory, home, and housing. Some specific instances include the dispossession and internment of Japanese Canadians during the Second World War (Oikawa, 2002), the destruction of Africville in Nova Scotia (Nelson, 2002), and the requirement that women entering Canada under the Live-In Caregiver Program reside with their employers (Arat-Kroc, 2001).

Feminist analyses of housing and homelessness (CERA, 2002; Farha, 2002; Klowdawsky, 2006; Novac, Brown, & Bourbonnais, 1996; Passaro, 1996; Watson & Austerberry, 1986) point out that under the patriarchal institutions of property and family, a woman's access to a home is often mediated through the income of a man. These analyses advocate an understanding of homelessness that incorporates the situation of women who may be physically housed but who lack the security, safety, and self-determination that are essential aspects of "home" (Bunston & Breton, 1992; Kappel Ramji, 2002).

Finally, scholars working within critical disability, anti-psychiatry, and penal abolitionist frameworks describe how social provision, physical confinement, and institutional surveillance are employed by the state to regulate "deviant" populations.[3] Such regimes of regulation are structured by pathologizing and criminalizing discourses, and are strongly gendered and raced in their application. Systems of "care and control" (Allen, 2000) relating to women's homelessness are often direct descendants of these regimes. For example, contemporary women's homelessness shelters resemble past residential settings for the control of women who stepped out of line, such as the Female Refuges of Toronto described by Minaker (2006) in which young women were criminalized for non-criminal behaviours, such as being sentenced to custody on charges of "incorrigibility."

Such state, church, and market projects utilized to sort out, punish, contain, and control surplus, colonized, racialized, and deviant populations find their contemporary descendants in laws and policies mandating discriminatory and excessive policing, criminalization, and incarceration of people facing homelessness. Local ordinances across the US and Canada (Foscarinis, 1996) explicitly criminalize homelessness by outlawing activities such as sitting or lying on the sidewalk, or camping in public parks. Ontario's *Safe Streets Act*, for example, places vague and broad restrictions on a number of ordinary activities—such as asking for money while standing near a bank machine—while the publicity surrounding the law and the arrests since its passage show that it creates status offences, applicable only to people who are or appear homeless (Hermer &

Mosher, 2002). Legal philosopher Jeremy Waldron (1991) explains that the convergence of laws protecting private property with local bylaws regulating use of public spaces often has the effect of denying people who are homeless the fundamental freedom to perform bodily functions such as sleep, because there is no place in which they are legally entitled to perform them. For example, a provision recently dropped from the Toronto Municipal Code would have prohibited camping, dwelling, and lodging on a street or other public place; for people without a place of their own, this would have had the effect of criminalizing their simple embodied presence (Wellesley Institute, 2011). Hermer and Mosher (2002) suggest that neoconservative laws restricting the civil rights of poor and homeless people operate to support neoliberal policies eliminating social rights (such as, most famously, in Ontario, the 21.6 percent cut to welfare in 1995, but also the recent restriction of the Special Diet Allowance and the 2013 elimination of the Community Start-Up and Maintenance Benefit).

In fact, the direct criminalization of absolute homelessness is only one area of the state's sphere of surveillance and control of women facing homelessness. In Ontario, a body of laws and policies enacted between 1995 and 2003 by the Conservative provincial governments of Mike Harris and Ernie Eves extended this sphere. For example, the *Ontario Works Act* mandates a frighteningly broad scope for the surveillance of welfare applicants and recipients, including seeking information about applicants from numerous authorities (such as the principals of their children's schools), and making unannounced home "visits" to check up on the relational/sexual lives of recipients (Mosher, 2002). Amendments to the *Health Care Consent Act* and *Mental Health Act* in 2000 under Bill 68 widened the criteria for involuntary psychiatric assessment and introduced Community Treatment Orders (CTOs), which enable forced drugging of psychiatric survivors outside of hospitals (Szigeti, 2001). As is the case with laws directed against other marginalized groups, legislation to restrict the civil rights of women facing homelessness brings the force of law to systemic violations that were already happening: police harassment of street people; welfare workers' intrusion into the private lives of recipients; psychiatric teams' regular visits to observe residents in shelters for homeless women; and landlords' practice of demanding criminal record checks from prospective tenants.

Many scholars would argue that women facing homelessness are not simply victims of the violation of social and civil rights; rather, they are implicitly excluded from the sphere of protection of liberal rights—that is, from citizenship. Kennett (1999) links homelessness in the UK to the shift from a Keynesian model of social citizenship to a market-based, competitive, and conditional model in which social rights become increasingly contingent on labour market participation. In the same vein, Porter (2007) holds that, in Canada, government cuts to social programs and courts' refusals to recognize social rights both form part of a pervasive system of discrimination against poor people in which they are denied equal citizenship. Following Patterson's work on slavery, Liggett (1991: 205) argues that people who are homeless are consigned to a radical denial of personhood that she calls a "social death." She explains that in addition to being identified with the powerlessness, alienation from systems of belonging, and dishonour that mark the social death of enslaved persons, people who are homeless are also seen as a surplus population who, unlike slaves, are economically unnecessary and therefore expendable.

The disenfranchisement of people facing homelessness, though, is more than just discursive or metaphorical. As previously noted, Razack (2002) demonstrates how the production of Canada as a White settler nation-state depends upon the designation of (White, bourgeois) citizens through the social and legal sorting-out of (racialized, degenerate) Others. Sharma (2004) extends this analysis, noting that the distinction between citizen and non-citizen is not only social but juridical, reliant upon the differential citizenship statuses legally accorded to various groups—from Aboriginal people to White Canadian-born people to racialized permanent residents to non-status migrants—all of whom physically reside in Canada, but who, as a result of juridical distinctions in citizenship status, have vastly different legal claims to social housing and civil rights.

Lived Experiences of Homelessness and Disenfranchisement

As it turns out, these analyses not only make sense on a theoretical level—they also resonate with the stories and theories women facing homelessness have shared in a number of feminist participatory research projects. These include a human rights project in which women at a Toronto drop-in centre prepared a report for a United Nations committee; a study based on open-ended interviews with mothers staying in shelters; and research to examine service practices in agencies serving women and families facing homelessness.[4]

When women speak about their experiences with "homelessness," their accounts are not limited to shelters and the street. Instead, they make reference to multiple and overlapping domains, including the housing and labour markets; state institutional systems, such as social assistance, child welfare, and the mental health system; civil society organizations, such as shelters, drop-ins, and food banks; and laws and policies that directly mediate women's and communities' citizenship rights and relationship to the Canadian state—most importantly, immigration law and Aboriginal policies. Women's accounts demonstrate that homelessness is produced through the laws, policies, practices, and discourses that operate through these domains. As it turns out, the material loss of housing is not the only—or even the most important—part of the story for many women. The dehumanizing treatment they receive is fundamental to how they understand homelessness.

Susan

Susan was in the midst of fighting her wrongful eviction at the Landlord and Tenant Board when she recounted this story in an interview. Her landlord had removed all her belongings from her apartment.

> You think, "Okay, well you know, you are right, this shouldn't have been done to you." But that doesn't make it better. You know? That doesn't bring back all your antique furniture, and your jewellery, your costume—you know I had flamenco costumes for dance work—and you know, theatre shoes, and costume pieces from Los Angeles ... all kinds of things that are just, every once in awhile I go, "Oh yeah!" I mean I owned that, and I can't dance in that Gypsy band wearing that costume anymore because I don't own it. I mean the gifts, the birthday gifts that people have given me, and the photographs of family, and souvenirs of friends from Europe that spent a holiday here, and we took photographs and logged the vacation and so forth. It's all gone! You know? And a medicine bag. That was the first thing, you know, Native cultural items that were stolen, and things like that. Just, gone! Never to be replaced again. So. No apology.
>
> And then, having turned my friends. If I go and ring their doorbell, I'm told I'm not allowed on the property. There's one woman who has had the courage. She's invited me in for tea. And my former best friend has been told that I'm not welcome on the property. And if he is answering the door to me, he's under threat. And [another friend in the same building] told me the same thing. She was afraid to let me in, because they told her that if she kept up—she had given me spare keys, when I had lost my keys, that belonged to her—and she said that if I was seen with her after I'd moved out, they were going to begin an eviction process on her as well.

Susan's story offers a fast-forward view of a process that is more subtle and protracted for many women. Losing home strips away material possessions that anchor a woman's personal and cultural identity, and it also represents a "social death" (Liggett, 1991) in which one's social status is radically altered from friend and neighbour to unwanted and threatening Other. Susan's eviction, though, also took place within a legal context structured by Ontario's Orwellian-named *Tenant Protection Act*, which was in force from 1998 to 2007. Seemingly intended to offer landlords protection from tenants, the act allowed landlords to raise rents an unlimited amount on vacant units, and introduced a number of measures to simplify and speed up eviction processes, including a provision for eviction by default if tenants failed to file a dispute in writing within five days of receiving an order of termination from their landlord (ACTO, 2005). These changes provided an incentive to private landlords to evict tenants considered undesirable, and those in long-term tenancies paying low rent. Women's accounts also reveal that the easy-to-obtain eviction orders (e.g., an order could be issued as soon as 24 hours after rent was due if the full amount was not yet paid) were used as a means of harassing tenants. This practice was not limited to private market housing: some women living in public housing described receiving automated orders from the (private) property management company that had taken over building management from their social housing provider.

In the year that Susan shared this story, more than 60,000 evictions were issued in Ontario. While there is no official count of how many of these orders were ultimately carried out, housing advocates point out that many tenants whose evictions were not warranted simply left after receiving an order, unaware that they had the right to contest it or incapable of completing the necessary administrative procedures within the prescribed timeline. Through the sustained efforts of advocates and tenants' organizations, the default eviction provision was finally removed in 2007.

Gab

Gab worked most of her life. Though back home in Eastern Europe she had held professional positions, since coming to Canada, her work was usually precarious. She provided this testimony for the United Nations report:

> I was fighting for more shifts, and they didn't like that, so they terminated me. They didn't like older workers, because we tried to organize unions. So they fired us and hired 19-year-olds. And then, because I couldn't get the extra shifts I needed, I was 24 hours short for EI (Employment Insurance). At another job, they paid me $400 per month for four hours per day, but I had to stay for a fifth hour that they called "lunch" even though I was the only one there and had to answer the phones.

At the time that she contributed this testimony, Gab was having a hard time making it to our weekly meetings because of a mandatory employment skills program she was required to attend in order to maintain her Ontario Works welfare benefits. The program seemed mainly to consist of developing a resumé, and then sending it, unsolicited, to every employer on a very long list. Surely these were "employment skills" Gab was already quite familiar with. Never mind that Gab, and many others in the program, were immigrant women in late middle age—the type of applicants, as she suggests above, that most employers will not even consider hiring. To say nothing of the fact that her experiences in the labour market belied the neoliberal promise that jobs are the route to a life of dignity and prosperity.

Gab's story reminds me of Peck's (2001) analysis of what he calls the "workfare state." Using case studies of jurisdictions, including Ontario, Peck shows how, in a neoliberal social and economic context, the welfare state's regimes of control work hand in hand with markets to provide workers to the most insecure, most dangerous, and lowest-paying sectors of the labour market. He suggests that they do this, in part, by holding recipients of social assistance "close to the market," in a perpetual state of employment readiness. Limitations to Employment Insurance eligibility, and involuntary workfare programs, are examples of how policy has shifted social security programs from universal entitlements to conditional, temporary measures offering the least possible respite between the precarious and often demeaning jobs that characterize the new labour market. Workfare policy employs emotional and relational, as well as technical, means for inducing recipients to return to work. Gab's experiences in the employment program are among what Herd, Mitchell, and Lightman (2005) refer to as the "rituals of degradation" mandated by regulations, policies, and procedures governing the delivery of Ontario Works. Other such rituals include the intrusive home visits and pervasive surveillance described above. In women's analyses of poverty and social assistance, these rituals figure at least as prominently as the material inadequacy of welfare.[5]

Chris

Chris was staying at a family shelter with her children when she attended a focus group and offered these insights:

> The one thing I really dislike is, every week, the staff and counsellors have a meeting and discuss every client together. So the whole staff knows my personal business, and it makes me not trust my counsellor. If you're having an issue, your counsellor will discuss it with the whole staff. They also might tell the management staff if they deem it's a "major concern." They decide what's "major" and if they deem it worth discussing. I think they should tell every client when you come in that they might share your information. And then they should ask your permission to share each piece of information. For example, why does the housing worker need

> to know what's going on in my personal life?... Every time you come in and out, every person at the front desk has to write something about you. Your counsellor can bring it up on her computer. "Went for 2 smoke breaks. Came in at 7 p.m."

These comments echo a theme that emerged repeatedly throughout all three projects: once in shelters, women lose their fundamental right to privacy. Of course, in shelters, women must perform the most basic daily activities of the private sphere—eating, sleeping, parenting, even bathing—in the presence of complete strangers, and there is rarely an opportunity to spend even a few minutes alone. But shelters are characterized by more than just a lack of physical privacy associated with congregate living: they are regulated by policies that mandate surveillance of residents and intrusion into the most private realms of their lives. Though Toronto's Shelter Standards include policies governing the sharing of resident information between agencies, the sharing of information among staff within a shelter is determined by the policies of the organization—and often, as in the case Chris describes, takes place in a culture where the lines between necessary information-sharing and gossip are blurred. Even the sharing of information between agencies is usually enabled through the signing of blanket waivers at intake and is not presented as something women have a choice about. For example, sharing of personal information between shelters and other municipally operated agencies such as Ontario Works and Housing Connections is enabled through the *Municipal Freedom of Information and Protection of Privacy Act* (MFIPPA). The process of getting women's permission for this information-sharing is so taken-for-granted that it has become a verb form: "Did you MFIPPA her?" one worker might ask another.

Meanwhile, the scene Chris describes of the front desk staff recording the minutiae of women's movements chillingly evokes the Foucauldian Panopticon normally associated with carceral settings. As women often pointed out in our discussions, when you are in a shelter you are treated like a criminal. In her study of federally sentenced women who successfully complete their conditional release and exit the penal system, Maidment (2006) explains that the majority nevertheless continue to be subjected to state-sponsored control through community-based services. She suggests that small local organizations increasingly must rely upon the penal and mental health systems for funding, and as a result, their programs and administration come to reflect those systems' mandate to surveil and control criminalized and psychiatrized populations. Chris's account demonstrates how these trans-carceral networks not only widen the net of state control for women in conflict with the law; they also draw women from outside the penal and psychiatric systems into a carceral regime of surveillance and control.

Nadine

Homelessness, criminalization, and psychiatrization—that is, the processes by which people come to be understood as homeless, criminals, and/or "mentally ill"—share a number of elements in common. One of these is the reinterpretation of people's words and actions through the lens of their presumed irrationality, unpredictability, and dangerousness (Ruddick, 2002). Nadine, a psychiatric survivor,[6] described how such a rereading of her words and actions prompted the activation of what she calls "the mental health unit."[7]

> If [the shelter manager] doesn't want people in "her" shelters, as she calls them, she calls the mental health unit.... The day that she did that to me, I had told her that she needs to give a pregnant woman milk. And when she saw that I stood up for that other lady, who needed milk because she was six month's pregnant, and she was the lady working at the shelter and wouldn't give that other lady a glass of milk, I said, "That pregnant woman needs a glass of milk each day." And I walked right into the kitchen, I walked right into the kitchen and I got a glass of milk. For the pregnant lady.... I said, "I'm not trying to challenge you, all I'm trying to do is get a glass of milk for this woman." You know what I mean? Like help, help another human being? And then she said to me, she doesn't want me in her shelter. And I think the reason she didn't want me in her shelter—it's not per se her shelter—but I think the reason why she didn't want me in "her" shelter is because I speak up.

The nominal requirement for a "mental health apprehension" under the *Mental Health Act* is that police or mental health workers directly witness someone behaving in a way that presents an immediate danger to themselves or others. While getting a glass of milk for a pregnant woman does not seem like it would meet this requirement, police are well known for overreacting to the danger posed by people they see as crazy. The police shooting deaths of Edmund Yu and Sylvia Klibingaitis—who were "armed" with a tack hammer and a kitchen knife, respectively—are clear evidence of this trend. In Ontario, the provincial government deliberately mobilized this harmful stereotype of the dangerous psychiatric survivor by way of the *Mental Health Act* amendments discussed above (Szigeti, 2001).

As in Chris's and Gab's stories, we see here the extension and seamless integration of the psychiatric-penal carceral net into the community. Nadine's story adds to this analysis, demonstrating the way in which this extension serves not only a state-imposed agenda of control, but also an internal managerial agenda of maintaining order and discipline.

What should have been understood as a reasonable dispute about the contradictions between the shelter's rigid rules and its obligation to provide for women's basic needs, was reinterpreted as a psychiatric "crisis" requiring police intervention.

Rose

Rose was living in a family homelessness shelter when she sat down with two researchers—one a graduate student, the other a mother who had been homeless in the past—to share her story. She had been living and working in Canada for about 20 years without permanent resident status. Her first experience of homelessness occurred about seven years before, when she fled with her children to a violence against women (VAW) shelter to escape physical and verbal abuse by her children's father. At that time, a lawyer advised her to apply for refugee status, which she was subsequently denied. Eventually she found a new place to live with her children and worked full-time until a few years later when she was injured at work. When complications from the injury led to a prolonged hospitalization, she was unable to pay the rent and had to enter a shelter for the second time with her children. In her interview, Rose explained how restrictions on her entitlements due to her lack of permanent resident status directly precipitated this current episode of homelessness:

> At that time [in the VAW shelter], if I did qualify for [subsidized] housing, I would've still been in the housing.[8] The kids, them would've been getting child tax benefit, and the dad was ordered to pay child support. So if I was getting that [subsidized housing], and if I get sick and I went to the hospital, I know I was coming home to my home still. But because I didn't qualify for housing, social assistance, or anything like that, [I ended up homeless] ... but if I did have that opportunity I wouldn't be in the shelter. I would've still been able to be in my home.

Not only was Rose, after 20 years in the workforce, excluded from social benefits—such as subsidized housing, workers' compensation benefits, Canada Pension Plan disability insurance, and provincial social assistance—that would normally protect a worker's income and housing in the event of a workplace injury, but her precarious citizenship status also means that her Canadian-born children are excluded from entitlements:

> It's a very hard road to travel down and especially when you have kids. They are Canadian-born but still because of you they have no rights. They have a birth certificate that is Canadian, they have a health card, but

> still they have no, they can't get no child tax benefit, they can't get no help from the government, no social assistance. Not even a drug plan.... So, it's really kind of affecting me and it affecting them in some way because things that they want, that they should be having, they can't have it because the parent is not a Canadian citizen.

Sharma (2006) suggests that the exclusion of people without citizenship status from social benefits, and the laws mandating their arrest, detention, and deportation, operate not to prevent people from migrating into Canada without status, but rather to maintain their vulnerability when in Canada. This serves a number of major industries—among them the garment and construction industries—that benefit from access to an easily exploited workforce. Though Rose entered Canada as a visitor and remained illegally, precarious status is also a feature of many of the legal channels through which migrants enter Canada, including family sponsorship, refugee claims, and temporary worker programs. Goldring, Berinstein, and Bernhard (2009) describe how immigration policy in Canada has shifted to prolong and maintain a precarious status for an ever-increasing proportion of the people entering Canada each year, leaving more and more residents of Canada with dramatically circumscribed legal rights and social entitlements.

Commando

Commando provided this testimony for the United Nations report:

> The only child I ever had was a daughter. CAS took my child as soon as she was born. I was all alone. So of course I had postpartum depression, and other issues to deal with such as defending myself on the street against attempted physical and sexual assault, and hunger. It is my experience that it is really demoralizing to the spirit when you are homeless, faced with the knowledge that I am walking on land that my ancestors had walked on since time immemorial.... The whole time I was fighting for custody of my daughter. On Jarvis Street [Family Court] I lost custody permanently because of my drinking and because I was still in recovery. They didn't give me a chance. When my child was being taken away I had a flashback of an old newspaper photo I had seen in a review in 1979 of children being taken away to the residential schools. To lose your child does something to your soul.

Though the events Commando recounts took place more than two decades ago, it is still commonplace for young women on the street to have their babies apprehended at birth (Novac, Paradis, Brown, & Morton, 2006). Once their children are removed, young women face daunting requirements to win custody back, including attendance at numerous court dates and mandated visits, and securing appropriate housing. Also, like women on welfare, mothers involved with child protection services are subject to a degree of surveillance and interference in parenting that no ordinary citizen would tolerate. Another Claiming Our Rights participant, for example, described the parenting-capacity assessment in which she was required to spend a period of time caring for her infant in a camera-equipped facility so that the parent and child's every interaction could be viewed and reviewed by clinicians. Commando's testimony also alludes to the fact that the surveillance, control, and forced separation of families are employed as tools in the colonization and cultural genocide against First Nations in Canada. She draws a link between residential schools and apprehensions of children by child welfare agencies, a link underlined by the oft-cited statistic that there are more Aboriginal children in state care today than there were at the height of the residential school era (cf. Peesker, 2012; Canadian Press, 2011).

Discussion

The experiences described above are, of course, unique, and have had particular impacts on the lives of the women who went through them. At the same time, they are also what the Kappel Ramji Consulting Group (2002) refers to as "common occurrences": incidents the like of which recur often in the lives of most women at the margins. They are recursive, or common, because they are socially organized and characteristic of the ways in which homelessness, housing, poverty, psychiatry, child protection, immigration, colonialism, and the regulation of public space operate to maintain the disadvantaged position of women who are poor, racialized, Aboriginal, disabled, and immigrants.

The experiences women described are characterized by a set of relations that are remarkably consistent across stories and scales. First, their security of the person and even their right to life are undermined: women experience physical and sexual violence; harms to their health, well-being, spirit, and dignity; and threats both overt and covert. Also, they are subject to restrictions on their autonomy and the normal freedoms of movement, thought, and self-expression; these restrictions are often enforced using the harms and threats described above. In addition, they encounter intrusion into and surveillance of realms normally recognized as private. Finally, the threats, restrictions, and surveillance combine to keep women in a state of constant precarity, risk, and insecurity. Women explain that the violence, harm, threats, control, surveillance, intrusion, precarity, and risk convey the message that they are "not seen as people"; indeed, dehumanizing representations both produce and legitimize these violations of their basic rights. In each domain, their poverty, homelessness, and need for support are the conditions that make these relations possible. Standing up for themselves in the face of threats, control, intrusion, precarity, and dehumanization means risking the withdrawal of the bare necessities of survival.

These relations are enacted in a multiplicity of local sites in women's everyday lives, including the streets, drop-ins, shelters, homes, workplaces, and social services. Further, they are carried out by a wide range of actors, including shelter managers, social housing providers, landlords, welfare workers, child protection agents, drop-in staff, and employers. These relations signal that women considered "homeless" are not afforded liberal rights such as privacy, liberty, freedom of expression, and security of the person. If these rights are guaranteed to all citizens, then women facing homelessness seem to belong to a category of people excluded from citizenship—they are disenfranchised. The social relations of disenfranchisement that women encounter in multiple everyday settings both enact and reflect the juridical disenfranchisement to which they are subject in policy and law. Women's homelessness, and their involvement or risk of involvement in systems such as welfare, psychiatry, and child protection, cause them to be subjected to different legal regimes than other citizens, with different and circumscribed rights and protections.

For example, because of the convergence of property law and laws governing the uses of parks and other public spaces, women who are literally homeless in Toronto have no access as of right to a place in which to erect a shelter in which to sleep, and conversely, they may legally be observed in the performance of private functions in their living places, whether these are shelters or outside. People on workfare are not protected by labour laws, such as minimum wage and the right to strike, and are effectively indentured to their "employer," the Ministry of Community and Social Services, under threat of deprivation of the means to survive, or even arrest and incarceration for welfare "fraud." Mothers on social assistance, and those involved with the child protection system, are subject to mandated intrusions by agents of the state into realms normally designated as private, including their sexual relationships (Mosher, 2002). Psychiatric survivors, unlike anyone else in Canadian society, can be compelled by law to take medications; since 2000, with Community Treatment Orders, this power to compel extends beyond hospitalized people who have been declared incompetent to also cover people who are legally competent and living in the community (Szigeti, 2001). Both Alberta and British Columbia have passed laws mandating the forced confinement of young women involved in the sex trade, without criminal charge, for their own "protection" (Czapska, Webb, & Taefi, 2008).

How homelessness affects women is, however, only half of the story. Women's experiential accounts not only reveal the impacts of homelessness, but also their responses to it. Women are always actively engaged in their encounters with homelessness. This is the case whether they are going along with institutional and governmental regimes in hopes of avoiding punishment, or resisting attempts to control and monitor themselves and others, in spite of the risks they face in doing so. Susan fights her eviction in court and visits her friends in defiance of the landlord's threats; Gab fights for more shifts and tries to form unions; Chris scrutinizes the workers who are scrutinizing her, and makes fun of the mundane details they document; Nadine gets a glass of milk for a pregnant woman; Rose claims her place in Canada and questions the legitimacy of her exclusion from social entitlements; and Commando fights for custody of her daughter.

Women's accounts underscore the significance of disenfranchisement in the operations of homelessness because their responses often represent their assertion of self-determination—even at the expense of their immediate material circumstances. It seems, too, from women's accounts, that the decision to assert self-determination often emerges in the context of their conscious assessment of the larger ramifications of their negotiations with homelessness; that is, when they view their immediate situation in its historical, political, social, and/or ethical context. For example, in explaining her decision to stick up for another woman even though it caused her to be barred from a shelter, Nadine simply asked, "If they're pregnant, and their babies are growing, and somebody doesn't stick up for them while they're in the shelters, what's going to happen?"

In this way, women's accounts teach us not only about the operations of homelessness, but also about resistance to it. To resist homelessness requires not only discourses and actions that promote access to material necessities, but more importantly, actions and discourses that confront disenfranchisement and assert the self-determination, worth, and dignity of people facing homelessness.

The many valences of this understanding of homelessness are perhaps best exemplified in the insights of participants who identify as Aboriginal. Commando's and Susan's descriptions of their experience of homelessness seamlessly bind together its localized manifestations and its broadest significance, allowing us to understand how homelessness has historically operated and currently operates in Canada and also how its processes are resisted in women's everyday thoughts and actions. Mass Aboriginal homelessness at this moment in Canada is continuous with colonial legacies of land theft, forced displacement, and residential schools (Menzies, 2005). At the same time, it is ideologically and functionally interlocked with other contemporary colonial practices, including the rape, murder, and disappearance of Aboriginal women and girls (Amnesty International, 2004; Native Women's Association of Canada, 2009; Smith, 2005), the rupture of family and community relations by child protection practices (Sinha et al., 2011), the mass criminalization of Aboriginal people (LaPrairie, 1996), and the police and legal suppression of community actions to protect territories from exploitation.

In their testimonies and interviews, Commando and Susan clearly articulated how their immediate experience of homelessness was informed by these connections. For example, Susan placed her eviction in the context of the displacement of the Lubicon Cree, and said losing her home was "like a re-enactment of Christopher Columbus landing all over again," while Commando described how the moment her daughter was taken from her brought to mind the image of children being taken to residential schools. When she concluded, "To lose your child does something to your soul," she was speaking not only of her own soul, but of the intergenerational soul wound (Duran & Duran, 1995) caused by Canada's "Indian" policies.[9]

For Commando and Susan, homelessness was at once an immediate personal crisis and a manifestation of a centuries-long project of colonialism. This doubled resonance of homelessness amplified its emotional and spiritual impacts, which Commando described as "demoralizing to the spirit." However, viewing their experiences through this lens also increased their strength and determination to stand up for their rights. For example, understanding her unlawful eviction in the context of the displacements of First Nations communities, Susan persisted in seeking justice at the Landlord and Tenant Board; and seeing the continuities between her child's apprehension and the theft of Aboriginal children into residential schools, Commando fought for custody. In these ways, they joined their everyday acts of resistance to the greater struggle for self-determination waged by their communities and ancestors. At the same time, their testimonies express recognition that their individual acts of resistance will not be sufficient to change the conditions that perpetuate colonialism, homelessness, and disenfranchisement. Self-determination requires ongoing collective struggle. As one participant in a recent focus group put it, "I would like us to unite and fight for our rights together, because we haven't been able to do it alone."

To conclude, the stories and theories explored here suggest that women's homelessness is far more than the de-housing and inadequate housing faced by growing numbers of women in the context of neoliberal economic restructuring. For the women speaking here, homelessness is a treacherous landscape in which their disenfranchisement by legal and policy regimes is repeatedly enacted in a multiplicity of local settings and moments, via relations of harm, control, surveillance, precarity, and dehumanization. That they are not seen as people is as much a characteristic of homelessness as of being de-housed and hungry. Finding a way through homelessness means securing the material necessities of survival, but it also means negotiating an identity of worth and dignity in the face of discourses and relations that harm, demean, restrain, intrude, degrade, and dehumanize. Often, acquiescence to dominant expectations is presented as the only road to having basic needs fulfilled. But in their everyday negotiations with homelessness, women mark countless alternate paths by which to secure what they need while holding on to their personhood. As they stand up for their own and each other's right to self-determination, they blaze trails for a movement of resistance.

Notes

1 Understanding homelessness as a state has given rise to contested definitions of what does and does not constitute homelessness, and many qualifiers of "homelessness"—such as "visible" and "invisible," "absolute" and "relative," "shelter" and "street," "hidden" or "at risk of"—have been proposed in order to delimit or enlarge the circumstances that are seen to count as homelessness. The recently published Canadian Definition of Homelessness (Canadian Homelessness Research Network, 2012) incorporates the full breadth of these circumstances.

2 While no national statistics on any aspect of homelessness exist in Canada, the overrepresentation of Aboriginal people among homeless populations has been documented in Vancouver, Calgary, Edmonton, and Toronto (Layton, 2000).

3 Some collections that examine these issues include those edited by Burstow and Weitz (1988) on psychiatry, Sudbury (2005) on women and criminalization, and Davis (1997) on disability.

4 These accounts are drawn from several projects I have been involved with. The stories of Susan, Gab, Nadine, and Commando were shared during Claiming Our Rights, in which women attended weekly meetings at Sistering, a women's drop-in, for 18 months and participated in actions including the development of a report on women's homelessness for the May 2006 review of Canada by the United Nations Committee on Economic, Social and Cultural Rights (For Women's Autonomy, Rights and Dignity (FORWARD), 2009; Paradis, 2009). Some stories are drawn from that report while others were shared in individual interviews or testimony given before the group. Rose shared her story through a project called Diverse Homeless Families, in which women who had been homeless worked with graduate students to interview mothers staying in Toronto shelters (Paradis, 2012). Chris's story, and the quote for the title of the paper, come from the project We're Not Asking, We're Telling, which aimed to identify and disseminate practices that promote the autonomy, dignity, and self-determination of women facing homelessness (Paradis et al., 2012). I wish to gratefully acknowledge funding from the following programs, without which the projects would not have been possible: SSHRC Graduate Fellowship program (Claiming Our Rights), SSHRC Homelessness and Diversity Issues program (Diverse Homeless Families), and the Homelessness Knowledge Development Program of the Homelessness Partnering Strategy, Human Resources and Skills Development Canada (We're Not Asking, We're Telling).

5 Another important aspect of Gab's story is that this program was based at a neighbourhood women's centre. In a context of deep funding cuts to community agencies, and especially the elimination of core funding for functions such as counselling and community development, small local organizations are faced with a trade-off: scale way down and maintain a grassroots mission, or keep the doors open through program funding that downloads former state functions onto the community level. The implications of deputizing local organizations as agents of the neoliberal workfare state's agenda of control and surveillance are discussed further below.

6 Feminist anti-psychiatry theorist and activist Bonnie Burstow (2013) distinguishes the term "psychiatric survivor" from the more common "consumer-survivor," explaining that it is part of a lexicon of "fighting words" (8) developed within the anti-psychiatry movement. In using it to describe Nadine, therefore, I not only signal her history in the psychiatric system, but also her political and discursive engagement against it. Though I did not have the opportunity to ask Nadine whether she identified with this term, or others, to describe her experiences with psychiatry, I knew her to participate in anti-psychiatry events and discourses (e.g., in a group meeting, she asserted, "I feel raped by the psychiatrists. They raped my brain. They took my intelligence and tried to zap it out of my head.").

7 A Toronto police unit specifically designated to respond to calls involving a mental health crisis. See www.torontopolice.on.ca/community/mentalhealth.php

8 Women leaving situations of violence are given priority on the social housing waiting list, enabling some women to move from VAW shelters into social housing with rent geared to their incomes. As a woman without status, Rose could not be placed on the wait list and was not entitled to social assistance or Workers' Compensation benefits—even though she paid income tax on her wages. Had she been in social housing at the time of her injury and hospitalization, her inability to pay rent would not have resulted in her family's eviction.

9 Duran and Duran (1995) distinguish the Indigenous understanding of the soul wound from Eurocentric psychological constructs of "mental illness." They explain that it has individual, family, and collective dimensions; it originates not in individual psychopathology but in collective, cumulative, and intergenerational experiences of violence, injustice, loss, enforced powerlessness, and family rupture; and it manifests itself in individual struggles with emotional well-being and substance use, as well as in family violence and community-wide struggles. Unlike the European Christian understanding of "soul," here, soul is understood to be a shared collective entity, on a continuum with culture.

References

ACTO (Advocacy Centre for Tenants of Ontario) & CERA (Centre for Equality Rights in Accommodation). (2005). Extract from *Submission to the United Nations Human Rights Committee Fifth Periodic Review of Canada,* October 17, 2005. Retrieved from www.acto.ca/assets/files/docs/LR_RTA_Extract_SubmissiontoOHCHR.pdf

Allen, T. (2000). *Someone to Talk To: Care and Control of the Homeless.* Halifax: Fernwood Publishing.

Amnesty International. (2004). "Canada: Stolen Sisters: A human rights response to discrimination and violence against Indigenous women in Canada." Ottawa: Amnesty International Canada. Retrieved from www.amnesty.ca/research/reports/stolen-sisters-a-human-rights-response-to-discrimination-and-violence-against-indig

Arat-Koc, S. (2001). *Caregivers Break the Silence: A Participatory Action Research on the Abuse and Violence, Including the Impact of Family Separation, Experienced by Women in the Live-In Caregiver Program.* Toronto: Intercede.

Blomley, N. (2004). *Unsettling the City: Urban Land and the Politics of Property.* New York: Routledge.

Bunston, T., & Breton, M. (1992). "Homes and homeless women." *Journal of Environmental Psychology,* 12: 149–162.

Burstow, B. (2013). "A rose by any other name: Naming and the battle against psychiatry." In B. LeFrançois, R. Menzies, & G. Reaume, eds., *Mad Matters* (pp. 79–90). Toronto: Canadian Scholars' Press.

Burstow, B., & Weitz, D. (1988). *Shrink Resistant: The Struggle against Psychiatry in Canada.* Vancouver: New Star Books.

Bussidor, I., & Bilgen-Rienart, U. (1997). *Night Spirits: The Story of the Relocation of the Sayisi Dene.* Winnipeg: University of Manitoba Press.

Canadian Homelessness Research Network. (2012). *Canadian Definition of Homelessness.* Homeless Hub: www.homelesshub.ca/CHRNhomelessdefinition/

Canadian Press. (2011, August 2). "First Nations children still taken from parents. Analysis finds more First Nations children in care than at height of residential school system." *CBC News.* Retrieved from www.cbc.ca/news/politics/story/2011/08/02/pol-first-nations-kids.html

CERA (Centre for Equality Rights in Accommodation), Women's Program. (2002). *Women and housing in Canada: Barriers to equality.* Toronto: CERA. Retrieved from www.equalityrights.org/cera/docs/CERAWomenHous.htm

Cheung, A., & Hwang, S. (2004). "Risk of death among homeless women: A cohort study and review of the literature." *CMAJ (Canadian Medical Association Journal),* 170(8): 1243–1247. Retrieved from www.cmaj.ca/cgi/content/full/170/8/1243

Czapska, A., Webb, A., & Taefi, N. (2008). *More Than Bricks and Mortar: A Rights-Based Strategy to Prevent Girl Homelessness in Canada.* Vancouver: Justice for Girls.

da Cunha, M. (2005). "From neighbourhood to prison: Women and the war on the drugs in Portugal." In J. Sudbury, ed., *Global Lockdown: Race, Gender, and the Prison-Industrial Complex* (pp. 155–165). London: Routledge.

Davis, L. (1997). *The Disability Studies Reader.* New York: Routledge.

Duran, E., & Duran, B. (1995.) *Native American Postcolonial Psychology.* Albany, NY: State University of New York.

Echenberg, H., & Jensen, H. (2008). "Defining and enumerating homelessness in Canada." Ottawa: Library of Parliament. Retrieved from www.homelesshub.ca/Library/Defining-and-Enumerating-Homelessness-in-Canada-34178.aspx

Farha, L. (2002). "Is there a woman in the house? Re/conceiving the human right to housing." *Canadian Journal of Women and the Law*, 14: 118–141.

For Women's Autonomy, Rights and Dignity (FORWARD). (2009). "Burned by the system, burned at the stake: Poor, homeless and marginalized women speak out." In J.D. Hulchanski, P. Campsie, S. Chau, S. Hwang, & E. Paradis, eds., *Finding Home: Policy Options for Addressing Homelessness in Canada* (eBook, Chapter 9.1). Toronto: Cities Centre, University of Toronto. Available at www.homelesshub.ca/FindingHome

Foscarinis, M. (1996). "Downward spiral: Homelessness and its criminalization." *Yale Law & Policy Review*, 14(1): 1–63.

Goldring, L., Berinstein, C., & Bernhard, J. (2009). "Institutionalizing precarious migratory status in Canada." *Citizenship Studies*, 13(3): 239–265.

Goodman, L., Saxe, L., & Harvey, M. (1991). "Homelessness as psychological trauma: Broadening perspectives." *American Psychologist*, 46(11): 1219–1225.

Herd, D., Mitchell, A., & Lightman, E. (2005). "Rituals of degradation: Administration as policy in the Ontario Works programme." *Social Policy and Administration*, 39(1): 65–79.

Hermer, J., & Mosher, J. (2002). "Introduction." In J. Hermer & J. Mosher, eds., *Disorderly People: Law and the Politics of Exclusion in Ontario* (pp. 11–21). Halifax: Fernwood Publishing.

Hulchanski, D., Campsie, P., Chau, S., Hwang, S., & Paradis, E. (2009). "Homelessness: What's in a word?" In D. Hulchanski, P. Campsie, S. Chau, S. Hwang, & E. Paradis, eds., *Finding Home: Policy Options for Addressing Homelessness in Canada* (eBook). Toronto: Cities Centre, University of Toronto. Available at www.homelesshub.ca/FindingHome

Jahiel, R. (1992). "Homeless-making processes and the homeless-makers." In R. Jahiel, ed., *Homelessness: A Prevention-Oriented Approach* (pp. 269–296). Baltimore: Johns Hopkins University Press.

Kappel Ramji Consulting Group. (2002). *Common Occurrence: The Impact of Homelessness on Women's Health. Phase II: Community Based Action Research. Final Report.* Toronto: Sistering, A Woman's Place/Brown Books Inc.

Kennett, P. (1999). "Homelessness, citizenship, and social exclusion." In P. Kennett & A. Marsh, eds., *Homelessness: Exploring the New Terrain* (pp. 37–60). Bristol, UK: The Policy Press.

LaPrairie, C. (1996). *Examining Aboriginal Corrections in Canada.* Ottawa: Ministry of the Solicitor General.

Layton, J. (2000). *Homelessness: The Making and Unmaking of a Crisis.* Toronto: Penguin Canada.

Liggett, H. (1991). "Where they don't have to take you in: The representation of homelessness in public policy." *Journal of Planning Education and Research,* 10(3): 201–208.

Maidment, M. (2006). *Doing Time on the Outside: Deconstructing the Benevolent Community.* Toronto: University of Toronto Press.

Menzies, P. (2005). *Orphans within Our Family: Intergenerational Trauma and Homeless Aboriginal Men.* Unpublished doctoral dissertation, Ontario Institute for Studies in Education, University of Toronto.

Minaker, J. (2006). "Sluts and slags: The censuring of the erring female." In G. Balfour & E. Comack, eds., *Criminalizing Women: Gender and (In)justice in Neo-Liberal Times.* Halifax: Fernwood Publishing.

Mosher, J. (2002). "The shrinking of the public and private spaces of the poor." In J. Hermer & J. Mosher, eds., *Disorderly People: Law and the Politics of Exclusion in Ontario* (pp. 41–53). Halifax: Fernwood Publishing.

Native Women's Association of Canada. (2007). "Aboriginal women and Bill C-31: An issue paper." Ottawa: Native Women's Association of Canada. Retrieved from www.laa.gov.nl.ca/laa/naws/pdf/nwac-billc-31.pdf

Native Women's Association of Canada. (2009). *Voices of Our Sisters in Spirit: A Report to Families and Communities* (2nd ed.). Ottawa: Native Women's Association of Canada.

Nelson, J. (2002). "The space of Africville: Creating, regulating, and remembering the urban 'slum.'" In S. Razack, ed., *Race, Space and the Law: Unmapping a White Settler Society* (pp. 185–210). Toronto: Between the Lines.

Novac, S., Brown, J., & Bourbonnais, C. (1996). *No Room of Her Own: Literature Review on Women and Homelessness.* Ottawa: CMHC (Canadian Mortgage and Housing and Corporation).

Novac, S., Paradis, E., Brown, J., & Morton, H. (2006). *A Visceral Grief: Young Homeless Mothers and Loss of Child Custody.* Toronto: Cities Centre.

Novac, S., Serge, L., Eberle, M., & Brown, J. (2002). *On Her Own: Young Women and Homelessness in Canada.* Ottawa: Canadian Housing and Renewal Association, and Status of Women Canada.

Oikawa, M. (2002). "Cartographies of violence: Women, memory, and the subject(s) of the 'internment.'" In S. Razack, ed., *Race, Space and the Law: Unmapping a White Settler Society* (pp. 71–98). Toronto: Between the Lines.

Paradis, E. (2009). *A Little Room of Hope: Feminist Participatory Action Research with "Homeless" Women*. Ph.D. dissertation housed on University of Toronto T-Space. Retrieved from https://tspace.library.utoronto.ca/handle/1807/19158

Paradis, E. (2012). "'It's a very hard road to travel down, especially when you have kids': Experiences of homelessness among women and families with precarious status in Toronto." In S. Pashang & D. Douglas, eds., *Unsettled Settlers: Barriers to Integration*. Toronto: de Sitter Publishing.

Paradis, E., Athumani, F., Bardy, S., Cummings-Diaz, P., Pereira, I., & Smith, C. (2012). *We're Not Asking, We're Telling: An Inventory of Practices Promoting the Dignity, Autonomy, and Self-Determination of Women and Families Facing Homelessness.* Toronto: Canadian Homelessness Research Network Press. Retrieved from www.homelesshub.ca/Library/View.aspx?id=55039

Passaro, J. (1996). *The Unequal Homeless: Men on the Streets, Women in Their Place.* New York: Routledge.

Peck, J. (2001). *Workfare States.* New York: The Guilford Press.

Peesker, S. (2012, September 6). "Why aren't children on reserves receiving equal welfare funding?" *OpenFile*. Retrieved from www.openfile.ca/toronto/story/why-arent-children-reserves-receiving-equal-welfare-funding

Porter, B. (2007). "Claiming adjudicative space: Social rights and citizenship." In S. Boyd, G. Brodsky, S. Day, & M. Young, eds., *Poverty: Rights, Social Citizenship, and Legal Activism* (pp. 77–95). Vancouver: University of British Columbia Press.

Razack, S. (2002). "Introduction." In S. Razack, ed., *Race, Space and the Law: Unmapping a White Settler Society* (pp. 1–20). Toronto: Between the Lines.

Ruddick, S. (2002). "Metamorphosis revisited: Restricting discourses of citizenship." In J. Hermer & J. Mosher, eds., *Disorderly People: Law and the Politics of Exclusion in Ontario* (pp. 55–64). Halifax: Fernwood Publishing.

Salvation Army. (2010). "Poverty shouldn't be a life sentence: A report on the perceptions of homelessness and poverty in Canada." Retrieved from www.homelesshub.ca/Library/Poverty-shouldn%E2%80%99t-be-a-life-sentence-A-report-on-the-perceptions-of-homelessness-and-poverty-in-Canada-48539.aspx

Sharma, N. (2004). "No Borders," a presentation at the Faculty of Social Work, University of Toronto, 25 November, 2004.

Sharma, N. (2006). *Home Economics: Nationalism and the Making of "Migrant Workers" in Canada*. Toronto: University of Toronto Press.

Sinha, V., Trocmé, N., Fallon, B., MacLaurin, B., Fast, E., Prokop, S., … Richard, K. (2011). *Kiskisik Awasisak: Remember the Children. Understanding the Overrepresentation of First Nations Children in the Child Welfare System.* Ontario: Assembly of First Nations. Retrieved from www.fncaringsociety.com/sites/default/files/docs/FNCIS-2008-report.pdf

Smith, A. (2005). *Conquest: Sexual Violence and the American Indian Genocide*. Cambridge, MA: South End Press.

Street Health Toronto. (2007). *The Street Health Report*. Toronto: Street Health. Retrieved from www.streethealth.ca/Downloads/SHReport2007.pdf

Sudbury, J. (2005). *Global Lockdown: Race, Gender, and the Prison-Industrial Complex*. New York: Routledge.

Swanson, J. (2001). *Poor-Bashing: The Politics of Exclusion*. Toronto: Between the Lines.

Szigeti, A. (2001). "Ontario's community treatment orders: How did we get there and where do we go now? An advocate's perspective." *Health Law in Canada*, 21(3): 66–83.

Waldron, J. (1991). "Homelessness and the issue of freedom." *UCLA Law Review*, 39: 295–324.

Watson, S., & Austerberry, H. (1986). *Housing and Homelessness: A Feminist Perspective*. London: Routledge & Kegan Paul.

Wellesley Institute. (2011). "Anti-camping bylaw removed from proposed amendments to Toronto's streets by-law." Retrieved from www.wellesleyinstitute.com/housing/anti-camping-clause-removed-from-proposed-amendments-to-torontos-streets-by-law/

YWCA. (2012). "When there's no place like home: A snapshot of women's homelessness in Canada." Retrieved from www.homelesshub.ca/%28S%28zrq5bsyg3ui31aabiufbyn-jy%29%29/Library/When-Theres-No-Place-Like-Home—A-snapshot-of-womens-homelessness-in-Canada-54037.aspx

Legal Cases and Statutes

Health Care Consent Act, 1996, S.O. 1996, c. 2, Sched. A. Government of Ontario.

Mental Health Act, 1990, R.S.O. 1990, c. M7. Government of Ontario.

Municipal Freedom of Information and Protection of Privacy Act, 1990, R.S.O. 1990, c. M56. Government of Ontario.

Ontario Works Act, 1997, S.O. 1997, c. 25, Sched. A. Government of Ontario.

Tenant Protection Act, 1997, S.O 1997, c. 24. Government of Ontario.

Chapter 4

Women, Drugs, and the Law

Rebecca Jesseman and Florence Kellner

Introduction

A police officer, smelling cannabis smoke, approaches a pair of young women in a public park in Toronto. When confronted, the women turn over a joint they were sharing. The two young women ask for leniency—they are university students and just relaxing on a nice evening after writing a final exam. The police officer tells them to go home, and carries on.

~

The same police officer failed to notice another young woman, about the same age, half-hidden under a low tree nearby. Her sweater hides the track marks on her thin arms, but no longer hides her rounded belly. She has yet to see a doctor about her pregnancy. She heard that she could be arrested for using drugs while pregnant and could have her child taken away.

These short vignettes illustrate the complex nature of illicit drug use by Canadian women and identify some of the contexts of this use. Currently, those enforcing drug laws exercise considerable discretion, and illegal drug use in this country shows up far more often on surveys than it does in crime statistics. The second example depicts a worst-case scenario: a pregnant woman who is addicted to a powerful drug and unable to access supports. The real-life counterpart of this fictional woman may not come to the attention of health agents until she becomes criminalized, thus increasing the likelihood that she is exposed to a contaminated needle or other secondary health risks.

The vignettes also illustrate differences in illicit substances themselves, their modes of use, circumstances of use, types of user, and potential harms to the user. Drug use is experienced differently according to many and varied characteristics, including gender, socio-economic status, race, and age. Unfortunately, legislation relevant to psychoactive substances reflects long-held and well-entrenched stereotypes about drugs, their effects, and about the people who use them. From the introduction of the *Opium Act* in 1908 to the current *Safe Streets and Communities Act* of 2012 , women involved in illicit drug use have been depicted across a spectrum of helplessness, victimization, and deviance. There is a gap between the perception of individuals and situations that our drug laws were established to govern and regulate and the actual people and situations that the drug laws impact. This chapter describes this gap, provides an overview of the socio-legal contexts and impacts of illegal drug use[1] for women, and a review of the key criminal justice responses.

The Role of the Law

In a liberal society, the application of criminal law to control behaviour is intended as a last resort when the threat to social order cannot otherwise be managed (Beauchesne, 2000). Despite long-standing prohibitions, a substantial proportion of the Canadian population has used illegal drugs—close to half of men and over one-third of women (Health Canada, 2011). Most use occurs during youth and decreases significantly with age. Canada's sustained use of criminal prosecution to deal with a practice that is common throughout society indicates an approach to illicit drug legislation that goes beyond the protection of social order and individual well-being. The moralism and paternalism that informed the development of this Canadian drug legislation provide a lens through which its impacts—both direct and indirect—can be explored.

Moralism in law involves its use as a means of promoting a perceived common or universally accepted righteous position on a given issue (Beauchesne, 2000). The threat of moral corruption posed by drugs and their users has long been used as justification for the imposition of severe sanctions for the use, production, and trafficking of psychoactive substances. It also contributes to the gendered and racialized application of those sanctions and other legislative and social responses to drug use. The original *Opium Act* specifically targeted behaviour that was concentrated among Chinese immigrants in British Columbia. One of the images called up to generate a moral panic to help justify the *Opium Act* was that of a young White woman under the spell of opium being seduced by an older Asian man (Carstairs, 2006; Giffen, Endicott, & Lambert, 1991). Women are not always portrayed as victims, however. Women who use drugs are crossing both social and gender norms, particularly women who have children. The need to preserve historic Victorian values of femininity and motherhood continues to be used to justify harsh social and criminal sanctions for women (Boyd & Faith, 1999; Boyd, 2001; Kilty, 2011).

Drug use by mothers is viewed as dangerously compromising the nurturing character they are expected to exemplify as primary caregivers.

While moral discourses about drug use involve judgments about the innate qualities and personality characteristics of the individual user, legal paternalism is based on the idea that a vulnerable group requires state protection from possible harms, including those they pose to themselves (Beauchesne, 2000). The paternal approach to drug legislation has been used both to protect and to prosecute. In Canada, the recently passed Bill C-10, for example, reschedules two substances, gamma hydroxybutyric acid (GHB) and flunitrazepam, in order to increase the penalties associated with their use, trafficking, and possession. The justification for this move provided by the Minister of Justice was that these substances are known "date rape" drugs, implying that this rescheduling would increase the protection offered to women from sexual predators. Similar to the earlier desire to protect women from threatening, racialized Others with the advent of the *Opium Act*, we again see the paternal role of the state used to justify the imposition of severe sanctions associated with illegal substances—despite limited supporting evidence for the efficacy of increased sanctions either for restricting illegal drug activity or protecting women (Gabor & Crutcher, 2002; Moore & Valverde, 2000).

Canada's Drug Control Legislation

Canada's legislative prosecution of the production, possession, distribution, and consumption of illicit drugs began in the early twentieth century with the introduction of the *Opium Act* in 1908 (Giffen, Endicott, & Lambert, 1991). Canada's legislation continued to expand throughout the century, with milestones including the expansion to cocaine and additional forms of opium in 1911, the addition of cannabis to the schedule of prohibited drugs in 1923, the expansion of the schedule to include increased pharmacological preparations in 1938, the separation of possession from trafficking offences in 1954, the introduction of treatment considerations in the *Narcotic Control Act* of 1961, and the enactment of the *Controlled Drugs and Substances Act* in 1996 (Giffen, Endicott, & Lambert, 1991).

The *Controlled Drugs and Substances Act* (CDSA) prohibits the possession, trafficking, and production of substances such as cannabis, cocaine, opium, amphetamines (including ecstasy), and LSD (acid). Offences under the CDSA are subject to criminal prosecution. The CDSA divides controlled substances into different schedules that determine each substance's associated regulations and sanctions. Table 4.1 provides examples of the penalties associated with the possession of a selection of substances in Schedules I, II, and III of the CDSA.

Table 4.1: Sample CDSA Offences and Penalties

Schedule	Offence	Prosecution	Penalty
I: Heroin, cocaine, ketamine	Possession, first offence	Indictable	Prison not exceeding 7 years
		Summary	Fine up to $1,000 and/or prison not exceeding 6 months
	Possession for the purpose of trafficking	Indictable	Prison up to life
II: Cannabis	Possession, first offence, more than 3 kg	Indictable	Prison not exceeding 5 years
		Summary	Fine up to $1,000 and/or prison not exceeding 6 months
	Possession, up to 3 kg	Summary	Fine up to $1,000 and/or prison not exceeding 6 months
	Possession for the purpose of trafficking, more than 3 kg	Indictable	Prison up to life
	Possession for the purpose of trafficking, up to 3 kg	Indictable	Prison not exceeding 5 years less a day
III: Amphetamines, LSD (acid), psilocybin, mescaline	Possession, first offence	Indictable	Prison not exceeding 3 years
		Summary	Fine up to $1,000 and/or prison not exceeding 6 months
	Possession for the purpose of trafficking	Indictable	Prison not exceeding 10 years
		Summary	Prison not exceeding 18 months

Note: The penalties outlined above are current as of April 15, 2012. They do not include offences where aggravating factors such as use of a weapon are present.

Canada's illicit drug legislation is situated within a complex international context. Canada is a signatory to several United Nations conventions that outline how member states are to regulate controlled substances, including identifying which substances should be deemed illegal and what related activities should be subject to criminal prosecution. The conventions are intended to limit the production and supply of controlled substances to medical and scientific purposes. The *Single Convention on Narcotic Drugs*, introduced in 1961, remains the foundational document guiding responses to opioids, cocaine, cannabis, and related derivatives. The 1971 *Convention on Psychotropic*

Substances provided additional controls over the broader range of psychotropics such as LSD (acid), MDMA (ecstasy), and other synthetics. And finally the 1988 *Convention against Illicit Traffic in Narcotic Drugs and Psychotropic Substances* addressed emerging issues such as precursor chemicals, money laundering, and facilitating international collaboration for prosecutions.

A significant revision to the CDSA is taking place as this chapter is being written. The *Safe Streets and Communities Act* of 2012, a large omnibus bill proposed and passed by the majority Conservative federal government, introduced mandatory minimum sentences[2] for a range of illicit drug offences, spanning from possession for the purpose of trafficking to production. Similarly, and reflecting the aforementioned roots of drug legislation in paternalist discourse, the act also changes the scheduling of certain substances linked to date rape in order to increase the associated penalties. Paternalism again featured strongly in the passage of this legislation, which increased penalties for sexual offences against children and presented CDSA amendments as a suggested means of protecting children from drug traffickers (Senate of Canada, 2012).

Gendered Nature of Drug Use

Table 4.2 provides an overview of recent national statistics on alcohol and illegal drug use. Important findings from the Canadian Alcohol and Drug Use Monitoring Survey (CADUMS) include the extent of illegal drug use: a third of Canadian women and half of men have used cannabis during their lifetimes, and 10 and 20 percent of females and males, respectively, have had lifetime exposure to illegal drugs (e.g., cocaine, ecstasy, heroin) other than cannabis. The CADUMS clearly indicates the gendered nature of drug use, with men consistently reporting higher rates of use than women. Also important to note is that recent (past year) use of all drugs is considerably lower than lifetime use, indicating that a large majority of illicit drug users do not use illicit drugs throughout their lives. The dominant pattern in survey research is higher rates of illegal drug use among youth that diminishes and virtually disappears in older age cohorts. For example, according to the 2011 CADUMS, the rate of cannabis use for people between the ages of 15 and 24 was three times higher than for those 25 and over (22 percent and 7 percent, respectively). Younger people were five times more likely than older people to report the use of illegal drugs other than cannabis (5 percent versus 1 percent, respectively) (Health Canada, 2011). Gender differences tend to be lesser among youth, although male rates of use remain consistently higher (Young et al., 2011). Provincial student surveys also indicate differences according to patterns of use, with males more likely to use cannabis at a higher frequency than females (Young et al., 2011).

Table 4.2: Substance Use Prevalence by Gender

	Canada's Alcohol and Drug Use Monitoring Survey (CADUMS, 2009)		Canada's Alcohol and Drug Use Monitoring Survey (CADUMS, 2011)	
	Females (%)	Males (%)	Females (%)	Males (%)
Cannabis – past year	7.2	14.2	6.2	12.2
Cannabis – lifetime	37.2	48.0	33.6	45.5
Cocaine – past year	0.9	1.5	s	1.4
Cocaine – lifetime	5.5	8.2	4.2	8.5
Ecstasy – past year	0.7	1.1	s	0.9
Ecstasy – lifetime	3.4	4.4	2.8	4.8
Any illegal drug[1] (excluding cannabis) – past year	1.5	2.8	1.1*	2.7*
Any illegal drug (excluding cannabis) – lifetime	11.9	18.6	10.7	18.5
Any illegal drug (including cannabis) – past year	7.6	14.8	6.5	12.5
Any illegal drug (including cannabis) – lifetime	37.9	49.0	34.1	46.7

Note: *High levels of sampling variability, interpret with caution

[1] = cocaine/crack, speed, hallucinogens (including salvia), heroin, ecstasy

We often think of illicit drug use as a contravention of social norms. However, many of the pharmacological properties of illicit drugs in fact support socially acceptable goals. Both licit and illicit drugs (e.g., ecstasy, cocaine, alcohol) are used to enhance confidence, reduce inhibitions, and increase sociability. These are considered socially acceptable goals for women. Particularly for young women, being confident, fun, and outgoing are associated with both popularity and romantic desirability. The social acceptance of use also depends on the context in which it is viewed, and gender is often a significant factor in that context (Measham, 2002). Qualitative research on women who use drugs recreationally indicates that most use drugs for personal enjoyment, physical pleasure, relaxing inhibitions, or as a kind of "time out." Women's freedom to pursue pleasure through recreational drug use, and to mobilize decision making concerning which drugs to use, as well as when, where, and the length of the drug-use occasion, suggest that recreational use is a normal, although somewhat risky, mainstream behaviour for those who have the resources to participate (Measham & Shiner, 2009). It is also important to note the emerging body of research and theoretical literature that examines drug taking as edgework or voluntary risk taking, and the socio-cultural value of drug taking as a pleasurable "risky" activity (Hunt, Evans, & Kares, 2007; Peratti-Watel & Moatti, 2006; Reith, 2005).

Measham's (2002) research on women illicit drug users in the UK suggests a deliberate use of psychoactive substances for a variety of purposes related to identity formation. For example, Measham's female respondents reported taking amphetamines when attending dance clubs. Not only does this practice accomplish the usual "night out" recreation, it also suppresses their appetite, activates their metabolism, and thus helps to control their weight.[3] Given that women face tremendous social pressure to be slim, taking stimulants such as amphetamines to suppress appetite and enhance energy levels may allow some women to restrict their calorie intake while still conducting professional, domestic, fitness, and other recreational and social activities.

Women have also reported using drugs as a means of coping. Links between drug use and trauma, victimization, and mental illness are well documented (Boyd & Faith, 1999; Boyd, 2001; Kilty, 2011). There is evidence that both men and women use illegal drugs to self-medicate and to alleviate symptoms associated with mental illness. Given that women in Canada are more likely to be diagnosed with a mental disorder than are men (Statistics Canada, 2002) and they are also more likely to be prescribed psycho-pharmaceuticals to treat those disorders (Tannenbaum, 2006), it is not surprising that some women take illicit substances to cope with the symptoms associated with mental illness. Cannabis, for example, may be used to decrease symptoms related to anxiety disorders (Canadian Centre on Substance Abuse, 2009). While women are more subject to the expertise of the state-approved and often paternal psychiatric and medical interventions than are men, those who assert agency by attempting to address mental distress through the use of psychoactive substances not prescribed by a physician—be they legal or illegal—are subject to criminalization and increased institutional punishment once incarcerated (Kilty, 2008, 2012).

Women in Canada are more likely than men to experience sexual and violent victimization at the hands of a partner or family member. Drug use is often cited as a means of escaping the emotional after-effects of this reality—be it the result of current victimization such as recurring domestic violence or memories of past victimization (Buchanan et al., 2011; Bungay, Johnson, Varcoe, & Boyd, 2010). Despite many women using drugs to cope with their experiences of distress and victimization, women's patterns of drug use are also frequently influenced by familial and other interpersonal relationships. Women often report that male partners played an influential role in their entry into drug use or progression to more high-risk drug use, for example, shifting from inhalation to injection use or to a more damaging and/or addictive substance (Buchanan et al., 2011).

Illegal drugs can also play a functional role among the marginalized populations within which use is most prevalent. Street youth, for example, report using amphetamines to stay awake at night to protect themselves from victimization. The association between street-level sex trade workers and illegal drugs is more complex; at a purely functional level, stimulants can provide the energy needed to work long hours (Bungay et al., 2010).

Some sex trade workers report that drug effects provide a level of depersonalization that enables them to do work that they find degrading. On the other hand, many drug users enter or remain in the sex trade in order to fund a drug addiction, which creates and reinforces a vicious cycle (Erickson, Adlaf, Smart, & Murray, 1994; Erickson, Butters, McGillicuddy, & Halgran, 2000).

Women's various reasons for drug use and the differing social stigmas associated with each result in the need for strategies of identity and stigma management. Interviews with formerly incarcerated women indicate that they often create dual identities—the "addict" and the "true" self—to manage both social stigma and personal guilt and shame associated with drug-using behaviour (Kilty, 2011). This division of selves or identities reflects women's internalization of society's moral and paternal judgment of their criminal and drug-using behaviours. It also reflects gendered expectations of ideal standards of motherhood and femininity that facilitate the compartmentalization of both criminal and drug user identities as the "non-true" and thus innately problematic constructions of self. Normative state discourses on motherhood and femininity may also set women up to fail in their recovery from addiction, as any relapse, use, or deviation from that hegemonic standard indicates failure in their role and identity as a mother and as a woman (Kilty & Dej, 2012).

The gendered nature of drug use means that men and women present with different treatment needs. Programs that are informed by gender and cultural diversity remain a commonly identified gap across the country (National Treatment Strategy Working Group, 2008), yet services based on a male delivery model do not respond to women's needs. Many services, for example, are confrontational and group-based, whereas women respond better to an environment of safety and acceptance (Niccols, Dell, & Clarke, 2010). One of the most common motivations for women seeking treatment is to provide better care for, or retaining/regaining custody of, their children; however, very few residential treatment services offer child care options. Many mothers must face the loss of contact with their children for an extended period of time in order to access drug treatment services. If the woman is a single mother without family support, her only option may be placing her children in foster care. The feelings of loss and guilt created by these choices can result in non-completion of the treatment program (Poole & Isaac, 2001). Conversely, women that are approached in a non-judgmental manner and offered options for child care report being receptive to the opportunity to focus on self-care (Poole & Isaac, 2001). Current best-practice literature for substance use treatment endorses a cognitive behavioural approach; problematically, however, most of this literature is based on research that examined White men only. Cognitive behavioural approaches focus on helping the individual to develop better decision-making skills, thus reflecting the choice model of addiction that situates the individual as responsible for and in control of her substance use (Kilty, 2011). This approach is in contrast with the 12-step model, promoted by AA and NA, which is based on a model of addiction as a chronic disease, recovery from which begins with the acceptance that the individual is powerless over his or her addiction (Valverde, 1998; Kilty, 2011).

Gendered Risks Associated with Drug Use

The enhanced risks faced by women who inject drugs are largely the result of invoking a moral approach to drug use. The evidence for the ability of interventions that do not require cessation of drug use, such as opiate substitution, peer education, needle exchange programs, and supervised injection sites, to reduce disease transmission, engage clients with health care and social support, and reduce deaths due to overdose continues to accumulate (see, e.g., European Monitoring Centre for Drugs and Drug Addiction, 2010; Ritter & Cameron, 2006). However, widely spread moral aversion to interventions that may be interpreted as condoning drug use creates complicated socio-political barriers to implementing these programs.

The role of illegal drugs in victimization is far more complex than the construction of the ravaging of virginal women by racialized male predators. This complexity is rooted in the inter-relationship between victimization, trauma, mental health, socio-economic status, and gender. Substance use, trauma, and mental health are highly correlated. Women who have experienced violence or other trauma are at increased risk of harm from substance use and of mental health problems; this fact is further aggravated when considering some of the exacerbating effects of race and class (Niccols, Dell, & Clarke, 2010). Aboriginal women are more likely to have a number of risk factors for substance use problems, including family violence, poverty, and sexual violence (Dell & Lyons, 2007). Intergenerational trauma associated with colonialization and residential schools (which also reflects both moral and paternal influences associated with the assimilation of Aboriginals into the "superior" Western culture) is a further predictor of harm from substance use (Shannon, Spittal, & Thomas, 2007). Paternalism also justifies state interventions designed to protect the well-being of the children and fetuses of drug-using mothers. While Canada has not gone as far as the United States in terms of prosecuting pregnant mothers who use drugs for endangering their unborn children (Eckenwiler, 2004; Lester, Andreozzi, & Appiah, 2004), women in Canada who use drugs still face the apprehension of their children by child protection agencies (Public Health Agency of Canada, 2010). Ironically, despite prevailing moral and paternal interpretations of women's drug use that might evoke sympathetic and supportive responses and interventions to arrest drug use, the state focuses on criminal justice interventions that are rooted in theories of deterrence. This fact reflects the neoliberal ideal of holding individuals accountable for their choices without consideration of the state, institutional, and other structural barriers that affect circumstance, behaviour, and decision making.

Women who are dependent upon illegal drugs experience many health problems, particularly those who are street-involved or otherwise marginalized. These health and other social problems are compounded by structural and interpersonal violence associated with drug use (Bungay et al., 2010; Fairbairn, Small, Shannon, Wood, & Kerr, 2008). Structural violence refers to social factors such as legislation and enforcement practices that limit access to safe spaces for sex trade work and drug use, and social norms and stereotypes that place women in a subordinate role in gendered power relations (Canadian HIV/AIDS Legal Network, 2012; Shannon et al., 2008). Interpersonal violence includes violence associated with the sex trade, robbery for drugs and/or money, and domestic violence. Research in Vancouver's Downtown Eastside, for example, found that women under age 30 who inject drugs were 54 times more likely to die prematurely than women of the same age in the general population, with homicide the most frequent cause of death (Miller, Kerr, Strathdee, Li, & Wood, 2007).

Women often have less control over the supply and use of illegal drugs than men (Boyd & Faith, 1999; Fairbairn et al., 2008). According to a study in San Francisco (Bourgois, Prince, & Moss, 2004), women who inject drugs are more likely than men to receive assistance with drug injections. Letting men (usually their male partners) inject them results in decreasing their control over the injection process itself, including ensuring the proper sanitation of the equipment and injection site, the cleanliness and accuracy of the injection itself, and the quantity of the drug that is injected. All of these steps in the injection process are vital in preventing soft tissue and vein injury, disease transmission, and overdose. The reason for this lies predominantly in the patriarchal culture of drug use. Women's subordinate role in acquisition and use affirms men's position of power and role as protector in street drug culture (Bourgois et al., 2004). Further associated with this reduced agency, women are also more likely to be "second on the needle," increasing the likelihood of disease transmission and soft tissue injury (Csete, 2006). Approximately 33 percent of women with HIV in Canada report injection drug use as their exposure category (Public Health Agency of Canada, 2012). Women are also more likely than men to work in the sex trade in order to support their drug use. Crack cocaine use in particular is associated with a decreased likelihood of safe sex practices such as condom use (Brewer, Zhao, Metsch, Coltes, & Zenilman, 2007; Logan & Leukefeld, 2000), which further increases the risk of blood-borne virus transmission among women who use drugs.

Responses to Women's Drug Use

Canada, like most Western nations, primarily responds to drug use via criminal justice interventions, most recently evidenced by the introduction of mandatory minimum sentencing under the *Safe Streets and Communities Act* (2012).This approach is in opposition to the growing recognition that drug use is a health issue (e.g., United Nations, 2010) and that the prosecution of drug users is the driving force behind mass incarceration in the US (e.g., Christie, 2000) and of human rights violations internationally (e.g., Iakobishvili, 2011). In this last section we highlight the key responses to women's drug use, illustrate that they continue to reflect earlier paternal and moral policy approaches, and provide a brief discussion of possible alternatives to incarceration.

Enforcement

As illustrated in the opening vignettes, Canadian police forces have a range of options available—from ignoring violations, to warnings, to arrest—to respond to women's illicit drug use, all of which can significantly impact the risks and harms experienced by women who use drugs. For example, police crackdowns or sweeps of specified areas, during which officers more aggressively seek out and charge people engaging in a targeted activity, often drive that activity further underground. Although justifiable in moralist and paternalist terms as directed toward or intending to express social disapproval and removing dangerous substances from public streets, the actual impact on women subject to these sweeps can be higher rates of victimization. Interviews with women who use drugs in Vancouver's Downtown Eastside indicate that drug users respond to crackdowns by retreating to less visible locations, such as alleyways, and that they are less able to protect themselves or to seek medical or public health counselling and assistance. This reduced visibility also minimizes women's capacity to look out for one another and places them at greater risk of physical and sexual victimization (Bungay et al., 2010). Confiscation and/or destruction of drug-use paraphernalia also results in the use of lower quality and shared equipment and the consequent increase in health risks; namely, infection and transmission of blood-borne diseases and viruses (Bungay et al., 2010; Kerr, Small, & Wood, 2005).

Prosecution

While women are less likely than men to be involved with the criminal justice system, the proportion of women charged with crimes in Canada is increasing (Mahoney, 2011).

The rate of women in prison is growing more quickly than the rate of men in prison, with Aboriginal women as the most quickly growing demographic in the Canadian penal system (Public Safety Canada, 2011). There are considerable differences in both gender and age for arrests related to drug offences. According to 2009 figures, 104.5/100,000 women were accused of drug-related offences compared to 564.2/100,000 men. When divided by age, younger women (under 18) were more likely than adult women to be charged, at a rate of 236.1/100,000 versus 92.6/100,000 (Mahoney, 2011). Women represent approximately 20 percent of drug trafficking cases in the courts but remain less likely than men to receive a custodial sentence; women convicted of drug possession, however, are one of the few exceptions to this pattern (Mahoney, 2011). The rate of federally incarcerated women serving sentences for drug crimes is also increasing. In 1981, 16 percent of federally incarcerated women were in prison for drug-related crime. In 2007, this proportion reached approximately 28 percent (Gobeil, 2009).

Substance abuse is the most commonly identified treatment need among women in provincial custody (93.7 percent), and according to the Correctional Service of Canada, 80 percent of women in federal custody have substance abuse problems (Matheson, Doherty, & Grant, 2008). Women serving time in federal custody for drug-related offences have a very different offence profile than the rest of the population. These women are more likely to have concurrent non-drug offences relating to the administration of justice, such as breaching parole conditions, rather than concurrent violent or other index offences (Gobeil, 2009). Gobeil's (2009) study of women sentenced to federal prison between 2000 and 2004 for drug-related versus non-drug-related offences found that racial minority women were significantly more likely to be incarcerated for drug-related offences. Black women made up 20.9 percent of the drug offence group versus 4.7 percent of the non-drug offence group; White and Aboriginal women made up larger portions of the non-drug offence group.

Alternatives to Incarceration

Despite the current Canadian trend toward more punitive measures for drug use, public health and other bodies both within Canada and internationally recognize the need to address substance use as a health rather than a legal issue (e.g., Canadian Public Health Association, 2007; United Nations Office on Drugs and Crime and World Health Organization, 2009). In practice, the two approaches are often combined through criminal justice diversion or through court-ordered treatment.

Court-mandated treatment for the protection of an unborn fetus is clearly a gendered issue. In Canada, the question of whether or not a woman with a substance use problem can be detained for mandatory treatment pending the birth of a child was taken to the Supreme Court in *Winnipeg Child and Family Services (Northwest Area) v. G. (D.F.)* (1997). The majority ruling in this case found that the courts do not have *parens patriae*[4] authority over an unborn child. The Court also confirmed that tort law could not be applied to parents' lifestyle choices, recognizing that, although the relationship between mother and fetus meets duty of care criterion, the mother remains an autonomous decision-maker. That autonomy would be threatened by the imposition of regulations based solely on the best interests of the fetus (in an extreme case, for example, a mother may be required to avoid walking in public places where she may be exposed to second-hand smoke). In its decision, the Court recognized the "slippery slope" that extending duty of care would involve, that this would most likely have a negative and disproportionate impact on women of lower socio-economic status, and that pregnant women that engage in potentially harmful lifestyle behaviours would be driven underground rather than encouraged to seek assistance, counselling, or treatment. In Canada, the social stigma of being a substance-using mother is already strong enough to dissuade women from seeking medical attention during their pregnancy, without the added threat of legal intervention (Poole & Isaac, 2001). This stigma is, again, rooted in the paternal interest in protecting the unborn child and the moral judgment of the mother's defiance of social norms.

Drug treatment courts (DTCs) are currently receiving federal support in Canada through the recently passed *Safe Streets and Communities Act* (Government of Canada, 2012). DTCs essentially involve the suspension of sentence pending completion of a court-supervised drug treatment program. Participation in DTCs requires entering a guilty plea and compliance with a substance abuse treatment program under direct supervision of the courts with weekly or biweekly reporting directly to a judge. Participation in the program is then taken into consideration in sentencing, although a reduction in sentence severity is not guaranteed. While there is support for DTCs as a means of reducing recidivism (Latimer, Morton-Bourgon, & Chretien, 2006), there are also many concerns, including coercion, reliance on the criminal justice system as a gateway to treatment access, inefficient use of court resources, lack of reliable evaluation data, and low completion rates (Allard, Lyons, & Elliott, 2011; Weekes, Mugford, Bourgon, & Price, 2007). Concerns with DTCs are amplified for women. The majority of treatment offered to DTC participants in Canada is not gender-specific. Both Toronto and Vancouver have offered some gender-specific options; however, these have been limited by operational demands and resource constraints (Department of Justice Canada, 2009). Concern has also been expressed that eligibility rules disqualifying applicants whose offences involved or were committed in the presence of children under 18 disproportionally impacts women, and particularly minority and low-income women, who are more likely to be primary caregivers (Allard et al., 2011). These women are also likely to face increased barriers in complying with required treatment and drug-testing schedules and bail conditions, given childcare demands. These restrictions likely contribute to the finding that women are less likely to engage in or complete DTC programs, despite the fact that federal funding provided in Canada mandated DTCs to target Aboriginal women, sex trade workers, and women in general (Department of Justice Canada, 2009).

Conclusion

There are ongoing calls to reform Canadian drug laws as well as the international treaties that govern them. Canada's drug laws were not created to further marginalize women with already complex health, social, and economic needs, and the criminal justice system was certainly not designed to meet those needs. In order to achieve a system that truly reduces the harms associated with illicit drug use, any legal reform should start from the position that drug use is primarily a health—not a criminal justice—issue. Reforms must be grounded in evidence and informed by gender- and diversity-based analyses, rather than social stigmas and stereotypes associated with moral and paternal discursive traditions. Such reforms would mean that the pregnant, marginalized, and thus vulnerable drug user characterized in the second opening vignette would be contacted by an outreach worker, and connected to supportive, comprehensive, and non-judgmental services to meet her physical and mental health, housing, economic, and substance use needs without criminal justice involvement. Programs that offer these services do exist (for an example, see the Fir Square program in Vancouver); however, the reach of these programs remains limited in comparison to that of Canada's archaic and punitive criminal justice sanctions. In order to implement a health policy approach to women's harmful involvement with drugs, it is necessary to eschew the attitudes and practices responsible for generating and maintaining their harmful involvement with law. Recent decades have seen considerable progress in recognizing the human rights of Canadian women in political participation, in the labour force, in marriage, and in other family matters. It is time to recognize these rights in the Canadian justice system.

Notes

1 The authors recognize that the social and economic impact of legal drug use, i.e., alcohol and pharmaceutical use, exceeds that of illicit drugs (Rehm et al., 2006). However, sufficient exploration of these issues is beyond the scope of this chapter.

2 Sentence length varies from six months to three years depending on substance involved, activity (i.e., trafficking vs. production), and presence of aggravating factors such as proximity to a public place frequented by minors or presence of weapons.

3 A third of the sample of women club dancers were clinically underweight with a Body Mass Index under 20 (Measham, 2002: 365).

4 The right of the court to make decisions concerning those unable to decide for themselves.

References

Allard, P., Lyons, T., & Elliott, R. (2011). *Impaired Judgment: Assessing the Appropriateness of Drug Treatment Courts as a Response to Drug Use in Canada.* Toronto: Canadian HIV/AIDS Legal Network.

Beauchesne, L. (2000). *What Do We in Canada Want?* Brief submitted to the Senate Special Committee on Illegal Drugs. Retrieved from www.parl.gc.ca/Content/SEN/Committee/371/ille/presentation/beauchesne-e.htm

Bourgois, P., Prince, B., & Moss, A. (2004). "The everyday violence of hepatitis C among young women who inject drugs in San Francisco." *Human Organization*, 63(3): 253–264.

Boyd, S. (2001). "The regulation of altered states of consciousness: A history of repression and resistance." *Contemporary Justice Review*, 4(1): 75–100.

Boyd, S., & Faith, K. (1999). "Women, illicit drugs and prison: Views from Canada." *International Journal of Drug Policy*, 10: 195–207.

Brewer, T.H., Zhao, W., Metsch, L.R., Coltes, A., & Zenilman, J. (2007). "High-risk behaviours in women who use crack: Knowledge of HIV serostatus and risk behavior." *Annals of Epidemiology*, 17(7): 533–539.

Buchanan, M., Murphy, K., Smith Martin, M., Korchinski, M., Buxton, J., Granger-Brown, A., ... & Hislop, G. (2011). "Understanding incarcerated women's perspectives on substance use: Catalysts, reasons for use, consequences, and desire for change." *Journal of Offender Rehabilitation*, 50(2): 81–100.

Bungay, V., Johnson, J.L., Varcoe, C., & Boyd, S. (2010). "Women's health and use of crack cocaine in context: Structural and 'everyday' violence." *International Journal of Drug Policy*, 21(4): 321–329.

Canadian Centre on Substance Abuse. (2009). *Substance Abuse in Canada: Concurrent Disorders.* Ottawa: Canadian Centre on Substance Abuse. Retrieved from www.ccsa.ca/2010%20CCSA%20Documents/ccsa-011811-2010.pdf

Canadian HIV/AIDS Legal Network. (2012). *Women, Sex Work, and HIV.* Toronto: Canadian HIV/AIDS Legal Network. Retrieved from www.aidslaw.ca/publications/interfaces/downloadFile.php?ref=2010

Canadian Public Health Association. (2007, September 17). "2007 Canadian Public Health Association resolution no. 2: Regulation of psychoactive substances in Canada." *Canadian Public Health Association 2007 Resolutions.* Ottawa. Retrieved from www.cpha.ca/uploads/resolutions/2007_e.pdf

Carstairs, C. (2006). *Jailed for Possession: Illegal Drug Use, Regulation, and Power in Canada, 1920–1961.* Toronto: University of Toronto Press.

Csete, J. (2006). "Second on the needle: Two-level strategy for claiming the rights of women who use drugs." XVI International AIDS Conference, Toronto, August 13–18. Retrieved from www.aidslaw.ca/publications/interfaces/downloadFile.php?ref=743

Christie, N. (2000). *Crime Control as Industry: Towards Gulags, Western Style.* New York: Routledge.

Department of Justice Canada. (2009). *Drug Treatment Court Funding Program: Summative Evaluation. Final Report.* Ottawa: Department of Justice Canada. Retrieved from www.justice.gc.ca/eng/pi/eval/rep-rap/09/dtcfp-pfttt/dtcfp.pdf

Dell, C., & Lyons, T. (2007). "Harm reduction policies and programs for persons of Aboriginal descent." Ottawa: Canadian Centre on Substance Abuse. Retrieved from www.ccsa.ca/2007%20CCSA%20Documents/ccsa-011515-2007.pdf

Eckenwiler, L. (2004). "Why not retribution? The particularized imagination and justice for pregnant addicts." *Journal of Law, Medicine, and Ethics*, 32: 89–99.

Erickson, P.G., Butters, J., McGillicuddy, P., & Halgren, A. (2000). "Crack and prostitution: Gender, myths and experiences." *Journal of Drug Issues*, 30(4): 767–788.

Erickson, P.G., Adlaf, E.M., Smart, R.G., & Murray, G.F. (1994). *The Steel Drug: Cocaine and Crack in Perspective* (2nd ed.). New York: Lexington.

European Monitoring Centre for Drugs and Drug Addiction. (2006). *Annual Report 2006: Selected Issues.* Luxembourg: Office for Official Publications of the European Communities. Retrieved from www.emcdda.europa.eu/html.cfm/index34880EN.html

European Monitoring Centre for Drugs and Drug Addiction. (2010). "Harm reduction: Evidence, impacts, and challenges." *Monographs*, 10. Luxembourg: European Monitoring Centre for Drugs and Drug Addiction.

Fairbairn, N., Small, W., Shannon, K., Wood, E., & Kerr, T. (2008). "Seeking refuge from violence in street-based drug scenes: Women's experiences in North America's first supervised injection facility." *Social Science and Medicine*, 67: 817–823.

Gabor, T., & Crutcher, T. (2002). *Mandatory Minimum Penalties: Their Effects on Crime, Sentencing Disparities, and Justice System Expenditures.* Prepared for the Research and Statistics Division, Department of Justice Canada. Retrieved from www.justice.gc.ca/eng/pi/rs/rep-rap/2002/rr02_1/rr02_1.pdf

Giffen, P.J., Endicott, S., & Lambert, S. (1991). *Panic and Indifference: The Politics of Canada's Drug Laws.* Ottawa: Canadian Centre on Substance Abuse.

Gobeil, R. (2009). *Profile of Federally Sentenced Women Drug Offenders.* (Rep. No. R-204). Ottawa: Correctional Service Canada. Retrieved from www.csc-scc.gc.ca/text/rsrch/reports/r204/r204-eng.shtml

Government of Canada. (2012). *Safe Streets and Communities Act.* Retrieved from http://laws-lois.justice.gc.ca/eng/annualstatutes/2012_1/

Health Canada. (2011). *Canadian Alcohol and Other Drug Use Monitoring Survey: Summary of Results for 2010*. Retrieved from www.hc-sc.gc.ca/hc-ps/drugs-drogues/stat/_2010/summary-sommaire-eng.php

Hunt, G.P., Evans, K., & Kares, F. (2007). "Drug use and the meanings of risk and pleasure." *Journal of Youth Studies*, 10(1): 73–96.

Iakobishvili, E. (2011). *Inflicting Harm: Judicial Corporal Punishment for Drug and Alcohol Offenses in Selected Countries*. London: Harm Reduction International. Retrieved from www.ihra.net/files/2011/11/08/IHRA_CorporalPunishmentReport_Web.pdf

Kerr, T., Small, W., & Wood, E. (2005). "The public health and social impacts of drug market enforcement: A review of the evidence." *International Journal of Drug Policy*, 16(4): 210–220.

Kilty, J. (2008). *Resisting Confined Identities: Women's Strategies of Coping in Prison*. Unpublished doctoral dissertation, Simon Fraser University, Burnaby, BC.

Kilty, J. (2011). "Tensions within identity: Notes on how criminalized women negotiate identity through addiction." *Aporia: The Nursing Journal*, 3(3): 5–15.

Kilty, J. (2012). "'It's like they don't want you to get better': Psy control of women in the carceral context." *Feminism & Psychology*, 22(2): 162–182.

Kilty, J., & Dej, E. (2012). "Anchoring amongst the waves: Discursive constructions of motherhood and addiction." *Qualitative Sociology Review*, 8(3): 6–23.

Latimer, J., Morton-Bourgon, K., & Chretien, J. (2006). *A Meta-Analytic Examination of Drug Treatment Courts: Do They Reduce Recidivism*. Ottawa: Department of Justice Canada. Retrieved from www.justice.gc.ca/eng/pi/rs/rep-rap/2006/rr06_7/rr06_7.pdf

Lester, B.M., Andreozzi, L., & Appiah, L. (2004). "Substance use during pregnancy: Time for policy to catch up with research." *Harm Reduction Journal*, 1(5). Retrieved from www.harmreductionjournal.com/content/pdf/1477-7517-1-5.pdf

Logan, T.K., & Leukefeld, C. (2000). "Sexual and drug use behaviors among female crack users: A multi-site sample." *Drug and Alcohol Dependence*, 58(3): 237–245.

Mahoney, T. (2011). *Women in the Criminal Justice System*. Ottawa: Statistics Canada. Retrieved from www.statcan.gc.ca/pub/89-503-x/2010001/article/11416-eng.pdf

Matheson, F.I., Doherty, S., & Grant, B. (2008). *Women Offender Substance Abuse Programming and Community Integration*. (Rep. No. R-202). Ottawa: Correctional Service Canada.

Measham, F. (2002). "'Doing gender—doing drugs': Conceptualizing the gendering of drugs cultures." *Contemporary Drug Problems*, 29: 335–373.

Measham, F., & Shiner, M. (2009). "The legacy of 'normalisation': The role of classical and contemporary criminological theory in understanding young people's drug use." *International Journal of Drug Policy*, 20: 502–508.

Miller, C.L., Kerr, T., Strathdee, S.A., Li, K., & Wood, E. (2007). "Factors associated with premature mortality among young injection drug users in Vancouver." *Harm Reduction Journal*, 4(1). Retrieved from www.ncbi.nlm.nih.gov/pmc/articles/PMC1769365/

Moore, D., & Valverde, M. (2000). "Maidens at risk: 'Date rape drugs' and the formation of hybrid risk knowledges." *Economy and Society*, 29(4): 514–531.

National Treatment Strategy Working Group. (2008). *A Systems Approach to Substance Use in Canada: Recommendations for a National Treatment Strategy.* Ottawa: National Treatment Strategy Working Group.

Niccols, A., Dell, C.A., & Clarke, S. (2010). "Treatment issues for Aboriginal mothers with substance use problems and their children." *International Journal of Mental Health and Addiction*, 8(1): 320–335.

Peratti-Watel, P., & Moatti, J.P. (2006). "Understanding risk behaviours: How the sociology of deviance may contribute? The case of drug taking." *Social Science & Medicine*, 63(3): 675–679.

Poole, N., & Isaac, B. (2001). *Apprehensions: Barriers to Treatment for Substance-Using Mothers.* Vancouver: British Columbia Centre of Excellence for Women's Health. Retrieved from www.bccewh.bc.ca/publications-resources/documents/apprehensions.pdf

Public Health Agency of Canada. (2010). *Canadian Incidence Study of Reported Child Abuse and Neglect 2008: Major Findings*. Retrieved from www.phac-aspc.gc.ca/ncfv-cnivf/pdfs/nfnts-cis-2008-rprt-eng.pdf

Public Health Agency of Canada. (2012). *Population-Specific HIV/AIDS Status Report: Women.* Ottawa: Public Health Agency of Canada. Retrieved from http://library.catie.ca/pdf/ATI-20000s/26407.pdf

Public Safety Canada. (2011). *Corrections and Conditional Release Statistical Overview*. Ottawa: Public Works and Government Services Canada. Retrieved from www.publicsafety.gc.ca/res/cor/rep/2011-ccrso-eng.aspx#c4

Rehm, J., Baliunas, D., Brochu, S., Fischer, B., Gnam, W., Patra, J., … & Taylor, B. (2006). *The Costs of Substance Abuse in Canada: Highlights Report*. Ottawa: Canadian Centre on Substance Abuse. Retrieved from www.ccsa.ca/2006%20CCSA%20Documents/ccsa-011332-2006.pdf

Reith, G. (2005). "Drugs and the consumption of risk in late modernity." In S. Lyng, ed., *Edgework: The Sociology of Risk-Taking* (pp. 227–246). New York: Routledge.

Ritter, A., & Cameron, J. (2006). "A review of the efficacy and effectiveness of harm reduction strategies for alcohol, tobacco, and illicit drugs." *Drug and Alcohol Review*, 25(6): 611–624.

Senate of Canada. (2012, February 1). Proceedings of the Standing Senate Committee on Legal and Constitutional Affairs, Issue 9. Testimony of the Hon. Robert Nicholson, P.C., M.P., Minister of Justice and Attorney General of Canada.

Shannon, K., Kerr, T., Allinott, S., Chettiar, J., Shoveller, J., & Tyndall, M.W. (2008). "Social and structural violence and power relations in mitigating HIV risk of drug-using women in survival sex work." *Social Science & Medicine*, 66: 911–921.

Shannon, K., Spittal, P., & Thomas, V. (2007). "Intersections of trauma, substance use, and HIV vulnerability among Aboriginal girls and young women who use drugs." In N. Poole

& L. Greaves, eds., *Highs & Lows: Canadian Perspectives on Women and Substance Use* (pp. 169–175). Toronto: Centre for Addiction and Mental Health.

Statistics Canada. (2002). *Canadian Community Health Survey (CCHS): Mental Health and Well-Being, Cycle 1.2.* Retrieved from www.statcan.gc.ca/concepts/health-sante/cycle1_2/index-eng.htm

Tannenbaum, C. (2006). *Towards a Better Understanding of Women's Mental Health and Its Indicators.* Ottawa: Health Canada. Retrieved from www.hc-sc.gc.ca/sr-sr/pubs/hpr-rpms/2006-tannenbaum-eng.php#_1

United Nations. (2010). *From Coercion to Cohesion: Treating Drug Dependence through Health Care, Not Punishment.* Vienna: United Nations. Retrieved from www.unodc.org/docs/treatment/Coercion/From_coercion_to_cohesion.pdf

United Nations Office on Drugs and Crime and World Health Organization. (2009). *UNODC-WHO Joint Programme on Drug Dependence Treatment and Care.* Austria: United Nations Office on Drugs and Crime and World Health Organization. Retrieved from www.unodc.org/documents/drug-treatment/UNODC-WHO-brochure.pdf

Valverde, M. (1998). *Diseases of the Will: Alcohol and the Dilemmas of Freedom.* Cambridge and New York: Cambridge University Press.

Weekes, J., Mugford, R., Bourgon, G., & Price, S. (2007). *Drug Treatment Courts: FAQs.* Ottawa: Canadian Centre on Substance Abuse. Retrieved from www.ccsa.ca/2007%20CCSA%20Documents/ccsa-011348-2007.pdf

Young, M.M., Saewyc, E., Boak, A., Jahrig, J., Anderson, B., Doiron, Y., ... & Clark, H. (2011). *Cross-Canada Report on Student Alcohol and Drug Use: Technical Report.* Ottawa: Canadian Centre on Substance Abuse. Retrieved from www.ccsa.ca/2011%20CCSA%20Documents/2011_CCSA_Student_Alcohol_and_Drug_Use_en.pdf

Legal Cases and Statutes

Controlled Drugs and Substances Act, S.C. 1996, c.19.

Convention Against Illicit Traffic in Narcotic Drugs and other Psychotropic Substances, 1988 United Nations Treaty Series, vol. 1582. Vienna.

Convention on Psychotropic Substances, 1971. United Nations Treaty Series, vol. 1019. Vienna.

Narcotic Control Act, 1961 c. 35.

An Act to Prohibit the Importation, Manufacture, and Sale of Opium for Other than Medicinal Purposes, 1908. c. 50.

Single Convention on Narcotic Drugs, 1961. United Nations Treaty Series, vol. 570. New York.

Safe Streets and Communities Act, S.C. 2012, c.1.

Winnipeg Child and Family Services (Northwest Area) v. G. (D.F.), [1997] 3 S.C.R. 925. *Safe Streets and Communities Act,* S.C. 2012, c. 1.

Chapter 5

Sentencing Aboriginal Women to Prison

Gillian Balfour

Criminalizing and Imprisoning Aboriginal Women in Canada

Racialized women are the fastest growing proportion of prisoner populations in the world, a trend described by some as a gendered "global lockdown" (Sudbury, 2005). Women prisoners, however, remain "too few to count" (Adelburg & Currie, 1987) as their absolute numbers fade in the shadow of men's rates of incarceration. Critical race scholars and penologists have pointed to the use of mass incarceration in the US as a form of cultural genocide of African Americans: two-thirds of African American males will be under some form of criminal sentence in their lifetime (Brotherton, 2008; Wacquant, 2001). Yet a closer look at the prison population data tells us another story. In the US, between 1977 and 2004 the rate of female incarceration increased by 750 percent, and this escalation of women being jailed is almost double the rate of men (Frost, 2006). In 2006, Black women were incarcerated at a rate of 148 per 100,000, Hispanic women at a rate of 81 per 100,000, and White women at a rate of 48 per 100,000 (Sabol, Couture, & Harrison, 2007). In the United Kingdom, over the past decade, the female prisoner population has almost tripled (Walmsley, 2006). And in 2010, the Australian Institute of Criminology reported that, between 1984 and 2003, there was a 209 percent increase in the number of female prisoners (Balfour, 2013b).

Incarceration rates are the best proximate measure we have in Canada of sentencing trends. Unlike the United States, Canada does not keep comprehensive longitudinal sentencing data to allow for time series analysis of the effectiveness of law reforms, nor to determine possible trends in the sentencing of racialized groups (Roberts & Melchers, 2003). In addition, not all provinces and territories consistently report annual criminal court data, limiting our understanding of criminal case processing. Prison data

Table 5.1: Offence Profile: All Admission Types, Aboriginal Women, 2005–2010, OOHL and EIFW

	Fiscal Year	First-Degree Murder	Second-Degree Murder	Schedule I (Violent Offences)	Schedule II (Non-Violent)	Other Offences	Total
OOHL	2005–2006	0	0	10	2	1	**13**
	2006–2007	0	0	11	1	2	**14**
	2007–2008	0	1	14	7	3	**25**
	2008–2009	1	0	12	15	4	**32**
	2009–2010	0	0	9	4	3	**16**
EIFW	2005–2006	0	2	47	22	7	**78**
	2006–2007	0	2	58	27	6	**93**
	2007–2008	0	1	47	22	6	**76**
	2008–2009	1	1	38	17	3	**60**
	2009–2010	0	3	45	25	10	**83**

Note: OOHL = Okimaw Ohci Healing Lodge, EIFW = Edmonton Institute for Women

Source: Adapted from Correctional Service Canada. (2009–2010). "Women offenders programs and issues 2009–2010." *Women Offender Statistical Overview*. Retrieved from www.csc-scc.gc.ca/publications/fsw/wos_Stat_09_10/wos_stat_09_10-eng.shtml#_Toc280867098

is problematic: it is a daily snapshot of prisoner populations and represents the smallest proportion of criminalized people as most offenders plead guilty to receive a lesser sentence; plea negotiations are unregulated and unreported and are thus not open to empirical study. Prison data also do not take into account trends over time. Examining existing data on the various stages of the criminalization and incarceration process—pretrial custody, sentencing, and length of time in custody before parole—shows that Aboriginal women are vastly overrepresented.

In spite of the empirical limits of prison data, the federal government reported that between 1998 and 2008, Aboriginal peoples represented 21 percent of prisoners held in remand (Porter & Calverley, 2011), and the proportion of Aboriginal men sentenced to custody increased from 13 percent to 18 percent. For Aboriginal women, however, the increase in their imprisonment was greater, moving from 7 percent to 24 percent (Perrault, 2009). In 2006, data showed that 75 percent of Aboriginal women prisoners are convicted of violent offences such as homicide, robbery, and assault, whereas non-Aboriginal women are more likely to be convicted of drug-related offences (Kong & AuCoin, 2008). In 2010, Correctional Services Canada (CSC) reported that 66 percent of federally sentenced women were incarcerated for violent crimes; 79 percent of

Table 5.2: Distribution of the Total Federal Women Offender Population: Incarcerated and in the Community, 2005–2010

Fiscal Year	Aboriginal Women					Non-Aboriginal Women				
	Incarcerated	%	Community	%	Total	Incarcerated	%	Community	%	Total
2005–2006	128	56	100	44	**228**	280	41	400	59	**680**
2006–2007	148	59	103	41	**251**	328	44	410	56	**738**
2007–2008	164	59	115	41	**279**	331	43	446	57	**777**
2008–2009	157	58	113	42	**270**	343	43	462	57	**805**
2009–2010	164	62	99	38	**263**	339	42	465	58	**804**

Source: Adapted from Correctional Service Canada. (2009–2010). "Women offenders programs and issues 2009–2010." *Women Offender Statistical Overview*. Retrieved from www.csc-scc.gc.ca/publications/fsw/wos_Stat_09_10/wos_stat_09_10-eng.shtml#_Toc280867098

incarcerated Aboriginal women were serving time for a violent offence. A disproportionate number of Aboriginal women prisoners are classified as maximum security and confined to the Edmonton Institute for Women (EIFW). By comparison, the Okimaw Ohci Healing Lodge (OOHL) on Nekaneet First Nation territory holds approximately only one-third of all federally sentenced Aboriginal women prisoners (see Table 5.1). OOHL was purpose-built to house Aboriginal women on traditional lands with the intent to deliver culturally appropriate programming and involve traditional elders (Hayman, 2006; Monture, 2000). Since its inception, the OOHL has not housed any Aboriginal women classified as maximum security.

In addition to increasing Aboriginal prisoner populations, data also reveals regional differences in the uses of incarceration, as well as racialized trends in parole release decisions. For example, in the Prairie provinces of Manitoba and Saskatchewan, Aboriginal women represent 80–90 percent of provincial female prisoners, yet account for only 5 percent of the provincial population. In the territories of Yukon and Northwest Territories, Aboriginal women account for 85–95 percent of prison populations. In all cases, the rate of imprisonment of Aboriginal women exceeds the rate for Aboriginal men by approximately 20 percent (Brzozowski, Taylor-Butts, and Johnson, 2006). When examining the release of women prisoners into the community on day parole, full parole, and statutory release, we also see disparities between Aboriginal and non-Aboriginal women (see Table 5.2). Although the actual numbers of non-Aboriginal women are higher than Aboriginal women, proportionally we can see that in 2009–2010, 62 percent of criminalized Aboriginal women were incarcerated, and only 38 percent were released into the community; whereas 42 percent of non-Aboriginal women were incarcerated, and 58 percent of non-Aboriginal women were released into the community (CSC, 2009–2010).

In sum, an increasing proportion of Aboriginal women are being criminalized and incarcerated for violent offences, especially women in the Prairie region, and are serving more of their prison sentence in custody, whereas non-Aboriginal women are returning to the community sooner. As these data reveal, there is a continuum of penality that follows Aboriginal women from pretrial custody, to sentencing decisions that do not seek alternatives to incarceration, to restricted access to the Aboriginal healing lodge, and to limited success in achieving parole. If we wish to address the spiral of Aboriginal women's rate of incarceration, we need to attend to this continuum or spiral of penality. In the next section of this chapter, I consider how sentencing methodologies followed by the courts enable the carceral control of Aboriginal women.

Sentencing Law Reforms in Canada: Special Consideration for Aboriginal Offenders and Conditional Sentences

Progressive sentencing law reforms enacted in 1996 (Bill C-41, an act to amend the *Criminal Code of Canada* with regard to sentencing) introduced sentencing objectives and principles to reduce the overall level of incarceration in Canada, and to move toward a restorative justice framework that allows for the special consideration of Aboriginal offenders. Section 718 of the *Criminal Code* directs judges to fashion their sentencing decisions in accordance with the "fundamental principle of contributing to a respect for the law and the maintenance of a just, peaceful, and safe society by imposing a just sanction." Thus, a just sanction must be proportionate to the seriousness of the harm caused and the degree of responsibility of the offender, and can be increased or reduced depending on several aggravating factors, such as "evidence that the offender, in committing the offence, abused the offender's spouse or common-law partner." Moreover, "an offender should not be deprived of liberty, if less restrictive sanctions may be appropriate in the circumstances"; and "all available sanctions other than imprisonment that are reasonable in the circumstances should be considered for all offenders, with particular attention to the circumstances of aboriginal offenders" (*Criminal Code of Canada*, s. 718.2(e))

The spiralling rates of Aboriginal women's incarceration come sharply into view when we consider these progressive sentencing principles and objectives that emphasize seeking alternatives to incarceration, especially in cases involving Aboriginal offenders.

As well, the recognition of domestic violence as an aggravating factor by sentencing judges should enable greater safety for Aboriginal women in their communities, given their high rates of victimization. In addition to these reforms, the *Criminal Code* sets out a remedial sanction for those offenders sentenced to less than two years: conditional sentences are intended to allow offenders deserving incarceration to serve their prison terms in the community under various conditions. The conditions can include house arrest, curfews, community service, victim-offender reconciliation, treatment programs, and restitution to the victim or community.

Despite the promise of Bill C-41, the rate of incarceration has not slowed; indeed, it has increased for Aboriginal people, especially women. For us to understand how progressive legislation does not accomplish its desired ends, we need to examine the implementation of the legislation at the level of legal practice. In the years following the enactment of Bill C-41, the Supreme Court of Canada was asked to interpret section 718.2(e) upon appeal from lower court rulings in the sentencing of Aboriginal peoples convicted of serious offences. The case of Jamie Gladue—a young Aboriginal woman from B.C. convicted in the death of her common law spouse after years of documented domestic violence—created an opportunity for decolonizing sentencing practices in Canada that took into account the unique circumstances of Aboriginal peoples' lives, but was also an opportunity for the prevalence of violence against Aboriginal women to be considered as a unique circumstance resulting from colonialism.

R. v. Gladue

In 1997, shortly after Bill C-41 was enacted, Jamie Gladue was convicted of manslaughter in the death of her abusive common law husband, Reuben Beaver, and received a three-year prison sentence. In 1999, her defence lawyers filed a successful appeal with the Supreme Court of Canada on the grounds that the lower provincial and appeal courts did not take into account Ms. Gladue's Aboriginal status under section 718.2(e). The provincial court of appeal instead found that, while the lower court had erred in not taking into account Ms. Gladue's Cree ancestry, the offence she committed involved deliberation, motivation, and "an element of viciousness and persistence in the attack." It also found that the killing constituted a "near murder" (*R. v. Gladue*, 1999, at para. 20) and was more serious and deserving of imprisonment because she killed her common law spouse. As set out in section 718.2(ii), domestic violence is an aggravating factor. In their decision, the justices of the Supreme Court reaffirmed the importance of section 718.2(e) and found that the lower court had not given consideration to the unique circumstances of Ms. Gladue's life as an Aboriginal person. However, the Court also held that restorative justice should not be the primary goal of sentencing in all cases involving Aboriginal offenders (see Murdocca, 2013).

Thus, the sentencing narrative in this decision reflects a conflicted and contradictory sentencing methodology. On one hand, the Supreme Court of Canada upheld the custodial sentence because of the seriousness of the offence calling for denunciation and deterrence, yet on the other hand, set out procedural requirements for the defence to provide courts with detailed background information about Aboriginal offenders, and directed judges to give appropriate notice to information about the offender and his/her community. "The sentencing judge must consider some of the following issues/factors and query counsel or unrepresented offenders" (Turpel-LaFond, 1999: 8):

- has this offender been affected by substance abuse in the community?
- has this offender been affected by poverty?
- has this offender been affected by overt racism?
- has this offender been affected by family or community breakdown?
- has this offender been affected by unemployment, low income and a lack of employment opportunity?
- has this offender been affected by dislocation from an Aboriginal community, loneliness and community fragmentation?
- has the offender been affected by residential school education? (*R v. Gladue*, 1999, at paras. 67, 80, at 222 & 226)

These conditions, known as Gladue factors, are to be given judicial notice. They are to be properly documented in a "Gladue Report" and are to be submitted to the sentencing judge. The Gladue Report should also outline available alternatives to incarceration and document consultation with community leaders and Elders (Turpel-LaFond, 1999).

In light of the increasing rates of Aboriginal women's imprisonment, we could well ask if Aboriginal women receive special consideration, and why alternatives to incarceration are seldom utilized for women. Do law reforms matter, and can they ameliorate the high rates of Aboriginal women's incarceration? For example, Ms. Gladue's own experiences of domestic violence were not paid judicial notice; indeed, her victimization seemed to disappear (Comack & Balfour, 2004: 109).[1] Thus, while seemingly progressive in that domestic violence is to be given judicial notice as an aggravating factor at sentencing, the interpretation of the provision has been the increased criminalization and incarceration of Aboriginal women whose violence takes place in the context of their own victimization. Aboriginal women appear to have "fallen between the cracks of retributive and restorative justice" (Balfour, 2008). In the next part of the chapter, I consider the gendered conditions of endangerment: those social and economic conditions that uniquely impact upon Aboriginal women in a manner that jeopardizes their safety and resilience, such as domestic violence, unstable housing, single parenting, socio-economic and political marginality, and sexual exploitation. Through an examination of sentencing decisions in cases of Aboriginal women convicted of violent offences, I explore if these gendered conditions are accorded special consideration by sentencing courts under section 718.2(e) and thus examine the legacy of the "Gladue methodology" and "Gladue factors" in the 13 years since that landmark ruling by the Supreme Court of Canada.

Gendered Conditions of Endangerment and the Punishment of Aboriginal Women

Aboriginal women's bodies not only languish in jails and prisons across Canada. They also survive on the streets and strolls of urban centres, in overcrowded reserve housing, and on welfare as single mothers. In efforts to understand why progressive sentencing reforms have not slowed the rate of Aboriginal women's incarceration, it is important to consider the interconnections between the conditions of these women's lives and how sentencing laws are implemented. I call these circumstances of Aboriginal women's lives "gendered conditions of endangerment," as they directly affect women's physical and sexual safety and their economic security, and are legacies of colonial systems such as residential schools, band councils, and police forces that have ignored the prevalence of violence against women in their communities. For Aboriginal communities, the legacy of residential schools has been the intergenerational cycle of physical and sexual violence, resulting in chronic addictions to drugs and alcohol, family violence, sexual exploitation of children, and deep poverty (Evans-Campbell, 2008; Milloy, 1999; Smith, 2005).

Under these conditions, Aboriginal women are poorly educated, rarely employed, and repeatedly victimized and prostituted.[2] These forms of structural violence are rooted in the ravages of colonialism, and are the context of women's own use of violence. Based on a synthesis of findings from the General Social Survey, the Adult Criminal Court Survey, and offender population data collected by Correctional Services Canada, violence against Aboriginal women is three and a half times greater than that against non-Aboriginal women. Twenty-one percent of Aboriginal women experience "much higher levels of spousal violence by current or ex-partners than non-Aboriginal women (6%) ... suggesting that the prevalence of family violence is more extensive in Aboriginal communities" (Brzozowski et al., 2006: 9). Aboriginal women are five times more likely to be victims of homicide than are non-Aboriginal women (Cameron, 2006; Crnkovich, 1995). Not surprisingly, given the prevalence of gendered violence in Aboriginal communities, many women reported profound fear of victimization and death (Brzozowski et al., 2006). These fears are compounded by severe overcrowding due to housing shortages, as well as by the limited availability of emergency shelters and services for women who seek support or safety from violence (O'Donnell & Tait, 2003).

Despite these conditions of endangerment in urban and reserve communities, Aboriginal women are more likely to be charged with, and imprisoned for, violent offences than non-Aboriginal women. Assault is the largest crime category where charges were laid against Aboriginal women living on and off reserves, and Aboriginal women are four times more likely to be charged with homicide than non-Aboriginal women (Brzozowski et al., 2006). Comparatively speaking, Aboriginal women living on-reserve are twice as likely to be charged with homicide than Aboriginal women living off-reserve (Brzozowski et al., 2006).

Why do Aboriginal women living on reserves use violence more often than in urban communities? Carol La Prairie (2002) points to the variations in reserve band council composition and practices as instrumental in the allocation of resources and opportunities, as well as reporting of crimes to the police; oftentimes Aboriginal women in these communities have very little power and are highly vulnerable, particularly when seeking protection from abusers in their communities. In an earlier study of domestic violence in Northern Manitoba reserves, McGillivray and Comansky (1999) found that police often disregarded women's calls for help, and band councils would force women to recant their testimony against their abuser (McGillvray & Comaskey, 1999). Moreover, many of these women were themselves charged by the police for domestic violence when they attempted to defend themselves against their abusers (McGillvray & Comaskey, cited in Comack & Balfour, 2004: 157).

Thus, Aboriginal women's victimization appears to be more serious on reserves, yet police resources seem less effective, and reserve governance seems dismissive of women's needs for safety. It is in this context of overcrowding and diminished social supports that women's violence takes place. Yet, as we will see, sentencing judges seldom acknowledge these gendered conditions of endangerment as deserving of special consideration under law.

Do Law Reforms Matter?

What is the connection between the conditions of women's lives and how they are punished? In this section of the chapter we will review some empirical evidence that maps over a decade of sentencing decisions in cases of Aboriginal men and women convicted of violent crimes. As most Aboriginal prisoners are not advantaged by the sentencing provisions that allow for special consideration of their unique circumstances, it is important to consider how these reforms are being implemented in cases that would have the most benefit for Aboriginal peoples, and whether sentencing law reforms further marginalize Aboriginal women by placing them at greater risk of incarceration and revictimization.

Hannah-Moffat and Maurutto (2010) found in their study of pre-sentence reports involving Aboriginal women offenders that Gladue Reports provided courts with a narrative of the offender that typically described her remorse and the circumstances of her offence. These reports can be used to outline the role of socio-cultural and structural remedies for the conditions of Aboriginal offender's lives, such as poverty, homelessness, and lack of education. However, the authors also found that Gladue Reports are interpreted through standardized pre-sentence offender assessments or Level of Security Inventory (LSI).[3] The authors warn that sentencing processes in cases of Aboriginal offenders are mediated by actuarial risk-based tools such as the LSI that reframe Aboriginal offenders' social histories as evidence of rehabilitation needs and risk factors (such as additions treatment, anger management, and parenting classes). In the end, the increase in rates of incarceration could be due in part to how Gladue Reports are interpreted as evidence of an Aboriginal offender's high need for treatment—and therefore her high risk to reoffend. As many Aboriginal communities struggle with limited resources and complex social problems, appropriate and meaningful levels of supervision and treatment to address the offender's risk to the community are difficult to achieve. Thus, incarceration is viewed by the sentencing court as being in the best interest of the offender and the community.

Critics of the *R. v. Gladue* decision focus on the sentencing methodology devised in the wake of the decision, which presupposes that the problem of over-incarcerating Aboriginal peoples is an inappropriate sentencing method (Stennings & Roberts, cited in Murdocca, 2009). Murdocca (2009) reminds us that by framing Aboriginal offenders as deserving of special consideration, Canadian law accomplishes two aims. First, the Crown is absolved of its responsibility for the harms wrought by colonialism; rather, it seeks to assist the offender to better cope with these harms through culturally appropriate treatment programs aimed at individual needs. Second, section 718.2(e) places the individual offender within a narrative of inferior cultural differences (addiction and violence) rather than colonial violence.

Williams (2009: 89) asserts that a "more specific process may be at work in the penalization of Aboriginal women" given the increase in the rates of their imprisonment since the enactment of the sentencing reforms under section 718.2(e). In Williams's qualitative study of 18 sentencing decisions in cases of Aboriginal women, she found that there was little discernible difference in the criminal offence characteristics between those women who were sentenced to federal custody, and those women who received conditional sentences: "each of the 5 federally sentenced women had killed somebody and so had the 9 women who received a conditional sentence" (89). Williams noted that while courts appeared to implement the sentencing methodology set out in *R. v. Gladue*, the focus of the judges' decisions appeared not to recognize the historical and contemporary discriminatory treatment of Aboriginal women. This was especially apparent in cases where the offender was convicted of a serious violent offence, where judges focused on the prevalence of alcohol abuse (90).

Across almost all cases, judicial notice was consistently paid to "women's experiences of sexual and physical violence, childhood, substance dependency, educational disadvantage, under or un-employment, dislocation, parental abandonment, and family dysfunction as factors that had shaped her identity, stunted the development of essential coping skills and led her to reproduce toxic and dangerous relationships in adulthood" (Williams, 2009: 91). Judges also documented the number of early pregnancies and number of children that remained in the care of the offender (91). Williams's critique of the implementation of section 718.2(e) was echoed in research by Hannah-Moffat and Maurutto (2010) wherein the unique background and systemic factors were found to function as justifications for prison terms to "contain the threat the defendant poses and custodial correctional programming to reduce it" (92). In short, Williams's assessment of the implementation of section 718.2(e) also raises the question of whether law reforms matter if Aboriginal women's lives are reduced to risk/need factors. In the next section we examine how Gladue factors and the Gladue methodology are conceptualized and implemented in sentencing studies, including those involving Aboriginal men and women. The first study focuses on conditional sentences in cases of 13 convicted sex offenders in Ontario, and the second study examines 168 sentencing decisions in cases of Aboriginal men and women convicted of violent offences reported between 1997 and 2004.

In a large sentencing study of 221 sex offenders in Ontario between 1993 and 2001, Du Mont, Forte, and Badgely (2008) found that almost half of the perpetrators received a provincial sentence of two years less a day—well below the possible sentencing ranges prescribed in the *Criminal Code*. However, authors of that study also uncovered a small sub-sample of 13 sentencing decisions in which perpetrators received a conditional sentence, despite the seriousness of the offence and multiple aggravating factors. In a subsequent study of those 13 cases, Balfour and Du Mont (2012) explored how progressive sentencing law reforms (community-based sentences as alternatives to incarceration) may also be regressive when addressing gendered violence. A qualitative analysis of sentencing narratives in these cases revealed how non-Aboriginal men were given conditional sentences because they were deemed more amenable to treatment and supervision in the community because they were professionally employed and married. For example, in a case of *R. v. K.R.G.* (1996), the perpetrator was convicted of repeatedly sexually assaulting his stepdaughter over an extended period of time. He denied committing the assaults, expressed no remorse, and yet received a conditional sentence of nine months. The perpetrator's conduct was described as an "aberration," and his character above reproach as he had demonstrated "an enduring work ethic":

> [H]e has otherwise responsibly discharged parental duties, most recently as a single parent for and the sole support of his teenage son and daughter by his first marriage. With a special interest in coaching and in organizing bone marrow donors, he has actively participated in community volunteer work. There is no reason to question the multitude of references attesting to his otherwise good character as an active member of society. (*R. v. K.R.G.*, 1996, at para. 15)

When deliberating on a term of imprisonment in this case, the judge asserted "that the fallout may be more impactive if the offender has made substantial progress on a career path for which status may be lost" (*R. v. K.R.G.*, 1996, at para. 28). Balfour and Du Mont (2012) also found that conditional sentences were justified in cases involving poorly educated men for whom incarceration would be excessively punitive. For example, sentencing judges in *R. v. Tulk* (2000) and *R. v. Ridings* (1998) accepted that the offenders were not predators, but instead men of limited intellect and low self-esteem. In fact, in *R. v. Tulk*, the offender was convicted of a serious sexual assault of a female acquaintance in a comatose state due to diabetic shock. He expressed no remorse for his actions, yet the sentencing judge explained in his decision that the offender's lack of remorse was more about his "lack of sophistication than moral turpitude" (*R. v. Tulk*, 2000, at para. 15). As well, in *R. v. Ridings* (1998), the judge described the sexual assault involving a 15-year-old victim and a 43-year-old perpetrator as

> an isolated incident not in keeping with his general character. His inferior personality does not lend itself to manipulation. He did not use violence or the threat of violence to control the victim. He is not a threat to the community to re-offend. On the contrary there is a greater threat that the perpetrator with his limited intellect would be in danger in a custodial situation. (at para. 13)

In contrast, in cases involving Aboriginal men convicted of sexual assault, the legal narratives were much different. In *R. v. Kakepetum* (2001), the offender was from an isolated reserve community in Northern Ontario and had sexually assaulted two young girls as they slept. While on bail awaiting trial, he completed a treatment program, secured a full-time job, abstained from drugs and alcohol, and expressed profound remorse for his actions. What is remarkable about this case is that the girls and community were consulted in the sentencing process in accordance with the principles of restorative justice. The Elders of the community requested that the offender reside in a different community out of respect for the girls and to denounce his behaviour. In this context, the restorative justice model appeared to be linked to the needs of the young women as victims of sexual violence and the consequences of high rates of incarceration for Aboriginal peoples. In his judgment, he stated:

> A substantial jail sentence would provide a powerful disincentive for men to come forward to acknowledge their sexual offending behaviour. Considering how widespread a problem that is in so many of our northern communities, it is my view that it is far more important to create an environment where men are encouraged to come forward and take responsibility for what they have done.... It would be bad public policy to be zealous about imposing a harsh sentence on this man if the net result is that we bury so many other cases. (*R. v. Kakepetum*, 2001, at para. 9)

In another case involving an Aboriginal man, *R. v. B.K.* (2000), the perpetrator pled guilty to sexually assaulting his former girlfriend. The offender, the woman, and their families participated in a "community accountability conference." This restorative circle process required that he publicly acknowledge his responsibility as well as meet certain conditions agreed upon by the community. These included a six-month conditional sentence with extensive conditions and two years on probation:

> The process resulted in agreement on the part of B.K. to complete ... a series of undertakings which address his rehabilitation and which include attempts to raise awareness within the community of the spectre of sexual abuse and to enhance the respect for the safety and integrity of women in the community. (at para. 6)

In sum, Balfour and Du Mont (2012) found that the legal narratives in the sexual assault cases of these two male Aboriginal offenders illustrate the decolonizing potential of sections 718 and 742 of the *Criminal Code*. Although these men were convicted of serious violent offences, the sentencing methodology used in these cases suggests judges applied the Gladue methodology that acknowledges the historical and contemporary contexts of violence in Aboriginal communities. Are the sentencing methodologies similar for Aboriginal women convicted of serious violent offences? In another study of 168 sentencing decisions involving Aboriginal men and women convicted of violent offences, it seems the Gladue methodology is not consistently implemented, and renders Aboriginal women almost invisible in sentencing narratives.

Gladue Methodology

The cases analyzed for this study included all reported sentencing decisions available through Quicklaw—an online repository of reported trial and appeal court judgments and sentencing decisions. Cases were selected based on the Aboriginal identity of the offender and violent crime category (all levels of assault, all levels of sexual assault, manslaughter, second- and first-degree murder). Overall, 168 cases were reported between 1997 and 2004. An initial finding was that, of the 168 cases examined, the offender's Aboriginal background was mentioned by judges in their reasons for sentence in only 19 percent of cases. Within these 40 cases, 39 involved a male offender, and only 1 case involved a female offender. These data clearly illustrate that Aboriginal women are marginalized in legal discourse. Although they represent an increasing proportion of criminalized and incarcerated Aboriginal people, their place in sentencing narratives is relatively invisible. While we cannot generalize the findings presented below given the limited number of Aboriginal women offenders, we need to recognize this as an important finding: more Aboriginal women are going to jail and yet we know little about the administration of justice in their cases.

Sentencing outcomes generally indicated a strong punitive response to violent crimes and Aboriginal offenders. For example, Table 5.3 shows that denunciation, general deterrence, and public safety were the key reported sentencing objectives; approximately 10 percent of cases reported reduction of incarceration rates as a sentencing goal, and less than 10 percent stated reparation of harm for victims and communities in their sentencing aims.

Table 5.3: Sentencing Objectives Cited, 1997–2004

Sentencing Objectives	Count	Percentage of Responses	Percentage of Cases
Denunciation	105	27.8	66.9
General deterrence	71	18.8	45.2
Individual deterrence	45	11.9	28.7
Public safety	74	19.6	47.1
Rehab of offender	57	15.1	36.3
Reparation	11	2.9	7.0
Lower prison rate	15	4.0	9.6

Notes: 11 missing cases, 157 valid cases. Total percentage greater than 100 due to multiple responses.

Source: Balfour, G. (2013a). "Do law reforms matter? Exploring the victimization-criminalization continuum in the sentencing of Aboriginal women in Canada." *International Review of Victimology*, 19(1): 85–102.

Overall, judges were far more likely to hand down carceral sentences (83 percent of cases) than non-carceral community-based alternative sanctions such as conditional sentences (16 percent of cases). Following these findings, I assessed the implementation of the Gladue methodology: pre-sentence reports, defence and Crown sentencing submissions, community support for the offender, and the involvement of Elders in sentencing recommendations.

Pre-sentence reports (Gladue Reports) were not mentioned by the sentencing judge in approximately 70 percent of cases, and when the report was mentioned, it was a positive account of the offender in 16 percent of cases and a negative account in 8 percent of cases. Given these data, it is unclear as to the value or role of pre-sentence reports in the sentencing process. In terms of the lawyering strategies of defence counsel, submissions regarding the special consideration of the unique circumstances of Aboriginal people were made in only 45 percent of cases—which is remarkable, given that all cases in the sample (168) were Aboriginal persons. In 30 percent of cases, defence counsel sought a term of incarceration for their client that was lower than that prescribed by the Crown prosecutor; and in 35 percent of cases, defence counsel sought a conditional sentence. By contrast, in 62 percent of cases, the Crown requested a carceral sentence and agreed with a conditional sentence in only 5 percent of cases. Community submissions made by Aboriginal organizations with regards to treatment programs, education, housing, or employment were not mentioned in 80 percent of cases. Overall, we see relative disregard for the requirements of the Gladue methodology set out by the Supreme Court in *R. v. Gladue*, which leads us to ask what factors sentencing judges took into account when constructing their decision.

Sentencing Factors

This study demonstrates that the courts highly rely on incarceration and the privileging of sentencing aims, such as denunciation, deterrence, and public safety; however, we should consider the various elements that comprise a sentencing decision, including mitigating and aggravating factors, as well as the Gladue factors identified by the court under section 718.2(e).

One of the most striking and concerning findings of this study was that only 54 percent (91 of 168) of the reported decisions analyzed included consideration of the Gladue factors expressly outlined by the Supreme Court. In those cases where Gladue factors were considered, 35 percent of judges (n=50) cited the offender's personal history of victimization. As noted earlier, victimization of Aboriginal people on reserve is 8 times higher than the national average; Aboriginal women in particular are more likely to experience physical or sexual violence (3.5 times higher than for non-Aboriginal women)

Table 5.4: Gladue Factors, 1997–2004

Dichotomy Label	Name	Count	Percentage of Responses	Percentage of Cases
Offender native background	NATIVE	40	28.0	44.0
Res school survivor	RESSCHOOL	8	5.6	8.8
Fetal alcohol syndrome	FAS	10	7.0	11.0
Offender employment	OFFEMP	24	16.8	26.4
Low level of education	LOWEDU	3	2.1	3.3
Drug/alcohol use at time of offense	DRUGUSE	8	5.6	8.8
Offender victim of abuse	ABUSEHIS	50	35.0	54.9
Total responses		**143**	**100.0**	**157.1**

Note: 77 missing cases, 91 valid cases.

Source: Balfour, G. (2013a). "Do law reforms matter? Exploring the victimization-criminalization continuum in the sentencing of Aboriginal women in Canada." *International Review of Victimology*, 19(1): 85–102.

(Brzozowski et al., 2006). Thus, we could expect sentencing judges to give special consideration to victimization histories of offenders as a Gladue factor. However, this study indicates personal victimization of the offender is a mitigating factor in only 30 percent of sentencing decisions (51 of 168). Of these 51 cases, 29 percent were male offenders and 41 percent were female offenders. Thus, it would seem that violence against women is receiving judicial notice, but not in such a way that it reduces the use of imprisonment in favour of community-based alternatives. Toni Williams (2009: 87) asserts that the sentencing methodology prescribed under section 718.2(e) "requires specific evidence of ... the defendant's experiences of abuse and victimization" although this logic erases "crucial knowledge about the structures and social relationships that shape the context of Aboriginal women's lives." Violence against women is rooted in substantive gender inequalities produced by historical and contemporary colonial practices. Yet, as Williams (2009: 87) reported in her study of sentencing decisions, the courts preferred to "scrutinize the defendant's experience of disadvantage and trauma in the home, in the family and the community to explain her offences.... This move ... revives and reinforces stereotypes about Aboriginal criminality." Thus, Aboriginal women who have personal histories of abuse and have been convicted of violent offences are viewed as in need of control and confinement.

In *R. v. Gladue* (1999), the Supreme Court recognized that low levels of education—an outcome of colonialism whereby numerous Aboriginal communities do not have adequate educational resources—force many young people to migrate to large urban centres to attend high school. This results in chronic poverty and poor economic development in those communities. In this study, limited education was rarely mentioned (only 7 percent of cases), yet other studies consistently report a strong association between lack of education, unemployment, and incarceration (Brzozowski et al., 2006; LaPrairie, 2002). Census data shows that 38 percent of Aboriginal people had not completed high school (compared to 19 percent of non-Aboriginals), and unemployment for Aboriginal people is 14 percent as compared to only 6 percent for non-Aboriginal people (averaged across all regions) (Perreault, 2009). However, sentencing judges did note if the offender was unemployed at the time of the offence (26 percent).

Another surprising finding was the lack of judicial notice paid to the impact of residential schools upon the personal lives of Aboriginal offenders. The traumatic intergenerational effect of residential schools is well documented (see Milloy, 1999; Royal Commission on Aboriginal Peoples, 1996). However, the complicated pathway of residential school survival to federal prison is less empirically understood (Corrado, Cohen, & Cale, 2004). Various studies of federally sentenced prisoners indicate a high proportion of Aboriginal offenders were apprehended and placed under child protection services as a result of poor parenting and community dysfunction produced by residential school trauma. In addition to the breakdown of family life, substance abuse is well documented as a serious social problem in Aboriginal communities, stemming from the impacts of sexual and physical abuse. In this study, substance abuse was recognized in only 9 percent of cases, but fetal alcohol syndrome was documented in 11 percent of cases.

Substance abuse has long been recognized as a key factor in the criminalization and incarceration of Aboriginal peoples. For example, in the Prairie region, 82 percent of Aboriginal offenders were found to have profound substance abuse problems, compared to 62 percent of non-Aboriginal offenders (Perreault, 2009). In *R. v. Gladue*, the Supreme Court of Canada recognized substance abuse as a serious social problem in most Aboriginal communities that requires culturally appropriate treatment. However, in this study we see substance abuse as the context for the violent offence considered by sentencing judges as an aggravating factor used to justify the use incarceration in over a third of cases.

Murdocca (2009) writes in her critical study of section 718.2(e) that restorative sentencing objectives were imagined to be reparative or compensatory for the historical mistreatment of Aboriginal peoples. Yet, these reforms operate ideologically as a practice of containment and control through a cultural difference paradigm; colonialism is never recognized as the cause of multi-dimensional social problems. Instead, substance abuse is an ahistorical fact of Aboriginal culture that operates to "obscure the ongoing material violence of colonization and exploitation faced by Aboriginal communities" (25). Instead, substance abuse is constituted as a predictor of future violence, justifying

Table 5.5: Aggravating Factors, 1997–2004

Dichotomy Label	Name	Count	Percentage of Responses	Percentage of Cases
Vulnerability of victim	VULNVIC	35	6.1	22.0
Weapon used	WEAPONUS	26	4.6	16.4
Seriousness of the offence	SERIOUSN	104	18.2	65.4
Domestic relation	DOMESTIC	19	3.3	11.9
Breach of trust (dependency)	BREACHTR	28	4.9	17.6
Violence and harm	VIOLENCE	69	12.1	43.4
Held in pretrial custody	REMAND	111	19.5	69.8
On statutory release	BREACHRE	40	7.0	25.2
Risk of reoffending	RISKREOF	52	9.1	32.7
Criminal record for violence	RECORDVI	86	15.1	54.1
Total responses		**570**	**100**	**358.5**

Note: 9 missing cases, 159 valid cases.

Source: Balfour, G. (2013a). "Do law reforms matter? Exploring the victimization-criminalization continuum in the sentencing of Aboriginal women in Canada." *International Review of Victimology*, 19(1): 85–102.

retributive sentencing for the "colonial management of degenerate populations" (26).

As these data suggest, sentencing judges refer more directly to conventional mitigating and aggravating factors. Overall, the strongest mitigating effect for both men and women was expressions of remorse and entering a guilty plea; in over half of the cases, sentencing judges noted the offenders' expressions of remorse or if a guilty plea was entered. Women's rehabilitative efforts (program participation while in pretrial custody) had a more mitigating effect (58 percent) on sentencing than men's participation in programming (35 percent). Across all sentencing decisions examined in this study, the most commonly mentioned aggravating factors justifying the term of incarceration for both Aboriginal men and women was if the offender was held in pretrial custody (69 percent), the seriousness of the offence (65 percent), if the offender had a criminal record for violence (54 percent), and the use of violence and harm (43 percent).

When we consider other aggravating factors mentioned by the sentencing judges, a gendered effect is noticeable with regard to the context of the relationship between the victim and the offender: an Aboriginal woman was more likely to be incarcerated when violence took place in the context of a familial or domestic relationship (27 percent of cases versus 12 percent for Aboriginal men). Deep poverty and overcrowding in

Aboriginal communities operate as conditions of endangerment as women are often socially isolated and responsible for caregiving. Another concern raised by this data, however, is the unintended consequence of feminist-inspired law reforms in the areas of domestic violence. Mandatory charging protocols for police as well as retributive and denunciatory sentencing of domestic violence offenders was envisioned as a means for achieving women's safety. However, we should consider the implications of compulsory criminalization of domestic violence for Aboriginal women whose own victimization within families and communities is the context in which their own violence occurs.

The characteristics of the offender noted by the sentencing judge as aggravating factors were consistent with previous sentencing studies with the exception of pretrial custody: for both men and women, being held in remand was the most common aggravating factor noted by the sentencing judge (approximately 85 percent of cases). This was followed by an accused's criminal record for violence (60 percent of cases), as well as whether the accused was on statutory release when the offence was committed (29 percent of cases). Thus, the increasing use of pretrial custody is influencing the likelihood of Aboriginal men and women being incarcerated. Finally, data indicates that sentencing judges often determine Aboriginal offenders to be at risk to reoffend but the basis for this assessment is not identified. It would seem that such a decision is based on a composite of indices such as unemployment, history of personal victimization, and substance abuse problems. However, we could ask why such measures of risk are not considered measures of need, and thus deserving of unique and culturally appropriate resources.

Conclusion

The removal of Aboriginal women from their families and communities through the criminal justice system is a re-colonizing process that severs women's roles as mothers and leaders in their communities. Once incarcerated, Aboriginal women continue to experience discriminatory and re-colonizing treatment; oftentimes women are confined at higher levels of security, denied access to culturally appropriate healing lodges, and are deemed to be too high risk for release back into the community as correctional plans are incomplete or inadequate. The sentencing data presented here suggest that over the past decade sentencing practices have moved away from the principles prescribed under section 718 that call for the least restrictive measures and special consideration of Aboriginal offenders. Moreover, Aboriginal women are more likely to be imprisoned than Aboriginal men. In this way, these data are striking in that they appear to contradict the intention of sentencing law reforms enacted over 16 years ago, aimed at reducing the rate of incarceration for Aboriginal people. Data presented here also suggest, however, that in addition to sentencing courts not consistently implementing the Gladue methodology set out by the Supreme Court, Aboriginal communities are ill-equipped to respond to the needs of offenders and cannot fully participate in developing alternative sentencing plans. It is difficult to discern if the relative silence of Aboriginal community leaders and Elders in these sentencing decisions is a measure of their lack of consultation.

Finally, while the limits of law as a means of social transformation and decolonization are evident, there are reasons for optimism. Recent provincial court decisions have upheld that section 718.2(e) must be applied in bail and parole hearings (see *R. v. Sim*, 2005; *R. v. Jensen*, 2005; and *R. v. Bain*, 2004). Also, the Aboriginal Legal Services of Toronto have expanded their services throughout Southwestern Ontario to provide court support to Aboriginal offenders convicted of non-violent crimes, and to ensure that Gladue Reports are written and presented to the courts. Since the completion of this study, 19 cases have been heard before the Ontario Superior Court with regard to Aboriginal offenders convicted of serious personal injury offences seeking application of section 718.2(e). However, of these cases, only 4 are Aboriginal women.

Aboriginal women are being increasingly criminalized and imprisoned regardless of the conditions of endangerment that tragically define their lives. There is a complicated relationship between the prevalence of gendered violence in Aboriginal communities and violence committed by Aboriginal women. In this way, a victimization-criminalization continuum appears, but one that is situated in historical, cultural, economic, and political practices that deny Aboriginal women their dignity and respect, autonomy, and self-determination, thereby contributing to their endangerment (Balfour, 2008: 3).

Notes

1 In *R. v. Gladue*, the Supreme Court noted that Reuben Beaver had been arrested and convicted of domestic assault against Jamie Gladue, and forensic evidence of bruising was noted at Ms. Gladue's original trial.

2 In the United States, Aboriginal scholar Luana Ross (2004) documents the deep connection between violence, addiction, and incarceration in the lives of American Indian women. Ross (2004: 56) argues that Aboriginal women's addictions are tied to both historical and personal traumas, such as the "elevated rates of violence perpetrated against Native women, as well as residential schools, coercive migration, and non-Native custodial care."

3 The LSI—Revised (LSI-R) consists of eight risk/need factors: (1) criminal history (measured in terms of number of offences rather than type of offence); (2) education/employment; (3) family circumstances; (4) leisure/recreation; (5) pro-criminal attitude; (6) substance abuse; (7) antisocial patterns; and (8) acquaintances. "A series of questions is typically used to determine the relevance and strength of each factor. A numerical evaluation of these variables produces a total risk score that is used to classify an offender as

having a low, medium or high risk of recidivism. Currently, the LSI is used in jurisdictions throughout Canada, the United States, the United Kingdom, Australia and Europe" (see Bonta, Bourgon, Jesseman, & Yessine, 2005; Hannah-Moffat & Maurutto, 2010: 269).

References

Adelburg, E., & Currie, C. (1987). *Too Few to Count: Canadian Women in Conflict with the Law.* Vancouver: Press Gang Publishers.

Balfour, G. (2008). "Falling between the cracks of retributive and restorative justice: The victimization, criminalization, and incarceration of Aboriginal women in Canada." *Feminist Criminology*, 3(2): 101–120.

Balfour, G. (2013a). "Do law reforms matter? Exploring the victimization-criminalization continuum in the sentencing of Aboriginal women in Canada." *International Review of Victimology*, 19(1): 85–102.

Balfour, G. (2013b). "Women in custody." In J. Winterdyk & M. Weinrath, eds., *Adult Corrections in Canada: A Comprehensive Overview* (pp. 240–260). Whitby, ON: de Sitter Publications.

Balfour, G., & Du Mont, J. (2012). "Confronting restorative justice: Legal and rape narratives in conditional sentencing." In E. Sheehy, ed., *Sexual Assault, Practice, Activism in a Post Jane Doe Era* (pp. 164–168). Ottawa: University of Ottawa Press.

Bonta, J., Bourgon, G., Jesseman, R., & Yessine, A.K. (2005). "Presentence reports in Canada." Ottawa: Public Safety and Emergency Preparedness Canada.

Brotherton, D.C. (2008). "Beyond social reproduction: Bringing resistance back in gang theory." *Theoretical Criminology*, 12(1): 55–77.

Brzozowski, J., Taylor-Butts, T., & Johnson, S. (2006). "Victimization and offending among the Aboriginal population in Canada." *Juristat*, 26(3). Ottawa: Statistics Canada. Retrieved from www5.statcan.gc.ca/bsolc/olc-cel/olc-cel?lang=eng&catno=85-002-X20060039199

Cameron, A. (2006). "Stopping the violence: Canadian feminist debates on restorative justice and intimate violence." *Theoretical Criminology*, 10(1): 49–66.

Comack, E., & Balfour, G. (2004). *The Power to Criminalize: Violence, Inequality and the Law.* Halifax: Fernwood Publishing.

Corrado, R., Cohen, I., & Cale, J. (2004). "Aboriginal resource access in response to criminal victimization in an urban context." *Aboriginal Policy Research: Setting the Agenda for Change. Volume II.* Toronto: Thompson Educational Publishing, Inc.

Correctional Services Canada (CSC). (2009–2010). "Women offenders programs and issues 2009–2010." *Women Offender Statistical Overview*. Ottawa. Retrieved from www.csc-scc.gc.ca/text/prgrm/fsw/wos_Stat_09_10/wos_stat_09_10-eng.shtml#_Toc280867078

Criminal Code of Canada. Purpose and Principles of Sentencing. (R.S.C., 1985, c. C-46, s. 718; R.S., 1985, c. 27 (1st Supp.), s. 155; 1995, c. 22, s. 6.

Crnkovich, M. (1995). "The role of the victim in the criminal justice system—Circle sentencing in Inuit communities." Paper presented at the Canadian Institute for the Administration of Justice Conference, Banff, Alberta, October 11–14.

Du Mont, J., Forte, T., & Badgley, R. (2008). "Does the punishment fit the crime? Judicial sentencing in adolescent and adult sexual assault cases." *Medicine and Law*, 27(2): 477–498.

Evans-Campbell, J. (2008). "Historical trauma in American Indian/Native Alaska communities: A multi-level framework for exploring impacts on individuals, families, and communities." *Journal of Interpersonal Violence*, 23(3): 316–338.

Frost, N. (2006). *The Punitiveness Report: Hard Hit, The Growth in the Imprisonment of Women, 1977–2004.* Retrieved from www.wpaonline.org/institute/hardhit/part2.htm

Hannah-Moffat, K., & Maurutto, P. (2010). "Recontextualizing pre-sentence reports: Risk and race." *Punishment and Society*, 12(3): 262–286.

Hayman, S. (2006). *Imprisoning Our Sisters: The New Federal Women's Prisons in Canada.* Montreal: McGill-Queen's University Press.

Kong, R., & AuCoin, K. (2008). "Female offenders in Canada." *Juristat*, 28. Ottawa: Statistics Canada.

La Prairie, C. (2002). "Aboriginal over-representation in the criminal justice system." *Canadian Journal of Criminology*, 44(2): 181–208.

Milloy, J. (1999). *A National Crime: Canadian Government and Residential Schools 1878–1996.* Winnipeg: University of Manitoba Press.

Monture, P. (2000). "Aboriginal women and correctional practice: Reflections on the Task Force on Federally Sentenced Women." In K. Hannah-Moffat & M. Shaw, eds., *An Ideal Prison? Critical Essays on Women's Imprisonment in Canada* (pp. 52–60). Halifax: Fernwood Publishing.

Murdocca, C. (2009). "From incarceration to restoration: National responsibility, gender, and the production of cultural difference." *Social & Legal Studies*, 18(1): 23–45.

Murdocca, C. (2013). *To Right Historical Wrongs: Race, Gender, and Sentencing in Canada.* Vancouver: UBC Press.

McGillivray, A., & Comaskey, B. (1999). *Black Eyes All the Time: Intimate Violence, Aboriginal Women and the Justice System*. Toronto: University of Toronto Press.

O'Donnell, V., & Tait, H. (2003). "Aboriginal peoples survey 2001—Initial findings: Well-being of the non-reserve Aboriginal population." Ottawa: Statistics Canada, Housing, Family and Social Statistics Division.

Perreault, S. (2009). "The incarceration of Aboriginal people in adult correctional services." *Juristat*, 29(3). Ottawa: Statistics Canada.

Porter, L., & Calverley, D. (2010). "Trends in the use of remand in Canada 1999–2009." *Juristat*, 85-002-X. Ottawa: Statistics Canada. Retrieved from www5.statcan.gc.ca/bsolc/olc-cel/olc-cel?catno=85-002-X&lang=eng

Roberts, J., & Melchers, R. (2003). "The incarceration of Aboriginal offenders: Trends from 1978 to 2001." *Canadian Journal of Criminology and Criminal Justice*, 45(2): 211–242.

Ross, L. (2004). "Native women, mean-spirited drugs, and punishing policies." *Social Justice*, 31(4): 54–62.

Royal Commission on Aboriginal Peoples. (1996). *Bridging the Cultural Divide: A Report on Aboriginal People and Criminal Justice in Canada*. Ottawa: Minister of Supply and Services Canada.

Sabol, C., Couture, H., & Harrison, P. (2007, December). "Prisoners in 2006." *Bureau of Justice Statistics Bulletin*. Washington, DC: Office of Justice Programs, US Department of Justice.

Smith, A. (2005). *Conquest: Sexual Violence and American Indian Genocide*. Cambridge, MA: South End Press.

Sudbury, J. (2005). *Global Lockdown: Race, Gender, and the Prison Industrial Context*. New York: Routledge.

Turpel-LaFond, M.E. (1999). "Sentencing within a restorative justice paradigm: Procedural implications of *R. v. Gladue*." *Criminal Law Quarterly*, 43: 34–50.

Wacquant, L. (2001). "The penalism of poverty and rise of neo-liberalism." *European Journal on Criminal Policy and Research*, 9: 401–412.

Walmsley, R. (2006). *World Female Imprisonment List*. London: Kings College, International Centre for Prison Studies.

Williams, T. (2009). "Intersectionality analysis in the sentencing of Aboriginal women in Canada: What difference does it make?" In E. Grabham, D. Cooper, J. Krishnadas, & D. Herman, eds., *Intersectionality and Beyond: Law, Power, and the Politics of Location* (pp. 79–104). Abingdon: Routledge-Cavendish.

Legal Cases and Statutes

R. v. B.K., [2000] ON CJ No. 2708 (Q.L.).

R. v. Bain, [2004] ON SC.

R. v. Gladue, [1999] 1 S.C.C. 688 (Q.L.).

R. v. Jensen, [2005] ON CA No. 37975.

R. v. K.R.G., [1996] ON CJ No. 3867 (Q.L.).

R. v. Kakepetum, [2001] ON CJ No. 1511 (Q.L.).

R. v. Ridings, [1998] ON CJ No. 183 (Q.L.).

R. v. Sim, [2005] No. 43385.

R. v. Tulk, [2000] ON CJ No. 4315 (Q.L.).

Part 2

Facets of Families, Motherhood, and Violence

Chapter 6

Agency and Choice: Gendered Constructions of Victim Worthiness in Domestic Violence Court

Holly Johnson and Ashley McConnell

The success of feminist activists in de-privatizing and bringing to public attention the prevalence and severity of violence inflicted on women by intimate partners, and convincing governments to enact social policies in response to this crime, stands as one of the most important social changes in the last 40 years. Heightened public awareness helped build support for prevention initiatives, services and shelters for abused women, and sanctions for violent men. In Canada, aggressive application of the criminal law is a cornerstone of a strategy designed to condemn this violence, protect women, and punish offenders. All provinces and territories now have pro-charge and no-drop prosecution policies that direct police and Crown Attorneys to prosecute independent of victims' wishes, and in many jurisdictions, these procedures are formalized in specialized domestic violence courts (Ursel, Tutty, & Lemaistre, 2008).

The battered women's movement has long been divided on the wisdom of promoting expansion of legal institutions as a feminist strategy. Aggressive criminal justice policies are seen by some as a way to equalize power between women and their male abusers, provide a credible threat of prosecution, and empower abused women by "witnessing a place where the batterer's control does not extend" (Corsilles, 1994: 879). While there continues to be broad agreement that the criminal law cannot be permitted to take a non-interventionist stand toward violence in the domestic sphere, some are of the view that many legal interventions are repressive and controlling and that women's interests cannot be met with an approach that concentrates power within a patriarchal justice system (Currie, 1990; Dobash & Dobash, 1992). Critics argue that strict no-drop policies characterize women as incapable of making rational decisions about their safety and at least partly responsible for the violence continuing if they reject state protection (Dayton, 2002–2003; Hanna, 1996). It is argued that abused women have lost the ability to make choices that are at odds with choices the justice system has determined for them, and that when their actions run counter to criminal justice policy, women rather than abusers become the problem that needs to be managed. In large measure, aggressive no-drop policies fail to recognize that women "use the law, purposefully and actively, as a part of a strategic process of challenge and resistance" and that a call to police does not imply an intention or need to hand over autonomy and decision-making authority to the state (Lewis, Dobash, Dobash, & Cavanagh, 2000: 184).

Despite the good intentions of advocates and bureaucratic reformers, there is evidence that criminal justice reforms have harmed some women and compounded their powerlessness. This happens, for example, when strict arrest and prosecution policies lead to situations where women are charged and convicted alongside or instead of violent partners and are then denied access to victim services, subjected to increased violence by partners or ostracism by their communities, or have children removed by child welfare authorities or by court decisions that grant custody to violent partners (Dayton, 2002–2003; Durfee, 2012; Hirschel & Buzawa, 2002; Hoyle & Sanders, 2000; Minaker, 2001; Osthoff, 2002). Although it is not well documented, women are at risk of incarceration when they retract their complaint. Such was the case for pregnant 19-year-old Noellee Mowatt, who, in 2008, was ordered by a Toronto judge to be imprisoned to ensure she would testify against her boyfriend who was charged with assault and forcible confinement against her (Canadian Press, 2008). The reasons for not wanting to prosecute following a call to police are many and varied: violent partners are often able to pressure women to drop charges through the threat of retaliatory violence; many women report negative past experiences with police and courts or feel the cost of engaging with the justice system is not worth the potential benefits; and others cite practical reasons related to their inability to live independently, and concerns about their children and breaking up the family (Erez & Belknap, 1998; Hoyle, 1998). Rigid one-dimensional laws and policies devised to respond to a singular image of a helpless victim who is in need of guidance and direction from professionals ignore the great diversity in the lived realities of abused women—which are conditioned not only by gender but by race, ethnicity, religion, colonialism, level of ability, economic situation, and intersections among these—and the multiple ways in which choices and decisions are negotiated within these realities (Minaker, 2001).

Apart from practical concerns about inflexible policies, many feminist scholars have long urged caution in engaging with law as a solution to gendered violence because of its claims to truth, its power to disqualify alternative knowledge and experiences, especially those of women, and for the way in which language, procedures, statutes, and the administration of law are imbued with patriarchal beliefs and values (Smart,

1989; Snider, 1994). From this perspective, extending legal intervention succeeds only in strengthening the power of institutions whose primary role is to punish and extend social control (Snider, 1994). Law is an exercise in power, and while women themselves can and have used the power of law, their interests are subordinated to dominant masculine interests and ideals within law (Currie, 1990). Laureen Snider (1994, 1998) and others are adamant that a patriarchal justice system historically has offered neither empowerment nor real change for women but extends its reach over already-criminalized and vulnerable populations. They are convinced that no amount of revision to these policies and practices can rectify inherently patriarchal, racist, and class-biased legal institutions. Law reform receives widespread support because it appears from the outside to be progressive and fits nicely within a law-and-order political agenda, but it offers no real restructuring of social and gender hierarchies and, in fact, has helped portray feminist claims for more radical transformation as extreme and marginal to the views and interests of the majority of women (Brodie, 2008; Currie, 1990). According to Carol Smart (1989), as a feminist strategy, using law to promote women's interests is flawed, as it empowers law, not women, to define women's interests, and because those with feminist sympathies have control over neither the application of the law nor the outcomes. Rather than moving toward more law, Smart (1989) advocates a strategy to "decentre" law as the dominant means of social control by challenging the law's claims to truth and power to disqualify.

This chapter lays out the claims-making processes by which aggressive criminal justice responses came to dominate at the expense of broader, more meaningful social changes needed to transform the social relations at the root of male violence against women, and the consequences for abused women who use the law for redress. Analysts of claims-making processes do not take for granted that victims and victimization exist as an objective fact; their main concern is how we arrive at a social understanding of victims, how victims are "created" in public discourse, and the power struggles among advocates, therapists, criminal justice professionals, and those affected by violence that go on behind this naming (Lamb, 1999). From a constructionist perspective, Sharon Lamb (1999: 3) defines a victim as "someone not only made a victim by her victimization but also made a 'victim' by our culture's understanding of what that word means, of social practices ... and of gender relations." A victim therefore is "a product of social relations, culture, and language," a label that is infused with power.

The typification of the helpless battered woman was considered strategic during second wave feminism to persuade a broad audience that the problem exists, that it is harmful and widespread, and that certain responses are needed to eradicate it (Loseke, 2003). However, the subjective experience of abused women fails to conform precisely to this image. Partner violence is not unambiguously experienced as severe and frequent with serious and ongoing consequences, and some women attribute positive feelings toward the abusive "brutes" and resist the label of "victim" (Loseke, 1987). Further, a central tension in the public framing of abused women by claims-makers is a falsely constructed dichotomy between victimhood and agency. In their efforts to have violence against women recognized as a serious social issue worthy of policy change and public resources, advocates have struggled to present these women as sympathetic victims needing protection while recognizing and celebrating their strength and agency. By contrast, aggressive pro-charging and pro-prosecution policies operate under images of undifferentiated victims whose needs and interests are subordinated to criminal justice ideals and normative expectations, even though justice system policies are incapable of guaranteeing long-term protection (Babcock & Steiner, 1999; Babcock, Green, & Robie, 2004; Klein, 1996; Maxwell, Garner, & Fagan, 2001).

Despite all the efforts to improve police and prosecutor training, fast-track cases, and provide court-based support to victims, substantial numbers of women attempt to withdraw from or halt the prosecution using the only lever available to them: recanting their testimony in court. In a study of five specialist domestic violence courts in England and Wales, one-half of women retracted or withdrew their testimony (Robinson & Cook, 2006). Although firm figures are not available in Canada, Crown Attorneys in Ontario estimate that between 40 percent and 65 percent of victims recant or otherwise do not participate in the prosecution (PRA Inc., 2006). For this study, a content analysis was undertaken of a sample of Ontario judicial decisions between 1995 and 2009 to explore judicial constructions of intimate partner violence victims. By comparing women who recant their testimony to those who co-operate with the prosecution, we assess how women's agency challenges dominant typifications of victims in need and worthy of state protection, and how judges construct these women in response.

Constructing Victims

Social policies are the result of a lengthy process of claims-making, where a social problem is constructed and contested and a solution found in the form of a response about what to do about it. Powerful images of victims are essential to any claims-making process, but because it is not possible to know, represent, or describe the unique experiences of every woman harmed by an intimate partner, an image of a "typical" abused woman is presented to characterize all abused women (Loseke, 2003). These "typifications" serve the added purpose of constructing collective identities among victims and their advocates that are central to the ongoing task of framing social problems (Dunn, 2005).

Donileen Loseke (2003) charts a claims-making process in which the grounds of a social problem must be constructed through the presentation of facts about how the problem is defined, the size and parameters of the problem, and the nature and degree of the harm to victims. In their efforts to draw public attention to the victims of a social problem, claims-makers often ignore the complexity of the social world and human experience by constructing simple and unambiguous frames that evoke emotion and sympathy and inspire action (Loseke, 1987). A common strategy is to cite statistics that portray the problem as widespread, then to use one or two typifying examples of extreme harm through compelling personal stories or dramatizations that lead the audience to conclude that these are average cases. Casting the net too widely can result in a loss of credibility, and so the problem of wife battering is portrayed as purposeful, extreme, and repetitive physical violence that results in serious physical and psychological injuries (Loseke, 1987). It is more convincing and palatable for the general public to say, for example, that one-quarter of women have been assaulted by a partner or that a small percentage are assaulted in a given year than to say all women have been victims of some form of male violence, despite scientific evidence that 80 percent of young women in Canada experience sexual harassment in a single year and 40 percent of women have been sexually assaulted in their adult lifetimes (Johnson, 1996).[1]

Encouraging audience members to evaluate a social condition as intolerable and requiring urgent action is accomplished by presenting the grounds that form the basis of this claim, but intricately related to how we think about problems is how we feel about them (Loseke, 2003). According to Loseke (2003), claims-makers tap into "cultural feeling rules," which are general conventions about how we think we should respond emotionally to a particular issue and are used by claims-makers to encourage audience members to feel sympathy for victims and loathing for the villains. However, cultural feeling rules entail biases in terms of who merits sympathy; to be sure, many people who experience real harm are effectively denied sympathy and support. For example, stigmatized and "degenerate" people, such as sex trade workers and street-involved drug users are not likely to elicit the same sympathy or acquire legitimate victim status when they are assaulted in the same way as a middle-class employed family man. Nor will an Aboriginal mother living in a common law relationship be able to acquire victim status in the same way as a married mother of European descent. Widespread racist stereotypes of "drunken Indians" and "squaws" evoke images of Aboriginal communities as spaces of degeneracy and create massive obstacles to Aboriginal peoples' claims for sympathy or support to the point where they are considered to deserve what they get (Comack & Balfour, 2004; Razak, 2000).

According to Nils Christie (1984), "ideal victims" possess certain attributes: they are weak (e.g., sick, young, or old); engaged in a respectable project (e.g., caring for a relative); found in a situation no one could possibly be blamed for (e.g., on the street during the day); and victimized by an offender who is big and bad and in no way known to them. Victims in possession of these characteristics warrant support and sympathy; others do not. This construction of the ideal victim plays out regularly in the media. A recent example is the media portrayal of the 1997 murder of Reena Virk, a South Asian teenager who was murdered by a group of other young people in Victoria, British Columbia. Kilty and Fabian (2010) argue that media portrayals of Reena Virk did not meet the prescribed criteria of what an "ideal victim" should embody: she was not seen as weak, but as a healthy and able-bodied teenage girl; she was not carrying out a respectable project, as she was meeting a group of teenagers to smoke and drink under a bridge during the night; and she was not in a blameless space, since she was away from parental supervision and authority figures. By centring her "otherness," media constructions reduced her victim status and our ability to feel sympathy for her. For example, while Virk was presented as "different," "a runaway," "a foster kid," "heavy," "unattractive," and "masculine," one of her attackers, Kelly Ellard, who was convicted of second-degree murder for her role in the killing, was presented as "pretty," "pale," "thin," and "beautiful," characteristics in keeping with hegemonic femininity. Even though the offenders were not big and bad or unknown, ethnocentric notions of normalcy that dictate what it means to be a worthy victim deserving of support and sympathy dominated the media portrayal of both the victim and offender.

Victims are not always constructed as deserving sympathy; in fact, it is often only those we perceive as morally "good" or "pure" that we see as innocent in terms of the harm they suffer (Loseke, 2003). Any hint of responsibility for their plight casts grave doubt on the worthiness of their claims to victimhood. To establish and reinforce the claim of innocence, activists in the battered women's movement worked hard to position victims as helpless against the attacker and against social and psychological constraints holding her captive in a violent relationship (Dunn, 2010; Dunn & Powell-Williams, 2007).

The plot of these "formula stories" is narrow and transforms women into one-dimensional victims and men into irredeemable and evil villains (Loseke, 2003). Throughout the 1970s and 1980s, a key feminist claims-making strategy was to construct grounds that portray extreme consequences, which required claims-makers to leave out ways in which victims of violence fight back, manage to live with the abuse, come out relatively unscathed, or find strength in the experience. As Loseke (2003) points out, the victim identity can be attractive, since cultural feeling rules judge a victim as a moral and pure person deserving of sympathy and assistance and as absolved from responsibility. But there are costs to assuming this identity: victims are object, not subject; they are weak, not in control; and they are objects of sympathy, which is easily transformed to pity, itself a stigmatized status (Lamb, 1999). The victim identity is readily discredited in individualistic cultures where responsibility and self-sufficiency are highly valued. Given that the "cultural code of agency"—the deeply held belief that we all have free and unconstrained choice—so resonates in North American society, it can trump cultural feeling rules governing sympathy for victims (Dunn, 2010: 7). The result is that victims are harshly and morally judged for not taking action, and when we deny them victim status, we instead pity and stigmatize them.

Critics of this portrayal of abused women as passive victims can be found both within and outside the women's movement. The cultural image of the passive victim has been the target of very public attacks by those who situate their arguments in the cultural code of agency and assert that victims are expected to exercise their autonomy and take responsibility for their actions. The "vocabularies of victimism" employed by so-called victim feminists are seen to be responsible for creating a victim culture where women are duped into conflating minor and more egregious offences (Dunn, 2010: 27). Victims, like everyone else, after all, have free choice; this position resulted in strong negative reactions to the battered woman syndrome (BWS) when it was established as a legal defence for women charged with killing abusive partners following the Supreme Court of Canada decision in the case of *R. v. Lavallee* in 1993 (Comack, 1993). The basis of these concerns, fuelled by the media, was that BWS provides an excuse for women's passivity and inaction in the face of domestic violence and gives them an unbridled "licence to kill," thus opening the door to vigilante justice (Downs, 1996; Loseke, Gelles, & Cavanaugh, 2005). From a feminist standpoint, problems with the BWS lie elsewhere: the defence highlights abused women's dysfunctional psychological state, lack of agency, and passive victimhood while simultaneously failing to examine the social, political, and economic conditions in which male violence in intimate relationships is permitted to occur and to escalate (Comack, 1993; Downs, 1996). The typification of abused women set out by the BWS is so narrow and so medicalized that those who fail to conform do not benefit. In fact, far from excusing women for vigilantism, women accused of killing violent partners often plead guilty to manslaughter to avoid the lengthy prison sentence mandated by a murder conviction that will result if the self-defence claim fails (Sheehy, 2001). As a result, very few women have been acquitted based on the battered woman defence.

The overemphasis on passivity in the usual typification of the battered woman has long been troublesome for many feminist advocates, as it leaves no room for acknowledging strength, agency, and choices made under extremely difficult circumstances. According to Jennifer Dunn (2010, p. 193):

> [V]ictimization presents an identity dilemma. This holds for people who must claim to be victims and for the social movements and individuals who advocate for them, because victims need compassion and the help that goes with it, but the identity of "victim" is not one we value very much. Moreover, we have a cultural predisposition toward blaming victims, effectively denying them this identity and our sympathy.

Many women reject the victim label, even when they suffer grievous injury, because it fails to encapsulate their personal experiences and because of the weakness and dysfunction it implies. As a result they counter formulaic stories of victimization with stories of strength that are culturally valued (Lamb, 1999). What is more, focusing on extreme or highly traumatic consequences of male violence makes it possible in public discourse and policy to deny the pervasiveness and diversity of ways in which women are subjected to violence in the public and private spheres, and the multiplicity of ways they resist and cope (Lamb, 1999). There is an additional and very real risk that victims who fail to meet normative expectations that result from the typification of the helpless victim will meet with blame and see support withdrawn, or will fail to recognize their own situation as worthy of assistance and state response (Dunn, 2005; Randall, 2004).

The alarm was raised early on by activists in the battered women and rape crisis movements about how the dominant typification of battered women pathologizes them, failing to recognize their agency when in fact they never cease to be active agents negotiating their survival (Barry, 1979: 38; see also Kelly, 1988, and Gondolf & Fisher, 1988). To counter the image of the "pathetic victim," to celebrate the great strength women have shown in surviving very severe conditions, and to explain women's apparent decisions to stay, leave, or return to a violent man, feminist advocates have worked to exchange the language of "victim" for the language of "survivor" (Dunn, 2005). The reasons offered for failing to leave in the face of terrible violence—concerns about children, gender socialization, lack of support, learned helplessness, guilt, or feelings of being trapped by poverty, religion, family tradition, or fear—that portray victims as moral but as lacking in options aid in countering victim blaming linked to the cultural code of agency. However, if staying, leaving, and returning to an abusive relationship are constructed or are implied to be choices, victims can lose our sympathy, so claims-makers framed this apparent deviance as a survival tactic and even as a virtue, a form of strength, a heroic measure designed to protect children and others (Dunn, 2005: 19; Dunn 2010: 196). If the deviant act of staying with or returning to a violent partner can be de-stigmatized, it "confers agency on battered women even as it excuses them from responsibility for their deviance" (Dunn, 2005: 18). Survivors can then be depicted as strong and heroic, as "admirable victims" (Dunn, 2010: 27). The vocabulary of surviving helps produce identities that simultaneously oppose and affirm the cultural code of agency and thus finds broad appeal to participants of the women's movement as well as the wider public (Dunn, 2010).

Constructing Solutions

Claims making around social problems produces collective identities of specific "types" of people who are offered specific "types" of services to respond to their situation according to how it was framed (Loseke, 2003). The typification of battered women suffering extreme and brutal consequences and as trapped with nowhere to go for assistance successfully led to public support for an expanded network of shelters. It was Lenore Walker's (1979) portrayal of battered women as suffering from "learned helplessness" and trapped in an escalating cycle of violence that culminated in the use of battered woman syndrome to challenge the legal definition of self-defence. These portrayals also produced support for pro-arrest and pro-prosecution policies that remove decision making from individual women and assign it to state actors who are seen as better positioned to know what is in a battered woman's best interests.

As Loseke (2003) points out, the construction of social problems and the policy responses to them are made within a political context where policy-makers and politicians are more or less sympathetic to the claims and draw on competing cultural codes to construct policies that are often the most politically feasible rather than the most logical, effective, or comprehensive. Early claims making around battered women was situated within a broader social movement advocating for women's rights within a culture that is individualistic, therapeutic, and gendered (Dunn, 2010: 53). Walker's (1979) portrayal of abused women as victims of a pathological learned helplessness, proposed to explain their passivity in the face of severe danger, fit easily with a prevailing culture already oriented toward individualized, therapeutic approaches to a wide range of problems, and with cultural images of women as weak, susceptible to mental health problems, and in need of treatment (Dobash & Dobash, 1992; Lamb, 1999). In law's disqualification of certain knowledges, experiences, and claims, it has granted legitimacy to and extended its power through the "psy" professions such as psychiatry and psychology, thus empowering mental health professionals to speak for and on behalf of women (Comack, 1993; Smart, 1989). Out of a construction of the pure and moral victim as suffering from symptoms caused by external forces outside her control arises the need for responses where professionals are required to rescue her; the counter and more culturally resonant expectation that victims are imbued with choice suggests a need for professionals who can enlighten and empower women as to their choices and assist them with safety planning and risk assessment (Dunn & Powell-Williams, 2007).

Access to victim assistance will depend on the extent to which abused women live up to narrow and simplistic typifications and cultural themes. Of course, the complexity and messiness of real life means they very often do not. Many abused women fail to live up to normative expectations when they actively fight back or fail to fight back, stay with or return to a violent partner, refuse police intervention or express a wish not to prosecute, all of which may be realistic and rational choices undertaken within the context and constraints of their lives. Minimizing the material and social realities of abused women overlooks the many ways they use agency and opportunity to assert some control, where striking back is a rational reaction to extreme frustration and anger, or staying with or returning to a violent man is a strategy for managing or avoiding the violence (Goodkind, Sullivan, & Bybee, 2004; Kelly & Johnson, 2008).

Here abused women are caught between victimhood and agency in what Loseke (1987) characterizes as "reality-definition contests." They are damned if they are not helpless enough or demonstrate too much agency, and damned if they are too passive or helpless (Dunn, 2010). In an analysis of the victim-agent dichotomy of domestic violence victims under the law, Melanie Randall (2004, p. 110) maintains that

> [t]he legal construction of both women who suffer from the "battered woman syndrome" and women who refuse to cooperate with the prosecution of their violent partners are built on stereotypical representations, one constructed as helpless and ineffective in her failure to act and one as demonstrating excessive agency in her refusal to live up to their obligations to the justice system once they engage the protection of the police.

As a result, the assertion of agency by non-compliant victims "in opposition to the needs of the criminal justice system undercuts their victim status" (Randall, 2004: 110).

The Cultural Code of the Masculinist Protector

In a society stratified by gender, in addition to cultural codes of agency and victimhood, women must navigate special rules related to what it means to be female. Iris Young's (2003: 3) conceptualization of the "logic of masculinist protection" that extends from the patriarchal head of household who is protector of the family to male leaders who are protectors of the population has relevance for our inquiry into the judicial construction of women in domestic violence court. In this conceptualization, there are "bad" men who aim to dominate women and "good" men who are courageous and responsible and who assume the role of chivalrous protector of subordinate members of the household. Protective masculinity is constituted in opposition to, and cannot exist without, dominative masculinity. But "central to the logic of masculinist protection is the subordinate relation of those in the protected position. In return for male protection, the woman concedes critical distance from decision-making autonomy" (Young, 2003: 4). Young develops this thesis in relation to state security, drawing analogies to the position of the masculinist protector toward his wife and other subordinates. We can also draw parallels with the experience of an abused woman and her relationship to her male abuser and the male-dominated state: in the household, the woman submits to a violent dominating bully, but in the courtroom, she submits with gratitude to the benevolent protection afforded by a protector in the form of an androcentric criminal justice system and its rules and practices. This chivalrous protection is expressed in terms of caring and concern for the abused woman, but in return for protection, the woman is expected to accept subordination and submit to the court's direction. The power exerted over the woman by the state is thus not in the form of overt, repressive power but in what Michel Foucault (1988, cited in Young, 2003: 6) refers to as "pastoral" power, which may appear benevolent to all concerned but is no less powerful. The subordinate woman in this scenario "neither resents nor resists the man's dominance, but rather she admires it and is grateful for its promise of protection" (Young, 2003: 9).

Of course, not all women are seen as equally deserving of masculinist protection. There are "good" women who submit to judgment about what is necessary for their protection and "bad" women who refuse protection and claim the right to make decisions about their own lives. The implicit bargain is that unless women submit to the governance of a masculine protector, they will be cast out to fend for themselves; part of the bargain is that they must trade some autonomy for this protection (Young 2003: 14). Women who refuse this protection and seek to be free of a position of subordination and dependence become suspect and constructed as threats to the agents assigned to protect them. The analogy in the courtroom is that the judge will have an expectation that, since the court knows what is best, the woman will be submissive and obey whatever action or decision is rendered on her behalf. The power of the victim or "client" is reduced when she comes before the law, the potential provider of sympathy: she "owes" the law something, at a minimum, gratitude and respect (Loseke, 2003: 145). The woman who defies the power of the state is labelled an undeserving victim whereas a co-operative woman who fulfills her role as the grateful, willing subordinate and who does not disrupt the administration of justice is labelled a deserving victim. The woman must entrust in the judge and the criminal justice system in order to demonstrate good citizenship and remain protected. She must concede decision-making distance and follow the will of the judge and prosecutor by dutifully testifying.

Method

This study employs the central concepts of Loseke (2003) and Young (2003) in an analysis of a sample of judicial decisions in Ontario courts. Analysis of judicial decisions provides a window into the extent to which case law and the decisions made by criminal justice actors are embedded in particular ideologies and discourses that dictate meanings and assumptions in the language used, and in the way the world and individuals are interpreted and made sense of (Comack & Balfour, 2004; Naffine, 1990). This study employs content analysis techniques that combine qualitative and quantitative methods to attempt "to make sense of, or interpret, phenomena in terms of the meanings people bring to them" (Denzin & Lincoln, 1994: 2) to examine how women who recant their testimony are constructed from the perspective of domestic violence court judges in Ontario and how this compares to the judicial construction of women who co-operate with the prosecution. Judicial decisions were drawn from Quicklaw, a publicly available database of full-text decisions from trial and appellate courts in all jurisdictions in Canada. It has coverage from January 1876 through to the present and is regularly updated. This study covers the 15-year time frame from January 1, 1995, to December 31, 2009. A starting point of 1995 was selected to allow sufficient time following the implementation of pro-prosecution policies in the early 1980s for courts and Crown Attorneys to become familiar with them and to have worked through challenges associated with the implementation of new policies and procedures. It is a limitation of this study that there is no comparison of cases to a time prior to pro-prosecution policies, due to the fact that police or prosecutors would have dropped the majority of cases with reluctant victims.

There are other limitations of Quicklaw as a source of empirical evidence of judicial discourse. In Canada, a comprehensive or exhaustive set of judicial decisions does not exist. Quicklaw publishes every written decision and, although not all decisions are written, it does include decisions judges consider to be precedent setting and of significant import to share with the legal community (Crocker, 2005). It is not known what proportion of domestic violence cases the database holds or how representative these cases are of the total. There is currently no data available from individual domestic violence courts or the Ontario Ministry of the Attorney General that would provide helpful contextual information, such as the number of intimate partner cases referred by police each year, the percentage that do not proceed to prosecution due to victim reluctance to testify, the percentage of victims who recant their statement in court as a form of resistance to no-drop policies or as a result of intimidation from violent partners, or the number of cases that proceed and are successful despite a recantation.

Analyzing judicial decisions offers a fruitful avenue for exploring some of the dilemmas women face when engaged with an inflexible criminal justice system that erects barriers to acting with individual agency. In an analysis of judicial decisions of intimate partner violence cases between 1970 and 2000 in the province of Ontario, Crocker (2005) found that, although many judges condemn intimate partner violence, issue harsh sentences, and consider the intimate nature of the relationship to be an aggravating factor, many rely on stereotypes and traditional notions of marriage, the family, and femininity. Harsh sentences were often given in the interests of deterring other violent men, but these tended to contain rationales that were simultaneously progressive and paternalistic. Very often, condemnations of violence were grounded in a discourse of vulnerability and protection instead of safety, and in stereotypes of feminine vulnerability and defencelessness that are based on the "disempowering notion that women are powerless" (Crocker, 2005: 219).

Specific search criteria applied to select recantation cases from the database were "domestic violence" OR "spousal abuse" AND "recant!" AND NOT "children's aid." Children's Aid cases were excluded because these cases centre on the best interests of the child and not the issue of victim recantation, and therefore did not fit with the objectives of this study. These criteria resulted in 16 cases in total. A control group of non-recantation cases was selected using the search terms ("domestic violence" OR "spousal abuse" AND "testimony" AND NOT "children's aid"); this yielded 249 cases. To reduce bias in the selection of non-recantation cases, a systematic random sampling method was used to select 16 comparison cases. The sampling interval of 249:16 determined that every fifteenth case would be selected, thus ensuring an evenly distributed sample. The study does not claim to have external validity, since only a small number of cases from one province were assessed; it is therefore inappropriate to make generalizations to other provinces or locations either within or outside Canada.

Table 6.1 outlines how each theme related to Loseke's (2003) "deserving" and "undeserving" victims, and Young's (2003) conceptualization of "masculinist protection" was conceptualized and operationalized. The categories of moral/pure and immoral/impure were treated as mutually exclusive categories because one, both, or neither could be included in a decision. Responsible and not responsible were also treated as separate categories since it was possible to have both or neither included in a decision. The overlapping categories of moral/pure were grouped, as were immoral/impure. When treated as separate categories, it was difficult to distinguish into which category the evidence should be coded, which would have resulted in reliability problems.

The internal validity of this study is strengthened by the use of both latent and manifest coding techniques. Manifest coding counts the frequency with which specific words or phrases appear in the text (Neuman, 2008). This is accomplished using a coding scheme in which the three central themes of "deserving victims," "undeserving victims," and "masculinist protector" and the corresponding indicators determined which words and phrases from the judicial decisions would be counted. In this study, the units of analysis are words and phrases, each of which are coded for existence rather than frequency. This results in single counting of each indicator (rather than multiple counting) in each judicial decision and counting of each case wherever an indicator appears at least once. This study also employs latent coding, which entails looking for underlying, implicit meaning of words and phrases within the specific content of the text (Neuman, 2008). This allows for the interpretation of statements made by judges

Table 6.1: Operationalization of Central Concepts

	Concept	Indicators
Deserving Victims	1 Not responsible for the violence	• Responsibility is placed on the actions and behaviours of the accused • The accused is acknowledged as the problem • Any delay of reporting, or blurred memory of the incident, is not problematized • The victim discontinued relationship with the accused
	2 Moral/pure	• Victim is constructed as a good mother or wife • The victim is seen as protecting her child(ren) from harm • The victim was not drinking or using drugs • The victim's occupation does not affect the judge's perception of her
Undeserving Victims	1 Responsible for the violence	• The responsibility is placed on the actions and behaviours of the victim • The victim is seen to have made poor choices (e.g., by staying with the accused, not calling the police) • Any delay in reporting, or blurred memory of the incident, is problematized • Continued relationship with the accused
	2 Immoral/impure	• Victim is constructed as a bad mother or wife • The victim is seen as not protecting her child(ren) from harm • The victim was drinking or using drugs and is seen as the aggressor • The victim's occupation affects the judge's perception of her
Masculinist Protector	1 Expresses chivalry	• Judge expresses concern about the victim being harmed • Judge expresses the need to protect other women from the defendant • Judge expresses concern about the dynamics of domestic violence • Judge expresses concern that the victim was not treated properly by the police
	2 Resists masculine protection	• The judge challenges the victim's recantation and conceptualizes it as preventing the administration of justice from doing its job

with respect to how they construct women who recant and those who co-operate with the prosecution. Together, manifest and latent coding capture the implicit and explicit meanings present in the text. Quotations were selected from the decisions to illustrate the central themes that emerged from this analysis.

Results

This study finds support for the hypothesis that judges construct recanting women as less deserving of state support when compared to women who co-operate with the prosecution. Of the 32 cases included in the analysis, defendants were convicted in 24 cases and not convicted in 8 cases. Seven of the 8 acquittals were recantation cases while 67 percent of convictions involved women who co-operated and testified. Women were constructed as not responsible in half of cases, and co-operative victims were more likely to be perceived as not responsible than women who recanted their testimony (75 percent compared to 25 percent). Contrastingly, holding victims responsible in some way for the violence more often involved recantation cases (77 percent) than women who testified (23 percent). In cases where judges constructed the women as moral/pure, the women were more often co-operative (67 percent) than recanting (33 percent). Conversely, women constructed as immoral/impure had recanted in 67 percent and testified in 33 percent. All of the women who were constructed by judges as resisting masculine protection recanted. Chivalry was expressed in a total of 12 cases, and 75 percent of these had co-operated with the prosecution.

Discussion

According to Loseke (2003), not all individuals who have experienced harm or violence are ascribed the status of victim due to "cultural feeling rules" that dictate general standards of how we should feel about certain individuals. The judicial decisions were examined for indicators of the three "cultural feeling rules" of responsibility, morality, and purity. Support was found for the argument that judges construct women who recant more negatively compared to women who co-operate and testify. Recanting victims were more likely to be constructed as responsible and immoral/impure than women who co-operated with the prosecution. Support for these "cultural feeling rules" leads to a determination of victims who recant as undeserving of state support.

Regarding to the "cultural feeling rule" of responsibility, Loseke (2003) argues that, for an individual to be ascribed victim status, that person must not be seen as in any way responsible for the harm they have suffered. Support for this argument was found

Table 6.2: Presence of Major Concepts

Major Concepts	No Recantation		Recantation		Total	
	(% row total)	No = 16	(% row total)	No = 16	(% column total)	No = 32
Conviction	67	16	33	8	75	24
No conviction	13	1	88	7	25	8
Not responsible	75	12	25	4	50	16
Responsible	23	3	77	10	41	13
Moral/pure	67	2	33	1	9	3
Immoral/impure	33	2	67	4	19	6
Resists masculine protection	0	0	100	4	13	4
Expresses chivalry	75	9	25	3	38	12

in this sample of judicial decisions, with judges constructing women who recanted as responsible far more often than women who co-operated with the prosecution. Even in cases where women were injured in the assault, and the injuries were visible and documented, judges proceeded to construct some of these women as responsible for the injuries and consequently as not deserving of victim status.

Women were constructed as responsible and undeserving when judges viewed them as failing to exercise the appropriate level of agency by staying with the violent partner, not staying in contact with the police, or delaying reporting the incident. In the recantation case of *R. v. Sanderson*, the judge shifted responsibility from the accused to the actions of the victim due to her decision to continue her relationship with the defendant. The judge stated that "it was pointed out the reconciliation was at the instigation of Ms. Phillips" (*R. v. Sanderson*, 2004: 2, lines 29–30). The word "instigation" reveals the woman's wrongdoing and the judge's disapproval of her actions. The judge constructs the woman as responsible and makes her undeserving behaviour known. This can also be seen in the case *R. v. Harbin*, where the judge declared that "the Crown has met its high onus of proof of these criminal offences beyond a reasonable doubt, resting its case as it must, on the words of a woman who has admittedly lied time and again" (*R. v. Harbin*, 2008: 4, lines 22–24). By constructing the woman as a liar and a manipulator of the justice system due to her decision to recant her testimony, which is conceptualized as an act of defiance rather than of an act of agency or a choice the woman has made in her own best interest, the judge also constructs her as an undeserving victim.

Lewis (2000: 184) argues that "women's agency or empowerment has generally equated to looking solely at enabling women to leave violent men." A woman who fails to concede decision making to the justice system and the officials who know what is best for her thus concedes victim status. Like in the case of *R. v. Harbin* (2008) cited above, a woman's recantation is reconstructed as lying to the court and not as a way to actively exercise agency in a situation where options are limited and choices constrained. In this sense, being an active agent is equated with being "undeserving," especially if her decision is not what criminal justice policy has determined is in her best interest.

The "cultural feeling rules" of morality and purity were combined in the analysis due to their common underlying meanings and concerns about the ability to reliably identify indicators of the two concepts separately. Loseke (2003) argues that "devalued groups" will not only be constructed as less moral and less pure but also as less deserving. Support for this argument was found: judges constructed women who recanted their testimony as immoral and impure 25 percent of the time compared to none of the women who co-operated and testified. This is exemplified in the recantation case of *R. v. W.C.D.*, where the judge categorized the woman as immoral/impure due to her perceived disregard for her children by staying with the accused. The judge explained in his judgment that "whether or not you feel the need to protect yourself, you must protect your children" (*R. v. W.C.D.*, 2002: 27, lines 30–31). The judge condemned the woman for not placing the needs of her children before her apparent (and deviant) need to continue her relationship with the defendant. Whether the woman cares about her health and safety, the judge makes it clear that she has a responsibility to act to ensure the protection of her children. The woman in this case is consequently relegated to the category of "bad mother" for failing to meet her responsibilities toward her children, and as a bad mother she is both immoral/impure and undeserving.

Motherhood is central to normative standards of femininity, and women are judged on the decisions they make to protect their children, judgments that are based on idealistic standards and on social constructions of "good" and "bad" mothers that often fail to consider the socio-economic and structural context in which these decisions are made (Greaves et al., 2004; Kilty & Dej, 2012). A good mother is selflessly devoted to and has an instinctive ability to care for and make sacrifices for their welfare (Douglas & Michaels, 2004). These normative expectations of motherhood are codified in "failure-to-protect" policies and practices in child protection systems across Canada, which hold mothers solely responsible for protecting children against violent men and imply that women are neglectful or abusive if they cannot protect them (Strega & Janzen, 2013). These expectations are based on false assumptions that support systems for abused mothers are effective at protecting women and their children, and that prosecuting violent men actually stops the violence (Strega & Janzen, 2013: 57). The judge in the case of *R. v. W.C.D.* further emphasizes the woman's need to leave her relationship with the defendant when he explains that "you must—you must—if you need to move, then you do that, you know" (*R. v. W.C.D.*, 2002: 27, lines 30–31). In the eyes of the court, a "good mother" is someone who leaves a violent relationship to shield her children from harm. The judge formally states his disapproval of her decision and proceeds to guide the woman to the proper standard of behaviour according to normative expectations of good motherhood.

Another case where the woman was constructed as immoral/impure is in the recantation case of *R. v. Handley*, where the woman was drinking on the night of the incident. The judge expresses disapproval of this behaviour and situates it as provocation for the abuse by stating how she "apparently is verbally abusive and aggressive when she drinks" (*R. v. Handley*, 2005: 7, line 20). The judge constructed the woman as the problem, with no disapproving remarks made toward the violent partner who was also drinking on the night of the incident. The judge categorizes the woman as immoral/impure for having been intoxicated and disregards the injuries she suffered. Instead, the woman's drinking is held as evidence of her immorality and impurity, which diminishes her victim status.

Support was also found for Young's (2003) logic of masculinist protection, which was operationalized as women accepting or resisting the masculine protection of the court and judges expressing or withdrawing chivalry. According to Young (2003: 2), in order to warrant masculine protection, women and children must be "in a subordinate position of dependence and obedience." A key requirement for benefiting from masculine protection is for the woman to "[concede] critical distance from decision-making autonomy" (4). In order for a good and deserving woman to receive male protection, there must be no "divided wills" (4) since the male protector knows what is best for her. The consequence of women exercising their own decision making and refusing male protection is that judges construct them as undeserving of state sympathy and support. Four cases showed judges expressing disapproval toward women for resisting masculine protection, all of which involved recantation.

One of the most blatant examples of a judge condemning the woman for her resistance to masculine protection is in the recantation case of *R. v. Harbin*. This case involved a pregnant 20-year-old woman who had recently moved with the defendant to Toronto at Christmastime. The woman accused the defendant of punching her to the point of blackouts, cutting her foot with a knife, and beating her over several days during the Christmas holidays. This was documented by photographs taken by the police showing considerable bruising to her face and body along with a sharp cut on her foot. During the trial, the woman was unwilling to testify in court, and when she was forced to do so by court order, she retracted all previous allegations. From this action, the judge explained in his judgment how "Ms. Mowatt did not present as a vulnerable complainant, but rather as an assertive and motivated woman intent on stopping the wheels of justice" (*R. v. Harbin*, 2008: 7, lines 49–50). The judge goes on to state that "in her various recantations and admitted deceit, she has thwarted the best attempts of the administration of justice to mete out justice" (*R. v. Harbin*, 2008: 7/8, line 52). The judge then places the blame on the woman by declaring "but for her testimony, the case of the Crown might have succeeded" (*R. v. Harbin*, 2008: 7, lines 24–25). The idea that one woman's expression of agency in a form that expressly runs counter to justice system goals could throw the justice system into disrepute demonstrates the strength of the good/bad victim divide. The judge's strong disapproval constructs the woman as a bad and undeserving victim, far from blameless, whose aim in exercising her autonomy by recanting her testimony is to obstruct justice rather than to pursue a course of action that is best for her. The woman is reduced to being a deceitful manipulator and someone who does not deserve the protection of the court.

This also emerged in the recantation case of *R. v. Bartlett*, where the judge made forthright statements about the problems that recanting victims create for the court in administrating justice. The trial judge "feels quite strongly that there are simply not enough convictions being recorded in cases of domestic violence. This is a problem because too many complainants recant at trial" (*R. v. Bartlett*, 1999: 2, lines 18–19). The judge is expressing his frustration with this particular woman as well as others who have recanted their testimony in court and have forced, in the judge's eyes, the court to fail in its responsibility to protect. This again constructs the victim as the source of the court's trouble. If the woman would only follow the standards of being a "good" victim by testifying and following the directions of the Crown, justice could be properly served.

The concept of expressing chivalry comes from the central tenet that "real men are neither selfish nor do they seek to enslave or overpower others for the sake of enhancing themselves" (Young, 2003: 4). What the chivalrous man does is "face the world's difficulties and dangers in order to shield women from harm" (4). Evidence of chivalry was found when judges expressed concern for the woman, her children, women in general, or the public being in need of protection. For the women who recanted their testimony, judges expressed chivalry in three of those cases as compared to nine cases where victims co-operated with the prosecution. Judges therefore construct recanting women less often as deserving of protection and chivalry of the court. According to Young (2003: 14), "[A] good woman stands under the male protection of a father or husband, submits to his judgment about what is necessary for her protection, and remains loyal to him." As a consequence, judges expressed minimal concern for victims who recanted their testimony and showed minimal regard for their safety.

This is exemplified in the non-recantation case of *R. v. Jabaerizad* where the woman testified against her husband who had assaulted her for most of their 20-year marriage. This couple had only been in Canada for four days when the defendant uttered death threats and assaulted his wife. Since the woman co-operated with the prosecution, the judge expressed concern for the woman by remarking "if his [the defendant's] behaviour is not curbed, he will kill the complainant or one of the children" (*R. v. Jabaerizad*, 2002: 14, lines 36–38). The judge took on the role of the chivalrous man who needs to protect subordinate and co-operative women from further danger. Since the victim did her duty as a good victim, immediately sought assistance from the justice system, and did not challenge the prosecution, the judge constructed the woman and her children as worthy of his protection.

This can also be seen in the non-recantation case of *R. v. W.C.D.* where the judge was chivalrous and expressed concern for the woman and others in the community. The judge stated that "the focus of this court today must be to protect the community, the women who have had the misfortune of being in relationships with him and his children from further abusive and violent behaviour" (*R. v. W.C.D.*, 2002: 23, lines 4–6). The judge again constructed the woman, her children, and the community as being in need of the court's protection. The judge ordered the defendant to serve a prison sentence of two years less a day, which allowed him to impose a probation order that, in his view, "will serve as further protection for Ms. C.C. and her children" (*R. v. W.C.D.*, 2002: 24, lines 5–6). The woman can be seen as gratefully conceding her decision-making power to the judge, who in return extended protection to her through a prison sentence and a subsequent probation order. The judge adopted the chivalrous role of the protector and tailored the defendant's sentence to provide long-term protection for the co-operative victim.

The findings from this research project lend credence to the two hypotheses: (1) women who recant are more likely to be constructed as undeserving victims compared to women who co-operate with the prosecution; and (2) judges are more likely to express chivalry toward women who co-operate and testify. These findings highlight a discourse on the part of domestic violence court judges that draws on certain cultural codes to construct abused women as deserving or not of the court's protection depending on their demeanour and their autonomous decision making. Research has shown that women's objectives in enlisting the help of police at the time of the assault may in fact be strategic, with the criminal justice system representing but one response among many that women use to manage or escape from violent partners (Lewis et al., 2000). Enlisting the help of police does not automatically signify support for prosecution, and many women actively resist the coercive policies of the state by the only avenue available to them under pro-prosecution policies—recanting their testimony in court. These research findings contribute to the growing chorus of concern that the objectives of pro-charge and pro-prosecution policies are at odds with the objectives of many women when they engage with the criminal justice system.

Conclusion

The relationship between the state and feminists working to end violence against women and provide support to abused women has always been conflicted. While at times this relationship has been collaborative and at other times in opposition, feminist activists have been strategic about accepting gains and compromises. A strong and consistent criminal justice response to intimate partner violence has been hailed as both a victory and as co-optation of feminist concerns by the state in a format that is partial and non-threatening to existing patriarchal structures and that offers little in the way of empowerment to women (Currie, 1990; Han, 2003; Lewis, 2004; Snider, 1994; Ursel et al., 2008). The unintended trade-off for the widespread enactment of aggressive prosecution policies has been to shift violence against women from a social and political movement that advocates for an overhaul of gender power relations to a problem that can be addressed through individualized responses, primarily through efforts that continue to strengthen the patriarchal and masculinist criminal justice system.

While pro-prosecution policies are no doubt beneficial to women with strong agency and community support who are committed to having their partners prosecuted, this study suggests that they can disempower and deny women agency when Crown prosecutors are compelled to press forward with prosecution in the face of resistance from the women involved. Expressions of agency in the form of recanting are often constructed as acts of defiance to the chivalrous and protective function of the court rather than an exercise in autonomous decision making, where recanting victims are interpreted as resisting the court's benevolence and actively obstructing the course of justice. As Randall (2004: 109; emphasis in original) states, "[D]ominant images and legal representations of women who are victims of violence typically fail to apprehend the *co-existence* of women's victimization with women's agency that is often expressed through the context-specific strategies of resistance which most women employ," and that "most mainstream social and legal responses to the problem of ... violence against women in intimate relationships, remain inextricably bound up with and shaped by incomplete and distorted representations of the nature, causes and effects of that violence" (107) that have evolved from drawing on cultural codes of passive victims or victims in possession of unconstrained agency. While the judicial attitudes exposed in this study may be beneficial to co-operative victims, women who recant their testimony in an attempt to halt prosecution are constructed as a problem that impedes the objectives and intent of a system set up to ensure their protection. The courts rarely consider the fact that their actions may be quite rational and reasonable given their particular social and financial circumstances.

An obvious problem that ensures these policies will continue to fail to meet women's diverse needs is the way much research fails to incorporate the views of those most deeply affected—women themselves. Women have yet to be invited to contribute in any systematic and meaningful way regarding how their needs for safety and autonomy can best be met within the wide range of informal and formal supports, including friends, relatives, neighbours, and the workplace, as well as social service, health, and justice agencies. Thus, knowledge about the effectiveness of justice system responses and the development of more nuanced approaches that take into account the particular socio-economic circumstances that shape women's lives continue to be underdeveloped. Thirty years after the implementation of pro-prosecution policies, it is time to revisit their objectives in concert with those of abused women to determine whether they in fact make women safer or if their coercive nature undermines and jeopardizes women's safety and right to personal autonomy. The results of this study suggest that a coercive domestic violence policy may deter women from seeking further help as a result of a negative first engagement with the justice system, or may deter many from engaging with the justice system in the first place, thereby putting their lives and safety at risk.

Notes

1 The feminist analysis of male violence against women is that it exists on a continuum from sexual harassment and threats to severe assaults, rape, and murder, and any of these threats or assaults can result in severe consequences (Brown & Walklate, 2011; Kelly, 1988). However, the claims-making process requires advocates to strategically identify specific types of violence as needing specific responses in order to avoid accusations of exaggerating the extent of the problem by casting all men as potentially violent and all women as victims.

References

Babcock, J., Green, C., & Robie, C. (2004). "Does batterers' treatment work? A meta-analytic review of domestic violence treatment." *Clinical Psychology Review*, 23: 1023–1053.

Babcock, J., & Steiner, R. (1999). "The relationship between treatment, incarceration, and recidivism of battering: A program evaluation of Seattle's coordinated community response to domestic violence." *Journal of Family Psychology*, 13(1): 46–59.

Barry, K. (1979). *Female Sexual Slavery*. New York: New York University Press.

Brodie, J. (2008). "We are all equal now: Contemporary gender politics in Canada." *Feminist Theory*, 9: 145–164.

Brown, J.M., & Walklate, S. (Eds.) (2011). *Handbook on Sexual Violence*. London, UK: Routledge.

Canadian Press. (2008, April 11). "Pregnant teen tells court she lied about abuse." *Toronto Star.* Retrieved from www.thestar.com/News/GTA/article/413645

Christie, N. (1986). "The ideal victim." In E. Fattah, ed., *From Crime Policy to Victim Policy: Reorienting the Justice System* (pp. 17–30). London, UK: MacMillan Press.

Comack, E. (1993). *Feminist Engagement with the Law: The Legal Recognition of the Battered Woman Syndrome.* Ottawa: Canadian Research Institute for the Advancement of Women.

Comack, E., & Balfour, G. (2004). *The Power to Criminalize: Violence, Inequality, and Law.* Halifax: Fernwood Publishing.

Corsilles, A. (1994). "No-drop policies in the prosecution of domestic violence cases: Guarantee to action or dangerous situation?" *Fordham Law Review*, 63(3): 853–881.

Crocker, D. (2005). "Regulating intimacy: Judicial discourse in cases of wife assault (1970 to 2000)." *Violence Against Women*, 11(2): 197–226.

Currie, D. (1990). "Battered women and the state: From the failure of theory to a theory of failure." *The Journal of Human Justice*, 1(2): 77–96.

Dayton, J. (2002–2003). "The silencing of a woman's choice: Mandatory arrest and no drop prosecution policies in domestic violence cases." *Cardozo Women's Law Journal*, 9: 281–297.

Denzin, N., & Lincoln, Y. (1994). *Handbook of Qualitative Research.* Thousand Oaks, CA: Sage Publications.

Dobash, E., & Dobash, R. (1992). *Women, Violence and Social Change.* New York: Routledge.

Douglas, S.J., & Michaels, M.W. (2004). *The Mommy Myth: The Idealization of Motherhood and How It Has Undermined All Women.* New York: Free Press.

Downs, A. (1996). *More Than Victims: Battered Women, The Syndrome Society, and The Law.* Chicago: The University of Chicago Press.

Dunn, J.L. (2005). "'Victims' and 'survivors': Emerging vocabularies of motive for 'battered women who stay.'" *Sociological Inquiry*, 75(1): 1–30.

Dunn, J.L. (2010). *Judging Victims: Why We Stigmatize Survivors, and How They Reclaim Respect.* Boulder, CO: Lynne Reinner Publishers, Inc.

Dunn, J.L., & Powell-Williams, M. (2007). "'Everybody makes choices': Victim advocates and the social construction of battered women's victimization and agency." *Violence Against Women*, 13(10): 977–1001.

Durfee, A. (2012). "Situational ambiguity and gendered patterns of arrest for intimate partner violence." *Violence Against Women*, 18(1): 64–84.

Erez, E., & Belknap, J. (1998). "In their own words: Battered women's assessment of the criminal processing system's responses." *Violence and Victims*, 13(3): 251–268.

Gondolf, E., & Fisher, E. (1988). *Battered Women as Survivors: An Alternative to Treating Learned Helplessness.* Lexington, MA: Lexington Books.

Goodkind, J.R., Sullivan, C.M., & Bybee, D.I. (2004). "A contextual analysis of battered women's safety planning." *Violence Against Women*, 10(5): 514–533.

Greaves, L., Pederson, A., Varcoe, C., Poole, N., Morrow, M., Johnson, J., & Irwin, L. (2004). "Mothering under duress: Women caught in a web of discourses." *Journal of the Association for Research on Mothering*, 6(1): 16–27.

Han, E. (2003). "Mandatory arrest and no-drop policies: Victim empowerment in domestic violence cases." *Boston College Third World Law Journal*, 23: 159–191.

Hanna, C. (1996). "No right to choose: Mandated victim participation in domestic violence prosecutions." *Harvard Law Review*, 109(8): 1849–1910.

Hirschel, D., & Buzawa, E. (2002). "Understanding the context of dual arrest with directions for future research." *Violence Against Women*, 8(12): 1449–1473.

Hoyle, C. (1998). *Negotiating Domestic Violence: Police, Criminal Justice and Victims*. Oxford, UK: Oxford University Press.

Hoyle, C., & Sanders, A. (2000). "Police response to domestic violence: From victim choice to victim empowerment?" *British Journal of Criminology*, 40(1): 14–36.

Johnson, H. (1996). *Dangerous Domains: Violence Against Women in Canada*. Toronto: Nelson Canada.

Kelly, J.B., & Johnson, M.P. (2008). "Differentiation among types of intimate partner violence: Research update and implications for interventions." *Family Court Review*, 46(3): 476–499.

Kelly, L. (1988). *Surviving Sexual Violence*. Minneapolis: University of Minnesota Press.

Kilty, J., & Dej, E. (2012). "Anchoring amongst the waves: Discursive constructions of motherhood and addiction." *Qualitative Sociology Review*, 8(3): 6–23.

Kilty, J., & Fabian, S. (2010). "Deconstructing an invisible identity: The case of Reena Virk." In R. Mythili & S. Batacharya, eds., *Reena Virk: Critical Perspectives on a Canadian Murder* (pp. 122–158). Toronto: Canadian Scholars' Press.

Klein, A. (1996). "Re-abuse in a population of court restrained male batterers: Why restraining orders don't work." In E. Buzawa & C. Buzawa, eds., *Do Arrests and Restraining Orders Work?* (pp. 192–213). Thousand Oaks, CA: Sage Publications.

Lamb, S. (1999). "Constructing the victim: Popular images and lasting labels." In S. Lamb, ed., *New Versions of Victims: Feminists Struggle with the Concept*. New York: New York University Press.

Lewis, R. (2004). "Making justice work: Effective legal interventions for domestic violence." *British Journal of Criminology*, 44: 204–224.

Lewis, R., Dobash, R., Dobash, E., & Cavanagh, K. (2000). "Protection, prevention, rehabilitation or justice? Women's use of the law to challenge domestic violence." *International Review of Victimology*, 7: 179–205.

Loseke, D. (1987). "Lived realities and the construction of social problems: The case of wife abuse." *Symbolic Interaction*, 10(2): 229–243.

Loseke, D. (2003). *Thinking about Social Problems* (2nd ed.). New York: Walter de Gruyter Inc.

Loseke, D., Gelles, R., & Cavanaugh, M. (2005). *Current Controversies on Family Violence*. Thousand Oaks, CA: Sage Publications.

Maxwell, C.D., Garner, J.H., & Fagan, J.S. (2001). *The Effects of Arrest on Intimate Partner Violence: New Evidence From the Spouse Assault Replication Program*. Washington, DC: Department of Justice, National Institute of Justice.

Minaker, J.C. (2001). "Evaluating criminal justice responses to intimate abuse through the lens of women's needs." *Canadian Journal of Women and the Law*, 13(1): 74–106.

Naffine, N. (1990). *Law and the Sexes: Explorations in Feminist Jurisprudence*. Sydney: Allen and Unwin.

Neuman, L. (2008). *Understanding Research*. Boston: Pearson/Allyn & Bacon.

Osthoff, S. (2002). "But, Gertrude, I beg to differ, a hit is not a hit is not a hit." *Violence Against Women*, 8(12): 1521–1544.

PRA Inc. (2006). *Evaluation of the Domestic Violence Court Program*. Prepared for the Ontario Ministry of the Attorney General. Winnipeg: PRA Inc.

Randall, M. (2004). "Domestic violence and the construction of 'ideal victims': Assaulted women's 'image problems' in law." *St. Louis University Public Law Review*, 23: 107–154.

Razack, S. (2000). "Gendered racial violence and spatialized justice: The murder of Pamela George." *Canadian Journal of Law and Society*, 15(2): 91–130.

Robinson, A., & Cook, D. (2006). "Understanding victim retraction in cases of domestic violence: Specialist courts, government policy, and victim-centred justice." *Contemporary Justice Review*, 9(2): 189–213.

Sheehy, E. (2001). "Battered women and mandatory minimum sentences." *Osgoode Hall Law Journal*, 39(2 & 3): 529–554.

Smart, C. (1989). *Feminism and the Power of Law*. London: Routledge and Kegan Paul.

Snider, L. (1994). "Feminism, punishment and the potential of empowerment." *Canadian Journal of Law and Society*, 9(7): 75–104.

Snider, L. (1998). "Struggles for social justice: Criminalization and alternatives." In K. Bonnycastle & G. Rigakos, eds., *Battered Women: Law, State and Contemporary Research in Canada* (pp. 144–155). Toronto: Collective Press.

Strega, S., & Janzen, C. (2013). "Asking the impossible of mothers: Child protection systems and intimate partner violence." In S. Strega, J. Krane, S. Lapierre, C. Richardson, & R. Carlton, eds., *Failure to Protect: Moving Beyond Gendered Responses* (pp. 49–76). Halifax: Fernwood Publishing.

Ursel, J., Tutty, L.M., & Lemaistre, J. (Eds.). (2008). *Unsettling Truths: Battered Women, Policy, Politics, and Contemporary Research in Canada*. Vancouver: Vancouver Collective Press.

Walker, L. (1979). *The Battered Woman*. New York: Harper and Row.

Young, I. (2003). "The logic of masculinist protection: Reflections on the current security state." *Signs: Journal of Women in Culture and Society*, 29(1): 1–25.

Legal Cases and Statutes

R v. A.D., [2004] O.C.J. No. 4674. (O.J) (QL).

R. v. Assin, [2003] O.C.J. No. 5694. (O.J) (QL).

R. v. Bartlett, [1999] O.S.C.J. No. 5214. (O.J) (QL).

R. v. Beals, [2001] O.C.J. No. 5607. (O.J) (QL).

R. v. Benacquista, [2001] O.C.J. No. 3541. (O.J) (QL).

R. v. Bevan, [2009] O.C.J. No. 4311. (O.J) (QL).

R. v. Brierley, [2009] O.C.J. No. 4253. (O.J) (QL).

R. v. Carrington, [2002] O.C.J. No. 2818. (O.J) (QL).

R. v. Ceballo, [1997] O.C.J. No. 5035. (O.J) (QL) .

R. v. Chapman, [2006] O.A.C. No. 185. (O.J) (QL).

R. v. Chappell, [2003] O.A.C. No. 772. (O.J) (QL).

R. v. Chartrand, [2006] O.C.J. No. 2095. (O.J) (QL).

R. v. Chugh, [2004] O.C.J. No. 1650. (O.J) (QL).

R. v. Delmastro, [2007] O.C.J. No. 4444. (O.J) (QL).

R. v. Doucet, [2000] O.C.J. No. 2459. (O.J) (QL).

R. v. Elidrissielawad, [2002] O.C.J. No. 5274. (O.J) (QL).

R. v. Ferman, [2001] O.C.J. No. 5639. (O.J) (QL).

R. v. Haluszka, [2000] O.C.J. No. 2696. (O.J) (QL).

R. v. Handley, [2005] O.C.J. No. 5739. (O.J) (QL).

R. v. Harbin, [2008] O.C.J. No. 2159. (O.J) (QL).

R. v. Jabaerizad, [2002] O.C.J. No. 4600. (O.J) (QL).

R. v. Kelemen, [2004] O.C.J. No. 804. (O.J) (QL) .

R. v. Lukaniuk, [2009] O.C.J No. 454. (O.J) (QL) .

R. v. Malouf, [2006] O.S.C.J. No. 3342. (O.J) (QL).

R. v. M.D.R, [2004] O.C.J. No. 2196. (O.J) (QL).

R. v. Minott, [2001] O.C.J. No. 1854. (O.J) (QL).

R. v. Murray, [2008] O.C.J. No. 4746. (O.J) (QL).

R. v. Nash, [2000] O.C.J . No. 2626. (O.J) (QL).

R. v. Nazareth, [2002] O.C.J. No. 4085. (O.J) (QL) .

R. v. Paul, [2008] O.S.C.J. No. 711. (O.J) (QL).

R. v. Sanderson, [2004] O.C.J. No. 5148. (O.J) (QL).

R. v. W.C.D., [2002] O.S.C.J. No. 1623. (O.J) (QL).

Chapter 7

"If I Can't Have You, No One Can," and Other Gendered Constructions of Criminal Harassment

Sheryl C. Fabian

Without cultural change, legal change is window dressing.
—Margaret M. Wright

Introduction

Criminal harassment, more commonly known as stalking, became a criminal offence in Canada in 1993. Contrary to other jurisdictions, where harassment legislation was a response to instances of celebrity stalking, in Canada, harassment was criminalized to protect women from the dangers they often face when leaving a relationship.[1] While it is sometimes assumed that separation and divorce end the risk of violence for women leaving relationships, in fact, quite the opposite is true.[2] Section 264 of the *Criminal Code of Canada* criminalizes activities that include: repeated following, repeated communication, besetting or watching, and threatening persons or their family. These behaviours must cause the victims "reasonably, in all of the circumstances, to fear for their safety or the safety of anyone known to them."

Despite legislative attempts to address a specific social problem, tensions between law and patriarchy, and questions about the law's ability to address violence against women remain: "[h]istorically, to varying degrees, societal standards, cultural dictates and law have both tacitly and explicitly encouraged male dominance over women" (Minaker, 2001: 76). To further complicate these concerns, misleading media images of criminal harassment that overrepresent "unusual" cases ignore the primary underlying reasons that stalking exists. Romantic notions of courtship[3] are social constructions that suggest pursuit is flattering, and further, that it may even be required to "capture" the "object of one's affections." In addition, it appears there are specific gendered expectations to fulfill, at least from the "male heterosexual perspective," which assumes "men are the natural pursuers of women" and women are "passive objects of desire. The infallibility of male romantic persistence is emphasized and the autonomy of women concerning the choice of their sexual partners is ignored" (Anand, 2001: 410). The influence of these conceptions of "romance" and "courtship" appears in the academic literature that discusses stalking and in the judicial decisions discussed below.

Moreover, stalkers are frequently portrayed as mentally disordered,[4] yet most studies find that few stalkers are acting under the influence of a major mental illness (see, e.g., Anand, 2001: 406–407; Gill & Brockman, 1996: 24; Lyon, 1993: 27). In fact, many stalkers may simply be playing out culturally embedded romantic scripts, albeit in an extreme fashion. Anand (2001: 409) goes so far as to say, "far from condemning stalking behaviour, our culture provides a supportive context for it."

Given this contention, it is important to consider the legal discourse within judicial decisions relating to courtship, intimate relationships, and presentations of gender roles and stereotypes. This chapter is based on a critical socio-legal analysis of criminal harassment court decisions reported in Quicklaw between 1993 and 2006. The analysis presented here extends beyond official characterizations of the offence and considers the context in which these behaviours occur. Violence against women is more than a legal problem to be resolved through legal responses. Rather, intimate partner violence reflects pervasive social inequalities, distinguished by sexism, patriarchy, and chivalry.

An examination of judicial responses to criminal harassment provides interesting insights into the criminalization of relationship pursuit, especially when the cases are explored using a gendered lens that includes consideration of popular culture images of relationships. It is important, however, to recognize the context in which juridical decisions are made. Judges do not operate in a vacuum and, therefore, their decisions must be considered both within the broader political, systemic, and structural contexts that influence decision-making processes as well as the legal and structural constraints of an adversarial legal system. Some argue that in order for laws to be effective and legitimate, they must reflect social attitudes and require social support; however, there is evidence that social attitudes toward intimate partner violence are inconsistent.[5] Despite increased public awareness of the issues and complexities of intimate partner violence, conflicting evidence regarding the unacceptability of this behaviour and debate about appropriate responses remains. In this chapter, I present four key themes regarding the gendered construction of criminal harassment within the cases: (1) Can't let go ... or ... "if I can't have you, no one can"; (2) "I may be guilty but that doesn't mean I'm sorry"; (3) "I'll do anything to get your attention"; and (4) whose fault is it, anyway? While the results show inconsistency within the judicial decisions, they are also encouraging in that it appears judges take criminal harassment seriously, although there is also evidence that they maintain paternalistic attitudes that sometimes infantilize women and remove their agency. Prior to a presentation of these findings, I now turn my attention to a brief summary of the methods employed in this study.

Methods

This chapter is based on one component of my doctoral research in which I conducted a qualitative content analysis of Canadian criminal harassment legal decisions; I applied both quantitative and qualitative techniques using a critical and gendered lens and a constructivist and inductive approach. My data set was developed using comprehensive searches of the Quicklaw databases; cases were imported into NVivo as a means of electronic storage, and they were coded within this program to assist in textual analysis. According to some researchers, computer software helps to ensure rigour in these processes in part because it facilitates queries of the data (see, e.g., Bazeley, 2007; Corbin & Strauss, 2008; Hesse-Biber & Leavy, 2011). This facilitation of the iterative processes inherent in qualitative research led to a much more rigorous and sophisticated analysis and product. I found myself going back through the early rounds of coding and recoding to develop more refined and analytic themes. This involved extensive memo-writing and reorganizing data to identify links and relationships between the data. The final data set consisted of 526 distinct court decisions (44 French- and 482 English-language cases). Of these, 315 cases involved only one decision, and 87 distinct cases included multiple proceedings, for a total of 402 separate incidents.

Consistent with the literature, 90 percent of the accused were male; 9.5 percent female; (one accused was transgender);[6] while 86.3 percent of cases involved female victims and 7.5 percent male victims. The literature shows that criminal harassment is most common between former intimate partners; reported rates of intimate partner relationships when all types of criminal harassment are considered range between 65 and 80 percent. My study found the numbers were lower than official data regarding intimate partner violence and criminal harassment: 58.0 percent were former intimate or intimate partners (only 5 were current intimates); 8.2 percent strangers (all of the accused in these cases were men); and 6.2 percent of cases involved acquaintances with no intimate history. Additional relationship types included neighbours, professional and business relationships, and friends, and the relationship type was unknown in 11.9 percent of cases. The differences between my results and official data may reflect the reporting of "unusual" cases. The length of harassment ranged from one day to 14 years, although more than 50 percent of the harassment cases were less than three months in duration. In 80 percent of cases, the harassing behaviours involved direct contact in person or by phone, and indirect contact such as following, emailing, leaving notes or gifts, contacting the victim's family, friends, or acquaintances to deliver messages, and/or damage to property or mischief. Frequently, evidence showed that the behaviours escalated in frequency and severity over time.

This chapter now presents some of the themes that emerged in the sentencing decisions when judges try to explain the behaviour of the accused, and in some cases, the complainant, using what are often relationship stereotypes. I also note the gendered language used by the accused and complainants, although the extent to which the judges adopt such language is not always clear. I begin by looking at the cases where the accused is unwilling or unable to let go of a relationship.

Can't Let Go ... or ... "If I Can't Have You, No One Can"

The theme, "can't let go," refers to instances where the accused seems unable to relinquish a relationship and his behaviour escalates to criminal harassment. Frequently this occurs when the harasser's ex-partner has found a new romantic interest and "moved on," and the harasser becomes preoccupied with ensuring that "if he can't have her, no one can." Although this attitude is not explicitly a psy diagnosis, there are numerous discussions in the case law regarding the inability of an accused "to let go" of a former intimate, which are couched in psy language (language reflecting a psychiatric diagnosis or disorder) referring to characteristics such as fixation, obsession, narcissism, and delusion. Of the 526 cases in the data set, 131 were coded as including psy language. For example, the words "obsessive," "obsession," and "obsess" are used as a descriptor of the accused when there is no expert testimony or report provided in 72 decisions, with 118 references. Similarly, 23 decisions with 69 references to the accused used the terms "narcissism" or "narcissistic." Fifteen decisions and 20 references described the accused as "fixated" or as having a "fixation" on the victim, and 25 decisions with 108 references referred to the accused as "delusional" or "deluded." In many instances, judges use this "diagnosis" to explain or rationalize the accused's behaviour, although judicial responses to these pseudo-psychiatric attributions vary dramatically. This finding is consistent with the literature in that psy typologies frequently include similar conceptualizations of stalkers using language such as "focus, fixation, obsession and persistence" to explain stalking behaviour (Cupach & Spitzberg, 2004: 74). Further, the proposed (but unsuccessful) DSM addition of "Post-Traumatic Embitterment Disorder" supports the notion that "breaking up" can lead to mental disorder if not "handled" appropriately.[7] Of greater concern is that "psychiatrizing" a terminated relationship diminishes and, depending on the case, removes responsibility from the offender. Historically, these explanations have been used to rationalize or excuse violence against women (Crocker, 2005).

R. v. Archer (1999a) demonstrates some of the ways in which psy language is used to discuss and explain the accused's behaviour. Judge Killeen notes:

> The full narrative evidence going back many years to the 1970s shows that the accused could never, as it were, release Ms. Corbett from the relationship he had with her, and which ended, from her perspective, by 1980 or so. Ms. Corbett attempted to get one [*sic*] with her life apart from the accused, but it is clear that the accused obsessively refused to accept the termination of their relationship.
>
> I can only conclude that something snapped in the accused's psyche about 1997 or so and that his personal demons and obsessions led him to embark upon the campaign of terror reflected in the charges in the indictment and the evidence. (*R. v. Archer*, 1999a, at paras. 44–45)

Not only does the judge reference the patriarchal construction of male ownership of women in intimate relationships (i.e., "*release* Ms. Corbett from the relationship"), but using language such as "snapped in the accused's psyche," and "personal demons and obsessions," contain a notable psy dimension and flavour. Similar phrases appear within the cases that do not include psy diagnoses or expert evidence. In the sentencing decision related to the above case, the judge went on to say,

> Mr. Archer undoubtedly snapped in 1997 because Miss Corbett had established another relationship and did not want to have anything more to do with him.... His overall intention was to terrorize Miss Corbett, her new spouse and a host of family members, friends and business associates of hers.
>
> It is not unfair to describe Mr. Archer as an obsessional stalker, and to add that the arsons and attempted arsons he committed were part of the revenge plan he determined to wreak upon the hapless Miss Corbett. (*R. v. Archer*, 1999b, at paras. 9–10)

Although the judge assesses the accused as an "obsessional stalker," one of the specific typologies of stalkers,[8] there is no indication in the case that this was an assessment provided by a psy expert. In fact, one portion of the report specifically cites that the accused did not suffer from "any major mental illness" even though the psychiatrist who prepared the report for the sentencing hearing noted that the offender has "features of an anti-social personality disorder and a history of substance abuse" (*R. v. Archer*, 1999b, at para. 12). The judge appears to set up a gendered dichotomy; the accused is presented as having "personal demons," being "obsessed" and having a "revenge plan" while the victim is presented as "hapless." This division is consistent with historical notions that women and other populations perceived as vulnerable require protection.

R. v. Watson (2002) did not involve any reported psy expertise in the sentencing hearing, although there is mention that the accused attended counselling for his alcohol abuse and there was a pre-sentence report. Again illustrating that judges are taking up psy discourse as part of their own expertise, Judge Donnelly's comments are nevertheless encouraging as they indicate that he is taking the matter seriously, as reflected in the 17-month custodial sentence followed by a three-year probation period:

> The alarming incidence of domestic violence requires stern response to patently dangerous circumstances. Mr. Watson's warning signs are obvious and significant. The fixation on his former wife, the delusional thought process relating to the cause of his problems and the denial of culpability give rise to significant concern. The intransigent conduct suggests that emotion has established a facility for overcoming reason. (*R. v. Watson*, 2002, at para. 25)

Similar to other cases, the offender is seen as irrational and unable to accept the end of the relationship. These behavioural explanations seem to both pathologize and normalize the offender. As previously discussed, cultural representations of breaking up emphasize heartache and blame and encourage persistence to not let go. Judge Donnelly, however, did not accept the offender's excuses or rationalizations for his ongoing and relentless unwanted contact with the victim, noting that this works to produce legitimate fear:

> Stalking breeds fear. Experience teaches that fear in such circumstances is well founded against a domestic background. Mrs. Watson, on reasonable grounds, fears for her safety. In effect, she testified: "I know him very well. He harasses me all the time. I'm concerned when I'm alone. I'm scared. I don't know what he is going to do. All this makes me feel like a prisoner in my own life." (*R. v. Watson*, 2002, at para. 19)

Even more encouraging is Judge Donnelly's subsequent statement: "She [the complainant] is entitled not to spend her life as a full time victim under a shroud of fear and harassment" (*R. v. Watson*, 2002, at para. 20).

Similarly, in *R. v. Beer* (2000), Judge Fisher acknowledges that harassing behaviours are not the type that most "wives" seek:

> When he says he loves his wife, unfortunately, that is not the kind of love that many wives wish; it is an obsession, a power, an entitlement that some husbands think they have over their wives, and it is terribly dangerous for everybody. (*R. v. Beer*, 2000, at para. 4)

Once again, the trial judge took the offender's threats, including a bumper sticker on his vehicle that said "I miss my ex, but my aim is getting better" (*R. v. Beer*, 2000, at para. 11) very seriously, handing down a 10-month custodial sentence for the criminal harassment. The very fact that such a bumper sticker exists is alarming and reflects the tacitly accepted socio-cultural constructions of relationships and gender-power dynamics that condone humour about women's victimization. Similar to *R. v. Archer* discussed above, Judge Fisher's statement also acknowledges that harassers problematically believe they are entitled to treat their female partners as possessions and thus to express power in a way that demands fear and attention.

Consonantly, in *R. v. Vanderlinde* (2001), considerable attention is paid to the psy characteristics of the offender without mention of psy assessments in the pre-sentence report. Once again, the judge suggests a "deep-seated psychiatric reason" for the offender's behaviours even though there is no evidence supporting such a diagnosis.[9] In reviewing the arguments put forth regarding disparate recommendations for sentencing (the Crown wanted a penitentiary sentence while defence argued that a suspended sentence and probation were appropriate), Judge Douglas summarizes the opposing characterizations of the offender. The Crown puts forth that "[f]irst, the accused is a danger; second or alternatively, we don't know if he is dangerous, but he is part of a dangerous class; and third, whatever treatment is proposed is not likely to be effective" (*R. v. Vanderlinde*, 2001, at para. 10). The defence, however, suggests that the accused's criminal history and current offence do not indicate "escalating violence, but … clearly speak to a significant problem with alcohol and perhaps other substance abuse" (*R. v. Vanderlinde*, 2001, at para. 10). Regardless of whether or not the offender's behaviours are alcohol-related, there is no doubt they escalated based on the information presented to the court. Judge Douglas engages in a discussion regarding the rationality of the offender, ultimately finding that there is a reasonable and logical connection between his behaviour and motives. The offender's behaviour is characterized as "obsessive" and "narcissistic," and his anger at the court-enforced separation from his wife and at the police enforcement of restraining orders is used as the logical link between the offender's continued attempts at contact and

> intimidation by mere presence. To him, given his motives, this makes perfect sense. It makes perfect sense, particularly if you have little concern for the consequences of being caught, and particularly if your desires are inflamed and your judgment weakened by the consumption of alcohol. (*R. v. Vanderlinde*, 2001, at para. 11)

> In my view, the accused, as the Crown puts it, narcissistically sees the world as he wants to or must see it to be, and he is prepared to act selfishly; that is, in disregard of the rights of others such as his wife and the Courts, to have it as he wants it or must see it. Whether he does this from some deep-seated psychiatric reason not addressed by the report, whatever that might be, or just to be, to quote the Crown, "bad", is something perhaps beyond the evidence of this Court, or even, perhaps, human understanding. (*R. v. Vanderlinde*, 2001, at para. 12)

Here the judge has emphasized connections between rationality, motivations, and the apparent inhuman inability of an accused to let go of his former partner. Because the judge finds it incomprehensible for a rational man to behave as Vanderlinde has, he suggests that he is likely to be mentally unstable, as though applying a formal label to the individual means he is no longer perceived as a free willed, rational being. In other words, the application of a formal psy label both explains and excuses the behaviour. And once again, the offender's anger is problematically grounded in his separation from his wife. Regardless, Judge Douglas goes on to acknowledge that the most useful predictor of future behaviour is past behaviour (*R. v. Vanderlinde*, 2001, at para. 13), and based on the offender's history of breaching probation he finds that the offender's

> conduct will continue to seriously impair the right to live their [the accused's ex-wife and child] lives unimpeded and free from his interference; and if a custodial sentence does nothing more than give them some months of peace, this protection of them, the only innocents in this affair, then that custodial sentence is justified. (*R. v. Vanderlinde*, 2001, at para. 14)

Although the judge considers the link between a potential psy diagnosis and the offender's behaviour, in this case, it is not seen as a justification for keeping the offender out of prison.

I May Be Guilty but That Doesn't Mean I'm Sorry

In addition to themes of relentless pursuit and attempts to control and defame former partners, the cases also feature a lack of insight, remorse, and responsibility on the part of accused stalkers. Although these aspects are evident in some of the above-mentioned cases, themes of remorse and responsibility warrant further attention. A total of 94 decisions and 143 coding references depicted minimizing responsibility on the part of the accused. For example, *R. v. Perrier* (1999) depicts an offender, who, unable to accept the end of a relationship, goes to extreme efforts to gain the attention of the complainant. The offender offered an apology that was immediately "qualified ... by noting he 'had to have some peace of mind'" (*R. v. Perrier*, 1999, at para. 21), thereby minimizing his role and responsibility in the criminal harassment behaviours.

On the other hand, when an accused presents a sincere and believable demonstration of remorse in criminal court, it can be used to mitigate punishments (Weisman, 2009: 48). Further,

> wrongdoers who are regarded as remorseful are viewed as more worthy of mercy, safer for re-inclusion into the community, and more similar to their law-abiding neighbors than those who have not shown remorse or whose expressions of remorse are judged as not credible. (Weisman, 2009: 49)

Gender stereotypes are often reflected in judicial evaluations of offenders' remorse and acceptance of responsibility (Kilty, 2010). In addition, when the accused shows insight into his behaviours, it is sometimes couched in psy language. It may be that refusing to accept responsibility is a defence mechanism, as accepting responsibility necessitates feeling remorse, which is then further complicated by the emotions associated with apology and forgiveness.[10]

For example, in *R. v. Downes* (2006), Justice Rosenberg, writing for the Ontario Court of Appeal, noted that the probation officer's report "described the appellant as not being remorseful" and that the offender "has little insight into the harm he caused the complainant, whom he blames for disrupting his relationship with his daughter" (*R. v. Downes*, 2006, at para. 12). The relationship was "uneventful" for the first 10 months, after which the accused became extremely violent, accusing the complainant of cheating on him after an evening out (*R. v. Downes*, 2006, at para. 5). Following a not atypical period of apology and remorse,[11] the couple reconciled until signs of jealousy recurred and the complainant ended the relationship. The offender refused to accept this turn of events and began harassing her, becoming "possessive, angry and violent" (*R. v. Downes*, 2006, at para. 6). While the offender was unwilling to convey his remorse to the court, he did so to the victim when he believed there was the potential for reconciling the relationship. The remorse, however, can be read as a manipulative attempt to reconcile the relationship, an apology to show he had changed and to entice her back, yet the logic is contradictory in that he made no attempt to manipulate the court in a similar way. Given that apologies are just words and remorse is an emotion, it is difficult to determine the authenticity of the accused's actions.

Likewise, in *R. v. MacLean* (1994), the offender is categorized as confused, obsessive, evasive, self-delusionary, and contradictory—attributes that, in turn, are used to explain his actions. Although the accused was convicted in this case, throughout his decision, Judge Bentley repeatedly refers to the offender's confusion in presenting information to the court, commenting that "he put a spin on things that were not borne out by other witnesses" (*R. v. MacLean*, 1994, at para. 50). It seems the offender was selectively remembering events in specific ways designed to present himself in the best light possible. Further, Justice Bentley notes:

> I find it strange that while he confirms the essence of all the telephone calls, and admits the complainant is angry with him, he never admits that she said she never wanted to see him again. For example he confirms the contents of the December 18th call and the contents of the 2 a.m. call, but denies threatening her. Most telling in my opinion was his evidence that when the complainant called him the following day and demanded to know "if this is going to carry on." He interpreted this to mean only that she objected to the 2 a.m. call and not his ongoing contact with her. I find his response either a self-serving comment to justify his continued actions or an act of outright delusion. Such feelings of delusion unfortunately were not confined to a single episode. He continued calling her between Christmas and New Years (even though he knew that she was angry with him), because he states he still had deep feelings for her. (*R. v. MacLean*, 1994, at paras. 52–53)

Justice Bentley invokes psy language by referencing MacLean's "feelings of delusion" but he does not weight this heavily enough to mitigate responsibility. While the offender's testimony and discourse demonstrate that he neither feels remorse nor is willing to take responsibility for his actions, he does justify them because he "still [has] deep feelings for the victim" (*R. v. MacLean*, 1994, at para. 53), as though his feelings of desire (or possession) should legitimately or rationally supersede those of the victim.

R. v. Olivier (2002b) also includes comments regarding the offender's lack of remorse. At sentencing, Justice Grannary admonishes the offender for his behaviours and the impact of these behaviours on the accused.

> There is no excuse for this. I know you have no remorse because you say you did not even do it. I decided you did do it. I heard nothing to the contrary. There was no evidence to suggest that this had not happened. I found Ms. B. to be a credible individual and I believed her and it is too late to say you did not do it. (*R. v. Olivier*, 2002b, at para. 10)

When the offender attempts to interject, arguing with the judge that there were inconsistencies in the complainant's testimony, Judge Grannary responds:

> No there was not, not in the trial there was not. There may be in your head but there was not at the trial and I can only go on what is at the trial, not what is going on in your mind. You have no remorse. You show absolutely no remorse on the last conviction you had. You denied it then too, even though you were convicted. The probation has had very little effect, in my estimation, on you although you request more of it. (*R. v. Olivier*, 2002b, at para. 14)

Throughout the case, the offender appears to rationalize his behaviours, although, as in the above case, this is directly related to his efforts to reconcile with the complainant. This results in the judge admonishing the offender for his inability to show remorse and his denial of responsibility regarding the impact of his behaviours on the complainant. These factors, coupled with a history of being late for court and missing appointments, influenced the judge's sentence of four months' incarceration. Judge Grannary speaks extensively about the available options that would allow him to keep the offender out of jail, stating:

> [Y]ou have had a difficult year with the passing of members of your family. It has been very tragic for you but there is nothing in any of that grief and personal misery, that suggests any excuse for the way you have behaved or any excuse for not attending to court when you are supposed to be here. (*R. v. Olivier*, 2002b, at para. 21)

Regardless of the personal circumstances used by the offender to justify his actions, these arguments are not enough to keep the offender from a jail sentence. However speculative, a critical reading of this text suggests that had Olivier expressed remorse more sincerely, perhaps Justice Grannery would have considered his difficult and emotional personal circumstances in terms of offering a reduced sentence.

In *R. v. Basha* (2002), Judge Gorman draws attention to the offender's lack of remorse and insight into his conduct, in addition to highlighting the findings of a psychiatrist, which indicate that the offender

> for the most part ... has the capacity to restraint [*sic*] his actions and is not a danger to himself or anyone else. He has shown capacity to follow directions by people he trusts or people who are in authority and if he knows there will be consequences to his actions. This can be used to control his behaviour effectively. (*R. v. Basha*, 2002, at para. 11)

Judge Gorman then focuses on Basha's failure to demonstrate regret for his actions or to promise no harm to the complainant in the future, noting:

> [W]hen I asked Mr. Basha [...] if he wished to say anything before sentence was imposed, he responded by blaming Ms. White for his actions. He offered no apology nor assurance that he would refrain from harassing her in the future. It is obvious that Mr. Basha has absolutely no empathy for Ms. White nor any concern or insight into the harm he has caused her despite her emotional plea at the sentence hearing for him to leave her alone. He has not physically harmed her yet, though he has threatened her. He has however, harmed her by taking away her freedom and her ability to live her life. (*R. v. Basha*, 2002, at para. 12)

Mr. Basha received a five-month sentence for criminal harassment and two consecutive sentences of three and four months each for the breach of recognizance offences related to the initial charge of criminal harassment (*R. v. Basha*, 2002, at para. 59). Although Judge Gorman acknowledges psychological illness in this case, he determines that other factors, such as the offender's employment status and his apology, indicate that he understands his actions.

I'll Do Anything to Get Your Attention

In addition to an accused's inability to let go of his previous partner, the former sometimes engaged in behaviours best characterized as doing almost anything to get her attention, including instilling fear, putting up sexually explicit and fabricated posters of the complainant in public spaces, contacting the complainant's family members, friends, and/or employer, and causing substantial property damage. For example, in *R. v. Bensley* (1998), Judge Thackray cites the trial judge, who noted:

> I am satisfied in this case that the complainant's psychological and emotional well being and safety were indeed threatened. That was precisely Mr. Bensley's aim. He felt that he might be able to successfully frighten

> her into returning to him. As he said in his letter, it was the rejection that got him and he thought that he could, as he put it, "piss her off enough to turn around and start talking to him again." (as reproduced by the Court of Appeal in *R. v. Bensley*, 1998, at para. 21)

In what would be perceived by most as an unusual move, after having exhausted more typical means of convincing the victim to return to the relationship, the offender engaged in a concerted effort to "frighten" her into returning, once again echoing the link between criminal harassment and culturally embedded patriarchal notions of romantic courtship. Of course, "frightening" a victim is hardly a conventional way to entice someone to re-engage in a relationship, but the above scenario does indicate a sense of urgency and desperation on the part of the accused. The latter makes it clear that his inability to accept her "rejection" was the reason behind the criminal harassment. There is a sense of ownership implied, in that she will not be permitted to and thus does not have the power to end the relationship.

As long as a sense of ownership dominates an intimate relationship, there is little wonder that some continue to believe that "no actually means yes, just not yet." These concerns are specifically addressed in *R. v. Baszczynski* (1994). After reviewing the intended purposes of criminal harassment legislation in Canada, Judge Downie, in one of the premier criminal harassment cases appearing in the legal databases, notes:

> [Y]ou've got to apply a certain amount of common sense to the situation as well. We're still dealing with people's emotions which have been rubbed raw by a break up. We must also keep in mind that there's a certain amount of folklore that says that a certain amount of persistence is forgivable. I think there's an old saying that says "Faint heart n'er won fair lady." Such sentiments may not be totally a propos these days in view of this new legislation but it seems to imply that a certain amount of persistence might win over the reluctant person who is the object of suit. (*R. v. Baszczynski*, 1994, at para. 37)

Distinctions between persistence and harassment are blurred, and a patriarchal culture that encourages pursuit, even when one has been told repeatedly to stop, helps explain some of these cases. As the Crown reminds us in *R. v. Bhangal* (2005), criminal harassment legislation criminalizes activities that are in most circumstances not criminal. For example, when "a girlfriend ha[s] ended a relationship it would not be criminal conduct for the boyfriend to send one bunch of flowers to the girlfriend, but it would not be okay and [is] potentially criminal conduct to send ten to 20 bunches of flowers at regular intervals" (*R. v. Bhangal*, 2005, at para. 10).

R. v. Zunti (1997) provides yet another example of the extreme lengths employed by an accused in his efforts to encourage the complainant to engage in a relationship with him. The complainant had known the accused for nine years, and shortly after they met "he became enamoured of her and when she did not reciprocate his feelings he began to appear at functions which she attended; watch and approach her on the street; leave telephone messages; and telephone and then hang up on her" (*R. v. Zunti*, 1997, at para. 6). The accused also sent her 16 "missives" during a three-year period (at para. 6). While initially (notably prior to the implementation of criminal harassment legislation in 1993) these "missives" were sent privately, the behaviours eventually escalated. On repeated occasions and in at least four different public locations, the accused put up posters that included sexually explicit language directed at the complainant. Although details regarding the posters are minimal, it is apparent that they name the complainant and "convey short obscene message[s] containing explicit reference[s] to sexual activity with big members of a minority group" (*R. v. Zunti*, 1997, at para. 3). In the words of the trial judge "the accused ... placed the posters ... in a further, obsessive attempt to get the attention of the complainant" (as reproduced by the Court of Appeal in *R. v. Zunti*, 1997, at para. 28). Once again, gender stereotypes are evident. The accused engages in a concerted effort to sour the reputation of the woman who is rejecting him, using sexually explicit messages (that appear to include a racial element although the accused's motivation is unclear[12]). Further, at least in this case, a steady dose of rejection speaks to men as the pursuers in courtship. It is as though the accused in this case followed the courtship manual of "romance": "Men will eventually be rewarded if they persistently pursue women" (Anand, 2001: 411). Unfortunately, the manual left out a discussion of the reality of gender relations: most women are not swooned by unwanted "romantic persistence."

The accused in *R. v. Gowing* (1994) experienced similar difficulties in letting go of his relationship with the complainant. Although the complainant made it clear to the accused that their relationship was over, the latter was unable to accept this situation and "felt he had a right to be told, in a manner acceptable to him, why the relationship was over. Rage, hostility, betrayal leaped from the pages of the letters delivered to the complainant during the period of time set out in the information" (*R. v. Gowing*, 1994, at para. 2). Despite repeated police warnings to stay away from the victim, "[t]he accused stated under oath that he took certain steps to provoke her to communicate with him when it became obvious that she did not wish to communicate (*R. v. Gowing*, 1994, at para. 2). Once again, a man's right to pursue (according to the accused), even when she says no, is evident. Moreover, the accused in this case felt that if the complainant wanted to leave she owed him a satisfactory explanation regardless of her wishes.

R. v. Bakhtari (2002)[13] also includes some interesting comments about the gendered power dynamics of relationships. As previously discussed, the judge was most impressed by Ms. Poleselo (complainant) as evidenced by his assessment of her testimony. Judge Kerr places specific emphasis on the courteous pleasantries the complainant offered the accused when she first met him, followed by a notation that Ms. Poleselo specifically told the accused she had a boyfriend.

> She testified that she did not want anything to do with him. She was not remotely attracted to him in any sort of romantic way. She did have a boyfriend, I believe she told him, or led him to believe at one point she was living with her boyfriend, which wasn't true, perhaps to discourage him. But nothing would discourage this man. (*R. v. Bakhtari*, 2002, at para. 2)

It is unclear whether this information was factual, or if the complainant had conscientiously lied in telling him that she was living with her boyfriend. Regardless, the implication is that it is somehow even more inappropriate for an accused to harass a woman who is "taken" or "owned" by another man, rendering the woman's voice and decision about whether to be in a relationship as ancillary to the man's.

Likewise, in *R. v. Pastore* (2005), Judge Lampkin makes noteworthy comments about the nature of intimate relationships. The accused denied all activities relating to the harassment of his estranged wife that involved threatening her; he also believed that he was entitled to the SUV she was driving. The judge finds "Mr. Pastore is a stranger to the truth. Mr. Pastore is not a fool" (*R. v. Pastore*, 2005, at para. 36). He then goes on to chastise the accused, stating:

> It appears that Mr. Pastore is living in the past. He believes that because he paid for the SUV he is entitled to pick it up whenever he wants it despite the fact that his wife has had the use of that vehicle and in the context of family proceedings between them. There was a time, many centuries ago, when the law was in such a state that the cynics said: "Husband and wife are one in law and the husband is that one." In those days all family property belonged to the husband. The wife had no separate estate. But times have changed, Mr. Pastore. The law now acknowledges what marriage has always been from the days of Adam and Eve—a partnership in which two people come together to share their lives, their successes and their failures, their joys and their sorrows, and also their property. And that is what you have failed to recognize. (*R. v. Pastore*, 2005, at para. 43)

The judge's comment that the accused is living in a past that no longer exists is constructive. As Judge Lampkin underscores, the end of marriage no longer means that everything accrued throughout its tenure belongs to the man. By emphasizing the accused's lack of insight into appropriate intimate relationship behaviours, the judge is effectively justifying not only the accused's failure to express remorse or to take responsibility for his actions, but he is also setting grounds for a conviction.

Whose Fault Is It, Anyway?

The final theme to be discussed is related to blame, and the assessment of who is at fault in the case and who is responsible for keeping the victim safe. These evaluations often include discussions of the impact of criminal harassment on the victim. These issues arise, in part, because the victim's fear is an integral part of the legal definition of criminal harassment. Of the 526 decisions, 183 cases and 384 specific references to victim impact were coded in the data set.

In some cases, there appears to be a law enforcement expectation that female victims manage their fears by changing their behaviours to keep themselves safe and free from harassment. This fact points to the neoliberal ethos of responsibilization making its way into legal rhetoric. Rather than placing blame on the typically male party who engages in the harassing behaviour, women are expected to find ways to ensure the harassment stops and, in some instances, they are even tasked with investigatory work. In *R. v. Gill* (2002), Judge Gorman chastised the Royal Newfoundland Constabulary who

> advised her [the complainant] to make a log of the harassing telephone calls that she was receiving and to come back later. Providing such advice to complainants can only serve to discourage women who are or have been harassed by their spouses or boyfriends from complaining to the police and it must have been disheartening to Ms. Alexander to have received such a reaction to her request for police assistance. (*R. v. Gill*, 2005, at paras. 4–5)

While it may be necessary for women to do what they can to protect themselves, they should not be made to feel responsible for being stalked (Sinwelski & Vinton, 2001: 59) nor should they be held accountable for the investigation. That said, women may be encouraged to keep a diary of attempted contacts, which can be helpful as evidence in court (Sinwelski & Vinton, 2001: 60). In addition, women are sometimes advised to change their phone numbers, licence plates, and even quit their jobs or move to protect themselves from their stalker (Anand, 2001: 399). For example, in *R. v. Gowing* (1994), the victim made extensive efforts to avoid the accused[14]—efforts that are acknowledged by Judge Zuraw:

> She left her apartment and stayed with a friend. She changed her phone number. She avoided him at the Y., and had friends escort her to her car. She was upset. She was seeking professional help. The friends called the police on her behalf and later she called the police. The police told the accused to leave the complainant alone. The accused knew this and was frustrated, dismayed and enraged. Thus the letters and the threats. The explicit video, the explicit photos of the two of them together left on her car. (*R. v. Gowing*, 1994, at para. 3)

Likewise, in *R. v. Ivory* (2004), Judge Lampkin acknowledges the lifestyle changes and the impact of criminal harassment on the victim:

> Ms. Pichler felt the telephone calls would not stop. It appeared to her that Mr. Ivory would not listen to her request not to call nor Constable Cheung's caution not to contact her. She did not feel safe anymore. She felt panicky and paranoid about going out. At the end of July 2002 she gave sixty days' notice to her landlord to surrender the premises. (*R. v. Ivory*, 2004, at para. 45)

Here the use of the term "paranoid" does not appear to be psychiatrized. Instead, there is an implication that the victim had good reason for concern, and yet, one could argue that you can only be "paranoid" if the object of your paranoia is not "out to get you." In this case, the victim's relationship with the accused included a history of violence and the criminal harassment charges came about because he would not leave her alone. According to the judge, the victim stated that

> the relationship was toxic. They argued a lot. There was a lot of verbal abuse. Arguments would escalate. Mr. Ivory would throw and smash things on the floor. There would be spitting and kicking. There was a lot of violence. They would hit each other. She suffered bruises on her legs, on her hairline and on her arm from the top of her shoulder to her elbow. She never reported any of that to the police because she felt guilty. She felt it was her fault. (*R. v. Ivory*, 2004, at para. 6)

In some cases, the fact that the female victim sought help from a psychologist or psychiatrist as a consequence of the stalking behaviour was actually used to support a conviction for criminal harassment because it was thought to empirically demonstrate the impact of the criminal harassment on the victim.[15] For example, in *R. v. Davis* (1999), Judge Beard reports that

> the complainant testified that immediately following the break-up ... the accused again began calling her and sending flowers and letters, as he had done before. She testified that she told him that their relationship was over this time and that he should get on with his life with this girlfriend and leave her out of it. He persisted and began calling her friends, asking how she was doing, whether she had a new boyfriend, etc. She began getting counseling from a psychologist who suggested that she stop talking to the accused and that she document all of his attempts to contact her. The complainant had her telephone number changed and got an unlisted number. (*R. v. Davis*, 1999, at para. 5)

The fact that the victim was seeing a psychologist was included as partial evidence for the accused's conviction for criminal harassment in that it indicated the victim was truly harassed (*R. v. Davis*, 1999, at paras. 52–53).

Literature suggests, however, that the woman is often blamed for causing the stalking by answering the perpetrator's phone calls, or by refusing to move or change her phone number. As seen above, in *R. v. Gill* (2005), the judge chastised the police for putting the onus on the victim to stop the behaviour and to establish proof of the offence before calling for police assistance again (at paras. 4–5). When women are not viewed as doing everything in their power to prevent the harassment, it seems that they are considered to be somehow complicit in it. Others have found evidence of condescending prescriptions for how to avoid harassment that seem designed to make the victim responsible: "If she doesn't tell him 'right' then he can't be expected to understand" (Mullen, Pathé, & Purcell, 2001: 223–224). When the victim is blamed, the stalker's behaviour is excused. Interestingly, cases such as these were rare in the data set, although in a few instances, authorities suggested that the victim was encouraging the offender.[16] That said, there are examples of the silencing of women through the use of gendered language describing women's dissatisfaction—notably, that they "nag," "moan," "whinge," and "bitch" (Astbury, 1996: 27–28).[17] And yet, within the cases that show an accused's attempts to explain, rationalize, or justify his behaviour, typically judges did not support these rationalizations.

Moreover, disproportionate (but not unexpected) gendered representations materialized in the case law. Women were more likely to be characterized as "paranoid" when reporting criminally harassing behaviour, which, depending on the context of the case, may be read as a gendered "hysterical" response, while the men who perpetrate this offence were more apt to be afforded some sort of psy explanation (supported or otherwise), which in turn is used to rationalize and sometimes excuse their behaviours.[18] For example, in *R. v. Meyerson* (2000), a case that hinged on issues of credibility, Judge Perozak states:

> This court finds the evidence of the complainant to be, in many material respects, vague and uncertain and fraught with unreasonable emotion.
>
> In Cross-examination, particularly, she was evasive and overwrought almost to the point of paranoia, for her own safety and that of her children, which this court finds entirely unreasonable, in the circumstances.
>
> Her inflexibility, with respect to communications concerning the children's welfare, was inconsistent with her own communications with the accused outside the strict terms of the civil court order and weakened her credibility. (*R. v. Meyerson*, 2000, at paras. 12–14)

This kind of pathologization of the victim, who is described as inflexible, unreasonably "emotional," and "overwrought almost to the point of paranoia," is disconcerting. The judge seems to overlook the traumatic effect of stalking on many victims that is well documented in the literature (Cupach & Spitzberg, 2004: 123; Meloy, 2007: 4–5). Further, when women do not react to harassment behaviours in prescribed ways, they are characterized as inferior, deviant, inadequate, and abnormal (Raitt & Zeedyk, 2000: 8). This reflects what feminists have long since exposed—that social life is gendered in profound ways, notably in and through power relations that call attention to the experiences of violence, intimidation, and abuse in intimate relations and domestic life (Marecek, 2002: 24).

On the other hand, victims sometimes used psy language themselves when describing the impact of criminal harassment.

> I found it very upsetting because the incidents were happen … happening more and more frequently, way more frequently, and since I'd told him, hoping to resolve it informally by telling him to leave me alone, I hoped that that would do the trick, and it seemed to make things worse. Every time I looked out my window it seemed the blue car was driving past. It was constant.

> I was concerned enough to tell my neighbours to keep an eye on my house. I was getting … you don't want to say you're getting paranoid, but it was making me very uncomfortable.
>
> Every time I'd hear a vehicle pull up, I'd look out the window. Every time I was away from home I was worried. My neighbours knew that if they ever saw that car out there, to page me right away, or to phone the office if they had to. I was … I was getting a little bit concerned at that time. (*R. v. Hoang*, 2002, at para. 6)

Again, given the escalation of the harassing behaviours, there is no doubt that the victim in this case was concerned with good reason. Notably, she was also a police officer, which sheds additional insights into the meaning of her response. Perhaps at issue is the use of the term "paranoid," which does not apply when one encounters a very real threat to one's life.

In some cases, judicial decisions include assessments of the appropriateness of a victim's behaviour. For example, in *R. v. Olivier* (2002a), the judge acknowledges that the victim had done the right thing in making it clear that she was not interested in resuming her relationship with the accused: "She told him. It was clear to him, it must have been clear to Mr. Olivier that she did not want him at her house" (*R. v. Olivier*, 2002a, at para. 39). Further, Judge Grannary concedes that the accused's intention was to "drive her crazy and he succeeded" (*R. v. Olivier*, 2002a, at para. 41). In the sentencing judgment, Olivier's impact on the victim and her family is made even more explicit:

> [T]here was a whole pattern of rather disturbing obsessive behaviour that led to Ms. B. becoming ill, physically ill as a result of it. She already had had a significant operation and you were doing some of these things while she was on medication and while she was recovering from surgery, and you made her condition worse. You terrified her child and what did she say about her cat, her cat spazzes every time she sees you or something like that. There was something like that. You upset the whole household, everybody, including the animals. (*R. v. Olivier*, 2002b, at paras. 8–9)

Likewise, in *R. v. Boaz* (1999), Judge Kilpatrick discusses the "profound" effects of the harassing behaviours on the "complainant's emotional and psychological well-being." The "fear generated by the persistent threatening behavior of Mr. Boaz," he writes, "has resulted in a significant dislocation of the complainant's lifestyle" (at para. 14). Further:

> This fear has resulted in sleep deprivation, memory loss and anxiety. It has adversely effected [*sic*] the complainant's ability to nurture and parent her infant son. The complainant's fear of the unknown caused her to become paranoid. She now sleeps with her clothes on. She locks doors unnecessarily. She waits, she watches, she listens for signs of an attack that may come at any moment.
>
> The psychological harm to the complainant in this case might not be as apparent as a cut, a bruise, or a wound that is the visible legacy of an assault. But the pain caused to victims of this offence is as real as the pain and anguish associated with crimes of actual violence. It is violence of a different sort. It is violence of the mind. It is the emotional damage so often associated with this offence that S. 264 attempts to prevent. (*R. v. Boaz*, 1999, at paras. 14–15)

Boaz was sentenced to nine months in jail followed by a three-year probation order.

The above discussion demonstrates that for the most part judges appear to have a reasonable understanding of criminal harassment, and the potential for such activities to have a profound impact on victims. Contrary to my expectations based on findings in other research, Canadian judges rarely blamed the complainant for the harassing behaviour and actually went so far as to chastise law enforcement for failing to respond appropriately to harassment incidents.

Conclusion

This chapter examined the gendered constructions of responsibility, remorse, and blameworthiness found in 13 years of criminal harassment case law. The theme describing an accused's inability to "let go" of a relationship was often supported using psy language and explanations that partially justify the behaviours. In some cases, the easiest way to explain criminal harassment is through common-sense conceptions of psy characteristics (i.e., obsession, paranoia, and narcissism, among others) even when there is no expert evidence that the parties involved were assessed or diagnosed with a mental illness. More problematic, however, was that on occasion the victims were referred to as "paranoid" by judges. Notably, this depiction did not emerge as a dominant theme and thus cannot be described as a systematic effort to pathologize the women involved in these cases. A more appropriate response might be to acknowledge the accused's flawed social construction of relationships, and the role of patriarchy in the power and control dynamics in heterosexual relationships. Similarly, psy characterizations were sometimes used to rationalize the extreme lengths to which some men go to hang on to a failed relationship. Amid these discussions, traditional descriptions of gender roles and stereotypes do emerge, which may perpetuate the romanticization of intense relationship pursuit.

A recurring theme in the cases was the image of an offender who, unable to "let go" of a relationship, "crosses a line" when his behaviour escalates to criminal harassment. This scenario is sometimes accompanied by mention of the fact that the harasser's ex-partner found a new romantic interest and "moved on." In these cases, the harasser refuses to permit this, giving credence to the title of this chapter: "If I can't have you, no one can." As noted at the outset of this chapter, when the harassing behaviours escalate, the cases sometimes end tragically in murder. In response, psy terms such as "obsessive," "fixated," "delusional," or "narcissistic" are typically evoked to explain stalking behaviours. In fact, at times, explanations for harassing behaviour seem to both pathologize and normalize the offender. Consistent with these findings, Comack and Balfour (2004) found that the psy disciplines are used together to "situate and explain" behaviours (59), and lawyering strategies involve "discursive constructions that render men's violence an expected outcome of masculine scripts" (76), demonstrating the gendered nature of power relations. Cultural constructions suggest men are the controllers and that women are to be controlled by men. Moreover, as seen in some of the cases presented in this section, women are hapless, and therefore need to be safeguarded from men with personal demons and revenge plans that are explained away as psy obsessions. These narratives suggest an underlying acceptance that these power dynamics are inevitable in heterosexual relationships. Such conceptions reflect a much broader issue regarding the gendered nature of power and control dynamics in relationships where men control and women are to be controlled; at times control manifests itself by instilling fear. That said, it is encouraging to see that in many cases, even though judges considered the links between a potential psy diagnosis and the offender's behaviour, and despite attempts on the part of defence, it was not effective in mitigating sentences.

Similarly, when examining the accused's rationale for his actions against what appeared to be disingenuous apologies, for the most part judges did not permit an offender's expression of remorse to mitigate punishments, even though gender stereotypes were still sometimes reflected in judicial evaluations of offenders' remorse and acceptance of responsibility in the criminal harassment cases. Further, elements of denial, or refusing to accept responsibility for one's actions, are viewed as aggravating factors that were used to support a sentence of incarceration. The nexus between remorse and responsibility is fluid, and there is no doubt that the two concepts are intricately connected, but the findings here suggest once again that the courts take criminal harassment seriously.

The finding that the accused minimize their responsibility often reflected stereotypical gender roles. Some accused argued that the victim "deserved" to be harassed because she had failed to offer a satisfactory explanation for leaving him, or because he was unable to "handle" the pain of breaking up and unrequited love—suggesting that only men possess the power to end a relationship and that the female complainant was simply playing hard to get. Some accused went to extreme lengths to get the victim's attention and convince her to resume the relationship, implying a sense of ownership, and suggesting that some men continue to believe that "no actually means yes, just not yet." These points demonstrate that, for many men, there are no clear distinctions between persistence and harassment, which supports the claim that patriarchal cultures encourage the relentless romantic pursuit of women. Once again, a man's right to pursue (according to the accused), even when she says no, is evident. Moreover, the accused in this case felt that if the complainant wanted to leave she owed him a satisfactory explanation regardless of her wishes.

Although I anticipated that the cases might include many instances of victim blaming consistent with the available research on violence against women, more often than not the judicial discourse seemed to place responsibility on the accused. While some examples of victim blaming were found, these were not the norm. In fact, especially when looking at trends in the case law over time, it is apparent that judges are aware of the problem of intimate partner violence and that it is unacceptable and no longer fits with Canadian values. At the same time, there is an impression that at least some judges maintain paternalistic approaches that serve to infantilize women, assuming that they are in need of care and protection from their male partners, thereby removing women's agency. The judge, in his/her role as a representative of the state, takes on the role of the victim's father.

While judges rarely blamed victims for the harassing behaviour, the same cannot be said of the accused. Frequently, the data indicated that the accused twisted explanations of his actions and justified his behaviours through victim blaming. Instead, it was encouraging to see judicial responses to criminal harassment that both acknowledge and take into account the often devastating and traumatic impact of the events on the victim. Although my results echo Crocker's (2008)[19] questions regarding the law's ability to solve social problems, we both found many indicators that the courts appeared to be taking criminal harassment seriously based on official data and sentencing practices. The overrepresentation of unusual cases is likely to continue in that individual judges may sometimes blame victims or dismiss the seriousness of criminal harassment. It appears, however, that on the whole Canadian judges have moved away from this trend and are thus recognizing the severity and traumatic impact of criminal harassment—both on the victim and on socio-cultural understandings of gender roles in intimate heterosexual relationships.

Notes

1 See, among others, AuCoin (2005), Brzozowski (2004), Cairns Way (1994), Gill & Brockman (1996), Hackett (2000), Hotton (2001), and Kong (1996).

2 Despite the fact that incidents of violence against women are challenging to measure due to the private nature of these matters that tend to be underreported to the police (Johnson, 2006: 16), official data and the GSS victimization survey consistently indicate that ex-spouses report higher rates of violence in comparison to current spouses (Beattie, 2003, 2009; Bressan, 2008; Hotton, 2001; Johnson, 2006; Ogrodnik, 2009).

3 For an interesting discussion of the romanticization of stalking in literature, film, and song, see Anand (2001: 409–414). Lee (1998) also provides an in-depth examination of some of the historical representations of stalking in literature (389–403) and further notes that a myriad of "how-to" manuals are available that encourage women to "play hard to get," reinforcing traditional notions that women must allow men to "pursue" them while remaining mysterious and secretive so that the suitor remains interested (399).

4 Typical characterizations of stalking, especially in the media, present images of mentally ill, "crazed stalkers" who target celebrities (Spitzberg & Cupach, 2007: 79). For example, reports of Canadian singer Anne Murray's 21 years of being stalked by a fan who "bombarded her with thousands of phone calls, letters, and gifts" (Anand, 2001: 404) or the highly publicized stalking and murder of American actress Rebecca Schaeffer by a "disordered" fan (Mullen et al., 2001: 11) quickly come to mind. Further, popular films like *Fatal Attraction,* where Glenn Close's "crazed" character stalks and nearly kills the object of her obsession, perpetuate notions that stalkers are mentally disordered individuals, obsessed and unable to control their actions (Anand, 2001: 412; Mullen et al., 2001: 406–407). Such images can also be found in song, as exemplified by the title of the dissertation from which this chapter is written: "I'll be watching you," from "Every Breath You Take" by the Police (Anand, 2001: 411–412; Kamir, 2001). However, these characterizations of stalkers and criminal harassment are far from accurate. Criminal harassment is a crime of control and power that typically involves an estranged male intimate partner who stalks his female ex-partner because he is unable to let go of the relationship or accept that she has moved on without him (Albrecht, 2001: 86; Davis & Chipman, 2001: 12; Mechanic, Weaver, & Resick, 2002: 63).

5 See, for example, Leisenring (2011), Lewis, Dobash, Dobash, and Cavanagh (2001), Loue, (2001), Trujillo and Ross (2008), Ursel, Tutty, and leMaistre (2008), and Williams and Grant (2006), among others.

6 The percentage of male accused in my study is somewhat higher than in official statistics: the most recent *Juristat* reports that, as of 1999, 84 percent of stalkers were male and 16 percent were female (Hackett, 2000: 6). However, a study similar to my own work, examining criminal harassment cases located in Quicklaw, found the accused was male in 94 percent of cases (Grant, Bone, & Grant, 2003, at para. 19).

7 Post-Traumatic Embitterment Disorder (PTED) was proposed as a new category of mental disorder for inclusion in the fifth revision of the *Diagnostic and Statistical Manual of Mental Disorders* (DSM-V). The disorder is characterized as a prolonged feeling of embitterment that occurs following a negative life experience such as separation or divorce. It differs from Post-Traumatic Stress Disorder, because the event that causes the condition is neither life-threatening or fear-provoking (Dvir, 2007). The PTED Self-Rating Scale assesses "embitterment and associated psychological symptoms in reaction to negative life events" (Linden, Baumann, Lieberei, & Rotter, 2009: 140). PTED was not included in the DSM-V.

8 Harassment typologies tend to focus on one of three related elements: clinical factors, such as the presence of a mental disorder; structural factors that focus on the relationship between the victim and accused; or the motivations behind the stalking behaviour (Spitzberg & Cupach, 2001: 105). The most common stalker profiles involve an individual's "obsessive" behaviour toward another person, most often motivated by intense affection and/or extreme dislike of the victim (Davis & Chipman, 2001; Douglas & Dutton, 2001; Zona, Palarea, & Lane, 1998).

9 Although the judge refers to a pre-sentence report (PSR) and suggests there is no evidence of a psy disorder, it is not clear if the PSR involved a psy assessment.

10 Although beyond the scope of this paper, there are discussions in the literature regarding the relationship between apology, forgiveness, remorse, and accountability, especially within the realm of restorative justice. To further complicate the matter, there is also considerable debate regarding the appropriateness of applying these concepts to intimate partner violence. See, for example, Ashworth (2002); Cameron (2003, 2006); Hudson (2002, 2003); Petrucci (2002); and Stubbs (2007) among others.

11 The cycle of violence attributed to Lenore Walker (1979) describes three phases in intimate partner violence: (1) tension-building prior to a violent explosion; (2) acute abuse incident; and (3) a period characterized by remorse, apology, and avowal that the abuse will not happen again (Belknap, 2007: 329).

12 The emphasis on race seems to imply that not only is the complainant promiscuous but she is the worst kind of promiscuous because she is engaging in miscegenation with a Black man, another group that is also hypersexualized (Bowleg, 2004; Hill Collins, 2004; Lemelle, 2010).

13 The relationship in this case is not one between former intimate partners. Shortly after the accused moved to a new home, he became "fixated" on a woman living a block away from him.

14 The literature shows that many stalking victims make significant behavioural changes to protect themselves, often in the absence of criminal justice support (Cupach & Spitzberg, 2004: 123; Meloy, 2007: 4–5).

15 Notably, no similar examples were located when cases involved a male victim.

16 See *R. v. Distaulo* (2003) and *R. v. Fiendell* (2006).

17 Thirty-six of the 526 decisions noted that the accused called the female victim a "bitch."

18 When men were psychiatrized in criminal harassment cases, it had a different construction when compared to the ways in which female stalkers are psychiatrized.

19 Crocker (2008) conducted a discourse analysis of criminal harassment cases between 2001 and 2003.

References

Albrecht, S.F. (2001). "Stalking, stalkers, and domestic violence: Relentless fear and obsessive intimacy." In J.A. Davis, ed., *Stalking Crimes and Victim Protection: Prevention, Intervention, Threat Assessment and Case Management* (pp. 81–95). Boca Raton: CRC Press.

Anand, S. (2001). "Stopping stalking: A search for solutions, a blueprint for effective change." *Saskatchewan Law Review*, 34: 397–428.

Ashworth, A. (2002). "Responsibilities, rights and restorative justice." *The British Journal of Criminology*, 42(3): 578–595.

Astbury, J. (1996). *Crazy For You: The Making of Women's Madness.* Melbourne: Oxford University Press.

AuCoin, K. (2005). "Stalking: Criminal harassment." In K. AuCoin, ed., *Family Violence in Canada: A Statistical Profile, 2005* (pp. 33–47). Ottawa: Canadian Centre for Justice Statistics, Statistics Canada.

Bazeley, P. (2007). *Qualitative Data Analysis with NVivo*. Los Angeles: Sage Publications.

Beattie, S. (2003). "Criminal harassment." In H. Johnson & K. AuCoin, eds., *Family Violence in Canada: A Statistical Profile, 2003* (pp. 9–20). Ottawa: Canadian Centre for Justice Statistics, Statistics Canada.

Beattie, S. (2009). "Homicide in Canada 2008." *Juristat*, 29. Ottawa: Canadian Centre for Justice Statistics, Statistics Canada.

Belknap, J. (2007). *The Invisible Woman: Gender, Crime, and Justice*. Belmont, CA: Thomson Wadsworth.

Bowleg, L. (2004). "Love, sex, and masculinity in sociocultural context: HIV concerns and condom use among African American men in heterosexual relationships." *Men and Masculinities*, 7(2): 166–186.

Bressan, A. (2008). "Spousal violence in Canada's provinces and territories." In L. Ogrodnik, ed., *Family Violence in Canada: A Statistical Profile, 2008* (pp. 10–25). Ottawa: Canadian Centre for Justice Statistics, Statistics Canada.

Brzozowski, J.-A. (2004). "Spousal violence." In J.-A. Brzozowski, ed., *Family Violence in Canada: A Statistical Profile, 2004* (pp. 5–15). Ottawa: Canadian Centre for Justice Statistics, Statistics Canada.

Cairns Way, R. (1994). "The criminalisation of stalking: An exercise in media manipulation and political opportunism." *McGill Law Journal*, 39(2): 379–400.

Cameron, A. (2003). *Gender, Power and Justice: A Feminist Perspective on Restorative Justice and Intimate Violence*. Master of Laws dissertation, University of British Columbia, Vancouver.

Cameron, A. (2006). "Stopping the violence: Canadian feminist debates on restorative justice and intimate violence." *Theoretical Criminology*, 10(1): 49–66.

Comack, E., & Balfour, G. (2004). *The Power to Criminalize: Violence, Inequality and the Law*. Halifax: Fernwood Publishing.

Corbin, J., & Strauss, A. (2008). *Basics of Qualitative Research: Techniques and Procedures for Developing Grounded Theory* (3rd ed.). Thousand Oaks, CA: Sage Publications.

Crocker, D. (2005). "Regulating intimacy: Judicial discourse in cases of wife assault (1970 to 2000)." *Violence Against Women*, 11(2): 197–226.

Crocker, D. (2008). "Criminalizing harassment and the transformative potential of law." *Canadian Journal of Women and the Law*, 20(1), 87–110.

Cupach, W.R., & Spitzberg, B.H. (2004). *The Dark Side of Relationship Pursuit: From Attraction to Obsession to Stalking*. Mahwah, NJ: Lawrence Erlbaum Associates.

Davis, J.A., & Chipman, M.A. (2001). "Stalkers and other obsessional types: A review and forensic psychological typology of those who stalk." In J.A. Davis, ed., *Stalking Crimes and Victim Protection: Prevention, Intervention, Threat Assessment, and Case Management* (pp. 3–18). Boca Raton: CRC Press.

Douglas, K.S., & Dutton, D.G. (2001). "Assessing the link between stalking and domestic violence." *Aggression and Violent Behaviour: A Review Journal*, 6(6): 519–546.

Dvir, Y. (2007). "Review of the book *Posttraumatic Embitterment Disorder: Definition, Evidence, Diagnosis, Treatment*." *Psychiatric Services*, 58(11): 1507–1508.

Gill, R., & Brockman, J. (1996). *A Review of Section 264 (Criminal Harassment) of the Criminal Code of Canada—Working Document*. Canada: Research, Statistics and Evaluation Directorate, Policy Sector.

Grant, I., Bone, N., & Grant, K. (2003). "Canada's criminal harassment provisions: A Review of the first ten years." *Queen's Law Journal*, 29, 175–241.

Hackett, K. (2000). "Criminal harassment." *Juristat*, 20. Ottawa: Canadian Centre for Justice Statistics, Statistics Canada.

Hesse-Biber, S.N., & Leavy, P. (2011). *The Practice of Qualitative Research* (2nd ed.). Los Angeles: Sage Publications.

Hill Collins, P. (2004). *Black Sexual Politics: African Americans, Gender, and the New Racism*. New York: Routledge.

Hotton, T. (2001). "Spousal violence after marital separation." *Juristat*, 21. Ottawa: Canadian Centre for Justice Statistics, Statistics Canada.

Hudson, B. (2002). "Restorative justice and gendered violence: Diversion or effective justice?" *British Journal of Criminology*, 42(3): 616–634.

Hudson, B. (2003). "Victims and offenders." In A.V. Hirsch, J.V. Roberts, A. Bottoms, K. Roach, & M. Schiff, eds., *Restorative Justice and Criminal Justice: Competing or Reconcilable Paradigms?* (pp. 177–194). Portland, OR: Hart Publishing.

Johnson, H. (2006). *Measuring Violence Against Women: Statistical Trends, 2006.* (Cat. No. 85-570-XIE). Ottawa: Statistics Canada.

Kamir, O. (2001). *Every Breath You Take: Stalking Narratives and the Law.* Ann Arbor: University of Michigan Press.

Kilty, J.M. (2010). "Gendering violence, remorse, and the role of restorative justice: Deconstructing public perceptions of Kelly Ellard and Warren Glowatsk." *Contemporary Justice Review,* 13(2): 155–172.

Kong, R. (1996). "Criminal harassment." *Juristat,* 16. Ottawa: Canadian Centre for Justice Statistics, Statistics Canada.

Lee, R.K. (1998). "Romantic and electronic stalking in a college context [comments]." *William & Mary Journal of Women and the Law,* 4(2): 373–466.

Leisenring, A. (2011). "'Whoa! They could've arrested me!': Unsuccessful identity claims of women during police response to intimate partner violence." *Qualitative Sociology,* 34: 353–370.

Lemelle, A.J. (2010). *Black Masculinity and Sexual Politics.* New York: Routledge.

Lewis, R., Dobash, R.E., Dobash, R.P., & Cavanagh, K. (2001). "Law's progressive potential: The value of engagement with the law for domestic violence." *Social & Legal Studies,* 10(1): 105–130.

Linden, M., Baumann, K., Lieberei, B., & Rotter, M. (2009). "The Post-traumatic Embitterment Disorder self-rating scale (PTED Scale)." *Clinical Psychology & Psychotherapy,* 16(2), 139–147.

Loue, S. (2001). *Intimate Partner Violence: Societal, Medical, Legal, and Individual Responses.* New York: Plenum Publishers.

Lyon, D.R. (1993). *The Characteristics of Stalkers in British Columbia: A Statistical Comparison of Persons Charged with Criminal Harassment and Persons Charged with other Criminal Code Offences.* Master's dissertation, Simon Fraser University, Burnaby, BC.

Marecek, J. (2002). "Unfinished business: Postmodern feminism in personality psychology." In M. Ballou & L.S. Brown, eds., *Rethinking Mental Health and Disorder: Feminist Perspectives* (pp. 3–28). New York: Guilford Press.

Mechanic, M.B., Weaver, T.L., & Resick, P.A. (2002). "Intimate partner violence and stalking behaviour: Exploration of patterns and correlates in a sample of acutely battered women." In K.E. Davis, I.H. Frieze, & R.D. Maiuro, eds., *Stalking: Perspectives on Victims and Perpetrators* (pp. 62–84). New York: Springer Publishing Company.

Meloy, J.R. (2007). "Stalking: The state of the science." *Criminal Behaviour and Mental Health,* 17: 1–7.

Minaker, J.C. (2001). "Evaluating criminal justice response to intimate abuse through the lens of women's needs. *Canadian Journal of Women and Law*, 13(1): 72–106.

Mullen, P.E., Pathé, M., & Purcell, R. (2001). "Stalking: New constructions of human behaviour." *Australian and New Zealand of Psychiatry*, 35, 9–16.

Ogrodnik, L. (2009). *Family Violence in Canada: A Statistical Profile, 2008*. Ottawa: Statistics Canada.

Petrucci, C.J. (2002). "Apology in the criminal justice setting: Evidence for including apology as an additional component in the legal system." *Behavioral Sciences & the Law*, 20(4): 337–362.

Raitt, F.E., & Zeedyk, M.S. (2000). *The Implicit Relation of Psychology and Law: Women and Syndrome Evidence*. London: Routledge.

Sinwelski, S.A., & Vinton, L. (2001). "Stalking: The constant threat of violence." *Affilia*, 16(1): 46–65.

Spitzberg, B.H., & Cupach, W.R. (2001). "Paradoxes of pursuit: Toward a relational model of stalking-related phenomena." In J.A. Davis, ed., *Stalking Crimes and Victim Protection: Prevention, Intervention, Threat Assessment and Case Management* (pp. 97–136). Boca Raton: CRC Press.

Spitzberg, B.H., & Cupach, W.R. (2007). "The state of the art of stalking: Taking stock of the emerging literature." *Aggression and Violent Behaviour*, 12(1): 64–86.

Stubbs, J. (2007). "Beyond apology? Domestic violence and critical questions for restorative justice." *Criminology and Criminal Justice*, 7(2): 169–187.

Trujillo, M.P., & Ross, S. (2008). "Police response to domestic violence: Making decisions about risk and risk management." *Journal of Interpersonal Violence*, 23(4): 454–473.

Ursel, J., Tutty, L.M., & leMaistre, J. (2008). *What's Law Got to Do With It? The Law, Specialized Courts and Domestic Violence in Canada*. Toronto: Cormorant Books Inc.

Weisman, R. (2009). "Being and doing: The judicial use of remorse to construct character and community." *Social & Legal Studies*, 18(1): 47–69.

Williams, K.R., & Grant, S.R. (2006). "Empirically examining the risk of intimate partner violence: The revised domestic violence screening instrument (DVSI-R). *Public Health Reports*, 121(4): 400–408.

Wright, M.M. (2007). *Judicial Decision Making in Child Sexual Abuse Cases*. Vancouver: UBC Press.

Zona, M.A., Palarea, R.E., & Lane, J.C. (1998). "Psychiatric diagnosis and the offender-victim typology of stalking." In J.R. Meloy, ed., *The Psychology of Stalking: Clinical and Forensic Perspectives* (pp. 69–84). San Diego, CA: Academic Press.

Legal Cases and Statutes

R. v. Archer, [1999a] O.J. No. 950; 41 W.C.B. (2d) 501 (ON.Ct.G.D.).

R. v. Archer, [1999b] O.J. No. 5126 (ON.Sup.Ct.Jus.).

R. v. Bakhtari, [2002] O.J. No. 4948 (ON.Ct.Jus.).

R. v. Basha, [2002] N.J. No. 334; 56 W.C.B. (2d) 147 (NL.Prov.Ct.).

R. v. Baszczynski, [1994] O.J. No. 1749; 24 W.C.B. (2d) 153 (ON.Ct.Prov.D.).

R. v. Beer, [2000] O.J. No. 1108 (ON.Ct.Jus.).

R. v. Bensley, [1998] B.C.J. No. 3264 (B.C.S.C.).

R. v. Bhangal, [2005] B.C.J. No. 2885; 2005 BCPC 624 (B.C.Prov.Ct.).

R. v. Boaz, [1999] Nu.J. No. 4 (NU.Ct.Jus.).

R. v. Davis, [1999] M.J. No. 477 (MB.Q.B.).

R. v. Distaulo, [2003] O.J. No. 6004; 63 W.C.B. (2d) 318 (ON.Ct.Jus.).

R. v. Downes, [2006] O.J. No. 555; 79 O.R. (3d) 321; 208 O.A.C. 324; 205 C.C.C. (3d) 488; 37 C.R. (6th) 46; 69 W.C.B. (2d) 12; 2006 CarswellOnt 778 (Ont.C.A.).

R. v. Fiendell, [2006] B.C.J. No. 2677; 2006 BCPC 456 (B.C.Prov.Ct.).

R. v. Gill, [2005] O.J. No. 2648; [2005] O.T.C. 539; 67 W.C.B. (2d) 244 (ON.Sup.Ct.Jus.).

R. v. Gowing, [1994] O.J. No. 1696 (ON.Ct.Prov.D.).

R. v. Hoang, [2002] B.C.J. No. 3017; 2002 BCPC 593 (B.C.Prov.Ct.).

R. v. Ivory, [2004] O.J. No. 5376; 2004 ONCJ 355; 63 W.C.B. (2d) 317 (ON.Ct.Jus.).

R. v. MacLean, [1994] O.J. No. 2296 (ON.Ct.Prov.D.).

R. v. Meyerson, [2000] O.J. No. 4302 (ON.Ct.Jus.).

R. v. Olivier, [2002a] B.C.J. No. 3137; 2002 BCPC 672 (B.C.Prov.Ct.).

R. v. Olivier, [2002b] B.C.J. No. 3136; 2002 BCPC 673 (B.C.Prov.Ct.).

R. v. Pastore, [2005] O.J. No. 2807; 2005 ONCJ 332; 65 W.C.B. (2d) 730 (ON.Ct.Jus.).

R. v. Perrier, [1999] N.J. No. 190; 177 Nfld. & P.E.I.R. 225; 43 W.C.B. (2d) 95 (NL.S.C.T.D.).

R. v. Vanderlinde, [2001] O.J. No. 425 (ON.Ct.Jus.).

R. v. Watson, [2002] O.J. No. 5221 (ON.Sup.Ct.Jus.).

R. v. Zunti, [1997] S.J. No. 788; 161 Sask.R. 55; 37 W.C.B. (2d) 98 (Sask.Q.B.).

Chapter 8

Peddling the Margins of Gender-Based Violence: Canadian Media Coverage of Honour Killings

Mythili Rajiva and Amar Khoday

In Canada, men and women are equal under the law. Canada's openness and generosity do not extend to barbaric cultural practices that tolerate spousal abuse, "honour killings", female genital mutilation, forced marriage or other gender-based violence. Those guilty of these crimes are severely punished under Canada's criminal laws.
—Citizenship and Immigration Canada Study Guide[1]

In 2004, at least 200,000 Canadian women were physically assaulted and 106,000 were sexually assaulted by intimate partners; 460,000 sexual assaults were committed by other men ... sixty four women were murdered by intimate partners in 2008 ... approximately 100,000 women and children are admitted to emergency shelters each year.
—Johnson & Dawson, 2011

Introduction

In this chapter, we argue that the Canadian mainstream media's portrayal of honour killing draws upon racist and colonial imagery to demonize South Asian and/or Muslim cultures and masculinities. The construction of honour killing as endemic to certain cultures draws on a familiar binary of the uncivilized East in comparison to the civilized West. Additionally, in a post-9/11 era and through what Razack identifies as the new "racial fault lines" being drawn (2005: 345), media representations reinforce public perceptions around certain immigrant communities as inassimilable. This, in turn, affects laws and policies concerning Canadian immigration. The current obsession with honour killing displayed by the media, government, and the general population also deliberately obfuscates the grim reality of the gender-based violence that is perpetrated across all sections of Canadian society. Violence against women is problematically constructed as a problem found only in racialized communities rather than one that is also located in White Canadian culture.

We use a synthesis of theoretical approaches to analyze the "mediatization" (Kilty & Fabian, 2010: 125) of recent honour killings in Canada. We draw upon Foucauldian analysis in combination with feminist post-colonial theory to examine how the Canadian media, through its representations of honour killings, labours to produce particular kinds of "unnational subjects" (Smith & Watson, cited in Protschky, 2009: 370). Methodologically, we use discourse analysis to analyze over 40 mainstream news items on Canadian honour killings. We employ a close reading of these texts, identifying the consistent use of overarching themes or frames, words, phrases, tropes, and imagery to construct honour killings.

We begin by examining how the Canadian media's racialized "crime narratives" (Mopas & Moore, 2011) construct certain communities as permanently outside the national imaginary by focusing on the killers' and their accomplices' perceived cultural barbarity. This media pathologizing of South Asian and/or Muslim masculinity exemplifies how the production of legal normativity by non-state actors helps to shape public perception in ways that indirectly impact law and policy on this issue (Khoday, 2010). We then proceed to argue that expelling the problem of gender-based violence onto the bodies/cultures of the Other works to legitimize violence against women through what Ahmetbeyzade (2008), via Foucault, Agamben, and Mbembe, describes as necropolitics. Ahmetbeyzade (2008) argues that, in Turkey, the state's juridico-political interests work in tandem with tribal authority to establish a state of exception: Kurdish honour killings, which are not prosecuted under Turkish law, function as a spectacle that controls women by exposing subjects to the terror of death. We take up Ahmetbeyzade's argument to suggest that, in Canada, the state and media's construction of honour killing as a state of exception—that is, outside Canadian gender norms and laws—implicitly reinforces violence against all Canadian women. Honour killing becomes the only legitimate spectacle of gender-based violence, the only crime against women that can be condemned publicly, because it is "alien" to Canadian culture. There is, therefore, a refusal to explicitly locate honour killing in the broader context of "Canadian" men's ongoing capacity for gender-based violence, as evidenced by recent Statistics Canada reports on violence against women.[2] We contend that the disappearing of these statistics through the media's repeated focus on the so-called "wave" of honour killings (there is some confusion around the exact number, but several media accounts report approximately 12 cases between 1999 and 2012)[3] represents a form of necropolitical governance. Given that close to half of all Canadian women have experienced or will experience some form of gender-based violence at some point in their lives,[4] participating in the widespread indignation over "barbaric" immigrant customs enrols them in a spectacle of death that denies their own reality as potential victims of violence.

Framework of Analysis

Our analysis synthesizes a number of different but complementary theoretical frameworks. We draw upon a Foucauldian approach, where the state's regulation of populations within a given territory, what Foucault calls biopower, is partly shaped through juridico-legal mechanisms, and the construction of particular subsets of the population as posing greater risks than others to the security of the overall population (Welch, 2008). Furthermore, within the disciplinary regimes of modern Western societies, how law, order and justice are framed in mass communication becomes of central importance in the dissemination of what Mopas and Moore (2011: 11) call "crime narratives." Along the same lines, Khoday (2010), drawing on legal pluralist scholarship, argues that non-state civil society actors, including producers of popular culture, are norm-generative, norm-interpreting, and norm-enforcing beings. As an extension of this, journalists, editors, and media corporations (as components of civil society) significantly contribute to the shaping of policy and attitudes toward both the suspected perpetrators and victims of honour crimes. Media actors decide which crime narratives, victims, and perpetrators receive the public's attention, and which then hold the potential to direct where the formal legal system of the state ought to focus its energies.

Given the sensitive nature of the topic and its relevance to larger questions of violence against women, we also explicitly locate ourselves in a feminist post-colonial framework. The work of critiquing ongoing forms of gender inequality must coalesce with a critical eye toward the neo-colonial motives underlying yet another project, in an ongoing history of what Spivak (1988: 92) has so eloquently identified as "white men saving brown women from brown men." More recently, Mutua (2001) argues that international human rights discourse is substantially governed by an implied belief that Western governments and international non-governmental organizations must act as saviours to Other women, who need to be rescued from the savage men and "barbaric" cultures from which they emerge. But with such women no longer abroad but "here," we are seeing the domestication of the savage-victim-saviour paradigm and the eradication of space that separates the savages from the civilized. In the honour killing paradigm in Canada, the savages and victims are no longer living abroad but are now in "our" midst and, thus, infecting the national character with their "backward traditions."

Our position in this chapter should in no way be interpreted as an attempt to rationalize honour crimes. As citizens and scholars concerned with social justice, we are opposed to the continued oppression of women through culturally based notions of family and community honour, and we stand firmly on the side of the many women's groups in different countries fighting to eradicate this specific form of violence. As insiders to diasporic South Asian and/or Muslim communities, we have both written against patriarchal violence and oppression in these contexts (see Khoday, 2005; Rajiva, 2010). However, as minority scholars, we also have to question what amounts to a full-blown obsession in contemporary Western societies with so-called honour killings, particularly in the context of a worldwide epidemic of violence against women that does not confine itself to certain regions, religions, classes, or cultures.

In the Canadian context, we are highly skeptical of the taking up of feminist discourses by such unlikely allies as the mainstream media, the Conservative Harper government currently in power, and the Canadian public. The outraged protests emanating from these quarters do not, with a few exceptions (see Caplan, 2010; Muise, 2010), extend beyond the issue of honour killings to the larger problem of gender-based violence in Canadian society. The conspicuous absence of a sustained discussion on violence against Canadian women, coupled with a fervent desire to liberate young ethnicized women from their supposedly tyrannical and even murderous cultures, suggests White feminist missionary work that is undergirded by Western neo-imperial interests in certain regions of the world. As Meetoo and Mirza (2007: 188), writing in the context of the United Kingdom, pointedly ask, "Why has the issue of violence to young, ethnicised women been selected for attention now, at this time?" They go on to argue that since September 11, 2001, these women have become highly visible in Western media, but they are problematically constructed within discourses of fear and risk around the "Muslim alien Other" (188). Following Meetoo and Mirza, we attempt to answer two questions in this paper: Why honour killings? And why now?

Methodology

We use discourse analysis as a method of investigating the media's role in the construction of honour killings and the potential impact of these crime narratives on public opinion, public policy, and even law. Discourse analysis requires an examination of text(s), the larger social, political, and cultural context in which they emerge and are given meaning, as well as how they, in turn, shape these contexts. With regards to media texts, Butler (2010: 5) argues that the mainstream media draws on particular discourses to frame their stories, and these "frames of recognition" shape the "parameters of reality itself—including what can be seen and what can be heard" (xi). According to Butler, these interpretive frames structure how we respond to certain events, whether or not we grieve for victims or even define them as victims, and how we come to understand ourselves within particular political and national contexts.

The media texts that we chose to analyze were taken from Google searches, where we typed in the phrase "honour killings in Canada" and were given a list of 549,000 results. Out of this enormous list, we randomly chose approximately 40 articles, the bulk of which were recent and had been published by the following mainstream media outlets in Canada: *The Montreal Gazette; The Globe and Mail*; CTV news; *Le Devoir*; Radio-Canada; *Maclean's; National Post*; CanWest News Service; *The Vancouver Sun; Toronto Sun; Toronto Star; The Calgary Herald*; Canada.com; Global News; *Winnipeg Sun, The Chronicle Herald* (Halifax), and *The Province* (Vancouver). In addition, we selectively added a handful of news stories accessed from North American, European, and Australian media outlets, which we draw upon to convey the transnational nature of the current media discourse on honour killing.

We analyze the words, phrases, photographs, and images used in various articles written on Canadian honour killings to illustrate that there are consistent and instantly recognizable media frames around the issue. We move on to examine how this framing works to produce racialized and culturalized understandings of what Mopas and Moore (2011: 8) call the dichotomy between "the law abiding community and the criminal outlaw." In this case, the dichotomy takes the form of contrasting the barbarism and savagery of non-Western cultures and masculinities with the civilized, non-patriarchal, non-violent West and Western masculinity, a juxtaposition that has an indirect but not insignificant impact on public perception, public policy, and law.

Shaping and Transmitting Legal Normativity: The Power of the Mainstream Media

The representation of racialized minorities in mainstream Canadian media discourses has, for a long time, been dominated by Eurocentric and even blatantly racist stereotypes. Scholars such as Ralston (1999) and Indra (1979) have documented the history of media representations dating back to the early 1900s, and the construction of Asian workers as a danger to the building of a White Canadian nation. In more contemporary times, Jiwani (2006), Chan and Mirchandani (2002), and others have argued that the mainstream media plays a crucial role in constructing certain communities as permanently outside the national imaginary by drawing upon images of non-European and thus non-White minorities and immigrants as criminal, barbaric, and dangerous. However, what is at stake in these racialized media narratives is more than just the racialized imagery that plays into the general public's fears or biases concerning immigrant populations. There is also a crucial link between media texts and the realms of politics, policy, and law-making. Far from being simply a neutral source of information or even a popular source of misinformation to the general public, the media plays a central role in the governing and disciplining of populations in advanced liberal democracies.

According to Foucault, an understanding of modern governance must recognize that power extends beyond just that of the state (2007: 108–109). Legal pluralists have long argued that human society is governed by norms that are not only created by the state but by civil society and its constituent members (see Jutras, 2001). Flowing from this recognition of the multiplicity of sometimes competing legal orders operating within various social fields, Kleinhans and Macdonald (1997) contend that a greater emphasis should be placed on examining the role of individuals in creating and interpreting law, rather than their being seen simply as objects on which laws are imposed. Kleinhans and Macdonald (1997: 38) argue that legal subjects "possess a transformative capacity that enables them to produce legal knowledge and to fashion the very structures of law that contribute to constituting their legal subjectivity." (Therefore, a critical legal pluralism "focuses upon the citizen-subjects of these hypothesized orders, and calls attention to the role of these subjects in generating normativity" (38). We argue that this includes individuals working in media outlets and corporate bodies.

Along these lines, Bandes (2004: 585) and Beale (2006: 476) both argue that media actors not only transmit but also create norms. Bandes (2004: 585) articulates that civil society constructs and interprets notions of law and justice based on what people know or think they know. Because most people do not have direct contact with the criminal justice system, Bandes asserts that people's beliefs about what they know are largely rooted in media coverage (585). The media's consistent highlighting of crimes and particularly violent crime thus creates the skewed impression that crime is more rampant than it may actually be (401, 421–440). This creates the normative expectation that these issues must be dealt with politically and places politicians in a space where they must address the "problem" of crime (471–476). For example, honour killings in South Asian/Muslim communities represent a relatively small proportion of gender-based violence against women in Canadian society, yet they occupy a great deal of media air time (on radio, television, and in newsprint and Web journalism), in part, because violence and killing sells. Furthermore, the trope of the vulnerable women being violently suppressed by their savage fathers or kin satisfies a need to quash the barbarians in "our" midst while feeling a sense of accomplishment in having rendered justice to the fallen.

While members of civil society, government, and the justice system are influenced by many sources, media institutions are particularly powerful ones. There is more than a tenuous connection between media representations, policy, and law-making, whereby the media construction of certain groups as outside the Canadian national imaginary not only impacts on public views toward these groups but is implicated in trends in both immigration policy and law. In the case of honour killings, we see this relationship play out very specifically through media messages that both draw on and are used by government and law officials and lawmakers:

> "Cultural differences that may in fact be crimes will be prosecuted," said Public Safety Minister Vic Toews. "I'm very pleased that the jury was able to come to a conclusion and that Canadian law was applied I think in a very fair and even-handed manner and the law is upheld.[5]
>
> Prime Minister Stephen Harper deliver[ed] a speech in Montreal, Friday, March 16, 2012, to announce support by the Canadian government to address family violence and violence against women. [He] recalled the Shafia killings ... called honour crimes "barbaric" and "heinous" before promising nearly $350,000 to help fund a program led by The Shield of Athena Family Services to prevent these practices in the city. "Recently, the tragedy of the Shafia girls touched Canadians profoundly," Harper said in a speech at a community centre.[6]
>
> Canadian courts have done their part to render justice for the victims and to voice society's outrage. Justice Robert Maranger was withering in his contempt as he handed down mandatory life sentences on Mohammad Shafia, his wife Tooba ... and their son Hamed on Sunday in the first-degree murders. "The four completely innocent victims offended your twisted concept of honour," he said, "a notion of honour that is founded upon the domination and control of women, a sick notion of honour that has absolutely no place in any civilized society.[7]

Through these quotes on the recent Shafia case, we witness the intersecting positions of the individuals making these statements. The statements made by the prime minister, his public safety minister, and the judge presiding in the case identify a series of normative tropes used to make sense of honour killings: "rational" and civilized Canadian law is administered to individuals perpetrating "sick," "barbaric," "heinous," and "uncivilized" crimes. Money is allocated to prevent "these practices," but it is not clear that these monies may be used to respond to violence against women more generally. And, finally, justice is said to be dispensed with "withering" scorn toward such twisted notions of honour that have no place in a "civilized" world. Ultimately, members of the media, government, and judiciary seem to be working from a similar script vis-à-vis the issue of honour crimes. Media actors both project their sense of what is proper normative behaviour and whom should be targeted with punitive action, while also reproducing statements of government actors that take action in support of this position. The Canadian government is directed to a precise "cultural" problem, and the justice system successfully prosecutes, with the court condemning the individuals that are successfully constructed as barbaric criminals.

"An Ancient, Twisted Code": Gender-Based Violence as a Problem of the Barbaric Other

While racialized groups are represented differently in contemporary Canadian media, the post-9/11 era has seen a striking consistency in the portrayal of Muslims (either those from the Middle East, South Asia, or Africa) as backward, terrorists, and violently patriarchal, with the latter claim established through a Western obsession with what has come to be known as honour killing. In most Western countries, honour killing is defined as the premeditated murder of a woman by her male kin for supposedly having brought shame upon her family and community through either consensual or non-consensual sexual activity (Ahmetbeyzade, 2008: 188–189). Women's bodies are seen to be the property of their male kin and/or husbands, and their sexual agency is subsequently heavily policed. Meetoo and Mirza (2007: 187) contend that the burden of shame always rests on the woman so that, even in cases of rape or incest, a girl or woman is held responsible rather than the perpetrator.[8]

Again, it is not our intention to deny the reality of honour killings or to minimize their horror, but the fact remains that violence against women, of which the extreme is femicide (the systemic and/or systematic killing of females), is prevalent in all cultures and societies. Moreover, and short of a genuine act of self-defence or defence of others, can one reasonably call any act of gender-based violence "civilized"? Simply honing in on the most sensational instantiations of gender-based violence in any given culture or community will not efface its less sensational and more common incarnations—much of which represent the vast majority of violence against women. So why, at this moment in time, is there such an intense Western preoccupation with honour killing? Brown (2008: 132) suggests that in a penal state, law and order serve the public through the manipulation of "social anxieties," which are "loosely directed at an enemy ... perceived to be 'lurking everywhere' but subtly diffused into the control of a few, defined by race and class." In the specific case of honour killing, the Canadian media's manipulation of social anxieties over immigration with respect to uncivilized Others occurs through frames, images, words, and storylines that display a remarkable consistency across news items. These frames can be broken down roughly into three categories: (1) the amorphous but ubiquitous cultural Other who is polluting the West by introducing backward practices and whose growth as a migrant population must be severely curtailed or removed; (2) the barbaric masculinity and violent patriarchy characteristic of this amorphous cultural Other, which is a threat to the pro-feminist, gender parity of modern Western societies;

and (3) the young, beautiful victims of this violent patriarchy, whose deaths sanction a neo-colonial rescue project.

The Indistinguishable Brown Other

In mainstream Canadian media descriptions of honour killings, there is a collapsed distinction between ethnicized, religious, and racialized populations; South Asian communities (from India, Pakistan, Sri Lanka, and Bangladesh, or their descendants who arrived via former African colonies) are sometimes identified as maintaining this practice but, at other times, honour killing is located more generally as a problem of Muslim populations (a religious rather than an ethnic or racial category). Alternately, honour killing is identified with Middle Eastern populations, without distinction between Christian and Muslim populations or the different countries from which migrant communities come. The overarching frame, then, elides important distinctions between any of these "imagined communities" and groups them under one rubric, that of the non-Western, non-European Other. In descriptions from prominent news sources, the words "culture," "community," "Arab," "South Asian," "Muslim," and "immigrant" all seem to tell the same story—regardless of the specific religious, ethnicized, racialized communities described as being "home" to this particular tradition. The following news quotes demonstrate this point:

> Dr. Muhammad explains the term ["honour killing"] dates back to [an] old medieval Arab tradition of burying daughters alive.... Dr. Muhammad cites honour crime cases involving Sikh and Hindu families and says the issue is not specific to the Muslim religion.[9]

> Les statistiques montrent que la majorité de ces crimes ont lieu de ces pays musulmans.[10]

> All of the killers were immigrants ... most of the perpetrators were men, usually of Muslim or Sikh background and the average victim was 21 years old.[11]

> Is there a risk that future murder cases involving Afghan, Middle Eastern or South Asian people could be tried as honour killings, even when that is not the case?[12]

In the above excerpts, it is impossible to glean a clear-cut understanding of who this problematic population is and whether or not the problem of honour killing can be traced back to any specific culture, religion, or race. Everyone who belongs to a vague and constantly shifting frame of the barbaric Other is equally guilty. The interpretive frame used in these excerpts from diverse Canadian news sources seems to be one that draws upon a homogenized understanding of what, following Bhabha (1994), we might describe as the "third space" of racialization. If "Blackness" and indigeneity are the original menacing counterparts to "Whiteness" in a traditional Euro-American binary (with racialized Others occupying various points along a continuum at different historical points), then, post-9/11, something seems to be emerging as a new counterpoint. It is an indistinguishable but threatening "brownness," mobile in its menace, that can cut across several continents (South Asia, Africa, the Middle East), and is thus everywhere and, at all times, a danger. Identified variously as Muslim, terrorist, Hindu, Sikh, and (hyper)patriarchal, those gathered under its banner occupy a fluid identity space in this discourse, where they serve as arbitrary markers of a confused, but ultimately unsalvageable, racial difference.

The positioning of this amorphous Other also takes the form of using specific images and words to describe/construct the culture(s) predisposed toward honour killing, cultures that are represented as being the antithesis of Western liberal democracies. The use of these images and words draws upon a classic developmental narrative where "the West" is seen to be the apex of civilization and these other cultures are located in the stone age; what Razack describes as "a global script in which white nations view themselves as assisting the third world into modernity" (2005: 345). Below are some examples of mainstream Canadian reporting on the recent Shafia case that use this frame:

> Pakistan, where the Shafias fled in 1992 and lived for four years is to honour killing what Las Vegas is to gambling or Mecca to Islam—the holiest shrine.[13]

> More prevalent in the Muslim world, it's a phenomenon many parents here can't even begin to comprehend.... [I]n the West, it's increasingly popping up in courtrooms as first-generation Muslims struggle to balance the strict old-world ways of their parents with a desire to fit into a more liberal society.[14]

> Fundamentalist Christians and Jews do not kill their daughters who disappoint them; they may shun or abandon them, but they do not generally assault them—rather it is a problem in cultures, with more than one religion espousing the same codes, from very specific areas ... as a non-fatalist culture, we just don't get it.[15]

> It is a tragedy, a horror, a crime against humanity. The details ... are as barbaric as they are shameful ... to the "West", as we like to call it, where immigrant families have sometimes brought amid their baggage the cruel traditions of their home villages.[16]

Through words such as "barbaric," "old world," and "fatalist," the media draws readers' attention to the ways that certain communities—always non-European, mostly racialized—continue to lag behind in the great progress of world civilization and must, once again, be schooled by Western nations in how to become more humane and thus fully human.

The Construction of Barbaric Masculinity

Violence against women continues to be largely perpetrated by men, or by women in furtherance of the dictates or desires of certain men. As Gerald Caplan observes, in Ontario, between 2002 and 2007, 212 women were killed by their partners, and furthermore such "domestic homicides" barely receive mention, maybe because "there's just too many of them to be newsworthy."[17] It is the violence perpetrated in the name of family (read patriarchal) honour that captures our rapt attention, as well as societal scorn and disgust. As with female genital mutilation or dowry burnings, the sharp focus on honour killing serves to stigmatize non-Western masculinity as barbaric:

> "This is a real issue," said Tarek Fatah, founder of the Muslim Canadian Congress, a non-profit advocacy group. "Honour killing is the logical extreme of the belief that suggests that men are the guardians," he said.[18]
>
> The Afghan understanding of a father's place reinforced Shafia's lust for control over his family, he said. "The word father, in Afghanistan, that means he has to control everything."[19]
>
> Shahrzad Mojab, an expert in honour killing, told the Shafia jury that in "traditional, patriarchal families, the chastity, virginity and obedience of girls and women are vital to the maintenance of family honour. If a woman dresses immodestly or consorts with other men, or is believed to have done those things, she may be perceived to have shamed the patriarch and may be marked for death."[20]

South Asian/Muslim masculinity is painted in broad strokes as patriarchal and barbaric, and a patriarchal crime committed on the basis of honour is somehow deemed worse than all other motives that fuel violence against women. Meanwhile, ongoing domestic violence committed against White women by White men in Canadian society is not culturally attributed to villainy perpetrated by all White men as agents of mainstream Canadian or Western culture but is, instead, dismissed as "a private affair between intimate partners."[21] The masculinity of White men is, therefore, not constructed in monolithic terms as savage or as absolutely villainous, nor are Canadian men forced to carry the cross for the sins of Paul Bernardo or other notorious male perpetrators of femicide.

Honour is, thus, constructed as a deep-seated cultural malaise when it emerges from the Global South. In the case of Mohammed Shafia, the convicted patriarch found criminally responsible of the murders of his three teenage daughters and first wife, honour is portrayed as his all-consuming motivation. In one of the wiretapped conversations recorded between Shafia and his co-accused (his wife and son), he is heard saying, "Be I dead or alive, nothing in the world is above your honour."[22] To be sure, Shafia fit the role of the murderous, repugnant, and unreconstructed patriarch from "over there" extremely well. In the wiretapped conversations, Shafia characterized his daughters as "prostitutes," "whores," and "honourless" girls and expressed delight in their demise. Shafia epitomizes all that is grotesque about the caricatures many hold about the non-Western "ethnic villain" (Rajiva, 2010: 221).

As cruel and despicable as Shafia's actions and words were, violence against women for reasons of masculine honour did not originate from, and has not been the monopoly of, third-world persons and cultures. Common law jurisdictions in the West, including Canada, have long recognized, however questionably, the inability of men to control their rage brought on by a sudden trigger assaulting their sense of honour. This recognition found voice in the partial defence of provocation that reduces a murder conviction to manslaughter as a result of the perpetrator's "heat of passion" at the time that the killing took place. Provocation was constructed to respond to circumstances where male honour was challenged in some significant fashion such that it was impossible for the accused to control his actions, including but not limited to instances where a man suddenly became witness to his wife in an act of adultery with another man (Carline, 2011: 82).

There is a rich literature discussing the applicability of cultural norms and values in the context of criminal litigation and whether they should serve as part of criminal defences like provocation (see, e.g., Renteln, 2005; Van Broeck, 2001). There are concerns and divergent perspectives about the inclusion of cultural values in the context of criminal litigation concerning immigrant men committing honour crimes against their female kin for perceived lapses that threaten family honour (see *R. v. Nahar*, 2004; *R. v. Humaid*, 2006). Macklin suggests that the cultural defence discourse that haunts honour killing cases in Canada and the critiques of this defence by right-wing and mainstream media and public figures constructs the Canadian legal system as neutral when, in fact, the provocation defence also relies implicitly on a cultural understanding of the acceptable loss of control for a heterosexual man that results in murder because of a partner's infidelity:

> I am not the first to criticize this existing application of the provocation defence as implicitly sanctioning violence against women … in respect of the cultural defence, I contend that the question "should the law recognize a cultural defence?" is the wrong question. What we should be asking is why law privileges one particular cultural defence above all others. (Macklin, 2002: 96–97)

We are not suggesting that honour killing by South Asian/Muslim men should now be eligible for the provocation defence in an effort to achieve some notion of racial equality among those committing femicide. Indeed, we would argue that defences that legitimate or provide succour to the murderers of women regardless of community (from either mainstream or visible minorities) should be re-examined and perhaps abolished altogether. But if, as Carline (2011: 90) observes, "the law and the provocation defence is a cultural phenomenon which has continually mitigated Western forms of honour killing," it is only the non-European Other who remains the savage (as does his culture) (Mutua, 2001). His White male counterpart may be individually castigated but the society and culture to which he belongs, or is identified with, is not taken down with him.

Operation Save Brown Girl

Kapur observes that women in the Global South are typecast as victims shorn of any agency or other agentive identity (Kapur, 2001). She observes that the "'Third World victim subject has come to represent the more victimised subject, that is, the real or authentic victim subject" (2001: 85). Furthermore, Kapur (2001: 89) posits that "[the] image we are left with is that of a truncated third world woman, who is sexually constrained, tradition bound, incarcerated in the home, illiterate, poor and victimized." In a similar fashion, we have witnessed the rise of a homegrown rescue mission: no longer only "over there," these girls and young women must be rescued from their backward immigrant families, communities, and cultures. Moreover, what Jiwani (2006) has called the "death by culture" discourse occurs through a familiar colonial optic, whereby the feminine Other is constructed as an object of salvation in a rescue storyline that masks a more libidinal investment. This occurs in two ways. First, images and words are used to render these girls and women as courageous but, ultimately, helpless females who should have been rescued from the ethnic villainy of their fathers and brothers—presumably by white knights in the guise of Canadian men, Canadian social services, or the Canadian state. This racialized dynamic is interwoven with a misogynist perception, where the rescue mission is implicitly justified because of the women's youth and beauty, leading us to wonder how attentive the media would be if it were middle-aged or elderly women being murdered by their families:

> It's the next step toward possible justice in the sensational murder, the news of which was first broken by the Vancouver *Province* less than two weeks after the gruesome killing in 2000 of the young and beautiful Jassi Sidhu and the near-fatal beating of the devoted man she loved.[23]

> His [Shafia's] daughters died because they were defiant and beautiful and had dreams of their own. Because they were considered property, not people.[24]

> Outside court, Crown Attorney Gerard Larhuis said the verdict is a reflection of Canadian values that he hopes will resonate. "This jury found that four strong, vivacious and freedom-loving women were murdered by their own family in the most troubling of circumstances."[25]

In the above excerpts, the girls' and young women's desire for freedom to be liberal Western subjects also contains a subtext that tells readers/viewers that what they really desired is the freedom to be sexual subjects, a subtext that has its roots in colonial narratives of the licentious Other woman who invites sexual subjugation by White, imperial masculinity. Moreover, media adjectives such as "stylish," "vivacious beauty," and "freedom loving" are often coupled with images of the girls and women that confront us with a certain heteronormative aesthetic frame.[26] Unlike other prominent cases of murder (such as that of Reena Virk), where racialized Others are presented as the very antithesis of sexually desirable (Kilty & Fabian, 2010: 141–143), these images tell a different story, a story of eroticized female Otherness.

There is a second, more disturbing way in which the feminine Other is eroticized in some of these new stories. Farrah Khan, a counsellor in Toronto, has expressed discomfort around the general obsession with the "salacious details" of these cases,[27] an obsession that speaks to what Young describes as "an ambivalent driving desire at the heart of racism, a compulsive libidinal attraction disavowed by an equal insistence on repulsion" (Young, cited in Razack, 2005: 355). Underpinning a "pornography of violence" around media representations of honour killings (Meetoo & Mirza, 2007: 194), we find a preoccupation with the sexual underbelly of these crimes. The images evoked by certain phrases suggest an enthrallment with sexually motivated violence, as if both the media and Canadian public are reluctant but excited viewers of a cultural snuff film. The references to polygamy, marriage or sexual relations between cousins (viewed as culturally unacceptable in contemporary Western societies, although not illegal), and even vague nods to patriarchal incestuous desire hint at a fascination with the supposedly bizarre and violent sexuality of the cultural and/or religious Other.

> Mr. Hyderi, 31, who immigrated to Canada in 2000, said the message was clear that Shafia wanted total control over his children.... Shafia did not even want his girls mingling with their male cousins: "He said it was male cousins who opened the door for female cousins to be prostitutes." The first time he met Zainab at a family picnic, she was wearing a hijab and he avoided even shaking hands when he was introduced. "Normally I hug my cousins and kiss them on the cheeks," he said.[28]

> As Shafia once howled to Yahya, in what they imagined was the privacy of their minivan just days after their household had been almost halved: "Every night I used to think of myself as a cuckold. Every day I used to go and gather (her) from the arms of boys." If the question was downright creepy—why on earth would any father ever feel like a cuckold?—the answer was far worse: Because, of course, that father believed he was the one who had absolute control of his daughters' sexuality.[29]

The murdered women in these descriptions function as tropes of forbidden desire, and there is something almost romanticized about the language used in the above excerpts (references to hugging and kissing; being held in boys' arms). Furthermore, if, as Razack (2005: 345) argues, "it is through the sexual that racial power is violently articulated," what these narratives hint at is not simply the desire to have the eroticized Other but a violent envy toward the masculine Other who maintains the authority to control the female bodies of his kin so completely.

> Abdul Ghafoor walked into his daughter's Scarborough apartment on July 22 to visit her and his grandson. What he saw haunts him: his 21-year-old daughter lying on the bed, her neck at an odd angle, her hair tousled. She was dead.[30]

> Zainab was openly challenging her father's "traditional" authority. She was stylish, loved makeup and fashionable clothes, and shunned the hijab.... Describing his eldest child as a "whore" and a "prostitute," Shafia

> asked Jawid to invite the girl to Sweden and plan a barbecue or a beach vacation, something near water. Once there, he said, Shafia would join them—and throw Zainab in.[31]

> The police diver ... found Zainab Shafia in the front passenger seat ... her fingernails painted a light shade of blue.... Her black cardigan, drenched after hours underwater, was on backwards. Sahar, her younger sister, was ... dressed in a pair of tight jeans and a sleeveless top. Her belly button was pierced (a stud with twin stones).... Like Sahar—the big sister she idolized—Geeti had a navel ring underneath her brown shirt.... Only a mass execution (staged to look like a foolish wrong turn) could wash away the stain of their secret boyfriends and revealing clothes.[32]

As with the previous excerpts, there is a sexualized undertone to the above descriptions, a kind of discursive necrophilia that eroticizes the victims through their violent deaths. The first excerpt describes the murdered woman lying on a bed with tousled hair, her neck at an odd angle, an image very often used in advertising, film, and fiction to convey sexual desire. The second excerpt, which quotes Shafia calling his daughters "whores" and "prostitutes," might parallel biblical ranting about the sexual dangers that women symbolize, but it also conjures the abject and forbidden sexuality that prostitutes represent to heterosexual men and "proper" civilized society. The third quote explicitly describes what the three Shafia daughters were wearing, but the question remains, why do we, as readers, need to know this information? The description of Zainab Shafia's cardigan being on backwards brings to mind clothes being taken off and put back on in a hurry, suggesting some clandestine sexual rendezvous. What are we to make of the descriptions of pierced belly buttons and navel rings with studs, the secret boyfriends, the revealing clothes, or the washing away of these "stains"? All of these phrases seem too sexually suggestive to be written off as journalistic sensationalism. While the writer of the article was obviously trying to make the point that the girls were trying to fit in to the normative cultural practices of White, Western, middle-class girls, the description is filtered through a racialized pornographic gaze that entwines sexuality with violence. As such, all the above descriptions are vaguely chilling because they seem to gesture toward an unspeakable longing: perhaps it is in death that the eroticized Other becomes almost unbearably desirable, as the ultimate signifier of sexual and racial domination.

States of Exception: Honour Killings in Canada

At this point, we seem to have answered the two questions that we raised at the beginning of the paper: Why honour killings? And why now? The post-9/11 climate in Western nations has been consistently Islamophobic, with global political strategies of invading countries in the Middle East under the guise of anti-terrorism coinciding with a suspension of democratic rights for racialized subjects who are suspected of terrorist activities. The mainstream media in countries such as Canada and the US has contributed to this climate of fear and hostility through crime narratives that focus on the dangers that certain immigrant groups are assumed to pose to Western democratic societies. Honour killing, as part of this Islamaphobia, is constructed as a problem of the barbaric Other, and as a warning sign to Western populations of the dangers of welcoming certain groups into our midst. However, without detracting from these obvious reasons for the current political climate, we would speculate that there are other complex forces at work that suggest that the deeper answers to these two questions may actually be found in the domestic gender politics of Western countries. In this final section, we argue that in a similar fashion to historical forms of colonial governance, White Canadian women are enlisted as part of a neo-imperial project that ultimately subordinates both the neo-colonized Other and neo-colonial women themselves.

We locate our argument in Ahmetbeyzade's (2008) evocative piece on Kurdish honour killing in Turkey. Ahmetbeyzade draws upon Foucault, Agamben, and Mbembe to theorize the relationship between violence and the law, where the Turkish state, in creating a state of exception for tribal decisions that sanction honour killing in Kurdish communities, participates in a form of necropolitical governance: Kurdish women are either victims of, or terrified spectators to, the murder of girls and women by their male kin, with no recourse under Turkish law. Ahmetbeyzade (2008: 188) distinguishes between biopower (the sovereign or state control over the lives of its population) and necropolitics: "by necropower and necropolitical techniques I am referring to the capacity of sovereign state and tribal powers to establish exceptions to control life and death and expose subjects to the terror of death." Similarly, Mbembe (2003: 11) describes sovereign power as the power and capacity to dictate who lives and who must die (a contemporary example might be found in the death penalty that is carried out in certain American states, and the supposed deterrent it offers to potential criminals). In the context of Kurdish honour killings in Turkey, the concept of necropolitical governance refers to the state's refusal to act against tribal leaders, thus allowing for a spectacle of death that terrorizes all Kurdish women.

At first glance, it seems incongruous to import Ahmetbeyzade's arguments into an analysis of Canadian honour killings. After all, the Canadian state does not condone such crimes; in fact, the justice system, the media, and the public have all publically condemned these acts. However, a closer look reveals that the mainstream media actually frames honour killing as "exceptional," which creates what Mbembe (2003: 24) describes as "a zone where the violence of the state of exception is deemed to operate in the service of civilization." With respect to the state of exception created by discursive productions of honour killings, we find the justification for revisions to Canadian immigration policy (including handbooks, screening, and other tools of racialized surveillance). Another example includes spending money specifically and even exclusively on organizations that address culturally based violence against girls and women (as opposed to more general shelters and women's groups trying to combat gender-based violence), and the continued vilification of certain cultures and communities. Furthermore, all of these moves occur in a conservative political climate characterized by the state's funding cuts to women's organizations, its refusal to fund groups who "advocate for equality and freedom from violence,"[33] its cancelling of a national child care program supported by a majority of Canadians, its refusal to fund maternal care that deals with abortion, and its removal of the word "equality" from the Status of Women Canada's mandate. Gender equality, therefore, works as a mythology that allows for the policing and criminalizing of minority populations.

> It was, as the shy prosecutor Gerard Laarhuis said outside the lovely old Frontenac courthouse, "a good day for Canadian justice." And so it was: Mohammad Shafia, Tooba Mohammad Yahya, and Hamed Mohammad Shafia ... had just been convicted of four counts each of first degree murder moments earlier. "This verdict sends a very clear message about our Canadian values and the core principles in a free and democratic society that all Canadians enjoy, and even visitors to Canada enjoy," Laarhuis said.[34]

> Justice Minister Rob Nicholson is condemning so-called honour killings.... "This Government is committed to protecting women and other vulnerable persons from all forms of violence and to hold perpetrators accountable for their acts.... We have been clear that, like all murders, this practice is barbaric and unacceptable in Canada." Interim Liberal leader Bob Rae was asked about the verdicts in Vancouver. "It's almost unimaginable to think of what has taken place," he said. "The Canadian justice system has done its job."[35]

> Kenney is the federal minister of immigration. He's released the latest edition of a citizenship guide for new immigrants.... Trudeau is the Liberals' immigration critic. "There's nothing that the word 'barbaric' achieves that the words 'absolutely unacceptable' would not have achieved ... in an official Government of Canada publication, there needs to be a little bit of an attempt at responsible neutrality." Kenney followed up in person,

> first via Twitter. "Liberal cultural relativism is precisely what undermines public support for multiculturalism ... it's wrong and irresponsible."[36]

Mbembe (2003: 16) argues that "power (and not necessarily state power) continuously refers and appeals to exception, emergency, and a fictionalized notion of the enemy. It also labors to produce the same exception, emergency and fictionalized enemy." In all of these quotes, honour killing is presented as a state of exception that requires the Canadian state and its juridical arm, the justice system, to impose harsh penalties on those who transgress the rule of law, which is itself based on a larger, more transcendent law of civilized humanity. But if, as Foucault (2007: 56) argues, there is a fundamental relationship between the law and the norm and every system of law is related to a system of norms, what exactly is the norm being violated in these cases? If the norm is that of gender equality in Canadian society, and the prohibition against committing violence against women, this is a highly contested cultural norm, given its continued violation by Canadian men in statistically significant numbers. It is also a juridically contested norm because, as we mentioned earlier, there is a continued reliance on the provocation defence in Canadian cases concerning spousal homicide. Finally, it is a state contested norm, at least under the current Harper government, which recently cut funding by 38 percent to the Status of Women Canada, an agency that promotes gender equality; the same government also instituted mandate and funding rules that "prohibit women's organizations from engaging in advocacy or lobbying activities,"[37] advocacy that, incidentally, includes combatting violence against women. In light of these many contradictions, it appears as if the cultural, legal, and political norm being violated in honour crimes is not actually violence against women, which is a common enough occurrence in Canadian society. Perhaps honour crimes actually function to maintain the norm of violence against women that operates implicitly in Canadian society by enrolling Canadian women in a spectacle of violence that denies their own vulnerability to gender-based violence and even death.

The spectacle of honour killings thus appears to function in parallel ways to the Turkish context described by Ahmetbeyzade (2008: 188), where the necropolitical techniques of the Turkish state reinforce Kurdish women's existence on the threshold of political life, simultaneously included in and excluded from political rights. Similarly, Canadian women, feminist groups, and the public at large are called upon to perpetuate a myth of Canadian society as one that upholds gender equality and, as such, abhors violence against women in all forms. But this requires an active looking away from the ongoing forms of gender-based violence perpetrated by White Canadian men against White Canadian women; a denial that reinforces the continued political and social subordination of all women in Canadian society:

> Youth protection group Batshaw Youth Services had opened files on the Shafia daughters ... said Madeleine Bernard, director of youth protection for the agency. "This kind of event is so out of our realm of usual youth protection ... because this kind of crime is now coming to our door, we now need to take that into account in our analysis."[38]

> "In Canada, we're a very open and generous country, and we welcome the cultures of new Canadians because it enriches our country, but when it comes to violence against women in Canada, it is not tolerated; honour killings and gender-based violence is not tolerated and it's unacceptable. In Canada, men and women are equal under the law," says [Rona] Ambrose [M.P.].[39]

> Law Professor Marie-Pierre Robert ... suggested a focus on prevention that stresses an education in Canadian values for newcomers. "The culture of equality between men and women must be stressed," said Robert.[40]

All of the above speakers and/or writers are women, some of them prominent, such as Rona Ambrose (a Member of Parliament and Minister for Status of Women Canada), while others work in social services or academia; all style themselves as modern, liberated women and point to how tragic honour crimes are, especially in this progressive country. Again, the underlying point is that the killing of girls and women is antithetical to gender norms in Canadian society. Interestingly, the consideration of honour crimes as domestic violence was raised repeatedly in media reports, only to be dismissed by "experts"—many of whom are insiders to the communities under attack—as being completely dissimilar because of community collusion and premeditation. Macklin (2002) argues that the distinction is false, since murders incited by sexual infidelity often require premeditation as well. Some of these insider experts also openly state that if the victims had been White girls or women, their pleas would have been listened to; instead, Canadian society's confused multicultural tolerance of some forms of violence against women contributed to the conditions whereby these victims were denied the same rights as White females. For example, Tarek Fatah, co-founder of the Muslim Canadian Congress, offers the following purely speculative comment in a newspaper article:

> Fatah says his concern is that Canadian political correctness is getting in the way of a frank discussion of the problem: that some Muslims consider women the possession of men. "If these four women were white women, they would still be alive today," he said. "If a white student would

> go to the principal or the police and say they would be beaten up, no one would go to their parents and say 'can you repeat what you said to us?' These girls went to the school, the cops, child services and everyone wanted to protect multiculturalism."[41]

The above statement reinforces the false notion that, when a White girl or woman reaches out for help, she is taken care of by social services and youth protection agencies because Canadian society is so vigilant about maintaining the safety of its girls and women. In reality, the statistics tell a different and far more chilling story about the frequency of sexual and physical violence against girls and women, and the consistent refusal on the part of Canadian society, the Canadian state, and the Canadian justice system to respond to gender-based violence.

It should be noted that not all media stories are guilty of this framing; as the following articles bravely attempt to point out, violence against women is not the exclusive domain of non-Western cultures, but is rather a pervasive problem across cultural divides. Unfortunately, these "minority" voices remain at the margins of media coverage.

> James Ramage was released from prison last Friday, only eight years following his conviction for strangling and bashing his wife, Julie, to death in their house and burying her in a shallow grave.... The silencing argument that women of the Anglophone "Western Civilisation", or whatever you would like to call it, are completely liberated, done and dusted, and have no business complaining about anything, has continued unabated lately. In such a cultural climate, a few people were rocked on their heels when Phil Cleary and Julie Ramage's sister Jane described her murder as an "honour" killing. But you know what? They're right.... There is a pervasive myth in our "western" society that harsh and primitive crimes of misogyny only happen There, perpetrated by Them, those Others. Therefore, Western feminism is a hobby for genteel and well-off middle class women who enjoy perfect equality in their world. It's false.[42]

> I'm confident that not one in a million is aware that in Ontario alone, from 2002 until only 2007 (the latest data), 212 women have been killed by their partners. That's 42 every year, compared with 12 so-called honour killings in all of Canada in the past eight years.... Why do we know little or nothing about the larger epidemic of women killed, almost routinely it sometimes seems, by boyfriends or husbands? Is it less terrible to be strangled to death or shot or have your throat slit by them than by family members?... [B]oth kinds of murders have a common root.

> Both are honour killings, reflecting a twisted, pathological male sense of honour.... Have we smug white Canadians forgotten that you don't have to be a Muslim or South Asian to regard women this way?[43]

> The Canadian Council of Muslim Women is strongly opposed to the use of the term "honour killing" to describe the murder of women and girls.... For us Canadians to label these murders as "honour killings" is both divisive and dangerous. It makes these murders exotic, foreign, and alien to Western culture as if the West is free from all forms of patriarchy.... It encourages blatant racism for some, as it gives them permission to blame "those people" and demand their ousting from Canada.[44]

The first quote is written by a blogger in the context of an Australian murder, the second is from a Canadian journalist, and the third is from a Muslim Canadian advocacy group, but all three share the same political agenda: the authors are trying desperately to locate honour crimes in a cross-cultural paradigm of femicide, a losing battle in a current Western context of denial and denunciation that cuts across many countries, including Canada, the US, Great Britain, Germany, and Australia. The second writer, Caplan, goes on to ask why, in Canada, a country with so many immigrants, there are not more than 12 murders labelled honour killings over eight (and to date twelve) years, assuming honour crimes are endemic to and supported by these communities. He also suggests that if "the rest of us" so sincerely embrace a culture of gender equality, it seems odd that so many Canadian women are still being murdered. These are pointed questions that have not been addressed, thus far, in the mainstream media discourse on honour killings in Canada. But as the Canadian state continues to withdraw resources for feminist organizations and women's shelters, and mainstream media continues to suggest that feminism is no longer needed in contemporary Western societies, we have to wonder whether, though less obviously than Kurdish women in the Turkish state, White Canadian women are also frozen on the threshold of full political rights, silenced by a media spectacle of honour killing that sends the insidious message: "don't ask for more and don't complain—you could have it much worse."

Conclusion

> On that June night in a lovely place in one of the freest and luckiest nations in the world, at the hands of those who should have most loved and protected her, she [Sahar Shafia] was killed because, well, she was a girl.[45]

In this chapter, we have tried to situate the Canadian media's framing of honour killing in a series of broader and intersecting discourses. Like all forms of femicide and violence against women, honour crimes are despicable acts and must be punished. Yet, the relatively few instances of honour killings in Canada, contrasted with the greater number of Canadian femicides and still larger number of women who (regardless of race, class, sexual orientation, and/or age) experience physical, emotional, and sexual violence every day across the country, suggest a rather disproportionate media emphasis on these crimes. Drawing from Ahmetbeyzade (2008), we have argued that honour killings constitute a state of exception for Canadian media sources and government actors where such cultural and barbaric practices must be targeted and rooted out because they stand outside the purported norms and values of mainstream Canadian society. In addition, borrowing from Mutua's (2001) exegesis on international human rights discourse, we see a well-worn trope of saving (or avenging) victimized women and girls from the barbarism of their male kin, which expresses itself in incoherent rage and violence, culminating in death. The emphasis on honour killings also plays into concurrent anxieties about the growing numbers of visible non-Anglo and/or non-Francophone communities and how this growth leads to a perceived threat to Canadian society.

There is relatively little scholarly work thus far on Canadian honour killing or its treatment by the media. In critically analyzing this phenomenon, we are attempting to hold media actors accountable for their racialized representation of honour killing, and we hope to encourage citizens to see honour crimes as part of a larger epidemic of violence experienced by women across Canada and around the world. In short, we argue that both Canadian media workers and their readers/viewers should consider the larger pattern of violence as emblematic of a culture that is effectively more tolerant of violence against women than is normally believed. This hope, however, runs up against powerful political and cultural forces and media practices that seek to retain, if not increase, their audience by peddling the margins—namely gender-based violence perpetrated in and among racialized communities. White Canadians may then experience a certain satisfaction in expressing moral outrage at these brutal killings, all the while resting content in the belief that violence against women has, in some magical way, been eliminated from Canadian culture. This is a dangerous illusion, which implicitly encourages the perpetuation of that violence through public silence. Despite media-spun fairy tales that employ what Sherene Razack has, in another context, described as the trope of "dark threats and white knights,"[46] the unpleasant reality continues to be that, "in one of the freest and luckiest nations in the world," a significant portion of Canadian women are regularly abused, assaulted, and killed by those who should most love and protect them, for the same underlying reason that honour crimes are committed: because they're, well, women.

Notes

1 Retrieved October 7, 2012, from www.cic.gc.ca./english/pdf/pub/discover.pdf

2 Retrieved October 7, 2012, from www.statcan.gc.ca/pub/85-570-x/85-570-x2006001-eng.htm

3 Caplan, Gerald. (2010, July 23). "Honour killings in Canada: Even worse than we believe." *The Globe and Mail*. Retrieved April 13, 2012, from www.theglobeandmail.com/news/politics/second-reading/gerald/caplan/honour-killings-in-canada-even-worse-than-we-believe. Also see "Canada's latest 'honour killing' case raises troubling questions." (2012, January 30). *Toronto Star*. Retrieved April 13, 2012, from www.thestar.com/printarticle/1123834. Also see Daly, Brian. (2012, January 26). "Honour killings on the rise in Canada: University study shows 12 honour-killing victims in Canada since '99." *Toronto Sun*. Retrieved April 13, 2012, from www.torontosun.com/2012/01/26/honour-killings-on-the-rise-in-canada-study

4 "Fairness for Women." Retrieved October 7, 2011, from www.ndp.ca/fairnessforwomen

5 Tucker, Ericka. (2012, January 30). "Defining honour killings." *Global News*. Retrieved April 13, 2012, from www.globalnews.ca/defining+honour+killings/6442570211/story.html

6 Blatchford, Andy. (2012, March 17). "PM denounces honour killings." *The Chronicle Herald*. Retrieved May 23, 2012, from thechronicleherald.ca/canada174679-pm-denounces-honour-killings

7 "Canada's latest 'honour killing' case raises troubling questions." (2012, January 30). *Toronto Star*. Retrieved April 13, 2012, from www.thestar.com/printarticle/1123834

8 According to Meetoo and Mirza (2007: 187): "The U.N. estimates that 5000 women are being killed each year in the name of 'honour'. Honour killings have been documented in Bangladesh, Brazil, Ecuador, Egypt, India, Israel, Italy, Jordan, Morocco, Pakistan, Sweden, Turkey, Uganda and the U.K."

9 Tucker, Ericka. (2012, January 30). "Defining honour killings." *Global News*. Retrieved April 13, 2012, from www.globalnews.ca/defining+honour+killings/6442570211/story.html

10 "Des actes criminels mal connus." (2011, October 11). *Radio-Canada*. Retrieved October 20, 2011, from www.radio-canada.ca/nouvelles/societe

11 Daly, Brian. (2012, January 26). "Honour killings on the rise in Canada: University study shows 12 honour-killing victims in Canada since '99." *Toronto Sun*. Retrieved April 13, 2012, from www.torontosun.com/2012/01/26/honour-killings-on-the-rise-in-canada-study

12 Hopper, Tristan. (2012, January 30). "What does the Shafia guilty verdict mean for Canada's legal system?" *National Post*. Retrieved April 12, 2012, from nationalpost.com/2012/01/30/what-does-the-shafia-guilty-verdict-mean-for-canadas-legal-system/

13 Blatchford, Christie. (2012, January 29). "No honour in 'cold-blooded, shameless' murder of Shafia girls." *National Post*. Retrieved April 12, 2012, from fullcomment.nationalpost/2012/01/29/jury-reaches-verdict-in-Shafia-trial/

14 Cohen, Tobi. (n.d.). "'Honour killings' on the rise in Canada: Expert." *Vancouver Sun.* Retrieved April 12, 2012, from www.vancouversun.com/story

15 Barbara Kay, quoted in "Full comment forum: Canada and the culture of honour killings." (2010, June 21). *National Post.* Retrieved April 13, 2012, from www.barbarakay.ca/index

16 Fisk, Robert. (2010, September 7). "The crimewave that shames the world." *The Independent.* Retrieved May 23, 2012, from www.independent.co.uk/opinion/commentator/fisk/robert-fisk-the-crimewave-that-shames-the-world

17 Caplan, Gerald. (2010, July 23). "Honour killings in Canada: Even worse than we believe." *The Globe and Mail.* Retrieved April 13, 2012, from www.theglobeandmail.com/news/politics/second-reading/gerald/caplan/honour-killings-in-canada-even-worse-than-we-believe

18 Findlay, Stephanie. (2012, January 30). "Were Shafia murders 'honour killings' or domestic violence?" *Toronto Star.* Retrieved April 12, 2012, from www.thestar.com/news/article/1123403-were shafia-murders-honour-killings-or-domestic-violence

19 Hamilton, Graeme. (2012, January 30). "Mohammad Shafia was so obsessed, so close-minded." *National Post.* Retrieved May 23, 2012, from fullcomment.nationalpost.com/2012/01/30/mohammad-shafia-was-so-obsessed-so-closed-minded

20 Wilton, Katherine. (2012, January 24). "Canadian justice system has the tools to deal with 'honour killings': study." *National Post.* Retrieved April 13, 2012, from www.news.nationalpost.com/2012/01/24/canadian-justice-system-has-the-tools-deal-with-honour-killings-study

21 Barbara Kay, quoted in "Full comment forum: Canada and the culture of honour killings." (2010, June 21). *National Post.* Retrieved April 13, 2012, from www.barbarakay.ca/index

22 Hamilton, Graeme. (2012, January 30). "Mohammad Shafia was so obsessed, so close-minded." *National Post.* Retrieved May 23, 2012, from fullcomment.nationalpost.com/2012/01/30/mohammad-shafia-was-so-obsessed-so-closed-minded

23 Lazaruk, Susan. (2012, January 8). "B.C. woman, brother, arrested in alleged Indian honour killing of Jassi Sidhu." *Postmedia News.* Retrieved April 13, 2012, from www/the province.com/story

24 Frsicolanti, Michael. (2012, February 2). "The Shafia honour killing trial-chapter 1." *Maclean's.* Retrieved April 13, 2012, from www2.macleans.ca/2012/02/03/the-honour-killing-trial-chapter-1

25 Jones, Allison. (2012, January 30). "All 3 guilty in Shafia murder trial: judge condemns twisted concept of honour." *Canadian Press.* Retrieved April 13, 2012, from canews.yahoo.com/shafia-jury-enters-second-full-day-deliberations-kingston-090532874.html

26 See Blatchford, Christie. (2012, January 29). "No honour in 'cold-blooded, shameless' murder of Shafia girls." *National Post.* Retrieved April 12, 2012, from fullcomment.nationalpost/2012/01/29/jury-reaches-verdict-in-Shafia-trial/; see also Lazaruk, Susan. (2012, January 7). "B.C. woman, brother, arrested in alleged Indian honour killing of Jassi

Sidhu." *Postmedia News*. Retrieved April 13, 2012, from www/the province.com/story; and Findlay, Stephanie. (2012, January 30). "Were Shafia murders 'honour killings' or domestic violence?" *Toronto Star*. Retrieved April 12, 2012, from www.thestar.com/news/article/1123403-were shafia-murders-honour-killings-or-domesticviolence

27 Aulakh, Raveena. (2011, August 5). "Domestic violence or honour killing?" *Toronto Star*. Retrieved May 23, 2012, from www.thestar.com/news/article/1035512

28 Hamilton, Graeme. (2012, January 30). "Mohammad Shafia was so obsessed, so close-minded." *National Post*. Retrieved May 23, 2012, from fullcomment.nationalpost.com/2012/01/30/mohammad-shafia-was-so-obsessed-so-closed-minded

29 Blatchford, Christie. (2012, January 29). "No honour in 'cold-blooded, shameless' murder of Shafia girls." *National Post*. Retrieved April 12, 2012, from fullcomment.nationalpost/2012/01/29/jury-reaches-verdict-in-Shafia-trial/

30 Aulakh, Raveena. (2011, August 5). "Domestic violence or honour killing?" *Toronto Star*. Retrieved May 23, 2012, from www.thestar.com/news/article/1035512

31 Friscolanti, Michael. (2011, November 28). "Four funerals and a wedding." *Maclean's*. Retrieved March 26, 2012, from www.2.macleans.ca/2011/11/17/four-funerals-and-a-wedding

32 Friscolanti, Michael. (2012, February 2). "The Shafia honour killing trial-chapter 1." *Maclean's*. Retrieved April 13, 2012, from www2.macleans.ca/2012/02/03/the-honour-killing-trial-chapter-1

33 National Union of Public and General Employees. (2006, October 24). "NUPGE condemns Tory attack on Status of Women Canada." Retrieved April 21, 2012, from www.nupge.ca/print/1527.

34 Blatchford, Christie. (2012, January 29). "No honour in 'cold-blooded, shameless' murder of Shafia girls." *National Post*. Retrieved April 12, 2012, from fullcomment.nationalpost/2012/01/29/jury-reaches-verdict-in-Shafia-trial/

35 Proussalidis, Daniel. (2012, January 29). "Justice minister condemns 'honour killings.'" *Winnipeg Sun*. Retrieved April 13, 2012, from www.winnipegsun.com/2012/01/29/justice-minister-condemns-honour-killings

36 Wells, Paul. (2011, March 28). "Politics: the future: Trudeau vs. Kenney: Head-to-head: Trudeau lost the latest battle with Kenney, but there will be plenty more to come." *Maclean's*. Retrieved March 26, 2012, from www.2macleans.ca/2011/03/18/the-future-trudeau-vs-kenney

37 National Union of Public and General Employees. (2006, October 24). "NUPGE condemns Tory attack on Status of Women Canada." Retrieved April 21, 2012, from www.nupge.ca/print/1527. Also see CTV News Staff. (2010, May 4). "Harper government axes funding for 11 women's groups." *CTV News*. Retrieved May 21, 2012, from www.ctv.ca/servlet/ArticleNews/print/CTVnews/20100504/Harper-womens-funding. Also see Wood, Laura. (2011, January). "Chipping away gender equality: Harper's five year round-up." *Rabble*.

Retrieved May 21, 2012, from rabble.ca/print/news/2011/01/chipping-away-gender-equality-harper's-five-year-round. Also see Jacobs, John. (2006, November 3). "Conservative ideology dressed up in fiscal responsibility." *Canadian Centre for Policy Alternatives*. Retrieved May 21, 2012, from www.policyalternatives.ca/publications/commentary/conservative-ideology-dressed-rhetoric-fiscal-responsibility

38 "Honour killings bear important distinctions: Expert." (2012, January 30). *CTV Montreal*. Retrieved April 13, 2012, from montreal.ctv.ca/servlet/an/plocal/CTVNews/20120130/mtl_honourcrimes_120130/20120130/?hub+montreal.

39 Singh, Renu. (2012, March). "The reality of honour killings in Canada." *Darpan Magazine*. Retrieved April 13, 2012, from www.darpanmagazine.com/2012/03/the-reality-of-honour-killings-in-canada

40 Daly, Brian. (2012, January 26). "Honour killings on the rise in Canada: University study shows 12 honour-killing victims in Canada since '99." *Toronto Sun*. Retrieved April 13, 2012, from www.torontosun.com/2012/01/26/honour-killings-on-the-rise-in-canada-study

41 Tarek Fatah, quoted in Findlay, Stephanie. (2012, January 30). "Were Shafia murders 'honour killings' or domestic violence?" *Toronto Star*. Retrieved April 12, 2012, from www.thestar.com/news/article/1123403-were shafia-murders-honour-killings-or-domestic-violence

42 "Australia's Honour killings—in the end they're just as dead." (2011, July 11). *Hoyden About Town*. Retrieved May 23, 2012, from hoydenabouttown.com/20110711.10242/australias-honour-killings-in-the-end-theyre-just-as-dead

43 Caplan, Gerald. (2010, July 23). "Honour killings in Canada: Even worse than we believe." *The Globe and Mail*. Retrieved April 13, 2012, from www.theglobeandmail.com/news/politics/second-reading/gerald/caplan/honour-killings-in-canada-even-worse-than-we-believe

44 Canadian Council of Muslim Women. (2012, January). "CCMW position on femicide [not honour killing]." Retrieved April 23, 2012, from www.ccmw.com/documents/positionpaper.

45 Blatchford, Christie. (2012, January 29). "No honour in 'cold-blooded, shameless' murder of Shafia girls." *National Post*. Retrieved April 12, 2012, from fullcomment.nationalpost/2012/01/29/jury-reaches-verdict-in-Shafia-trial/

46 See Razack, Sherene. (2004). *Dark Threats, White Knights: The Somali Affair, Peacekeeping, and the New Imperialism*. Toronto: University of Toronto Press.

References

Ahmetbeyzade, C. (2008). "Gendering necropolitics: The juridical-political sociality of honor killings in Turkey." *Journal of Human Rights*, 7: 187–206.

Bandes, S. (2004). "Fear factor: The role of media in covering and shaping the death penalty." *Ohio State Journal of Criminal Law*, 1(2): 585–597.

Beale, S. (2006). "The news media's influence on criminal justice policy: How market-driven news promotes punitiveness." *William and Mary Law Review*, 48(2): 397–481.

Berger, B.L. (2008). "Moral judgment, criminal law and the constitutional protection of religion." *Supreme Court Law Review*, 40 S.C.L.R. (2d): 513–552.

Bhabha, H. (1994). *The Location of Culture*. London: Routledge.

Brown, M. (2008). "Aftermath: Living with the crisis; From PTC to governing through crime." *Crime Media Culture*, 4(1): 131–136.

Butler, J. (2010). *Frames of War: When is Life Grievable?* London and New York: Verso.

Caplan, G. (2010, July 23). "Honour killings in Canada: Even worse than we believe." *The Globe and Mail*. Retrieved from www.theglobeandmail.com/news/politics/second-reading/gerald/caplan/honour-killings-incanada-even-worse-than-we-believe

Carline, A. (2011). "Honour and shame in domestic homicide: A critical analysis of the provocation defence." In M. Idriss & T. Abbas, eds., *Honour, Violence, Women and Islam* (pp. 80–95). New York: Routledge.

Chan, W., & Mirchandani, K., (Eds.) (2002). *Crimes of Colour: Racialization and the Criminal Justice System in Canada*. Peterborough, ON: Broadview Press, Ltd.

Foucault, M. (2007). *Security, Territory, Population: Lectures at the Collège de France 1977–1978*. New York: Palgrave Macmillan.

Indra, D. (1979). "South Asian stereotypes in the Vancouver press." *Ethnic and Racial Studies*, 2: 166–189.

Jiwani, Y. (2006). *Discourses of Denial: Mediations of Race, Gender and Violence*. Vancouver: UBC Press.

Johnson, H., & Dawson, M. (2011). *Violence Against Women in Canada: Research and Policy Perspectives*. Oxford and New York: Oxford University Press.

Jutras, D. (2001). "The legal dimensions of everyday life." *Canadian Journal of Law and Society*, 16(1): 45–65.

Kapur, R. (2001). "Babe politics and the victim subject: Negotiating agency in women's human rights." In D. Barnhizer, ed., *Effective Strategies for Protecting Human Rights* (pp. 85–94). Burlington: Ashgate Dartmouth.

Khoday, A. (2005, March 8). Honour killings hide racist motives. *Toronto Star*, p. A19.

Khoday, A. (2010). "Prime-time saviors: The West Wing and the cultivation of a unilateral American responsibility to protect." *Southern California Interdisciplinary Law Journal*, 19(1): 1–54.

Kilty, J., & Fabian, S. (2010). "Deconstructing an invisible identity: The Reena Virk case." In M. Rajiva & S. Batacharya, eds., *Reena Virk: Critical Perspectives on a Canadian Murder* (pp. 122–155). Toronto: Canadian Scholars' Press.

Kleinhans, M., & Macdonald, R. (1997). "What is a critical legal pluralism?" *Canadian Journal of Law and Society*, 12(2): 25–46.

Macklin, A. (2002). "Looking at law through the lens of culture: A provocative." In W. Chan & K. Mirchandani, eds., *Crimes of Colour: Racialization and the Criminal Justice System in Canada* (pp. 87–99). Peterborough, ON: Broadview Press, Ltd.

Mbembe, A. (2003). "Necropolitics." *Public Culture*, 15(1): 11–45.

Meetoo, V., & Mirza, H.S. (2007). "'There is nothing honourable about honour killings': Gender, violence and the limits of multiculturalism." *Women's Studies International Forum*, 30(3): 187–200.

Mopas, M., & Moore, D. (2011). "Talking heads and bleeding hearts: Newsmaking, emotion and public criminology in the wake of a sexual assault." *Critical Criminology*, online publication, May 11, 1–14.

Muise, M. (2012, January 30). "Shafia verdict prompts debate: Was it an honour killing, or just plain murder?" *The Montreal Gazette*. Retrieved from www.montrealgazette.com/news/Shafia+verdict+prompts+debate+honour+killing+just+plain+murder/6069784/story.html

Mutua, M. (2001). "Savages, victims, and saviors: The metaphor of human rights." *Harvard International Law Review*, 42(1): 201–245.

Protschky, S. (2009). "The flavour of history: Food, family and subjectivity in two Indo-European women's memoirs." *History of the Family*, 14: 369–385.

Rajiva, M. (2010). "In Papaji's house: Representations of the father/daughter relationship in South Asian diasporic cinema." *Feminist Media Studies*, 10(2): 213–228.

Ralston, H. (1999). "Canadian immigration policy in the twentieth century: Its impact on South Asian women." *Canadian Woman Studies*, 19: 33–37.

Razack, S. (2005). "How is white supremacy embodied? Sexualised racial violence at Abu Ghraib." *Canadian Journal of Women and the Law*, 17(2): 341–363.

Renteln, A.D. (2005). "The use and abuse of the cultural defence." *Canadian Journal of Law and Society*, 20(1): 47–67.

Spivak, G.C. (1988). "Can the subaltern speak?" In L. Grossberg & C. Nelson, eds., *Marxism and the Interpretation of Culture* (pp. 271–311). Urbana: University of Illinois Press.

Van Broeck, J. (2001). "Cultural defence and culturally motivated crimes (cultural offences)." *European Journal of Crime, Criminal Law and Criminal Justice*, 9(1): 1–37.

Welch, M. (2008). "Ordering Iraq: Reflections on power, discourse, and neocolonialism." *Critical Criminology*, 16: 257–269.

Legal Cases and Statutes

Criminal Code, R.S.C. 1985, c. C-46, s.232.

R. v. Humaid, (2006) 81 O.R. (3d) 456, 208 C.C.C. (3d) 43.

R. v. Nahar, 2004 BCCA 77, 181 C.C.C. (3d) 449.

Chapter 9

Unwanted Motherhood and the Canadian Law of Infanticide

Kirsten Kramar

Introduction

Passed into Canadian law in 1948, and later amended in 1955, section 233 of the *Criminal Code of Canada* functions as an offence and defence to murder:

> A female person commits infanticide when by a wilful act or omission she causes the death of her newly-born child, if at the time of the act or omission she is not fully recovered from the effects of giving birth to the child and by reason thereof or of the effect of lactation consequent on the birth of the child her mind is then disturbed. R.S., c. C-34, s. 216.

Contemporary Canadian infanticide law, which only applies to the biological mother of a victim in the first year of life, and which offers a kind of mitigation from a possible murder conviction, seems to link women's deviance to reproductive difference and pathology in the most obvious and unequivocal way.

Officially, the infanticide law was adopted in Canada to offer a mitigation framework, such that convictions for a crime other than murder could be achieved through a reduced punishment framework (the maximum penalty for infanticide is now five years' imprisonment). The infanticide law is situated in a range of charges available for maternal neonaticide, which also include "concealment of birth" and "neglecting to obtain assistance in childbirth"; laws that were not removed from the books at the time of its passage. The Canadian provision adopted the earlier English version of infanticide law from 1922 that was passed in England at the height of psychological ambition in law.

The strong psychological language contained in the English version of 1922, adopted by Canadian legislators in 1948, linked lactation and childbirth but was intended to legally recognize that the young, often unmarried pregnant women newly arrived to Canada from Europe faced unique social, economic, and legal challenges at the turn of the twentieth century in Canada (Backhouse, 1984; Kramar, 2005; Osborne, 1987).

By the mid-1950s in Canada, the sorts of cases that came before the courts resulted in the common law expansion of the conceptual framework to include circumstances in which the mother was experiencing mental disturbance associated with what is now termed "postpartum depression." Cases where culpable actions did not rise to the level of mental incapacitation required for an insanity defence, and where older babies rather than newborns were killed, expanded the common law of infanticide to include mild mental disturbance. Historically, the defence recognized exhaustion brought on by breastfeeding and lack of sleep, combined with the real physical hardships associated with poverty and single motherhoods (including widowhood). Also, during that decade in Canada, the infanticide law was amended to include an additional provision whereby it became unnecessary for the Crown to prove the psychological mental element written into the law. This burden of proof was removed because Crown prosecutors continued to experience difficulties with securing convictions for infanticide. Elsewhere, I have argued that this was owing to the fact that judges and juries did not really view the women as being mentally unbalanced (Kramar, 2005; Kramar & Watson, 2008). In fact, they were viewed as acting to preserve their reputations, and to prevent a life of misery for the child in the context of poverty because the law of illegitimacy prevented children of unmarried mothers from acquiring legal status of their own. Children born out of wedlock could not take their father's name nor inherit property. Therefore, the women who killed their newly born children were often viewed as acting with the sort of moral integrity demanded by society at that time.

Taken as a whole, the 1954–55 amendments to the infanticide law brought the Canadian legal framework in line with the expanded English law of 1938 and can be seen as producing a kind of lay-social-psychological hybrid category to address a range of cases where babies are killed by their mothers (Kramar & Watson, 2008). In short, motherhood, both unwanted and otherwise fraught, continues to be provisionally recognized as exculpatory in law. Of course the will to mitigate punishment is also linked to the sociological knowledge claim that it is only women who kill newly born babies for socio-economic and cultural reasons, and that women who exhibit signs of mental distress as a result of postpartum psychosis kill their babies while labouring under the belief that the baby is in some kind of extreme danger. In both circumstances, the killing is usually wilful but not malicious.

Attempts would later be made to claw back the infanticide mitigation framework in the late twentieth and twenty-first centuries by judges and juries who did not want to allow for a reduced punishment when a single mother kills an unwanted baby in the context of postpartum depression, or when attempting to hide their sexual activity for religious or other kinds of socially prescribed moral reasons. This recent development can be linked to women's formal legal equality, the achievement of reproductive freedom, advocacy for the infant-victim on the part of the authorities, and retributive demands for vengeance in the name of the victim-baby on the part of law and order advocates, particularly those working in the Office of the Chief Coroner for Ontario (Kramar, 2006). Today, the infanticide law allows for an interpretation of a "disturbed mind" to include "a range of disturbances caused by the complex interaction of social, economic, psychological, cultural, religious, biological, hormonal and other factors" associated with childbirth and lactation (LEAF, 2010). Had the term "motherhood" been included along with childbirth and lactation, judges and juries might have been better able to find the women guilty because most understood the complexities associated with unwanted pregnancy and motherhood.

Theory and Methodology

This research employs the analytical tools and methodological approach introduced by Michel Foucault known as "governmentality" (Burchell, Gordon, & Miller, 1991; Foucault, 1991a, 1991b) to examine emerging justifications for reforming how infanticide cases are prosecuted. According to Rose, O'Malley, and Valverde (2006: 2, citing Foucault, 1997: 82), for Foucault, "governmentality" is in a "broad sense about the techniques and procedures for directing human behaviour. Government of children, government of souls and consciences, government of a household, of a state, or of oneself." The concept of "governmentality" or "governmental rationalities" refers to the ways of thinking and styles of reasoning that are embodied in particular sets of practices, and provides a framework for critique that brings into focus the analytics of government. The approach allows us to "ask questions about how we govern and the conduct of both the governed and the governors" (Dean, 1999: 28). By employing this "analytic of government" approach to law, I am able to ask questions about how certain governmental practices with respect to killing newborn babies take shape, and how they affect the self-government of individuals and collectives and/or lead to the intensification of power relations. This line of questioning allows us to "become clear on how forms of domination, relations of power and kinds of freedom and autonomy are linked, how such regimes are contested and resisted, and thus how it might be possible to do things differently" (Dean, 1999: 37). Social justice projects (such as those advanced by the various kinds of feminist arguments for empowerment, equality, and freedom, or other kinds of revolutionary or emancipatory programs for social change) can benefit from governmentality studies insofar as those activist programs often advance prescriptive arguments while ignoring the logic and power effects of their own governmental objectives. Feminist research has shown that when progressive or emancipatory rationalities are disciplinary, they often result in the solidification of governmental structures that are difficult to untangle once established. For example, the feminization of the state and the pro-arrest/no-drop criminal justice policies aimed at addressing violence against women and empowering the state apparatus is an example of the solidification of state power. These policies have resulted in the arrest and prosecution of victims of domestic violence who fight back against their abusers, and fail to address the relationship between punishment and the feminist aim of empowering women (Dean, 1999; Snider, 1994; Johnson & McConnell, this volume). Similarly, there is an uneasy alliance between conservatives and certain feminist groups who call for the criminalization of specific kinds of sexually explicit materials. Where these alliances exist, the use of state power in the form of criminalization and punishment is more easily justified and accepted as the best and even sole solution to a social problem (Jochelson & Kramar, 2011a; Hannem & Bruckert, this volume).

Crime control has been viewed through the "governmentality" lens as part of the constellation of changes associated with the decline of the penal-welfare strategies of social democratic governments (Garland, 1997). The prosecutorial project will be examined through this lens to investigate the processes by which various kinds of knowledge about infanticide are subjugated, the rights of women to access a diminished capacity framework are problematized on the grounds of formal legal equality, and particular practices of power are enhanced by the subordination of the feminist sociological and psychological discourse(s). This chapter is, then, located in the post-critical criminology literature informed by the work of Foucault (e.g., 1979, 1991a, 2003), extended by Dean (1997, 1999), and applied in a variety of substantive areas. Foucault's neologism "governmentality" refers to the calculated means used to think about the "conduct of conduct" and to dispose of things in the right manner (Dean, 1999; Foucault, 1979, 1991b). By focusing on the tactics used by government to respond to problems, we bring into focus the utopian aims of government in their quest for a better way of doing things, which presupposes a particular outcome or end result. The objective is to think about the way we govern and are governed by making explicit the forms of rationality that underpin practices of government, and to remove the taken-for-granted character of any form of "government" that seeks to achieve particular social or political objectives. Most importantly, the governmentality approach enables us to consider how the effects of particular sets of prescriptive arguments (such as those offered by various feminist emancipatory discourses) produce contradictory, often unintended, consequences with particular kinds of regulatory effects. This approach is particularly useful for considering the ramifications of adopting arguments or concepts such as emancipation, equality, victims' rights, or reproductive freedom and rights to advance particular regimes of governing. In relation to the prosecution of women for killing their newly born babies, it will be useful to understand how equality and reproductive rights discourses may result in enhanced law-and-order approaches to punishment that contradict the rationalities that underpin the aims of these emancipatory discourses.

The relational aspect of governmentality, where "[g]overnance ... is not about individuals in positions of power who exert direct, sovereign, and coercive control over territory but rather how it is that norms of a population are unconsciously produced and reproduced by citizen-subjects, thereby making governance at a distance possible" (Ettlinger, 2011: 538), brings into sharper focus the manner in which techniques of governance materialize as techniques of power and mentalities of the self. The research proposed here investigates both the production of expert forms of knowledge and the manner in which that knowledge is used in various contexts by different legal agents to produce legal norms that inform the right manner for disposing of infanticide cases. The legal norms within these discourses generate a conceptualization of the plights of "woman" that spark feminist rejection and demand for recognition of motherhood and reproductive difference. These historically contingent feminist politics can also be usefully explored as the "conduct of conduct," wherein the feminist politics of legal reform is accepted as a process of female subjectification in which different sorts of norms are given the power to identify the appropriate norms for the conduct of women (Drakopoulou, 2008: 351–352); each of these mentalities may in turn generate societal norms that govern the "conduct of conduct." The question of how women with unwanted pregnancies govern their own conduct as a result of the expert knowledge and material legal practices would require empirical study of the transformation of subjectivity and the constitution of the pregnant self, and falls outside the scope of this chapter.

The methodology adopted for this chapter is located in the post-critical criminology framework of "radical historicism," a methodology that can also be described as "genealogy," which is an historicist form of critique. According to Bevir (2010: 426), genealogy can overcome the problems associated with structuralism through an historicist mode of enquiry "that highlights nominalism, contingency, and contestability." The research methodology is nominalist in the sense that it "conceive[s] of human life as unfolding against a historical background" in which "human actions, practices, [and] institutions come into being in historical contexts that influence their content" (Bevir 2010: 427). It will highlight the contingent nature of interpretation and expression by social agents to show how various discursive formations solidify and become taken for granted at certain historical junctures and sometimes in concert with opposing political programs. This is not to say that change is inexplicable, but rather that observable patterns emerge that shed new light and explain how certain kinds of interpretation and expression become dominant. For example, in my research on obscenity law, I have argued that feminist legal arguments aimed at articulating equality-based interpretations that support the use of censorship through Canadian obscenity law have been most successful when they chime with morally conservative arguments that favour enhanced censorship, regulation, and punishment (Kramar, 2006; Jochelson & Kramar, 2011a, 2011b). Finally, contestability suggests that seemingly obdurate governmental rationalities used to justify legal interpretations and their application are always disputable social constructs open to transformation. Such an approach is consistent with a Foucauldian-inspired study of the governmentalities of the state, prosecutorial policies, and their broader effects (Bevir, 2010; Dean, 1999; Foucault, 1979, 1991a). However, these sorts of approaches do have a tendency to ignore the "contingent ruptures and displacements that arise from struggles among agents," resulting in monolithic or homogeneous accounts of the power/knowledge formations (Bevir, 2010: 424). This approach overcomes the tendency in governmentality studies toward synchronic analyses of power by examining the history of the struggles among different agents over the infanticide law, which is conceived as an expression of juridical power (its interpretation, proper meaning, and application). The higher courts' rejection of aspects of the prosecutorial strategy in both *R. v. Effert* (2011) and *R. v. L.B.* (2011) provides a special opportunity to study the formation and adaptation of governing strategies through these processes of contestation.

Finally, this approach to research on women and the law targets the mentalities expressed in expert discourses (legal, sociological, psychological, and lay) that inform the inchoate problem of infanticide, and the limitations placed on new governing strategies within the legal realm. These mentalities often include broader discourses of formal legal equality, reproductive rights and responsibility (and therefore enhanced criminal responsibility), and the security of the fetus-infant victim. The baby is conceived as having the highest value to the community—that of life (bio-value)[1]—for which women are responsibilized through a variety of gender-specific technologies of the self.[2] When those technologies of the self fail (and a woman kills a baby), the state reacts to restore order through a juridical normalization strategy. Where governmentalities break down, regulation is quick to respond (Tadros, 1998). The enhanced punishment framework for murder in use today is rationalized as a deterrent to crime. Following a line of inquiry developed by Foucault's later work, we can see this *dispositif* as bio-political in that "security mechanisms have to be installed around the random element[3] inherent in a population of living beings so as to optimize a state of life" (Foucault, 2003: 246).

I am particularly interested in examining how it is that certain kinds of power formations become dominant even in the face of overwhelming opposition. Here I am thinking of the decade-long struggle by accused mothers and their families, defence counsel, and other forensic experts to challenge the scientific assertions of Dr. Charles Smith, acting on behalf of the Office of the Chief Coroner for Ontario. These assertions were taken up as fact by the courts, resulting in practically unassailable truth claims that were eventually revealed to have resulted in multiple wrongful convictions (Kramar,

2006). Smith was eventually found to be an unqualified pathologist whose biased and unprofessional testimony was found in at least 19 cases where children died. The Office of the Chief Coroner for Ontario and Dr. Smith fabricated the notion that the children died under suspicious circumstances, which compelled the police and the Crown to investigate and prosecute the men and women who were deemed culpable. In 2008, the Goudge Inquiry into Pediatric Forensic Pathology in Ontario led to the exoneration of all those persons wrongfully prosecuted and convicted on the basis of the reports by the Office of the Chief Coroner for Ontario that contained the bogus forensic scientific claims (and subsequent testimony) provided by Dr. Charles Smith, in a number of child homicide cases that were prosecuted throughout the 1990s in Ontario. This is not a unique phenomenon. Cunliffe's (2011) research has documented how the interface between law and expert testimony has been adopted by the courts in many high-profile cases, resulting in wrongful convictions involving marginalized women in Australia and the UK.

Thinking by Case

The main sources of empirical data examined to understand the rationalities that inform governing strategies include reported legal cases and the building blocks for those cases (police reports, coroners' reports, autopsy findings, social workers' reports, psychiatrists' reports, trial transcripts, facti) as well as accompanying media stories. According to Berlant (2007: 663), "[T]he case represents a problem-event that has animated some kind of judgement." Thus, "thinking by case" enables the researcher to show how disparate expert knowledges can fold space and time to produce an "event" in the present (Berlant, 2007; Ettlinger, 2011), creating new discursive salience. My aim is to highlight the allegiances and disjunctures between the various competing interpretations and usages of the infanticide law and the accompanying prosecutorial and defence strategies. The objective of this work is to think about the way we govern and are governed by making explicit the forms of rationality that underpin practices of government and to remove the taken-for-granted character of any form of government that seeks to produce particular social or political outcomes or objectives. Most importantly, the governmentality approach enables us to consider the effects of particular sets of prescriptive arguments (such as those offered by various feminist arguments for social change) and the ways in which they produce contradictory, often unintended, consequences with particular kinds of regulatory effects. This approach is especially useful for considering the ramifications of using particular arguments or concepts (such as emancipation, equality, victims' rights, or freedom) to advance specific regimes of governing. There are no political programs (or prescriptions for social justice) that stand outside power relations. Through an examination of cases, we can be clear about how these discursive practices challenge and/or authorize particular courses of action to secure the life of the fetus-infant.

Infant Killing in Canadian History

In Canada, women commit infanticide to maintain the status quo. Whether the status quo is perceived to exist, or actually exists, the forces that maintain the status quo exist both at the micro-level of the family and the macro-level of society. The practice of concealing an unwanted pregnancy and giving birth in secret and disposing of the baby's body could lead to criminal charges for "murder," "concealment of birth," or "neglecting to obtain assistance in childbirth." However, jurors were so sympathetic to these women that they were disinclined to convict them, whatever the evidence, because infanticide was thought of as a quasi-criminal act. Prior to the passage of the 1948 infanticide law, women who killed children at birth or shortly afterward were rarely charged with the crime of murder. At that time, a murder conviction carried with it a mandatory penalty of death. Because of this harsh penalty, the state could rarely achieve convictions. In fact, only those women who confessed to the killings were convicted of murder and given a mandatory sentence of death (Kramar, 2005). Usually, the women were young (in their teens); sometimes they were victims of sexual assault at the hands of their employers or co-workers on farms and in domestic service. An open-door immigration policy for Irish and British citizens meant that many young women were sent to Canada in search of work between the mid-nineteenth and early twentieth centuries.

In some cases domestic violence played a key role in the baby's death. For example, in 1919 Viola Thompson was convicted in the death of her fifth baby following its discovery beside a railway track in Smith Falls, Ontario. Thompson was found guilty and sentenced to death by hanging. This sentence was later commuted to life imprisonment. Because her husband was extremely violent toward her and their four children, Thompson had left him for another man with whom she had the illegitimate child. When she was convicted of murder, the surviving children were left to live with their abusive father. Her sons, friends, and women's groups across the country wrote to the Minister of Justice demanding her release, and provided narrative evidence of extreme domestic violence to explain her actions and to plea for her early release. Eventually, after serving six and a half years in Kingston Penitentiary, Thompson was granted a ticket of leave when she was 40 years old. In other cases, women were compelled by social norms to hide their unwanted pregnancy and dispose of the infant at birth to conceal their ex-nuptial sexual activity. None were motivated by any malice towards the infants, who were rarely seen in lay or professional terms as victims of callous women-murderers.

Accordingly, throughout the nineteenth century and into the early twentieth century, there were a range of social factors that very strongly mitigated the women's responsibility. The women's "irrational" behaviour or "impulses" as it was described in court were seen as motivated not by evil but by morally pure intentions; women who killed their illegitimate babies were seen as conforming to society's moral standards, and were viewed in contradictory terms as acting both irrationally for legal purposes and reacting properly in relation to society's moral standards. In this regard, the infanticide offence/defence is one of the first laws to incorporate a gendered construction of the "reasonable woman" to mitigate punishment for violence. The mens rea of infanticide law requires that the killing be "wilful," and the actus reas requires that the woman was suffering from a "disturbed mind" consequent to childbirth and lactation (although the mental element need not be proven beyond a reasonable doubt). Written into the law is the hybrid category of a "disturbed mind," which applies to conduct wrought by a complex interaction of social, economic, psychological, cultural, religious, biological, and hormonal factors associated with new motherhood. Like the law of self-defence, which accommodates a variety of men's experiences to mitigate against harsh punishment when it applies both objective and subjective tests for the "reasonable man," the infanticide offence/defence allowed for a modest accommodation of the stresses of motherhood understood in layperson's terms as rooted in societal problems, albeit in the individualized language of psychological distress.

The removal of the requirement to prove the mental element beyond a reasonable doubt speaks directly to this point, since prosecutors had considerable difficulty convincing judges and juries that there was anything psychologically wrong with the women who committed infanticide. Before the law was amended in the 1950s to remove this burden, women were found not guilty of infanticide. This created a legal catch-22, because a not-guilty finding could mean the accused was in fact guilty of murder but could not be retried on account of the double jeopardy rule. Removing the burden to prove the mental element solved this problem by ostensibly allowing judges and juries to "read in" sociological factors as mitigating against a murder conviction. The women were thus understood to be acting reasonably to protect their reputations as well as the lives of the babies, who would experience a life of stigmatization and poverty. In those cases where incest was asserted to be the motivation for infanticide, societal revulsion led to extreme leniency. Men who, by seducing, abandoning, or abusing the women, failed to live up to society's moral standards were viewed as true criminals. In these contexts, the women's actions were "wilful" but also reasonable, given the range of circumstances that produced a "disturbed mind." It was surely recognized that women experience social inequality in relation to childbirth and child-rearing, given both the biological imperatives and the socially ascribed division of labour that produced socio-economic disparities between men and women. Thus, all that is required to be proven beyond a reasonable doubt for a conviction is that the baby is the biological child of the accused and that the accused had killed it before it reached the age of one year.

Although women sometimes killed their babies in states of what we now refer to as postpartum psychosis, the infanticide provision was originally enacted to address the killing of newly born babies by desperate women in desperate social circumstances for which the penalty for murder was entirely without basis in punishment theory. In summary, the infanticide law was passed following a significant increase in the population of young single women to Canada at a time when the *Criminal Code* prescribed the death penalty for murder. The stigma attached to illegitimacy enforced through bastardy laws prevented children born out of wedlock from inheriting property. Birth control and abortion were criminalized, and adoption, socialized medicine, hospital-based childbirth, and public K-12 education had yet to be implemented as part of the overall development of the Canadian welfare state. The victims' rights movement had yet to alter the prosecution process in the manner we see it today, such that Crown prosecutors and experts such as forensic pathologists see themselves as strategic legal advocates for infant-victims (see Roach, 1999, on victims' rights; and Kramar 2005, 2006, on the advocacy role played by forensic experts working for coroners' offices). It was not until the mid- to late twentieth century that infanticide cases became linked to child abuse homicide, and the infanticide law became a strategy that inventive lawyers could marshal in defence of their female clients charged with murder. In that victims' rights context, infanticide law came to be seen by some, particularly those in the prosecutorial law-and-order culture, as a kind of end-run around a murder conviction (Kramar, 2005, 2006).

The Disappearance of Infanticide: The Will to Punish

Despite Canadian legislators' enactment of a special infanticide law to address the socio-legal aspects of infanticide, Cunliffe's (2009) research on reported Canadian cases reveals a trend from the 2000s onwards of charging filicidal women with murder (see also Grant, 2011). These findings are consistent with my own research (Kramar, 2003, 2005, 2006) and form part of a broader climate of law-and-order approaches to crime in general. As recognition of the strains of new motherhood associated with the mid-nineteenth to mid-twentieth centuries is replaced by a zeal to protect newborn children, the authorities began to problematize the infanticide law as a threat to men's equality. Of course, this change in the societal understanding of the reasonable infanticidal woman occurs against a backdrop of sweeping social and economic changes that have reconfigured the responsibility of the state toward those very populations of women now targeted through enhanced law-and-order approaches to infanticide.

R. v. Effert

In September of 2006, a Wetaskiwin, Alberta, jury found 20-year-old Katrina Effert guilty of second-degree murder following a concealed pregnancy and secret birth in the basement of her parents' home. The media reported that Effert strangled the baby boy with her "thong panties in the early hours of April 14, 2005" (Farrell, 2006). Later, Effert confessed to having thrown the dead baby over a neighbour's fence in an effort to conceal the body. Katrina Effert was given the mandatory sentence of life imprisonment, without possibility of parole for 10 years. It was the first time that a woman had been found guilty of second-degree murder for maternal neonaticide since the passage of the infanticide provision in 1948. Very few women in Canadian history have ever served time in prison for the crime of infanticide (Kramar, 2005). Then, a year later in September 2007, the Alberta Court of Appeal overturned the jury conviction on the grounds that the judge's instructions to the jury with respect to the infanticide provision were flawed. A new trial was ordered. Katrina Effert was re-prosecuted and again found guilty of second-degree murder by a new jury. That jury rejected the infanticide defence and presumably the evidence from forensic psychiatrists that she suffered from an emotional disturbance at the time of the killing. Additional commentary at the time the case was unfolding from Mr. Sanjeev Anand, a professor of criminal and constitutional law at the University of Alberta, framed the law as "an anachronism that should be seriously amended, if not gotten rid of" (Arrowsmith, 2006). According to Mr. Anand, "[M]any legal experts consider the law on infanticide a holdover from paternalistic 19th century medicine, when women were considered weaker vessels ... women were considered more frail than men, and the act of having a child could unhinge certain women." Legal expert Mr. Anand advanced a sort of lay interpretation of the infanticide law and its purpose without having informed himself of the historic purpose of the defence. Of course, an amateurish reading of the law might lead one to conclude that the infanticide offence/defence "treat[s] women as a lesser human beings," as Anand was quoted as saying to a reporter (Canadian Press, September 27, 2006).

Incongruously, this misunderstanding of the intended purpose of the infanticide law chimes with contemporary feminist critiques of the medicalization of deviance that object to its individualization and pathologization. These sociological feminist critiques are theoretically opposed to the use of psychological mitigation frameworks because they fail to account for the social circumstances in which desperate mothers find themselves within patriarchal societies that privatize child-rearing. The infanticide offence/defence addresses these very issues, albeit in the psychological language demanded by criminal law at that time. What is more, because the social circumstances of the past have largely been reformed as a result of the women's movements and the reproductive rights movement in particular, legal experts and laypersons often assume that all women have the same options. This articulation of what is known as formal legal equality fails to account for a number of key factors, including: the high rates of unemployment among young Canadian women; the pressures faced by sexually active young women in strongly religious communities; the different experiences of children of immigrants whose families adhere to strict patriarchal rules of conduct for young women or that face language barriers; and those women that may not have access to their own health cards to seek independent medical services, let alone birth control or abortions. Women commit infanticide to maintain the status quo, yet legal experts and jurors have ignored the different experiences and material realities of young women. These legal actors fail to account for or understand, or choose to reject the fact that societal circumstances makes infanticide the best way to maintain the status quo for the women who commit the crime. This failure has led to jurors seeing life imprisonment with no possibility of parole as a just punishment, largely on the grounds that they are acting in the name of the innocent baby-victim who demands vengeance. In addition, certain Crown Attorneys' offices readily apply a deterrence-based rational actor model of criminal justice, ostensibly to deter populations of infanticidal women and to manage the risk of harm to infants. Effert's defence lawyer offered the Crown a guilty plea to the lesser and included offence of infanticide, which was rejected. The Court of Appeal for Alberta would later find this decision to be unreasonable, finding that the jury did not act judicially. In doing so, the court set aside the second-degree murder conviction and substituted a conviction for infanticide (*R. v. Effert*, 2011, at para. 30).

R. v. L.B.

On the other side of the country, in Southern Ontario, an infanticide finding provided the impetus for the government to challenge the validity of the infanticide law itself. In 2008, L.B. was convicted in Guelph, Ontario, on two counts of infanticide. This case was unlike the more typical infanticide scenario in Effert, because the accused was not suspected of having killed the babies until many years later when she confessed to smothering her babies while undergoing medical treatment at the Homewood Health Centre for mental health and addictions treatment. Nevertheless, the conditions of mothering in which the deaths occurred were not unlike a range of cases we have seen over the course of the twentieth century. A very young mother, herself an unwanted child born to a 19-year-old mother, spent three months in the care of Children's Aid because she was estranged from her father and socio-economically marginalized. These antecedent social conditions underpinned L.B.'s psychiatric diagnosis as both borderline personality disorder and postpartum depression.

L.B. was 17 years old when she gave birth to her first son in 1998. Six weeks later, the baby was found dead in his crib. The cause of death was given as Sudden Infant Death Syndrome (SIDS).[4] Shortly after the baby's death, L.B. ended her relationship with the father of the child. She married in March 2001 while pregnant at the age of 19 and gave birth to a second child in May of that year. By the end of that year, she was again pregnant and gave birth to her third child in September 2002. Ten weeks later, that child was found dead in its crib. The cause of death was this time attributed to Sudden Unexplained Death Syndrome (SUDS). By 2003, L.B. was pregnant again and gave birth to her fourth child in January of 2004. Prior to the birth of her first child, she had been admitted to Homewood Health Centre, an addictions and mental health facility, for two weeks. It was during her second stay at the Homewood Health Centre in 2004 that she admitted to smothering both her babies.

At trial the judge determined that the Crown had made out the elements of first-degree murder because there was evidence of planning and deliberation on the part of L.B., although she claimed she did so with the intent to save the children from harm. However, given that the defence had established the required elements for infanticide, the judge substituted a conviction on that charge. The Crown appealed this finding on the grounds that infanticide is not a partial defence to murder when the elements of murder are made out at trial. Because of the odd way in which infanticide is situated in Canadian law, which does not formally recognize diminished capacity provisions, the Crown contended in their appeal that infanticide is not a partial defence to murder. Moreover, the Crown argued that the psychological elements contained in the text of the law have been discredited in psychological circles, and that the "plight of young unwed mothers does not accord with present reality, and constitutes an unacceptable devaluation of the worth of a newborn child" (*R. v. L.B.*, 2011, at para. 49).

The matter of two children having been killed marshalled a governance strategy in which the Crown sought an order from the Court of Appeal that L.B. stand trial for first-degree murder, which carries a maximum penalty of life imprisonment with no possibility of parole. The case heard before the Ontario Court of Appeal centred on the legitimacy of the infanticide law as a lesser included defence to murder. The Crown's position was that, in cases where murder was proven with each of the elements of the infanticide scenario present, a substitute finding of the lesser included offence of infanticide should be excluded. They relied on a narrow reading of the lesser included text of the law contained in s. 662(3), which provides that where a count charges murder and the evidence proves infanticide but does not prove murder, the jury may convict of infanticide. The Crown sought to interpret the law the other way around, such that in cases were murder is proven (the mens rea of intentional killing is established), the accused does not have access to the infanticide defence even if the required elements of the infanticide offence/defence are present. The Women's Legal and Education Action

Fund (LEAF)[5] was granted leave to intervene in the case in order to present arguments on the proper interpretation of the infanticide provisions in the *Criminal Code.* According to LEAF, the Crown was seeking to render the infanticide law inoperative where the Crown chose to charge murder, thereby denying women the opportunity to access a regime of reduced culpability and sentence provided by the infanticide provision (LEAF, 2010, at paras. 2–7). LEAF argued that a successful appeal would effectively repeal s. 233 and submitted that "this cannot be correct" (LEAF, 2010, at para. 6) since infanticide was enacted by Parliament as a partial defence to murder. In short, the Crown's argument was an end-run around the infanticide provision in an effort to achieve a conviction for first-degree murder.

The humanitarian and psychological mitigation rationalities in infanticide law have given way to a rather more law-and-order style of governance, which attempts to manage the future through retributive-type sanctions that presume deterrence will be achieved through punishment for the rational actor. Challenges to these efforts to repeal the infanticide law on the part of equality-seeking groups such as LEAF continue to advance the rights of women to have the social context of pregnancy and mothering recognized in homicide law (LEAF, 2010). Ironically, retributive calls for infanticide law reform often seek to erase the gendered nature of infanticide while relying on discourses of formal equality, reproductive rights, and responsibility. These produce an abstract rational legal subject where social context has little or no role in the mitigation of responsibility. In addition, legal strategies adopted by Crown prosecutors suggest that the infanticide law ought to be repealed because, it is argued, postpartum mental disturbance has no connection to violence in these cases (CBC, 2010).

The will to provide a mitigation framework in cases of mothers who conceal their pregnancies and subsequently kill their babies at birth, and those in which the mother is suffering from a postpartum mental disturbance and who commit infanticide, has fallen out of favour in some provinces. Crowns, jurors, and the public increasingly argue that the social conditions that compel women to commit infanticide no longer exist, either because the feminist movement has achieved both formal legal equality and reproductive freedom for women, or because they simply do not want to extend the reduced culpability framework that recognizes the relative "powerlessness of women charged with infanticide and the social and economic imposition on them alone of the stigma and responsibility for pregnancy and child-rearing" (LEAF, 2010, at para. 13). In another ironic twist, retributive reformers view the law as a violation of the equality provision of the *Charter of Rights and Freedoms* because no such law exists for men (CBC, 2010).[6] Interviewed again in this matter, Mr. Anand, himself a former Crown prosecutor, argued that women ought to be treated equally to men and charged with murder. In other words, the category of equality (in the context of reproductive freedom) is deployed to allow for much harsher punishment of the women who commit infanticide rather than as a category used to understand women's unique experiences of pregnancy, childbirth, and motherhood.

Conclusion

Until the appearance of Dr. Charles Smith in Ontario and other forensic experts, forensic scientific uncertainty surrounding the question of live birth (for the purposes of a murder charge) interfered with prosecutors' attempts to secure murder convictions for infanticide (Kramar, 2006). Without the availability of this bogus forensic science to facilitate convictions, the infanticide defence continues to interfere with the will to punish, with the defence rejected by two juries in the Effert case, and the Crown in the L.B. case challenging its use by the lower courts. The proposed marginalization of the strains of new motherhood as a legal consideration is at odds with developments in other areas of law where the courts have sought to legally recognize socially induced inequalities to mitigate against the use of imprisonment, such as women's experiences of domestic violence (*R. v. Lavallee*) and the effects of colonialism in the everyday lives of Indigenous people (*R. v. Gladue*). Infanticide, one of the few laws originally incorporating "sociological" evidence (albeit informally), is now rejected and/or contested because women are presumed to be free from the earlier identified constraints of motherhood. Autonomous (free, equal, and responsible) motherhood is here a technology of citizenship through which women are made up as active citizens responsible for their own biological effects (children). However, the new governing initiative has not proceeded unhindered; the Court of Appeal in Ontario rejected the Crown's challenge to the use of the infanticide law as a defence to murder in L.B., a case in which the Women's Legal Education and Action Fund (LEAF) was granted intervener status to defend the infanticide provision, and the Court of Appeal in Alberta overturned the unreasonable murder conviction in Effert. The Supreme Court of Canada recently refused to hear appeals of both rulings.

Prosecutors will have to adapt to these rulings. They will still have the option to favour murder over infanticide charges, but with less assistance from the courts in securing convictions than they had demanded. The resultant regime of prosecutorial practice is likely to continue to develop over the next decade. Examining the effects of the contemporary move by claims-makers to abolish the infanticide mitigation framework, both de facto and de jure, and the limitations placed on this move, along with attempts to interpret the manner in which both subjects and authorities have been capacitated in the various contexts, will clarify how the outcomes are shaped in these cases. As this research demonstrates, there are emerging rationalities that privilege formal legal equality and/or retribution over the feminist recognition of ongoing inequality in their proposals for the abolishment of infanticide. These expert legal discourses dovetail directly into a governmentality of reproductive responsibility and therefore criminal responsibility in a context of formal, rather than substantive, equality.[7] The sociological feminist critique of laws that medicalize women's deviance (here I am thinking of the sociological critiques of battered woman syndrome) rather than recognize the relative powerlessness of women in abusive relationships in law has led to what is perhaps a not wholly justified critique of the psychological elements written into infanticide law. This critique of the law has been picked up on by critics of infanticide law who advocate formal legal equality and has been marshalled into their arsenal to discredit the offence/defence. This challenge to the legitimacy of the law is taken even further by retributivists, who advocate for enhanced punishment more broadly as a means of addressing social problems such as neonaticide. Formal legal equality has always been seen by feminist critics as producing inequalities, despite its face value appeal (Hudson, 2003; Naffine, 1990; Young, 1990).

The rise of law and order under neoliberalism further complicates the legitimacy of the infanticide offence/defence because responsibilization strategies are a hallmark of neoliberal citizenship and crime control (see Hannah-Moffat, 2004). These retributive mentalities marshal a reproductive responsibilization strategy that is gendered. Young, sexually active, single women have in some cases lost access to the mitigation framework offered by the infanticide defence to murder. When we examine the life experiences of the women who commit infanticide in the various Canadian provinces, we find that the typical woman who conceals her pregnancy, gives birth unaided and alone, and kills a newly born child is young, marginally employed, single, and White. In other cases, the women are of ethnic or immigrant background, with strong religious injunctions against premarital sex and the use of birth control and abortion, and for whom maternal neonaticide continues to be a "device of last resort" (Kramar, 2005). Interestingly, however, these latter cases are not necessarily the ones subject to aggressive prosecution; rather, it appears to be single White women such as Katrina Effert who are the main objects of government (Kramar, 2005, 2006). Examining these two kinds of cases side by side, we can speculate that the race and ethnicity of the women for whom culture is highly religious have access to that sociological experience that contours their reproductive lives, while White women from working-class backgrounds do not, meaning that race and religiosity mitigate while class does not. It is simply erased by the institutional power structures that are blind to the social and cultural strains of motherhood on these women.

In those unusual cases where postpartum depression is asserted as the cause of the homicide, the mothers are often older and middle class. In *R. v. L.B.*, the infanticide law incorporates socio-economic and cultural variables to offer a formal criminal response as a means of "securitizing" the "unwilling mother" against an unjust punishment framework that required the death penalty for murder. The infanticide law strikes this balance. Infanticide law was one of the few gender-specific laws where the underpinning rationality for exculpation was aimed at securitizing the mother against the punitive force of the state while still enabling a formal response that recognized harm to the victim-baby. The question remains as to whether the bio-politics of optimal life associated with governmental forms of power shifted this balance away from securitizing individual women against the power of the state and toward securitizing the fetus-baby against the malevolent mother.

Notes

1 The concept of "bio-value" is borrowed from Robert Ciccarelli (2008).

2 For example, girls and women are socialized throughout their life course to be nurturers and caregivers in preparation for their socially ascribed roles as mothers. We are taught to identify primarily with the roles of wife and mother, and are rewarded for exhibiting passive and nurturing personalities. Where the forces of socialization fail, there exist a variety of forms of moral regulation that target the behaviour of girls differently than boys. Sexual agency is prohibited (sex'ting, dress codes, etc.).

3 From the perspective of government, the aleatory event is maternal filicide (infanticide), which requires the security mechanism of punishment for murder to optimize a state of life.

4 Sudden Infant Death Syndrome (SIDS) and Sudden Unexplained Death Syndrome (SUDS) are causes of death that are given to babies when no other cause of death can be given. It is an absence of cause of death category that in other cases has cast considerable suspicion upon the mothers, some of whom have been wrongfully convicted of killing their babies (Cunliffe, 2010; Kramar, 2006).

5 Retrieved from www.leaf.ca/about/index.html#target

6 This claim is advanced despite the lack of any solid empirical evidence that men kill newly born children for the social reasons outlined herein or that they suffer from postpartum depression. In addition, *R. v. L.B.* had nothing to do with men and diminished responsibility for infant murder (CBC, 2010).

7 Formal equality treats different people in the same way, thereby producing inequalities of outcome, whereas substantive equality recognizes the importance of recognizing different social experiences to produce equality of outcome.

References

Arrowsmith, L. (2006, September 27). "Alberta baby-killing verdict discussions echo national infanticide debate." *Canadian Press.* Retrieved from http://www.canadiancrc.com/Newspaper_Articles/CP_Alberta_baby-killer_verdict_national_infanticide_debate_27SEP06.aspx

Backhouse, C. (1984). "Desperate women and compassionate courts: Infanticide in nineteenth century Canada." *University of Toronto Law Journal*, 34: 447–478.

Berlant, L. (2007). "On the case." *Critical Inquiry*, 33(Summer): 663–671.

Bevir, M. (2010). "Rethinking governmentality: Towards genealogies of governance." *European Journal of Social Theory*, 13(4): 423–441.

Burchell, G., Gordon, C., & Miller, P., eds. (1991). *The Foucault Effect.* Hemmel Hempstead: Harvester Wheatsheaf.

CBC. (2010, September 23). "Infanticide." *The Current*, with Anna-Maria Tremonte. Retrieved from www.cbc.ca/thecurrent/2010/09/sept-2310---pt-2-infanticide.html

Ciccarelli, R. (2008). "Reframing political freedom in the analytics of governmentality." *Law and Critique*, 19(3): 307–327.

Cunliffe, E. (2009). "Infanticide: Legislative history and current questions." *Criminal Law Quarterly*, 55: 94–119.

Cunliffe, E. (2011). *Murder, Medicine and Motherhood.* Oxford: Hart Publishing.

Dean, M. (1997). *Governing Societies.* New York: Open University Press.

Dean, M. (1999). *Governmentality: Power and Rule in Modern Society.* London: Sage Publications.

Drakopoulou, M. (2008). "Feminism, governmentality and the politics of legal reform." *Griffith Law Review*, 17(1): 330–356.

Ettlinger, N. (2011). "Governmentality as epistemology." *Annals of the Association of American Geographers*, 101(3): 537–560.

Farrell, J. (2006, September 27). "'No! How could they do it?'" *The Edmonton Journal.* Retrieved from www2.canada.com/edmontonjournal/news/story.html?id=8949a1c3-f4d9-45a3-ad6d-1b2663e67b84

Foucault, M. (1991a). "Governmentality." In G. Burchell, C. Gordon, & P. Miller, eds., *The Foucault Effect: Studies in Governmentality* (pp. 87–104). Chicago: University of Chicago Press.

Foucault, M. (1979). "On governmentality." *Ideology and Consciousness*, 6(Autumn): 5–22.

Foucault, M. (1991b). "On questions of method." In G. Burchell, C. Gordon, & P. Miller, eds., *The Foucault Effect: Studies in Governmentality* (pp. 87–104). Chicago: University of Chicago Press.

Foucault, M. (2003). "17 March 1976." In M. Bertani & A. Fontana, eds., *Society Must Be Defended: Lectures at the Collège de France 1975-1976* (pp. 239–264). New York: Picador.

Garland, D. (1997). "'Governmentality' and the problem of crime: Foucault, criminology, sociology." *Theoretical Criminology*, 1(2): 173–214.

Grant, I. (2011). "Desperate measures: Rationalizing the crime of infanticide." *Canadian Criminal Law Review*, 14: 253–271.

Hannah-Moffat, K. (2004). "Losing ground: Gender, responsibility and parole risk." *Social Politics*, 11(3): 363–385.

Hudson, B. (2003). *Justice in the Risk Society*. London: Sage Publications.

Jochelson, R., & Kramar, K. (2011a). *Sex and the Supreme Court: Obscenity and Indecency Law in Canada*. Halifax & Winnipeg: Fernwood Publishing.

Jochelson, R., & Kramar, K. (2011b). "Governing through precaution to protect equality and freedom: obscenity and indecency law in Canada after *R. v. Labaye* [2005]." *Canadian Journal of Sociology/Cahiers Canadiens de Sociologie*, 36(4): 283–312.

Kramar, K. (2003). "Vengeance for the innocents: The new medico-legal designation of 'infanticide' as 'child abuse homicide.'" In D. Brock, ed., *Making Normal: Social Regulation in Canada* (pp. 182–208). Toronto: Thomson Nelson.

Kramar, K. (2005). *Unwilling Mothers, Unwanted Babies: Infanticide in Canada*. Vancouver: UBC Press.

Kramar, K. (2006). "Coroners' interested advocacy: Understanding wrongful accusations and convictions." *Canadian Journal of Criminology and Criminal Justice*, 48(5): 811–830.

Kramar, K., & Watson, W. (2006). "The insanities of reproduction: Medico-legal knowledge and the development of infanticide law." *Social & Legal Studies*, 15(2): 237–255.

Kramar, K., & Watson, W. (2008). "Canadian infanticide legislation, 1948 and 1955: Reflections on the medicalization/autopoiesis debate." *Canadian Journal of Sociology*, 33(2): 237–263.

LEAF (Women's Legal and Education Action Fund). (2010). Factum of the Intervener, Ontario Court of Appeal, *R. v. L.B.* C49467/C49468.

Naffine, N. (1990). *Law and the Sexes: Explorations in Feminist Jurisprudence*. Toronto: Harper Collins.

Osborne, J. (1987). "The crime of infanticide: Throwing the baby out with the bathwater." *Canadian Journal of Family Law*, 6: 47–59.

Roach, K. (1999). *Due Process and Victims' Rights: The New Law and Politics of Criminal Justice*. Toronto: University of Toronto Press.

Rose, N., O'Malley, P., & Valverde, M. (2006). "Governmentality." *Annual Review of Law and Social Science*, 2: 83–104.

Snider, L, (1994). "Feminism, punishment and the potential of empowerment." *Canadian Journal of Law and Society* (Special Edition on Feminism and Justice), 9(1): 75–104.

Tadros, V. (1998). "Between governance and discipline: The law and Michel Foucault." *Oxford Journal of Legal Studies*, 18: 75–103.

Young, I.M. (1990). *Justice and the Politics of Difference*. New Jersey: Princeton University Press.

Legal Cases and Statutes

R. v. Effert, 2011 ABCA 134 (CanLII).

R. v. Gladue, [1999] 1 S.C.R. 688.

R. v. L.B., 2011 ONCA 153 (CanLII).

R. v. Lavallee, [1990] 1 S.C.R. 852.

Chapter 10

Women and Child Homicide: Exploring the Role of Stereotypes about Gender, Race, and Poverty in Contemporary Canadian Cases

Emma Cunliffe[1]

Contemplating the death of a child is deeply upsetting. It seems unimaginable that one might first lose a child and then face criminal charges—and even conviction—for a crime that never occurred. Yet this describes the experience of at least 20 Ontario parents and caregivers between 1990 and 2005 (Goudge, 2008a). This group, more than two-thirds of which were women, was unjustly accused of causing children's deaths. Thirteen were wrongly convicted of homicide offences. This chapter examines the role of gender stereotypes in these Canadian miscarriages of justice, and suggests that the official response to these errors would have benefited from greater attention to the manner in which those who were wrongly accused were subjected to adverse stereotypes about gender and other aspects of their identity throughout the criminal investigation and trial process. The chapter begins with an account of one wrongful accusation—the trial of a babysitter who was not convicted—and ends with an account of a trial conducted in Winnipeg in 2009, in which a young mother was convicted of manslaughter. Comparing these two cases, one of which is characterized as a wrongful accusation, and the other which has not been appealed or otherwise officially reviewed, raises questions about the extent to which the Canadian criminal justice system continues to rely on punitive assumptions about women and mothering to overcome uncertainties in medical knowledge about how very young children die.

The Case of Amber: *R. v. M.(S.)*

In the summer of 1988, 12-year-old Shelly M. had a summer job caring for 16-month-old Amber S. Three days a week, from early morning until late afternoon, Shelly babysat Amber in Amber's home in Timmins, Ontario. Amber's mother telephoned regularly to make sure that Shelly and Amber were doing well. Amber's mother later said that, while Shelly was occasionally late for work, Amber adored Shelly and Shelly cared affectionately and responsibly for Amber. Shelly stood five foot four and weighed 125 pounds the summer she cared for Amber. Amber weighed about 25 pounds.

On July 28, 1988, something happened to Amber to cause a serious brain injury. Shelly maintained that Amber had fallen down five stairs and hit her head, but pathologists and doctors who treated Amber said that they could see no signs of bruises or fractures that would corroborate Shelly's story. Amber died on July 30, 1988, and, after some delay, pediatric pathologist Dr. Charles Smith conducted an autopsy at the Toronto Hospital for Sick Children (HSC). A child abuse investigation was started, focusing on Shelly. Police charged Shelly with manslaughter on the theory that she had shaken Amber to the point where Amber's brain had been terminally injured. Shelly's trial began on October 2, 1989, and ran until November 6, 1990.

At trial, each side called several medical experts and Ontario Provincial Court Justice Dunn was given the unenviable task of adjudicating the conflicting evidence given by pediatric neuropathologists, biomechanics, neurosurgeons, pediatric radiologists, and pediatricians. At least in part, the trial turned on whether Justice Dunn could be satisfied that "pure shaking exists as a cause of infant death" (*R. v. M.(S.)*, 1991, at para. 68). In his judgment, Justice Dunn characterized the disagreement thus: some experts "said that pure shaking may exist, but neither they nor their colleagues have ... found examples of it," while others—both Crown and defence experts—"believe it does exist and they say they have seen examples of it" (*R. v. M.(S.)*, 1991, at para. 68).

In a lengthy judgment, Justice Dunn acquitted Shelly M. He preferred the evidence of defence experts, whom he found to be more learned, better versed in relevant literature, and less dogmatic than the experts called by the prosecution. Justice Dunn particularly criticized the work done by experts at the HSC, including Dr. Smith, holding that "the fact gathering process, the communication procedures, and the documentation of the medical opinions of the HSC doctors involved in this case are such that I am led to question the conclusion they drew" (*R. v. M.(S.)*, 1991, at para. 92). Justice Dunn did not reach a settled conclusion on the possibility that pure shaking exists as a cause of death, but his comments suggest that he preferred the evidence of those experts who questioned the reliability of the shaking theory.

Child Homicide in Canada

Homicides committed against very young children are among the very few violent crimes for which women are charged in relatively equal numbers to men. However, Statistics Canada has not adopted consistent policies in relation to reporting child homicide rates, and it can be difficult to discern the difference between suspected and proven homicides from reported figures. Academic commentary on child homicide frequently asserts that jurors and trial judges have difficulty believing that a woman could kill, and particularly that a mother could kill her children (e.g., Alder & Polk, 2001: 5–9; Prentice, 2001). The fear that child homicide might be under-detected arises repeatedly within the academic, medical, and statistical literature on child homicides. For example, the Canadian Centre for Justice Studies (2006) states:

> It is important to note that the incidence of child and youth homicide may be under-counted. This is because some deaths that are actually due to intentional injury or neglect may be misclassified as accidental or a natural or undetermined cause.

The concern about under-counting is widely shared in legal studies of child homicide statistics (Alder & Polk, 2001; Wilczynski, 1997) as well as medical studies of sudden, unexplained infant deaths (e.g., American Academy of Pediatrics, 2006; Levene & Bacon, 2004).

The source of fear that some child homicides may go undetected is the widely held medical belief that it can be difficult, if not impossible, to distinguish between natural, accidental, and inflicted causes of death in very young children. Remarkably little is known about how and why some children under the age of two years die, and medical research has raised the possibility that some deaths that appear natural or accidental may in fact be homicides. Two key areas in which this theory has gained traction are in relation to Sudden Infant Death Syndrome and in relation to head and brain injuries.

Sudden Infant Death Syndrome (SIDS) was first coined in the 1960s. The phrase is little more than a euphemism for an unknown cause of death. In a child that dies of SIDS, there is no evidence to suggest other causes of death, such as heart defects or diagnosable genetic disorders. As medical research advanced and autopsies improved, the number of SIDS deaths declined, but a few babies still die every year in Canada from unknown causes. In the 1990s, pathologists and pediatricians began to hypothesize that adult caretakers might be deliberately smothering a substantial minority of these babies. This theory gained currency after the 1995 conviction of Waneta Hoyt, a New York woman who was convicted of killing five children in this manner. The deaths in her family had previously been the subject of medical curiosity because they suggested the possibility of a genetic explanation for SIDS (Cunliffe, 2011: 34–37). However, the theory that SIDS might often mask smothering was most notoriously advanced by English pediatrician Sir Roy Meadow, who wrote: "[B]etween 2 and 10 percent of babies currently labelled as dying from the sudden infant death syndrome have probably been smothered by their mothers" (Meadow, 1989: 1242). Meadow was an expert witness in several trials that led to the wrongful convictions of English women for killing children who probably died naturally.

Head and brain injuries present different challenges to medical science. When a child presents at hospital with evidence of brain or head injuries, the challenge is to distinguish between injuries caused accidentally—for example, by a fall down a short set of stairs, or by an infant being dropped—and injuries that are deliberately inflicted by an abusive caretaker. For several decades, some experts have suggested that it is possible to diagnose abuse using the three indicia of the so-called Shaken Baby Syndrome, now renamed "Abusive Head Trauma." An enormous amount of medical research has been devoted to differentiating between homicidal and accidental head injuries in children, and much more research has been done since Justice Dunn decided *R. v. M.(S.)* in 1991. However, to this day, experts are engaged in heated disagreement about what evidence is sufficient to differentiate between accident and deliberately inflicted injury (Findley, Barnes, Moran, & Squier, 2012: 213–214.) Given that falls and shaking are rarely if ever recorded, there is very real uncertainty about how much force is required to cause serious head and brain injuries. Findley and colleagues (2012: 312) suggest that this field remains sufficiently unsettled that expert witnesses must clearly explain the degree of controversy and uncertainty to courts when caregivers are charged with shaking or other non-accidental forms of causing head and brain injury.

In Canada, England, and Australia, the recognition that homicide cannot be detected by autopsy alone in young children led police and doctors to focus considerable resources on investigating and prosecuting suspicious child deaths based on so-called psychosocial evidence about a caregiver's parenting ability. "Psychosocial" is a compendious term used by medical experts as shorthand for psychological, behavioural, financial, lifestyle, and cultural factors. Because very young children are most often cared for by their mothers or by other women—and therefore tend to be in a woman's care when they die—these investigations into psychosocial evidence often focused on the caregiving capacities, personality, and lifestyle of women. Given the challenges in medically distinguishing between homicidal, accidental, and natural manner of death, compliance with expected gender performance came to act as a substitute for reliable medical conclusions about how a child died. Racialized and Aboriginal women, those who were poor, and those who otherwise seemed like less than ideal caregivers became particularly vulnerable to false accusations of homicide.

Concerns about under-counting homicide—which were never particularly well supported by positive evidence—have been undermined by the identification of a large number of wrongful convictions of women in Canada and the United Kingdom. Far from under-detecting murder or failing to prosecute women, courts and prosecutors in these jurisdictions seem to have been too ready to accept allegations of homicide between 1990 and 2005. These wrongful convictions and an associated cohort of cases in which mothers were charged but not convicted tend to be blamed on misleading expert evidence given by a small number of pathologists and pediatricians who adopted an unusually suspicious stance toward unexplained infant deaths.

The prevailing tendency to blame individual experts for wrongful convictions is unsatisfying because it fails to explain why the views of these expert witnesses became influential despite the existence of trial safeguards that are designed to prevent miscarriages of justice. Likewise, it is possible to identify troubling similarities between the misleading evidence given by experts in trials that led to wrongful convictions and the evidence given in more recent cases. In order to obtain a more complete understanding of the wrongful convictions of women for child homicide, it is therefore necessary to consider the relationship between legal processes and medical understandings of infant death, and particularly the role of gendered expectations in investigating and prosecuting suspected child homicide.

The concept of stereotyping is crucial to exploring the role of gendered expectations in criminal law. Psychological research suggests that people draw upon their "attitudes, experience and beliefs about the social world" when investigating or judging suspected crime (Pennington & Hastie, 1986: 254). These beliefs are based on a combination of individual experience and hegemonic understandings of human relationships and society (Bennett & Feldman, 1981). Stereotypes are one form of belief about the social world. They are specifically defined by psychologists to mean "statements about the group that are (at least tentatively) accepted as facts about every member" (Kahneman, 2011: 168). In this usage, "stereotype" is a neutral term that describes how we think about categories—for example, a table can be stereotyped according to the proposition that most tables have four legs and a flat top. However, stereotypes can also lead to predictable errors in thinking. Particularly when unreliable information resonates with a pre-existing stereotype, decision-makers are apt to overvalue that information and thereby ignore other relevant data (Kahneman, 2011: 168).

Legal theorists and other social scientists tend to use the term "stereotype" more pejoratively, to indicate the harms of treating all members of a stereotyped group as if they were the same, rather than judging them as individuals (Moreau, 2009: 36–37). Decisions made on the basis of such a stereotype risk being unjust to members of the stereotyped group. For example, someone who believes that welfare-dependent mothers are lazy may be more likely to accept a suggestion that a particular welfare-dependent mother deliberately sabotaged a job interview that she was required to attend. Contemporary research suggests that judgments based on negative stereotypes are only rarely motivated by deliberate prejudice or hostility. Far more commonly, prejudice is "unwitting, unintentional and uncontrollable" (Hardin & Banaji, 2012: 14–15). This negative conception of stereotyping, and the psychological explanation on which it depends, form the heart of my suggestion that paying attention to the role of gendered (and raced and classed) expectations is a necessary element of understanding the wrongful convictions of parents in child homicide cases.

Miscarriages of Justice in Ontario Child Homicide Cases

Dr. Charles Smith worked at HSC between 1981 and 2005. A pediatric pathologist who lacked formal training in forensic pathology (as was common in his early career), he was appointed the director of the Ontario Pediatric Forensic Pathology Unit in 1992. During the 1990s, he gained eminence as an "unequalled" expert in pediatric forensic pathology (Goudge, 2008a, Vol. 1: 6). However, Shelly M.'s trial is an example of the early signs that Smith's work may not have been as independent or objective as courts normally expect of an expert witness. Despite Justice Dunn's decision in *R. v. M.(S.)* and subsequent warning signs about Smith, including complaints laid at the Ontario College of Physicians and Surgeons, those overseeing Smith's work did not seriously investigate his competence or the validity of his conclusions until 2006.

Dr. Barry McLellan, then Chief Coroner for Ontario, initiated the first formal investigation of Smith's work. McLellan commissioned independent pathologists to review all criminally suspicious cases (n = 45) in which Smith had become involved between 1991 and 2005. The reviewing pathologists identified mistakes in Smith's work in 20 of the cases. In the cases flagged as problematic, Smith had either exaggerated the likelihood of a criminally suspicious cause of death or misconstrued signs that were relevant to identifying the likely time or manner of death, thereby risking a police focus on the wrong suspect. The reviewers found that Dr. Smith provided biased testimony and lacked appreciation for the basic principles of evidence preservation when working in a forensic environment. In each of these 20 cases, individuals were accused of homicide on the basis of Smith's conclusions. Fourteen accused were convicted. Table 10.1 sets out the charges laid and verdicts obtained against individuals accused in the 20 cases flagged by the McLellan review.

Totals in Table 10.1 add up to more than 20 charges because, in several instances, more than one accused was charged and/or convicted. Notably, seven accused pleaded guilty to causing a child's death when the child probably died naturally.

The Province of Ontario established the Commission of Inquiry into Pediatric

Table 10.1: Charges Laid and Verdicts Obtained in Reviewed Smith Cases

	N Charged		N Guilty Verdicts		Guilty Pleas	
	All	Women	All	Women	All	Women
Infanticide	1	1	3	3	1	1
Manslaughter	6	4	7	4	6	3
Second-degree murder	12	8	2	1	0	0
First-degree murder	4	2	1	0	0	0
Aggravated assault	0	0	1	0	0	0
(No charge)	1	1	—	—	—	—
Total	**24**	**16**	**14**	**8**	**7**	**4**

Forensic Pathology in Ontario (Goudge Inquiry) soon after the conclusions of McLellan's review were released. The Goudge Inquiry focused on 18 of the 20 cases in which the experts from the McLellan review expressed concern with Smith's report or testimony. The two remaining cases, *R. v. Trotta* (2007) and *R. v. Kporwodu & Veno* (2005), were excluded from the Goudge Inquiry because they were at the time subject to continuing proceedings. These cases will be included in this analysis, as they are now concluded, and are not categorically different from the cases Justice Goudge reviewed. For the purpose of this chapter, I refer to these 20 cases collectively as the "Ontario cases."

The Role of Gender in the Ontario Cases

The following discussion seeks to identify trends within the Ontario cases. It is important to begin this discussion by remembering that the majority of children whose deaths were at stake in the Ontario cases are now believed to have died naturally or accidentally. In almost all of these cases, there is now considered to be inadequate evidence to support a finding of criminal guilt. This is an important reminder, because there is a significant difference between ascertaining whether a given death is, in fact, culpable homicide and investigating a death in circumstances where that death is believed to be a culpable homicide (in which case the focus often becomes the identity of the killer). Frequently, Smith and others involved in these cases focused on identifying the supposed killer without giving sufficiently careful consideration to the pathology evidence that could help to determine cause of death.

The two exceptions to the general principle that these children may not have been deliberately killed include the death of Paolo Trotta, for which Marco Trotta was convicted of manslaughter; and the death of Jenna Waudby, for which a teenage babysitter was convicted of manslaughter after confessing to physically assaulting her. Jenna's mother was charged with second-degree murder soon after Jenna's death, but these charges were withdrawn before trial. In a third case, *R. v. Kporwodu & Veno* (2005), charges were stayed after delays in prosecution, so the case was not tried on its merits. The stay was granted because the accused would not have been given a fair opportunity to contest the Crown's allegations in light of the passage of time. In the eyes of the law, Kporwodu and Veno must be regarded as not guilty of killing their daughter, Athena. In the remaining 17 cases, the McLellan review and subsequent appeal courts concluded that there is positive evidence of a natural or accidental cause of death, or at a minimum, that there is inadequate evidence to conclude that the child was killed.

Although there are only two infant deaths in which a "safe" conviction now holds, the other children whose deaths formed the basis of the Ontario cases did not have model upbringings. A number had demonstrably been physically abused during their lifetimes, or physical abuse was strongly suspected even after the cases were reviewed. Others lived in families in which illicit drug use or alcohol abuse was common. Many families were welfare dependent, and many of these children experienced multiple family forms during their brief lifetimes (e.g., living with both parents, living with one parent, living with at least one adult who was not biologically related, or having siblings who were half-siblings). In several families, there was a history of domestic violence between adults. In a paradigm in which medical experts were reliant upon psychosocial factors to diagnose manner of death, the families were especially vulnerable to negative stereotyping about the quality of care their children received.

Given the role of the psychosocial inquiry in establishing cause of death, I consider an appraisal of the sociological characteristics of the families who formed the core of the Ontario cases to be crucial to obtaining a full understanding of the miscarriages of justice that occurred. Specifically, my research suggests that pathologists, police, and courts were more ready to conclude that the child was killed when they perceived that child's circumstances or an adult's caregiving to be inadequate. While this dimension of the Ontario cases received little media attention and no scholarly consideration, studying the sociological dimensions of child death investigation seems important to preventing similar miscarriages from arising in future.

The children whose deaths were reviewed by Justice Goudge ranged in age between one day and seven years when they died. Table 10.2 describes the relationships between the deceased children and their accused killers in the Ontario cases. Table 10.2 also provides some sense of the gendered dynamics of the Ontario cases, and in particular the extent to which women were impacted by Smith's inadequate forensic pathology. A total of 16 women were charged as principals or participants in the Ontario cases. Eight men were similarly charged.

Table 10.2: Relationship between Accused and Deceased in Reviewed Smith Cases

Two parents charged (both or uncertain assailant)	6
Two parents charged (father assailant)	2
Two parents charged (mother assailant)	0
Mother or stepmother charged alone	9
Mother subject to child apprehension proceedings but not charged	1
Father charged alone	3
Caregiver or babysitter charged	3

Feminist commentators have observed a growing tendency to charge women as accessories to child homicide in circumstances where a woman fails to protect a child from her male partner's violence (Lothian, 2002; Roberts, 1993). This dynamic may also arise within some of the Ontario cases, and is most evident in *R. v. Trotta* (2007). In Trotta, a mother was convicted as an accessory in circumstances where a father is believed to have committed the fatal assault against the child. There was considerable evidence to suggest that Paolo Trotta was physically abused by his father throughout his lifetime, and Marco Trotta eventually pleaded guilty to manslaughter. Paolo's mother Anisa Trotta repeatedly denied that there was any cause for concern about Marco's treatment of Paolo. After Anisa was convicted alongside Marco Trotta, her parents wrote to the court:

> Anisa is not [malicious] nor do many people believe that she herself could harm anyone, especially her own flesh and blood. I believe that Anisa has taken her marriage vows beyond their intent in that she will stick by her man for better or worse.... Anisa is not a criminal. However, she needs to be made aware that she, today and for the future has a very important commitment towards her children. (*R. v. Trotta*, 2007, court record)

In this letter and in glimpses from the trial transcript, Anisa Trotta emerges as a woman raised by a conservative religious family to believe in the sanctity of marriage and family and who took those obligations seriously. However, she is also punished for failing to protect the welfare of her children when her husband became a threat to them. The double standard inherent in socializing women to respect marriage and religious teachings about obedience, and then punishing them for apparently upholding those lessons, is not explored within the trial or any of the appeal judgments. The nature of Marco's relationship with Anisa likewise seems never to have been the object of serious inquiry. The Supreme Court of Canada quashed the Trottas' convictions after the revelations about Charles Smith's errors, and the prosecution did not retry Anisa; Marco eventually pleaded guilty to manslaughter.

In another Ontario case, a mother was charged with second-degree murder along with the child's father in circumstances where the only possible evidence of physical abuse pointed to the father. Both parents were discharged after a preliminary inquiry, and the judge specifically observed that there was no evidence whatsoever that the mother had been involved in any criminal wrongdoing. In this instance, it seems possible that the mother was charged partly because the police were uncertain about the exact course of events and they perceived her as protecting the child's father from their investigation. Subsequently, the charges laid against the mother may have been designed in part to encourage her to be more co-operative with the investigation. Table 10.2 shows that in three cases, two parents were charged in circumstances where police were unable to determine which parent had caused the child's death (total number of accused = 6). When a mother was considered the primary assailant, the father was never charged.

When looking at the cases in which a parent was charged as a sole accused, different dynamics emerge. In nine cases, a mother was charged as the sole criminal actor. Three of these mothers had not cohabited with a male partner; two were young women who hid their pregnancies from family and were alleged to have killed the child immediately after birth. Two mothers were separated from their partners at the time of the child's death. In one case, this separation occurred at the request of a child welfare worker; the other mother was engaged in a custody dispute with the biological father. Three mothers were cohabiting with a male partner or married at the time of their children's deaths, and one stepmother was likewise cohabiting with the child's biological father. The stepmother had cared for the deceased child since the child was an infant. Only one of these cohabiting accused was alone with the child throughout the time in which an alleged fatal assault could have occurred. In several of the cases in which single or separated mothers were accused, the children had been in contact with babysitters or other adults in the time period in which an assault could potentially have occurred.

In many of the cases, the mother seemed an obvious suspect. For example, in those cases where the infant or child lived in a single-parent household at the time when the pathologist believed injuries were inflicted, the mother seemed the most likely perpetrator. The disproportionate number of women wrongly accused of killing young children reflects that women continue to perform the majority of childcare both during a heterosexual relationship and after the relationship ends. However, this analysis only holds if the police investigation into the identity of a possible killer is conducted subsequent to the forensic pathologist's task of ascribing cause, manner, and likely time of death, and if the pathologist's determination of time of death is independent from the police investigation.

Justice Goudge found that the pathologist's inquiry into cause of death and the policy investigation often proceeded in lockstep. For example, Smith "expressed expert opinions about the causes of death in some cases, with little or no pathology support, because the non-pathology evidence seemed to support those causes of death" (Goudge, 2008a, Vol. 3: 389). He was often wrong, or at least too firm, in his opinions about time of death. It therefore seems that the pathologist's opinion about time and manner of death was as likely to be influenced by police theories about what happened to the child, as it was to influence those theories. In two cases, police were seemingly quick to focus their investigation solely on a single mother in circumstances where others had access to the child during the relevant window.

In the three cases in which a father was charged alone, one accused was married and living with the child's mother and extended family, one had irregular contact with his biological daughter, and one had cared for the deceased child for the three days prior to the child's death in a context of family violence and potential separation. In the case in which the accused was married and cohabiting, the child's mother was seriously unwell and played no part in caring for the child. In each of these cases, mothers and other female adults had no access to the child during the time at which the fatal injury was believed to have occurred. Again, it is difficult to know how much the police investigation influenced the pathologist's conclusions about timing of injury and death, but it is possible to state that mothers were charged in every case in which they could conceivably have participated in the apparent crime, while fathers and other caregivers were not.

In summary, it was common for both parents to be charged in circumstances where both had access to the child during the time period in which Smith considered a fatal assault had occurred and the police could not determine which parent had harmed the child. Mothers were charged alongside fathers when it seemed that the father was the sole assailant and the mother was perceived as not co-operating fully with police. Fathers were only charged as sole actors in circumstances where a mother had no access to the child during the period in which Smith considered that a fatal assault had occurred. Mothers were charged as sole actors where they had exclusive access to the child, or where police reached the conclusion that a father or another person who had access to a child was not involved in the child's death. Given a similar lack of evidence of involvement, mothers were charged, but fathers were not. Lori Lothian suggests that the tendency to charge mothers comes from an expectation that mothers can protect children from harm in every instance, even when that harm is inflicted by a man who is also violent toward the mother (Lothian, 2002). Her hypothesis seems to be supported by several of the Ontario cases.

This précis of the gendered pattern of suspicion within the Ontario cases is closely based on the detailed information contained in case overviews prepared for the Goudge Commission (Goudge, 2007). Overall, the cases suggest a differential approach to mothers and fathers in the investigation and prosecution of child homicide. As noted, these cases support previous suggestions that women are vulnerable to being charged with failing to protect a child from abuse, but men are not similarly vulnerable. However, these cases also hint at other trends, including a tendency to charge both parents where a fatal assailant cannot be determined, and an occasional tendency to focus on the mother as the perpetrator of a fatal assault in circumstances where the father and other adults also had access to the child and (on the evidence presented to the Goudge Inquiry) their opportunity and potential involvement had not been conclusively ruled out. In fact, in at least one case in which a mother was charged alone, there was positive evidence suggesting that the father had previously physically assaulted the deceased child.

The proposition that gender stereotypes played an active role in identifying certain deaths as likely homicides, and in the decision about whom to charge, is further supported by information contained within the court records of the Ontario cases. The example of Tammy Marquardt, whose conviction was overturned by the Ontario Court of Appeal in 2011 after she had spent nearly 14 years in prison, is particularly apposite. When Marquardt's son Kenneth died, Smith attributed Kenneth's death to strangulation. He wrote in his autopsy report:

> Social history indicates that the mother's husband was not in the home at the time of the incident. [Marquardt's husband] (who married Kenneth's mother about three months ago) is not Kenneth's father. He was not present at the time because he was at a Scarborough hospital, attending to his girlfriend who was giving birth to his baby. (*R. v. Marquardt*, 2011, court record)

The inclusion of such information within a report that is intended to address the medical dimensions of cause and manner of death suggests how thoroughly social and familial factors were mixed with medical evidence in Smith's reasoning. It seems wholly possible that Smith was influenced by this information about Kenneth's family in reaching his conclusions about how Kenneth died, although he denied that proposition when he testified before the Goudge Inquiry (Goudge, 2008b: 123–124).

Marquardt gave birth to a second child while awaiting trial, and this child was immediately apprehended by child welfare services. In fact, all of the parents who were wrongly accused on the basis of Smith's conclusions lost their surviving children, at least temporarily, in this manner. A document prepared before Marquardt was sentenced offers a glimpse into Marquardt's awareness that she would be judged according to how well she fit with social expectations of good mothering:

> [Marquardt] expressed to the staff feeling very sad having to leave her son ... each Tuesday.... She expressed a desire to stop seeing [her son]

> because the pain she felt at leaving him each week was almost unbearable. She said she couldn't stop though because she would be deemed a "bad mother." (Goudge, 2007: 112)

In 2011, the Ontario Court of Appeal ultimately concluded that the Marquardt trial court had not heard evidence that supported the proposition that Kenneth died of a seizure, and so quashed her conviction. Marquardt has not been reunited with the two children who were removed from her care when she was imprisoned (Tyler, 2011).

On other occasions, Smith seemed to suggest that he regarded the relationship between manner of death and the social characteristics of an alleged assailant to be analytically useful in his work. During one preliminary hearing, he testified:

> Here are the principles and once again, you throw them out if you want to. Blunt force injuries, shaking, blunt impact head injury or abdominal injuries are much more likely to be inflicted by a man than a woman. That man is not likely the biological parent of the infant or child.... Asphyxial deaths are more likely to be caused by women. (Goudge, 2008b: 233)

In this case, a second-degree murder charge was laid against a child's stepmother after the child died of a head injury. The prosecution withdrew the charge when they became aware that reputable experts believed that children could on rare occasions die after minor household falls. Throughout the records of the 20 cases in which Smith made errors, it seems clear that Smith and others who worked on the Ontario cases used psychosocial factors, in particular, factors associated with gendered stereotypes, to focus their investigation, speculate about probable manner of death, and identify likely assailants.

Goudge paid relatively little attention to the role of gender stereotypes within Smith's reasoning or the prosecution of parents and caregivers, particularly mothers, in the Ontario cases. He included the following suggestions among his recommendations:

> As a general rule, police and coroners should not "filter out" relevant information that is to be provided to the forensic pathologist. The forensic pathologist is best situated to determine what is relevant to his or her work.... That being said, police and coroners should generally not transmit information that is clearly irrelevant, innuendo, or purely speculative.... The forensic pathologist should remain vigilant against confirmation bias or being affected by extraneous considerations. (Goudge, 2008a, Vol. 1: 69)

In light of the research that shows that much prejudice is unwitting and uncontrolled, these recommendations do not seem to go far enough to protect those who are suspected of criminal wrongdoing from the effect of bias and prejudice. I have argued elsewhere that courts should adopt a much more comprehensive approach to investigating the reasoning processes on which expert opinions depend in order to make sure that an expert does not base his or her conclusions on the same stereotypes that a juror may use in judging an accused person. I call this phenomenon "double counting" to reflect that it doubly penalizes an accused who is already vulnerable to having her parenting or lifestyle adversely judged by a jury (Cunliffe, 2013).

Other Psychosocial Factors: Race and Financial Status in the Ontario Cases

Having suggested that the Ontario cases cannot be fully understood without paying attention to the sociological characteristics of affected families, it is important to consider the impact of race and financial status, as well as gender. Race and financial status interact with gender to produce differential expectations of individuals depending on their social location. In turn, these differential expectations—or stereotypes—may make investigators and legal decision-makers more willing to conclude that a crime has occurred in the face of ambiguous evidence. In the US, for example, studies of women's wrongful convictions show that White women are more likely to be convicted of child abuse and Black women more likely to be convicted of murder and drug offences (Ruesnick & Free, 2007). Accordingly, it is impossible to fully understand the role of gender within the Ontario cases without also attending to race and financial status.

The race, ethnic origins, and immigrant status of the families affected by the Ontario cases have been almost wholly overlooked. I am unable to provide a complete sense of the racial dynamics within these cases because the record is often silent as to the race or ethnicity of family members and accused (see Backhouse, 1999). In this regard, race is unlike gender, which inevitably emerges through the use of standard English pronouns and other linguistic conventions. Even when the official position is that gender is irrelevant, it is possible to glimpse gendered stereotypes operating through the medico-legal discourses. However, identifying the role of race, ethnicity, and immigrant status from textual records requires more sleuthing. In some cases, race, ethnicity, or immigrant status became apparent from trial testimony. For example, in *R. v. Mullins-Johnson* (2007), much of the evidence centred on William Mullins-Johnson's activities with family on and off a nearby reserve, and his Aboriginality is clearly apparent from the trial transcript. However, the Ontario Court of Appeal decision acquitting Mullins-Johnson does not mention his status as a member of the Batchewana First Nation, nor does the Goudge

Table 10.3: Race and Ethnicity in the Smith Cases

Race/Ethnicity/ Nationality	Accused	Deceased	Other Adult Family Members
Aboriginal	2	2	2
Colombian	1	1	0
East Indian	1	1	1
Ghanaian	1	1	0
Jamaican	0	1	1
Portuguese	1	1	1
White	0	0	0
Not specified	18	13	n/a
Total specified non-White	6	7	5

Inquiry report consider whether Mullins-Johnson's Aboriginality influenced his wrongful conviction (*R. v. Mullins-Johnson*, 2007; Goudge, 2008b). In other cases, race, ethnicity, or nationality form an incidental part of the case narrative or are mentioned in news coverage of the original trial. Table 10.3 shows aggregated information from the Goudge Inquiry and overview reports, the media coverage, and those few trial transcripts and other court records that mention race, ethnicity, or immigrant status.

Table 10.3 somewhat mixes categories in an effort to remain true to the information gleaned from various sources. In cases where race, ethnicity, or nationality are unspecified, the relevant actors may be perceived as belonging to one or more socially dominant (White, Canadian) groups. This conclusion would be in keeping with suggestions that membership of these groups is largely unremarked in a society that codes certain races and ethnicities as different from an implicit norm. Silence on these matters could also, however, reflect the official position that race, ethnicity, and nationality are not relevant to legal proceedings or important for record-keeping purposes (Backhouse, 1999).

Given the silences within the official record, it can be particularly difficult to know by looking at judgments and official reports whether, for example, an accused person who was a member of a visible minority was perceived differently and/or treated differently within the process of death investigation and prosecution. For example, I cannot determine whether a deceased child whose mother was Jamaican by birth would have been perceived by hospital workers, police, and expert witnesses as non-White and, if so, whether this raised the index of suspicion in his death. The number of children and families who belonged to visible minorities is accordingly almost certainly under-counted within Table 10.3.

Race, ethnicity, and nationality are notoriously difficult to measure, and the social effects of being negatively racialized act through implicit perceptions of race as much, if not more, than by the explicit commitments of individuals (Greenwald, Poehlman, Uhlmann, & Banaji, 2009; Karpinski & Hilton, 2001). Greenwald and colleagues (2009) show that the same implicit operation is true of gender. Implicit prejudice is far more difficult to discern from a textual study than explicit prejudice. Sophisticated official actors are generally able to avoid speaking in terms that betray racial prejudice, even in cases where they seem relatively ready to stereotype the quality of a woman's mothering. A rare example of explicit prejudice is seen in the description of one deceased child as "mulatto" by a nurse witness. This term has highly derogatory connotations due to its historical connection with slavery, although it may not have (consciously) resonated in the same way with the witness. Lacking further information, this child's race and ethnicity is coded in Table 10.3 as unspecified. Despite the slipperiness of ascribing race and ethnicity through textual research, perceptions of race and ethnicity are worth attending to because these perceptions may affect how a particular death is investigated. While race and ethnicity were most often unremarked within the textual records, at least a third of the families in the Ontario cases included members who were identifiably racialized, Aboriginal, or immigrant.

A further axis along which the Ontario cases may be read is that of financial stability, as a proxy for the more difficult concept of class. This axis operated differently for women accused of neonaticide than for other deaths. Two young women (ages 18 and 21) were wrongly accused of killing newly born children (less than a day old) based on Smith's conclusions. They were both financially dependent upon their parents, with whom they lived, apparently in relatively comfortable circumstances. Most of those who were wrongly accused of killing older infants and children lived in far more precarious material circumstances. The overview reports, trial transcripts, and police reports contain references to welfare dependency, mouldy basement apartments, cramped and dirty housing, frequent financially motivated moves, parents having difficulty paying for infant food, and the deprived background of accused parents who had themselves been the victims of abuse or were wards of the state. Each of these factors likely increased the vulnerability of these children to natural causes of death because they have direct impacts on health. However, for police and doctors who investigated the deaths, they may also have raised suspicions about the quality of the caregiving provided by the relevant parents.

One member of a child abuse team testified at the Goudge Inquiry that risk factors for abuse included "financial hardships, number of children in the family, the housing situation, social network—often you found there were new arrivals in Canada with no social network" (Goudge, 2008b: 85). Each of these factors resonates with cultural tropes about the challenges of parenting—that it is easier when the family is financially stable, and has help to draw upon—and each is drawn from statistical studies of child abuse. However, errors arise when these factors shift from being a reason to offer more support to families at risk, or a reason to look more closely at an otherwise suspicious death, to becoming proof that a death was inflicted. Smith, and others involved in the Ontario cases, seemed at times to have made the slippage into using these factors as proof that parents and caregivers killed children. As is true with the use of gendered stereotypes to determine the likely manner of death and identify an assailant, the use of stereotypes about poor parents to determine cause of death in their children is profoundly inappropriate and may well help to explain the concentration of welfare-dependent parents among those who were wrongly accused in the Ontario cases.

At the start of his inquiry into the Ontario cases, Justice Goudge set out a list of systemic factors for investigation (Goudge, 2008a, Vol. 4: 310). These factors included attention to the training and role of forensic pathologists, coroners, and other actors in the Canadian criminal justice system. They also covered the mechanisms that might allow the criminal justice system to respond to changes in scientific knowledge and implement best practices when dealing with expert testimony. However, the list did not include factors that might relate to the operation of gender, race, and class stereotypes within criminal investigation and prosecution. Consequently, although many witnesses provided evidence that hinted at the role of stereotypes and prejudice within the work of investigating and prosecuting suspected child homicide, these hints were not pursued in Justice Goudge's report (2008a), or in the press coverage of the Inquiry.

Justice Goudge's report offers a nuanced and well-reasoned set of recommendations for improving the institutional arrangements and processes of child homicide investigation, and has led to considerable reform within the Ontario criminal justice system. However, within the media, the Ontario cases tend to be characterized as attributable to the failings of an individual expert witness. Concomitant to this characterization is that, having identified Smith's errors and corrected for them, the criminal justice system as a whole is presumed to (be continuing to) function at a high standard of reliability and objectivity. Unfortunately, the possibility that the criminal justice system might be vulnerable to the operation of negative stereotypes in place of careful evidence-based reasoning in child homicide cases was obscured. In the discussion of *R. v. Camire* (2009) that concludes this chapter, I question the belief that the child homicide trials conducted since 2008 are more rigorous and less susceptible to stereotype than those conducted when Dr. Smith was working in Ontario.

The Case of Michael: *R. v. Camire*

In the summer of 2004, Michelle Camire, already the mother of a 15-month-old girl, gave birth to triplets at 35 weeks' gestation. She spent four days in hospital recovering from the birth, and the triplets came home after 10 days. Camire's common law partner returned to work a week later. The family received assistance from Winnipeg Child and Family

Services, but the assigned carers often cancelled work, and some were poorly trained in caring for newborns. Camire received little help from her partner or extended family.

On the morning of October 22, 2004, Camire was alone with the four children. She fed the four-month-old triplets their bottles and placed two of them to sleep, but the third, Michael, was fussing. After Michael refused to finish his bottle and spit up some formula, Camire "slammed him down" into his bassinette, gave him a soother, and apologized to him for having laid him down more roughly than she should. Two hours later, two of the triplets awoke but Michael was pale and limp. Camire immediately called 911, but Michael did not respond to efforts at resuscitation. An autopsy found a large hemorrhage in the area between Michael's brain and skull, and a fracture in his skull. In an interview, Camire showed police how she had placed Michael into his bassinette. She demonstrated placing him roughly from about 8 inches above the mattress, and denied that he had hit his head on anything hard as he was put down. Experts suggested that the bleeding in Michael's skull could have been caused at any time in the preceding two days and that the fracture could not be dated from the autopsy alone; however, the subsequent investigation focused exclusively on Camire.

Camire was charged with manslaughter, and her surviving children were removed from her care. After two trials resulted in juries failing to agree on a verdict, the prosecution decided to pursue a third trial. The case relied primarily on two expert witnesses, who testified that Michael had likely been shaken and then subjected to an impact force that was analogous to the impact he would receive in a car crash (*R. v. Camire*, 2009, court record: 15). While acknowledging that it is difficult to date fractures, the experts suggested that the skull fracture could not have happened through any routine accident and was most likely caused by impact with a hard object. They proposed that the only plausible explanation for this combination of injuries was a severe impact, or a combination of shaking and impact, very shortly before death.

The caregivers who had assisted Camire testified that nothing had happened to Michael while in their care that could explain Michael's injuries. Answering questions asked by the defence, the caregivers agreed that Camire was a good mother who interacted well with the babies and showed genuine care and concern for them. The defence did not call any witnesses, including any medical experts. The court heard no information about the controversy regarding Abusive Head Trauma, or the degree of uncertainty expressed within the medical literature about how much force is necessary to cause the observed injuries in a very young baby. Nor was published research that suggests that the soft skull of a baby can readily be fractured by short falls, accidents, or even during birth presented at trial (see studies cited by Findley et al., 2012: 255). To the contrary, one Crown expert explained on cross-examination that "this is not a trivial injury, it's not a bump on the head, it's not a drop from someone's arms, not a roll off the sofa" (*R. v. Camire*, 2009, court record: 72). Another implied that literature reporting that toddlers may die from short falls does not cast doubt upon the proposition that considerable force must be used to cause the injuries seen in Michael (*R. v. Camire*, 2009, court record: 23). However, basic logic, neurological theory, and published research suggest that the softer skull and brain of an infant must be, if anything, more prone to injury than that of a toddler.

The prosecution ultimately suggested to the jury that the degree of force Camire used against Michael was "more similar to a car crash than falling from a bed," and that the use of such force showed that Camire intended to assault Michael (*R. v. Camire*, 2009, court record: 40). In this way, the expert testimony about the force needed to fracture an infant's skull was tied to the intent required for manslaughter and used to override the defence's argument that Camire's actions, while driven by frustration, were not intended to harm Michael and could not reasonably have been expected to cause serious injury. Throughout the case, experts, police, and prosecutors seem to have been influenced by Camire's choice of words in describing her handling of Michael, while rejecting her demonstration and her protestations that Michael had not hit anything hard. The investigation may have proceeded with too little attention to alternative possible explanations for his injuries.

Michelle Camire was convicted after the third trial. Camire received a conditional sentence from a judge who suggested that the care of her children be returned to her. She has not appealed her conviction. Soon after Camire was sentenced, an article appeared in the prestigious *Archives of Disease in Childhood*, reporting that two-thirds of newborns that fall less than a metre onto a hard surface in hospitals sustained a skull fracture (Ruddick, Ward Platt, & Lazaro, 2010). A growing body of research warns against using parents' statements about their handling of infants to corroborate prosecution theories of Abusive Head Trauma (Findley et al., 2012). However, research that demonstrates the need to proceed with caution in cases involving parental handling of young infants did not assist Camire to defend herself in Manitoba in 2009.

Conclusion

R. v. Camire (2009) illustrates that despite the courts' awareness of the miscarriages of justice that emerged as a result of Dr. Smith's zealous work, gendered stereotypes continue to affect investigation and decision making in cases of alleged child homicide. It seems likely that evidence of the continued operation of classed and racialized stereotypes would likewise emerge from a broader evaluation of contemporary child homicide trials. In this chapter, I have explained that stereotyping is a pervasive, unconscious process by which we make sense of our world. The biasing effects of negative stereotyping arguably played an important role in the wrongful convictions identified in Ontario.

Overlooking the role of these biasing effects in child homicide cases risks perpetuating error in this emotionally loaded corner of the criminal justice system. For as long as this dimension of legal decision-making processes remains little understood, mothers, the poor, and racialized suspects may continue to be vulnerable to being wrongly accused and improperly convicted based on the operation of stereotype rather than through the use of sound medical research and careful investigation into actual cause of death. Allowing the uncertainties that remain within the medical understanding of infant death to be resolved by negative stereotyping is antithetical to the rational and egalitarian model of fact determination that underlies most normative conceptions of criminal justice.

Notes

1 Thank you to Yun Li and Jennifer Dyck, who provided exceptional research assistance. The research on which this chapter is based is funded by the Social Sciences & Humanities Research Council of Canada.

References

American Academy of Pediatrics. (2006). "Distinguishing sudden infant death syndrome from child abuse fatalities." *Pediatrics*, 118: 421–427.

Alder, C., & Polk, K. (2001). *Child Victims of Homicide*. Cambridge: Cambridge University Press.

Backhouse, C. (1999). *Colour Coded: A Legal History of Racism in Canada, 1990–1950*. Toronto: University of Toronto Press for the Osgoode Society.

Bennett, W.L., & Feldman, M. (1981). *Reconstructing Reality in the Courtroom*. London and New York: Rutgers University Press.

Canadian Centre for Justice Statistics. (1998–2005). *Family Violence in Canada: A Statistical Profile*. Ottawa: Statistics Canada. Retrieved from www.statcan.ca/english/freepub/85-224-XIE/free.htm

Cunliffe, E. (2011). *Murder, Medicine and Motherhood*. Oxford: Hart Publishing.

Cunliffe, E. (2013). "Independence, reliability and expert reasoning in criminal trials." *Australian Journal of Forensic Sciences*, 45(3): 284–295.

Findley, K.A., Barnes, P.D., Moran, D.A., & Squier, W. (2012). "Shaken baby syndrome, abusive head trauma, and actual innocence: Getting it right." *Houston Journal of Law & Policy*, 12: 209–312.

Greenwald, A., Poehlman, T.A., Uhlmann, E.L., & Banaji, M.R. (2009). "Understanding and using the Implicit Association Test: III. Meta-analysis of predictive validity." *Journal of Personality and Social Psychology*, 97: 17–41.

Goudge, S.T. (2007). *Case Overview Reports*. Toronto: Government of Ontario.

Goudge, S.T. (2008a). *Report of the Inquiry into Ontario Pediatric Forensic Pathology in Ontario* (4 Volumes). Toronto: Queen's Printer.

Goudge, S.T. (2008b). Goudge Inquiry Transcripts. Retrieved from www.attorneygeneral.jus.gov.on.ca/inquiries/goudge/index.html

Hardin, C.D., & Banaji, M.R. (2012). "The nature of implicit prejudice: Implications for personal and public policy." In E. Shafir, ed., *The Behavioral Foundations of Public Policy* (pp. 13–31). Princeton, NJ: Princeton University Press.

Kahneman, D. (2011). *Thinking, Fast and Slow*. Toronto: Doubleday.

Karpinski, A., & Hilton, J. (2001). "Attitudes and the Implicit Association Test." *Journal of Personality and Social Psychology*, 81: 774–778.

Levene, S., & Bacon, C.J. (2004). "Sudden unexpected and covert homicide in infancy." *Archives of Disease in Childhood*, 89: 443–447.

Lothian, L.A. (2002). *Mapping Contested Terrain: The Doctrine of Failure to Protect in Canadian Criminal Law*. Master of Laws dissertation, University of British Columbia, Vancouver, BC.

Meadow, R. (1989). "ABC of child abuse: Suffocation." *British Medical Journal*, 298: 1572–1573.

Moreau, S. (2009). "The wrongs of unequal treatment." In F. Faraday & M. Denike, eds., *Making Equality Rights Real*. Toronto: Irwin Law.

Pennington, N., & Hastie, R. (1986). "Evidence evaluation in complex decision making." *Journal of Personality and Social Psychology*, 51: 242–258.

Prentice, M.A. (2001). "Prosecuting mothers who maim and kill." *American Journal of Criminal Law*, 28(3): 373–412.

Roberts, D. (1993). "Motherhood and crime." *Iowa Law Review*, 79: 95–142.

Ruddick, C., Ward Platt, M., & Lazaro, C. (2010). "Head trauma outcomes of verifiable falls in newborn babies." *Archives of Disease in Childhood, Fetal & Neonatal Edition*, 89: F144.

Ruesnick, M., & Free, M.D. (2007). "Wrongful convictions among women." *Women and Criminal Justice*, 16: 1–23.

Tyler, T. (2011, February 10). "15 years later, court overturns child murder conviction." *Toronto Star*. Retrieved from www.thestar.com/news/gta/2011/02/10/15_years_later_court_overturns_child_murder_conviction.html

Wilczynski, A. (1997). *Child Homicide*. London: Greenwich Medical Media.

Legal Cases and Statutes

R. v. Camire, [2009] 226 (MB.Q.B).

R. v. Kporwodu & Veno, [2005] O.J. No. 1405 (Quicklaw) (ON.Ct.A.).

R. v. Marquardt, [2011] 281 (ON.Ct.A.).

R. v. Mullins-Johnson, [2007] 720 (ON.Ct.A.).

R. v. M.(S.), [1991] O.J. No. 1383 (Quicklaw) (ON.Ct.Jus.).

R. v. Trotta [2007] 3 SCR 453, [2007] SCC 49.

Court Records

R. v. Camire, Manitoba Court of Queen's Bench docket Winnipeg Centre CR 06-01-26701.

R. v. Marquardt, Ontario Court of Appeal docket C24367.

R. v. Trotta, Ontario Court of Appeal docket CA M30565, C32352.

Part 3

Sex and the Social Context

Chapter 11

A Chip Off the Old (Ice) Block? Women-Led Families, Sperm Donors, and Family Law

Angela Cameron

This chapter provides a feminist analysis of an emerging issue at the nexus of reproductive technologies and family law; namely, the impact of changing regulations regarding sperm donor anonymity on women-led families.[1] While I strongly support the prospective de-anonymization of sperm donation (Cameron, Gruben, & Kelly, 2010), I argue that without prior family law reform, women-led families risk having an additional, unwanted third party inserted into their families by the law. This violates the family integrity that the law allows, and in some cases fiercely protects, in the context of heteronormative, nuclear families. Each province must urgently reform their family law to fully take into account parentage via artificial reproductive technologies. I argue they should do so in a way that facilitates three-parent, lesbian-led, and single-mother-led families' legal protection and autonomy.

Part I provides a short historical overview of the regulation of reproductive technologies generally, culminating with the December 2010 Supreme Court of Canada reference, striking down parts of the *Assisted Human Reproduction Act* (AHRA). Part II outlines the current state of the law regarding sperm donor anonymity and parental rights in light of these recent legal changes. Part III closely examines recent family law jurisprudence, which defines whether or not a sperm donor is a legal parent. In these cases I argue that heteronormative and nuclear-normative discourses function to justify the insertion of sperm donors into unwilling women-led families, while often simultaneously reducing or eclipsing the parental rights of one or more women parents within the family unit. In Part III I argue for a more transformative legal model of family, one that focuses on intentionality,[2] and (re)productive care[3] rather than biology or paternity.[4] Such a model would allow for the legal recognition of both women-led families and multiple-parent families that may include a sperm donor.

Part I

The history of the legal regulation of assisted human reproductive technologies in Canada is relatively short, but dynamic and complex. It was not until 1989 that the federal government began to consider legislating in the area, striking the Royal Commission on Reproductive Technologies (Baird, 1993). This was the first body in Canada to systematically consider the legal ramifications of these growing medical practices. The Commission heard from hundreds of private, professional, NGO, and government bodies and individuals across the country. In 1993 they released their final report (Baird, 1993) containing an exhaustive canvassing of many issues related to reproductive technologies, and issuing 293 detailed recommendations.

Among these recommendations, the Royal Commission dealt with parentage laws, warning that a lack of comprehensive legislation would be harmful to all members of families using reproductive technologies, as well as donors (Baird, 1993: 465). Twenty years later we still largely lack these important laws in most Canadian jurisdictions, and the negative effects alluded to by the Commission are being felt by many Canadian families.

The model legislation recommended by the Commission proposed to de-couple sperm donation from parenthood, allowing only donors who also filled the role of social parent to become legal parents (Baird, 1993: 467). Otherwise, the Commission recommended that the conjugal partner of the birth mother, regardless of their gender, be considered a legal parent. In families headed by single mothers by choice, the Commission points out their especial vulnerability to having a donor intercede as an unwanted legal parent, and recommends legislation that would allow these mothers to parent autonomously (Baird, 1993: 466). The Commission also notes that this type of law also protects donors from unwanted claims of paternity, child support, claims on their estates, or invasions of their own familial privacy (Baird, 1993: 468).[5]

In 2001, the federal government asked the House of Commons Standing Committee on Health to review the first draft of ground-breaking legislation based on the Commission's report, and to complete a report of their own (House of Commons, 2001). The Committee again solicited testimony from numerous stakeholders from across the country, releasing their report in 2001. The Committee recommended that donor anonymity be prohibited going forward, and that offspring be legally entitled to identifying information regarding the gamete donor (House of Commons, 2001: 18). As a necessary condition of known gamete donation, the Commission also recommended that

> [t]he federal Minister of Justice, in collaboration with provincial and territorial counterparts, seek to develop uniform legislation across the country establishing the legal status of donors in relation to offspring. (House of Commons, 2001: 34)

In particular, the Committee recommended that such laws should provide that donors hold neither legal liability toward any offspring (aside from revealing their identity at the age of majority of the child), nor any parenting rights.

The legislation itself, stemming from the report, purported to deal with all aspects of reproductive technologies, including cloning, stem cell research, and human reproduction. The legislation attempted to resolve the moral, ethical, and scientific controversies inherent in artificial reproductive practices (Cameron & Gruben, 2014). While numerous iterations were hotly debated in the House of Commons, the final version was not passed until 2006, creating Canada's first legislative regime governing reproductive technologies, the *Assisted Human Reproduction Act* (2004). Despite the recommendations of both the Commission and the Committee, however, due to the constitutional division of powers in Canada, issues of legal parentage were left to the provinces (Cameron & Gruben, 2014). Only Quebec moved to create a comprehensive family law regime, while the Yukon and Newfoundland passed partial laws. The result, which persists in most provinces, was a legal vacuum in the area of family law, despite federal legislation of other aspects of these medical practices.

Less than two years after the passage of the *Assisted Human Reproduction Act*, the province of Quebec launched a constitutional challenge, claiming that the federal act impinged upon their provincial powers to regulate the practice of medicine and the facilities where assisted human reproductive procedures were conducted. The challenge went to the Supreme Court of Canada, and in December 2010, the Court struck down large segments of the act (*Reference*, 2010), passing important aspects of the regulation of assisted reproductive technologies (ARTs) to the provinces, for example, whether or not sperm donors can and should remain anonymous (Cameron, Gruben, & Kelly, 2010). As with the family law provisions within their jurisdiction, most provinces have yet to regulate in these areas. The fallout is profound legal uncertainty in a number of key areas, but particularly around the legal parentage of sperm donors.

Part II

Who Are Women-Led Families?

Women-led families consist of either a lesbian couple or a single woman of any sexual orientation and their children. As with heterosexual family units, they are socially, legally, and economically interdependent and often live under the same roof. Children in women-led families may have been conceived either through a previous conjugal relationship with a man, where the man does not play the role of a social parent, or through reproductive technologies, involving a sperm donor. The chapter deals only with the legal status of those children born through reproductive technologies.

In many cases, single women and lesbian couples choose to use an anonymous[6] or identity-release[7] sperm donor because they plan to parent autonomously, and this kind of donor gives them the most legal security to do so (Kelly, 2011: 72; Mezey, 2008: 22–25). In other cases women choose a known donor for a variety of reasons, including a desire that their child be able to know both biological progenitors or have access to important health information (Mezey, 2008: 102–105), balancing this against the heightened legal security that an anonymous or identity-release donor can bring (Cameron, Gruben, & Kelly, 2010; Kelly, 2011: 41).

Finding a Sperm Donor in Canada: How Women-Led Families Conceive Children

In Canada, if a single woman or lesbian couple wants to use donor sperm to conceive a child, they have several choices. First, and most common, they can visit one of Canada's regulated,[8] private fertility clinics, where they will be offered a small catalogue of potential donors (see, e.g., www.repromed.ca/sperm_donor_catalogue). These donors are usually American, and sometimes Canadian, but all must comply with Canada's national health screening program for donated sperm (*Processing and Distribution of Semen for Assisted Conception Regulations*). The catalogues are generated by private, for-profit sperm banks, whose donor profiles contain wildly varied levels of information. For instance, some profiles show results for genetic screening, or contain both an adult and childhood photograph, or detailed family medical history. Other donors are depicted only as a sketched adult profile, with descriptors such as hair colour, eye colour, height, and IQ level. There is currently no legislative standard governing what information is to be contained in these profiles, or guaranteeing its accuracy. Fertility clinics in Canada are obliged to provide services to women regardless of their marital status or sexual orientation (AHRA, 2004: Preamble; *Potter*, 1995).

Clinics carry both anonymous and "identity release" donors (ReproMed, n.d.), although until very recently anonymous donors were the status quo. Under the sperm donation regulations, men who have had sexual contact with other men since 1977 are banned from donating sperm to the general supply available to fertility clinics (Cameron, 2008). The *Assisted Human Reproduction Act* also bans the commercialization of gametes; therefore, at least nominally, sperm is free at Canadian clinics. Clients pay for other services, including procedures and visits with doctors and clinicians (Ottawa Fertility Centre, 2013). The clinics themselves were heavily regulated under the AHRA (2004: s. 40), until many provisions were struck down by the Supreme Court of Canada in December 2010. While some sections affecting clinics remain in force (AHRA, 2004: ss. 5, 6, which prohibit anyone from performing certain activities), many aspects of the fertility industry are currently unregulated across Canada.

The second option is to use a known sperm donor. Again, since 1977, this can take place easily through a fertility clinic, so long as the donor has not had sexual contact with another man, or he is the sexual partner of the woman seeking treatment.[9] The donor's sperm is screened according to the sperm donation regulations to ensure that they meet health requirements. For sperm donors who have had sexual contact with other men during the prohibited time period, and are not the sexual partner of the woman who seeks to use their sperm, they and the recipient require a special dispensation from the Minister of Health to donate and receive this sperm in a fertility clinic (*Susan Doe*, 2007).

Known donation can also be accomplished at home, with self-insemination, using fresh or frozen sperm. This route circumvents many of the costs associated with a fertility clinic, and allows the recipient to choose a donor regardless of his sexual orientation or sexual practices. Resourceful families have relied on local medical clinics to mimic the screening procedures required under the national sperm regulations, ensuring that the sperm is free of body-fluid-borne pathogens (Kelly, 2010).

The Law Governing Sperm Donors in Canada: The Implications for Women-Led Families

Many aspects of anonymous and identity-release sperm donation remain unregulated in Canada. For instance, there is no legal limit to the number of offspring that can be born from a particular donor within a particular geographical area, no standards regarding the kinds of information that must be collected or updated from sperm donors, and no legislative mechanism for offspring to obtain health or other information from their donor on a one-time or ongoing basis. The number of children born to a particular donor is set by self-imposed guidelines through individual fertility clinics, and is based on self-reporting of a live birth by the parents of a child born through sperm donation.

Currently, the primary regulation of anonymous and identity-release sperm donors is through the health standards they must meet in order to donate sperm. Health Canada has strict Guidelines (*Food and Drug Regulations*) for the governing, screening, storage, transport, and distribution of sperm, including sperm that is imported from the United States. Aside from these regulations, the *Assisted Human Reproduction Act* dictates that neither sperm nor eggs can be bought or sold (AHRA, 2004: s. 7(1)), defines a sperm donor and sperm (AHRA, 2004: s. 3), and requires and regulates the consent of a donor for the use of their sperm in an artificial reproductive process (AHRA, 2004: ss. 8(1), 8(2), 9).[10] Since many provisions of the *Assisted Human Reproduction Act* were struck down, this represents the full legislative regime currently in place, outside of scattered family law provisions to be discussed below.

One important aspect of the law for women-led families is whether or not an anonymous or identity-release sperm donor may be deemed a parent for access, custody, and child support or inheritance purposes. Until 2010, it seemed settled in the law that anonymous and identity-release sperm donors were not legal parents, and did not have access or even contact rights to the children born using their gametes; nor were they obliged to pay child support or include donor offspring in their estates. In exchange, the anonymity of these donors was strictly protected, preventing offspring from receiving identifying information regarding their biological progenitors and from contacting them, unless they agreed to this as an identity-release donor.[11] However, as previously mentioned, in December 2010 the Supreme Court of Canada struck down parts of the *Assisted Human Reproduction Act*, leaving the provinces to fill this gap. As few provinces have moved to do so, the law is currently in flux.

Also, in 2010, a young adult born using anonymous donated sperm, Ms. Olivia Pratten, brought a case before British Columbia's courts, claiming that her inability to access identifying information about her sperm donor was a violation of her section 15 *Charter* right to equality (*Pratten*, 2011, 2012; *Adoption Act*, 1996).[12] She was successful in her lower court application (*Pratten*, 2010), but her claim was denied by the British Columbia Court of Appeal (*Pratten*, 2012).The Supreme Court of Canada upheld that decision, denying Ms. Pratten's appeal (*Pratten*, 2013). While this means that adult offspring like Olivia Pratten are not automatically able to contact or meet their *anonymous* sperm donors at will, or have donors contact them, this leaves several legal questions of significance to women-led families unanswered. First, the status of *known* sperm donors in relation to donor offspring is still in question. Second, even where an anonymous donor is used, not all provinces have family law legislation that facilitates either the legal protection of parenting rights for single mothers by choice, or for non-biological mothers in a same-sex relationship. In light of the jurisprudence discussed below, it seems clear that some judges, relying on gendered stereotypes about the need for a father or father figure in the lives of children, may insert an unwanted known sperm donor into women-led families with minor children, against their wishes.

The legal status of known sperm donors vis-à-vis single mothers by choice or lesbian mothers is also quite unclear, and is the primary subject of Part III of this chapter. These families rely on a variety of legal mechanisms in an attempt to clearly delineate legal parenting, access, and decision-making rights, including pre-birth contracts and adoption (Kelly, 2011). In the absence of clear legislation in many provinces, however, courts have been making inconsistent decisions, and in some cases, they have inserted an unwanted sperm donor as a parent into women-led families.

Province by Province: The Legal Status of Sperm Donors—Parents or Absent Gift-Givers?

Since the 2010 decision of the Supreme Court of Canada in the *Reference re Assisted Human Reproduction Act*, responsibility for the regulation of donor anonymity, including the collection and disclosure of identifying and non-identifying data, has passed from the federal government to the individual provinces and territories. For those few provinces who have taken steps to legislate in the area, most have made it clear that anonymous and identity-release sperm donors are not legal parents. However, they fail to regulate the collection and distribution of health or identifying information regarding sperm donors. There are many provinces, though, that have yet to legislate in either area, including Ontario. This is significant, due to the large population in this province and the presence of the largest number of fertility clinics in the country.

Below is a brief description of the current legal regime (or lack thereof) in a cross-section of provinces and territories, with an emphasis on the implications for women-led families. Each section describes three pertinent aspects of the provincial law in question: first, whether the act designates anonymous and identity-release sperm donors as legal parents or not; second, if the legislation allows for more than two legal parents; and third, if the act creates a legal presumption that non-biological lesbian mothers are legal parents. It is worth noting that all jurisdictions require that parenting rights be exercised within the boundaries of the best interests of the child; including but not limited to protecting children from abuse, and ensuring that they maintain contact with and have access to people with whom they have developed deep bonds.

Even in jurisdictions where legislation exists, such as Quebec, the parental status of *known* donors is still complicated and contested. Disputes between women-led families and known donors often require a court to decide if the donor is "simply" a sperm donor, or a parent, based on a number of factors.

Quebec[13]

Only two jurisdictions have comprehensive legislation on parentage via assisted human reproduction: British Columbia[14] and Quebec. Because Quebec's regime has been in place longer, the majority of cases discussed in Part III are from courts in this province. This also makes Quebec a jurisdiction worth closer study in general, as their legislative model may be emulated by other provincial lawmakers drafting family law to reflect the role of artificial reproductive technologies in their respective jurisdictions. As Part III will demonstrate, however, even having a liberal, comprehensive legislative scheme does not guarantee the parental autonomy of women-led families.

In 2002, amendments were made to the *Civil Code of Québec* (CCQ, 1991) regarding legal parental status and assisted procreation. The changes base filiation[15] on the "parental project"—essentially centring intentionality as a fundamental aspect of a legal family. A spouse is defined as someone either in a marriage or civil union with the birth mother, meaning that the spouses must have formalized their relationship. This differs from many common law jurisdictions, where common law couples can automatically make claims to legal parenthood in cases involving ARTs.[16] The CCQ also explicitly recognizes single mothers by choice, allowing the birth mother to legally declare that there is no other parent.[17] The legislation does not allow for more than two legal parents (Leckey, 2009: 70), eliminating the possibility that a lesbian couple and a known sperm donor could co-parent. In the final analysis this means that one of these three adults must be legally severed from children born through sperm donation.

Under the CCQ, sperm donors are not legal parents. Section 538.2 of the *Code* (1991) states:

> 538.2. The contribution of genetic material for the purposes of a third-party parental project does not create any bond of filiation between the contributor and the child born of the parental project.

Under this section there is no differentiation between anonymous, known, or identity-release sperm donors (Leckey, 2011c: 584). So long as it is clear that there was no intention on the part of the parties that the sperm donor be a parent, no donor, known or otherwise, has any filial ties to the children of others' parental projects unless the donation was made through intercourse.

However, if the genetic material is provided by way of sexual intercourse, a bond of filiation may be established, in the year following the birth, between the contributor and the child. During that period, the spouse of the woman who gave birth to the child cannot make a parentage claim that interferes with the claim for filiation by the donor (CCQ, 1991: s. 538.2). In other words in the case of donation through sexual intercourse, a 12-month period starting at conception is reserved for the donor to change his mind and assert parental rights (CCQ, 1991: s. 538.2, para. 2). This is done explicitly at the expense of the non-biological lesbian parent, whose legal footing in relation to her child is less certain to begin with.

Significantly, Quebec regulates the collection and distribution of identifying information from anonymous gamete donors and recipients.[18] Except for a circumstance where a child (or a close relative of the child) is in danger of serious harm, no identifying information from any donor is to be disclosed. Section 542 reads:

> Personal information relating to medically assisted procreation is confidential. However, where the health of a person born of medically assisted procreation or of any descendant of that person could be seriously harmed if the person were deprived of the information requested, the court may allow the information to be transmitted confidentially to the medical authorities concerned. A descendant of such a person may also exercise this right where the health of that descendant or of a close relative could be seriously harmed if the descendant were deprived of the information requested.

Alberta

Alberta's laws regarding the parental status of sperm donors and of women-led family members (such as non-biological lesbian mothers) have undergone important changes in the last year. Formerly, under Alberta's *Family Law Act* (FLA, 2003), a sperm donor had no parental rights unless he was the marital or conjugal partner of the birth mother. In fact, the male marital or conjugal partner of the birth mother, even if he did not contribute the sperm, was *presumed* to be a legal father. This legal presumption did not flow for lesbian partners who would have to take extra steps, such as adoption, to secure legal parenting rights.

The recent case of *D.W.H. v. D.J.R.* (2011), coupled with legislative amendments (*Family Law Statutes Amendment Act*, 2010), have addressed these problems. First, the presumption of parental status now applies to the birth mother's marital or conjugal partner regardless of gender. In other words, the non-biological mother in a lesbian relationship is granted presumptive legal parent status, as a male partner would be in her position (FLA, 2003: s. 8.1(2)(i)). There is no need to show a biological connection to the child, only a marital or conjugal relationship with the birth mother.

Second, the act dictates that a sperm donor who donates sperm "not for his own reproductive use" is not a legal parent:

> 7(2) The following persons are the parents of a child:
> (4) A person who donates human reproductive material or an embryo for

> use in assisted reproduction without the intention of using the material or embryo for his or her own reproductive use is not, by reason only of the donation, a parent of a child born as a result.

This section is potentially problematic for women-led families. First, the word "intention" in section 7(2) leaves it open for a *known* sperm donor to claim parenting rights in a woman-led family. A known donor could argue that he, rather than the birth mother's female marital or cohabiting partner, intended to co-parent, and that therefore he donated his sperm for his own reproductive use. This possibility is exacerbated by section 8.2(7), which prohibits the legal existence of more than two parents, making it impossible, for instance, for a lesbian couple and a known sperm donor to legally co-parent in a three-parent arrangement. In circumstances involving a conflict between a known donor and a lesbian couple, the outcome can name only two of them as legal parents.

Specifically in relation to single mothers by choice, the 2007 case of *Jane Doe v. Alberta*,[19] forecloses the possibility of a unilateral declaration of sole parenthood, even when using donated sperm. This is in sharp contrast to Quebec, where such a declaration is explicitly allowed for.

Newfoundland and Labrador

Newfoundland and Labrador was one of the first provinces to pass provincial legislation dealing specifically with sperm donors (*Children's Law Act*, 1990). Newfoundland's act states that unless a sperm donor is the marital or cohabitating partner of the birth mother, they are not considered a parent. The act is silent on the parental status of female partners of birth mothers.

> 12(4) A man whose semen is used to artificially inseminate a woman to whom he is not married or with whom he is not cohabiting at the time of the insemination is not in law the father of the resulting child. (*Children's Law Act*, 1990: s. 12(4))

From the perspective of women-led families, this closes the door on parental claims from anonymous, identity-disclosure, and known donors, unless the donor was also a marital or cohabiting partner of the birth mother at the time of the insemination. Unlike Alberta, Newfoundland allows for a presumption of legal parental status only for male partners of birth mothers (*Children's Law Act*, 1990: s. 10(2–5)), meaning that lesbian couples may have to take extra steps, such as adoption, to firmly secure full parenting rights for the non-biological parent. This, and other family law statutes in this jurisdiction, is silent on the number of legal parents each child may have.

Nova Scotia

Nova Scotia's statute mandates that if a birth mother is married, the spouse must be registered as the child's other parent (*Birth Registration Regulations* [BRR], 2009). This seems to function as a presumption of legal parental status only for married spouses, but should apply to married spouses of either gender, as marriage is now legal for both opposite and same-sex couples (*Reference re Same-Sex Marriage,* 2004). If a birth mother is unmarried, it is the person whom the birth mother acknowledges as the other parent who is permitted to file a Statutory Declaration stating that they intend to act as a parent to the child (BRR, 2009: s 3(2)). The act does not stipulate that the other parent must be of the male gender. For lesbian couples who are married, this creates an automatic right to legal parentage. For unmarried lesbian couples, this leaves the door open for the birth mother to immediately include her partner as a legal parent. Because the legislation seems to rely on a two-parent model, it is less clear whether a single mother by choice can easily protect her legal rights as a sole parent, particularly if using a known donor. This, and other family law statutes in this jurisdiction, are silent on the number of legal parents a child may have.[20]

Yukon

The Yukon's legislation is similar to that of Newfoundland, basically stating that unless the sperm donor is a marital or cohabiting partner with the birth mother, he is not a legal parent. The act is silent on the status of female partners to birth mothers (*Child and Family Services Act* [CFSA], 2002). Again, like Newfoundland, the Yukon act allows for a presumption of legal parental status only for male partners of birth mothers (CFSA, 2002: ss. 13(2), 12), meaning that lesbian couples may also have to take extra steps such as adoption to firmly secure full parenting rights for the non-biological parent in this jurisdiction. This, and other family law statutes in this jurisdiction, are silent on the number of legal parents each child may have, although section 12(2) of the act prohibits a court finding more than one legal father.

British Columbia

British Columbia has been actively reforming its legislation over the past several years to make the determination of legal parentage clearer. This has resulted in a new act that came into force on March 18, 2013. Like Quebec, it strives to provide comprehensive legal guidance on parentage where reproductive technologies are used.

Under BC's new law, the donor of gametes is never, simply by virtue of having donated, a parent. In other words, a donor must also act as a social parent, or he must be the birth mother's marital or conjugal partner (*Family Law Act*, 2011). As in Quebec, for single mothers by choice, this falls short of being able to declare that they are the child's only parent, but it does provide ample legal protection from unwanted intrusion by known and anonymous sperm donors. Non-biological mothers in lesbian relationships are also granted presumptive legal parental status, as a male partner would be in their position (*Family Law Act*, 2011: s. 27).

British Columbia's new legislation explicitly allows for the legal recognition of three parents under certain circumstances. Section 30 reads:

> This section applies if there is a written agreement that
> (a) is made before a child is conceived through assisted reproduction,
> (b) is made between
> (i) an intended parent or the intended parents and a potential birth mother who agrees to be a parent together with the intended parent or intended parents, or
> (ii) the potential birth mother, a person who is married to or in a marriage-like relationship with the potential birth mother, and a donor who agrees to be a parent together with the potential birth mother and a person married to or in a marriage-like relationship with the potential birth mother, and
> (c) provides that
> (i) the potential birth mother will be the birth mother of a child conceived through assisted reproduction, and
> (ii) on the child's birth, the parties to the agreement will be the parents of the child.
> (2) On the birth of a child born as a result of assisted reproduction in the circumstances described in subsection (1), the child's parents are the parties to the agreement.
> (3) If an agreement described in subsection (1) is made but, before a child is conceived, a party withdraws from the agreement or dies, the agreement is deemed to be revoked.

In other words, where donated gametes are used, and the parties enter into a pre-birth contract, a lesbian couple and their sperm donor could all have legal parenting rights, subject to the contract and the best interests of the child.

Ontario

While Ontario has yet to systemically reform its family law to take into account women-led families, as Quebec has done, there have been some piecemeal changes through litigation by queer families. In the 2006 case of *Rutherford*, a judge struck down as unconstitutional provisions of Ontario's birth registration legislation that discriminated against lesbian couples. The lesbian couple in *Rutherford* successfully argued that while the male partner of a woman using anonymously donated sperm could automatically register himself as the "other parent" on the relevant birth registration forms, the female partner of a birth mother could not.[21] It is striking to note that, unlike many other provinces, Ontario's presumption of legal parentage remains homophobic: only automatically recognizing a male partner of a birth mother as the legal parent of a child born of reproductive technologies (*Children's Law Reform Act*, 1990).

In 2007 a family consisting of a lesbian couple and a known sperm donor, all of whom had acted as social parents, made an application to allow for three parents to appear on the birth certificate of their child. The decision in *(A.)A. v. (B.)B.* (2007) permitted the legal recognition of a family made up of two mothers and a father, although this case was specific to the factual circumstances and should not be understood as automatically enabling three-parent families.

The lack of clarity in Ontario's legislation regarding parentage for families who use donated sperm has spawned at least one court case (*Deblois*, 2012). The *National Post*, in June 2012, reported that a lesbian couple who conceived using sperm from a known donor may become the subject of a lawsuit by the donor. Mr. Deblois was seeking a declaration that he is a parent to the boy born from the donation, and liberal access to the child. The lesbian parents contested his assertion, stating that the donor signed a pre-birth contract eschewing all parenting rights, and that with regard to their son, "[h]is family is complete." (Blackwell, 2012).

Part III

This part of the chapter examines two family law cases that define whether or not a sperm donor is a legal parent. In these cases, heteronormative and nuclear-normative discourses function to justify the insertion of sperm donors into unwilling women-led families while often simultaneously reducing or eclipsing the parental rights of one or more women parents within the family unit. Both cases below deal with lesbian-led families, where two women are seeking parental rights. Single mothers by choice, regardless of their sexual orientation, also fare badly when their parenting rights are placed against those of a known sperm donor. There is very little scope for a single woman to parent autonomously where a male biological progenitor seeks parenting rights, outside of the regime created in Quebec (see, e.g., *Droit de la famille*, 2008; *Johnson-Steeves*, 1997, 1998; *Caufield*, 2007; *Droit de la famille*, 2011).

I also argue for a more transformative legal model of family, one that focuses on intentionality and (re)productive care (Boyd, 2007, 2010; Kelly, 2009a, 2009b) rather than biology or paternity, which would avoid the heart-wrenching outcomes in these cases. Such a model would allow for the legal recognition of both women-led families and multiple-parent families, which may include a sperm donor within the confines of intention, parenting work, and the best interests of the child.

While the number of cases discussed below is fairly small, this fact does not render them unimportant. While judges alone do not, of course, shape either the law or our society, "judicial attitudes and expression grow out of and are manifestations of more general social and legal attitudes and expression" (MacDougall, 2000: 5).[22] This is especially true when provincial legislation itself is completely lacking, incomplete, or vague. Judges, through their common law jurisdiction, have the mandate to make the law as they see fit. This has the potential to create poor precedents with a major impact on large numbers of families, and to affect the lives of litigants in profound and troubling ways. In the case of women-led families, the legal lacunae left by the *Reference re Assisted Human Reproduction Act* (2010) makes these few pronouncements extremely important and precedent-setting.[23]

Parentage Cases

S.G. v. L.C. (2004)[24] is a Quebec case which, although eventually subject to a publication ban due to the stress placed on the family from media scrutiny (*S.G.*, 2004), tells the story of a married lesbian couple who, despite both being registered on the Act of Birth,[25] had their parenting rights displaced by a known sperm donor.

On May 4, 2004, Justice Courteau in the Quebec Superior Court granted an order for access by S.G. to M., a child born in 2003, then nine months old. Although S.G. had consistent access to M. since her birth, M. had been living with her two married lesbian mothers since her birth, and was conceived using S.G.'s sperm via artificial insemination by physician. When S.G. filed for recognition of his paternity, and therefore rights as a parent, the mothers cut off his access. The mothers filed no affidavits, so the findings of fact were based entirely on the assertion by S.G. that, despite being married to her lesbian partner, the birth mother of M. intended to enter into a "parental project" with S.G.

The mothers' position was that "S.G. has no legal standing to ask for any access to M. His participation to her medically assisted procreation does not give him any rights" (*S.G.*, 2004, at para. 19). Although Justice Courteau cited the relevant section of the 1991 *Civil Code of Québec*, namely, that without sexual intercourse, a sperm donor in S.G.'s situation has no parental rights, she goes on to find that he was, indeed, in a parental project with M.'s birth mother. This is, with all due respect, clearly a misreading of the *Civil Code*. Justice Courteau notes that, at the time her decision was made, "[t]here has been little, if any, interpretation of these provisions by the courts (*S.G.*, 2004, at para. 30). This, perhaps, could explain Justice Courteau's disregard of the *Civil Code*'s clear directive that

> 538.2 The contribution of genetic material for the purposes of a third-party parental project does not create any bond of filiation between the contributor and the child born of the parental project.
>
> However, if the genetic material is provided by way of sexual intercourse, a bond of filiation may be established, in the year following the birth, between the contributor and the child. During that period, the spouse of the woman who gave birth to the child may not invoke possession of status consistent with the act of birth in order to oppose the application for establishment of the filiation.

Justice Courteau rests her finding on the fact, alleged by S.G. in his affidavit, that he and the birth mother had intended to enter into a parental project. The fact that the mothers were married, cohabiting, and co-parenting M., and that they cut off S.G.'s access to M. when he attempted to change his legal status vis-à-vis M. indicates otherwise. M.'s mothers evinced a clear intention, and showed in their daily lives, that they were M.'s parents. While acrimony between the parties may have prevented a three-parent family from forming, the law in Quebec would have prevented legal recognition of three parents, making S.G.'s bid for legal recognition a zero-sum game. Either he or M.'s non-biological mother could be recognized as parents, not both.

Justice Courteau relies on a biologically essentialist view of procreation in erroneously applying the *Civil Code*, noting that "the Court believes that a person's status is of public order and cannot be created artificially" (*S.G.*, 2004, at para. 50). Presumably this means that ties of biology, regardless of the *Civil Code*'s elaborate regime establishing filiation outside blood bonds, should prevail. This, of course, must implicitly exclude lesbian couples as legitimate parents, due to their biological inability to create a filiation by blood with both parents. Justice Courteau also leans heavily on heteronormative notions of the importance of fatherhood in granting S.G. interim access to M., against the wishes of her mothers.[26] First, while declining to assign legal paternity to S.G. in this interim application, Justice Courteau quotes extensively from S.G.'s pleadings, which place a strong emphasis on his important role as "father." No mention is made in the judgment of the daily parenting work being done by both of M.'s mothers.

> This attitude is totally destructive and is made in an attempt to punish Defendant for exercising his rights as a parent and at the same time depriving M's rights to her *father*, preventing her from further developing a loving and stable relationship with Plaintiff; Plaintiff has seen his daughter on a regular basis, and is fully capable of tending to her needs and taking care of her, and it is certainly in the child's best interest to have contact with her *father*. (*S.G.*, 2004, at para. 54; emphasis added)

Second, Justice Courteau effectively ignores any legal integrity granted to lesbian-led families via the *Civil Code*. In granting S.G. access, Justice Courteau observes that the insertion of an unwanted male person into this family, against the express wishes of both parents, will cause no harm.

> If she continues seeing him until judgment is rendered on the merits, if the Motion is dismissed, no prejudice will have been caused to her by having a loving and caring person in her life, during all these months. (*S.G.*, 2004, at para. 64)

It is difficult to imagine a judge making a similar disposition in a case where, within a heterosexual family unit, a known sperm donor wanted access against the wishes of the birth mother and social father. That family, almost certainly, would be considered intact and inviolable. The kind of legal and social integrity to which heterosexual families are entitled is denied to M.'s mothers. Finally, despite having never been left alone with S.G., in fact, with access having been always held in the mothers' home, Justice Courteau orders M. to have frequent, unsupervised visits with him.[27] Having a "loving and caring" third party, no matter how long you have known them, allowed unsupervised access to your infant daughter against your wishes is an affront to parental autonomy and very difficult to imagine in cases involving an intact, heterosexual couple.

A. v. B., C. and X. (2003)[28] is a second case that speaks clearly to the interests of non-biological lesbian mothers in family law reform, which takes their caregiving work and intentional parenting into account in meaningful ways. Between 1990 and 1994, B. and A. lived as lesbian intimate partners. They bought a home together, shared finances, and cohabitated. During that time A. gave birth to a baby, C. Between C.'s birth and 1996, B. acted as parent to C., at which point A. cut off B.'s access. This application was brought in 2003 to take advantage of Quebec's newly changed laws that allow for lesbian mothers to be granted filiation where artificial reproductive technologies were used. B. alleged that A. became pregnant during their relationship via artificial insemination, using the sperm of D., and that B. was heavily involved in planning the pregnancy, in assisting at the birth, and in parenting C. after her birth. According to Quebec law, A. and B. had entered into a parental project together, thus making B. C.'s legal parent. A. claimed that, instead, C. had been conceived by sexual intercourse between herself and D., completely unbeknownst to and against the wishes of B., making the parental project either hers alone, or hers and D.'s. The record shows that A. travelled to visit D. for the purpose of becoming pregnant by artificial insemination, and told B. at the time that the conception occurred in this way.

In 2002, despite the fact that D. had never acted as a parent to C.,[29] A. supported a successful motion by D. to be recognized as C.'s father. B.'s initial application was to have

D.'s name removed as a legal parent to C., and hers substituted, giving her legal leverage to make an application for access to C. More than 10 years before her relationship with B., A. lived in a heterosexual, intimate relationship with D. When A. and D. broke up, the Court found that D. offered to act as a sperm donor, and not a father, upon finding out that A. was now in a lesbian relationship.

In his decision, the Honourable Gaétan Dumas found against B.'s application, instead granting parental status to D. Because of the fact that, in Quebec, a child cannot have three parents, this effectively excluded B. from parental status completely. Justice Dumas based his decision on a strict interpretation of the new *Civil Code* provisions, which deal with "friendly assisted reproduction" or the donation of sperm via sexual intercourse for the parental project of another. In this case, Justice Dumas reasoned, the legislation allows for the sperm donor by sexual intercourse to claim parental status within one year of conception, regardless of who is actually parenting the child. In this case, D. claimed parental status within one year *of the legislation being passed*, which was in fact almost five years after the birth of C. During the intervening period of C.'s childhood, B. acted as a parent but was prevented from claiming parental status due to D.'s exercising his legislative prerogative to be recognized as a parent. The retroactive nature of the *Civil Code* provisions in this case means that B. parented for four years, until A. denied access, while the provisions were not yet in place. The changes came into play only after C. was about seven years old.

B. appealed the decision denying her parental status, and the Quebec Court of Appeal upheld the lower court's decision, denying B. parental status. In their decision, the Court emphasizes D.'s role as a "parent," and compares B. and D.'s involvement in C.'s life in a way that renders invisible the fact that during the first four years of C.'s life B. acted in the capacity of a full parent, while D. was living in another city.

> D had been communicating with the child and sending him gifts since his birth. In May 1997, D was in City C for training. He visited the child for the first time and since then has spent a few days with him every summer. In October 1997, he spent five days with the child. In the summers of 1998, 1999, and 2000, he spent ten days with him. In the summer of 2001, they spent fourteen days together. During the summers of 2002, 2003, 2004, they spent three weeks together, and in the summer of 2005, one month. (*A. v. B., C. and X.*, 2003, at para. 22)

The Court also places heavy emphasis in the factual record (5 of the 28 paragraphs) on the previous heterosexual relationship between A. and D., which occurred more than a decade before C. was conceived and was of similar duration to the lesbian relationship between B. and A. The Court goes to great lengths to emphasize the fact that, during their heterosexual relationship, D. and A. were unsuccessful in conceiving a child, but leaves aside most of the extensive factual matrix outlined in the lower court's decision, which points to a carefully executed, fully intended parental project between A. and B. The emphasis on heterosexual reproduction to the detriment of intention and actual parenting effectively excludes B. from the legal and social picture, thus erasing her equal role in the planning, birth, and parenting of her son, leaving only a heterosexual couple whose reproductive goals were "interrupted" by time and circumstance. Imagine, from B.'s point of view, planning for the conception of your child with your partner, attending the birth, and parenting your son for four years, only to have him completely removed from your care and access denied with no legal recourse. To add insult to injury, the sperm donor is not only named legal father but history is reconstructed to give him an equal role as "parent," when in reality, as you parented your son, he lived in another city and did not even meet C. until the child was four years old. Ironically, if B. had been able to show that C. was conceived using artificial rather than "friendly" sperm donation, which the lesbian couple planned and tried twice, the outcome would have been very different, opening the door for B. to establish her status as parent based on the planned parental project, and her actual parenting of C. for the first four years of his life.

Currently, then, the "friendly assisted reproduction" provisions give sperm donors by sexual intercourse a trump card against non-biological mothers within the first year of their children's lives. If a donor by sexual intercourse, *despite the intentions of the lesbian couple and the donor before the conception*, decides to claim parental status, the non-biological lesbian mother must lose her parenting status, and possibly her parenting rights, even if she has been the primary caregiver. This is due to the fact that a child in Quebec cannot have more than two parents, leaving those legal titles for the biological mother and the sperm donor who claims parental status within one year.

Rethinking the Legal Family: Intentionality and Reproductive Care

These kinds of judicial outcomes[30] are the combined product of a number of factors that may be addressed and ameliorated. First, most provinces do not have comprehensive legislation dealing with assisted human reproduction and parentage, leaving a legal gap that allows for misguided judicial decision making. Provinces that do not have existing legislation must promulgate parentage laws, using British Columbia and Quebec as working examples. For reasons outlined below, the legislative regime must, like Quebec's, focus on intentionality, but require modification to allow for three-parent families and single-mother-by-choice families as in British Columbia, where it is intended by the parties, and where it is in the best interest of the child.

Second, in most provinces the law is explicitly unable and unwilling to recognize more than two parents, leading to a zero-sum game for queer families that might otherwise consist of a lesbian couple and a known sperm donor. In all provinces except British Columbia and Ontario, on a case-by case basis, one of the three possible parents must lose their parental status in order to allow for the legal recognition of a parenting duo. For example, in the Quebec case discussed above, *A. v. B., C. and X.* (2003), Justice Gaétan Dumas notes that, in part, his decision to sever the non-biological mother's parenting rights was dictated by the fact that it is impossible to have three parents under Quebec law. Further, in relation to the Quebec regime, it is worth noting that the provision for "friendly assisted reproduction" allows a donor by sexual intercourse, within one year, to intercede in an existing lesbian-led or single-mother-by-choice family, regardless of how much parenting a non-biological mother may do within that first year of the child's life, because the child can only have two legal parents. Rather than giving biology a trump card, donors by sexual intercourse must be held to the same standard of intentionality; that is, the adults who intend to hold legal parentage before the child is born, especially where they actually do parenting work, remain the legal parents regardless of how the sperm was donated.[31]

And finally, it is clear that judicial discourse is deeply informed by the heteronormative and heteronuclear assumption that a lone mother or two mothers are insufficient parents unto themselves, and that a child needs a father or father figure for healthy development.[32] A clear legal regime that protects women-led families explicitly would counter the prevailing heteronormative and heteronuclear tide, and would provide specific legal protection for these families. Particular legislation, such as Quebec's, which allows for a single mother by choice to unilaterally declare that she is the sole parent of her child, provides much needed security and autonomy for this family form.

Notes

1 For clarity, "woman" refers to cisgender women, and "man" refers to cisgender men. Cisgender means that your perception of your gender matches the biological sex you were assigned at birth.

2 Intentionality in relation to parentage laws focuses on the intentions of the adult parties regarding who will hold legal parentage. The relevant binding time period is during the conception of the child, and leading up to its birth. Any change to the parenting rights after that time—including access and custody—must be negotiated and consented to by the adults who are intended to be the child's parents. In several cases discussed below, we see the pre-birth intentions of women-led families stymied by the existing law, and the post-birth wishes of sperm donors substituted for the pre-birth agreement (Craig 2010; Leckey 2011a, 2011b; Millbank, 2008).

3 (Re)productive care refers to the ways in which women's actual parenting work, including carrying and nurturing children and the sacrifices made in the name of maternity, are eclipsed by an emphasis on biological connection with another parent who provides little or no (re)productive care. The need to "find fathers," especially biologically related fathers, for children in women-led families is part of this trend toward rendering women's (re) productive work invisible or of diminished importance (Boyd, 2007, 2010; Kelly, 2009a, 2009b).

4 A combination of intentionality and (re)productive care following the birth of the child will be necessary to equitably determine parental rights in women-led families, particularly in cases where lesbian couples split up, where single mothers by choice are faced with parentage claims by sperm donors, and in three-parent families where (re)productive care is unequally divided among the three involved adults. What the parties agreed to before the child was born, and who has been doing the actual parenting, I argue, must trump biology in all cases. Recent legislation passed in British Columbia (see below) does an admirable job of taking these factors into account.

5 For example, a sperm donor may choose not to disclose his donation to future intimate partners or children that he parents, making the intervention of donor offspring at a later date a threat to his family integrity and privacy.

6 In this chapter, anonymity means that no identifying information is disclosed to women using donor sperm, or to any offspring born from donor sperm. Non-identifying information, such as hair colour, height, weight, basic medical information, and social information, such as hobbies, favourite foods, colours, and so forth, are made available. This information may include photographs of the donor as a child or as an adult, and an essay or letter from the donor indicating why they chose to donate.

7 Identity-release donors have agreed to share identifying information with any offspring at a given age, usually 18. The information, however, is held by a private sperm bank, which has no legal obligation to keep track of the donor and offers no legal guarantee the identity will be on file as the offspring turn 18.

8 The clinics themselves were heavily regulated under the AHRA (2004: s, 40), until many provisions were struck down by the Supreme Court of Canada in December 2010. While some sections affecting clinics remain in force (AHRA, 2004: ss. 5, 6), many aspects of the fertility industry are currently unregulated across Canada.

9 This rule creates particular problems for queer families (Cameron, 2008; *Susan Doe*, 2007). The prohibition was challenged as a violation of constitutionally protected equality. The case was unsuccessful. See *Susan Doe v. Canada* (2007).

10 Sections 8(1), 8(2) (this includes posthumous use of sperm), s. 9 (includes the sperm of those under 18 years).

11 Formerly ss. 14, 15, 16 of the AHRA (2004).

12 Ms. Pratten compared herself to children who were adopted and able to access information about their biological progenitors at age 18 under British Columbia law.
13 For detailed accounts of the changes in Quebec's law, see Campbell, 2007; Giroux, 2006; Leckey, 2009, 2011c.
14 See below: British Columbia's comprehensive legislation came into force in March 2013.
15 For a detailed exploration of the concept of filiation in English, see Leckey (2009: 63–65).
16 This distinction between spouses who have registered a civil union or marriage, versus those living in common law relationships, was recently upheld by the Supreme Court of Canada in relation to spousal support. This likely means that in order for lesbian couples to take advantage of the automatic right of legal parenthood, they must have entered one of these two forms of legally recognized relationships. See *Quebec (Attorney General)* (2013).
17 As noted in Leckey (2011c: 587), this contrasts sharply with common law jurisprudence where a single mother was not permitted, even with the consent of the biological father, to declare herself a sole parent. See *Doe v. Alberta* (2007).
18 According to Leckey (2009: 67) this right to privacy does not extend to known gamete donors.
19 *Doe* (2007b), leave to appeal to SCC refused (*Doe*, 2007).
20 In fact, the *Maintenance and Custody Act* (1989) is preoccupied with finding biological fathers through heterosexual intercourse in order to make them responsible for child maintenance, and does not deal with artificial reproductive technologies at all.
21 The court suspended the effect of its decision in order to give the Ontario government time to change the offending law. They did so in 2006.
22 However, see Boyd (2003: 3) for the dangers of privileging legal discourses over all others.
23 It is worth noting that similar legal trends are found in other Western jurisdictions with whom Canada shares significant legal traditions. In Australia, see, e.g., *Fraser* (2012) and *Re Patrick* (2002). In the United States, see, e.g., *Thomas* (1994, 1995) and *KM* (2004). In New Zealand, see, e.g., *K.* (2002); *P. v. K. & M.* (2004, 2002); and *P v. K*, (2006, 2004, 2003). And in Scotland, see, e.g., *X.* (2002).
24 For the initial access decision, see *S.G.* (2004). For Quebec Court of Appeal interlocutory application, see *S.G.* (26 November 2004). Lesbian mothers divorce: *S.G.* (2005). But see *L.O.* (2006), where a known sperm donor's application to be declared a parent under the same provisions of the *Civil Code* is denied, and the parental project of the lesbian couple upheld. In this case the couple was intact, and the child was conceived using artificial insemination.
25 The Quebec equivalent to a birth certificate, registering who is part of the "parental project."
26 The Court, in fact, notes that, over a decade earlier, S.G. and M.'s birth mother had a dating relationship, setting them up as the cognizable heterosexual dyad couple (*S.G.*, 2004, at para. 1). Except to mention S.G.'s unsubstantiated assertion that she did not "want" M., the Court doesn't refer to M.'s non-biological mother except as being in a civil union with M.'s birth mother.

27 After a brief period of access accompanied by her mothers, which they are to facilitate.

28 See also *L.B.* (2004, 2006).

29 In fact, the record shows that he lived in another city, and did not meet C. until 1997, well after C.'s conception and birth.

30 Canada is not the only jurisdiction that is struggling with the legal role of sperm donors and where families are resorting to litigation. For a look at such cases in multiple jurisdictions, see Milbank (2008). Australia is seeing similar litigation (see, e.g., *Fraser*, 2012) as is California (see, e.g., *K.M.*, 2004).

31 In the Ontario case of *M.A.C.* (2009), a known donor blocked a bid by a non-biological lesbian mother to adopt the child that she had been parenting by withholding consent. In this case, the known donor had actually participated in parenting work up to the time of the legal intervention, and was in fact awarded continued interim access. It was due to this parenting work that he was granted parental rights. While this may have been an appropriate response to the donor's significant involvement, the effect of the decision was to negate the parental relationship between the non-biological mother and child. A legislative regime that mandated judicial recognition of three parents, rather than a case-by-case approach required in Ontario requiring the consent of all three adults, would go a great distance to supporting and recognizing how many three-parent families are already structured and functioning, even in cases where the three adults are not all in agreement.

32 In fact, recent research indicates that children from women-led families fare as well or better than families where a father is present. See Biblarz & Stacey (2010); U.S. National Longitudinal Lesbian Family Study (2012); MacCallum & Golombok (2004); van Gelderen, Bos, Hermanns, & Perrin (2012).

References

Baird, P. (1993). *Proceed with Care: Final Report of the Royal Commission on New Reproductive Technologies* (2 Volumes). Ottawa: Minister of Supply and Services Canada.

Biblarz, T.J., & Stacey, J. (2010). "How does the gender of parents matter?" *Journal of Marriage and Family*, 72(1): 3–22.

Blackwell, T. (2012, June 5). "Sperm donation laws on trial as man wants deal with lesbian couple voided." *National Post*. Retrieved from news.nationalpost.com/2012/06/05/sperm-donation-laws-on-trial-as-man-wants-deal-with-lesbian-couple-voided/

Boyd, S.B. (2003). *Child Custody, Law and Women's Work*. Don Mills, ON: Oxford University Press.

Boyd, S.B. (2007). "Gendering legal parenthood: Bio-genetic ties, intentionality and responsibility." *Windsor Yearbook of Access to Justice*, 25: 55.

Boyd, S.B. (2010). "Autonomy for mothers? Relational theory and parenting apart." *Feminist Legal Studies*, 18(2): 137–158.

Cameron, A. (2008). "Regulating the queer family: The *Assisted Human Reproduction Act*." *Canadian Journal of Family Law*, 24: 101–122.

Cameron, A., & Gruben, V. (2014). "Quebec's constitutional challenge to the AHRA: Overlooking women's reproductive autonomy?" In S. Patterson, F. Scala, & M. Sokolon, eds., *Fertile Ground: Exploring Reproduction in Canada* (pp. 125–151). Montreal: McGill-Queen's University Press.

Cameron, A., Gruben, V., & Kelly, F. (2010). "De-anonymising sperm donors in Canada: Some doubts and directions." *Canadian Journal of Family Law*, 26(1): 95–148.

Campbell, A. (2007). "Conceiving parents through law." *International Journal of Law, Policy & the Family*, 21: 242–273.

Craig, E. (2010). "Converging feminist and queer legal theories: Family feuds and family ties." *Windsor Yearbook of Access to Justice*, 28: 209–230.

Giroux, M. (2006). "Le droit fondamental de connaître ses origines biologiques: impact des droits fondamentaux sur le droit de la filiation." *Revue du Barreau*, 255.

House of Commons, Standing Committee on Health. (2001, December). *Assisted Human Reproduction: Building Families* (Chair: Bonnie Brown). Retrieved from http://cmte.parl.gc.ca/Content/HOC/committee/371/heal/reports/rp1032041/healrp02/healrp02-e.pdf

Kelly, F. (2009a). "(Re)forming parenthood: The assignment of legal parentage within planned lesbian families." *Ottawa Law Review*, 40: 185–224.

Kelly, F. (2009b). "Producing paternity: The role of legal fatherhood in maintaining the traditional family." *Canadian Journal of Women and the Law*, 21(2): 315–351.

Kelly, F. (2010). "An alternative conception: The legality of home insemination under Canada's *Assisted Human Reproduction Act*." *Canadian Journal of Family Law*, 26: 149–170.

Kelly, F. (2011). *Transforming Law's Family*. Vancouver: UBC Press.

Leckey, R. (2009). "Where the parents are of the same sex: Quebec's reforms to filiation." *International Journal of Law, Policy & the Family*, 23(1): 62–82.

Leckey, R. (2011a). "Law reform, lesbian parenting, and the reflective claim." *Sociology and Legal Studies*, 20: 331–348.

Leckey, R. (2011b). "Lesbian parental projects in word and deed." *Revue Juridique Thémis*, 45: 315–341.

Leckey, R. (2011c). "The practices of lesbian mothers and Quebec's reforms." *Canadian Journal of Women and the Law*, 23(2): 579–599.

MacCallum, F., & Golombok, S. (2004). "Children raised in fatherless families from infancy: A follow up of children of lesbian and single heterosexual mothers at early adolescence." *Journal of Child Psychology and Psychiatry*, 8: 1407–1419.

MacDougall, B. (2000). *Queer Judgments: Homosexuality, Expression, and the Courts in Canada*. Toronto: University of Toronto Press.

Mezey, N. (2008). *New Choices, New Families: How Lesbians Decide about Motherhood.* Baltimore: The Johns Hopkins University Press.

Millbank, J. (2008). "The limits of the functional family: Lesbian mother litigation in the era of the eternal biological family." *International Journal of Law, Policy and the Family*, 22: 149.

Ottawa Fertility Centre. (2013). "Fees for Fertility Services." Retrieved from www.conceive.ca/wp-content/uploads/2013/12/FEES-Brochure-E-1July2013.pdf

ReproMed. (n.d.). "Semen donor catalogue." The Toronto Institute for Reproductive Medicine. Retrieved from www.repromed.ca/sperm_donor_catalogue

U.S. National Longitudinal Lesbian Family Study. (2012). *U.S. National Longitudinal Lesbian Family Study.* Retrieved from www.nllfs.org/

van Gelderen, L., Bos, H.M., Hermanns, J., & Perrin, E.C. (2012). "Quality of life of adolescents raised by lesbian mothers." *Journal of Developmental and Behavioural Pediatrics*, 33(1): 1.

Legal Cases and Statutes

A. v. B., C. and X, [2003] J.Q. no 9254.

(A.)A. v. (B.)B., 2007 ONCA 2, 83 OR (3d) 561.

Adoption Act, RSBC 1996, c 5.

Assisted Human Reproduction Act, SC 2004, c 2.

Birth Registration Regulations, NS Reg 39/2009, s 3(1) [BRR].

Caufield v. Wong, 2007 ABQB 732, 162 ACWS (3d) 973.

Child and Family Services Act, RSY 2002, c 31, s 13(6).

Children's Law Act, RSNL 1990, c C-1 [CLA].

Children's Law Reform Act, RSO 1990, c 12, s 8.

Civil Code of Québec, SQ 1991, c 64.

Deblois v. Lavigne, 2012 ONSC 3949 (available on CanLII).

Doe v. Alberta, [2007] SCCA No 211.

Doe v. Alberta, 2007b ABCA 50, 404 AR 153.

Droit de la famille—111729, 2011 QCCA 1180 (available on CanLII).

Droit de la famille—081450, 2008 QCCS 2677, [2008] RDF 482.

D.W.H. v. D.J.R. 2011 ABQB 119, 516 AR 134.

Family Law Act, SBC 2011, c 25, s 24.

Family Law Act, SA 2003, c F-4.5, s 8.1.

Family Law Statutes Amendment Act, SA 2010, c 16.

Food and Drug Regulations, CRC, c 870.

Fraser v. Farwell, [2012] FMCAFAM 1088.

Johnson-Steeves v. Lee (1997), 203 AR 192, [1997] 6 WWR 608 (Alta QB).

Johnson- Steeves v. Lee (1997), 209 AR292, [1998] 3 WWR 410 (Alta CA).

K. v. M., [2002] 22 FRNZ 360.

K.M. v. E.G., 118 Cal App (4th) 477 (June 2004).

L.B. c L.B., 2006 QCCS 591, [2006] RJQ 862.

L.B. c L.B., [2004] RDF 456 (available on QL).

L.O. v. S.J., 2006 QCCS 302, [2006] RJQ 775.

M.A.C. v. M.K., 2009 ONCJ 18, 94 OR (3d) 756.

Maintenance and Custody Act, RSNS 1989, c 160.

P. v. K., [2006] NZFLR 22.

P. v. K., [2004] 2 NZLR 421.

P. v. K., [2003] 2 NZLR 787.

P. v. K. & M., [2004] NZFLR 752.

P. v. K. & M. (8 August 2002) (Fam Ct NZ).

Potter v. Korn, [1995] BCCHRD No 20.

Pratten v. British Columbia (Attorney General), 2012 BCCA 480, [2013] 2 WWR 6.

Pratten v. British Columbia (Attorney General), 2011 BCSC 656, [2011] 10 WWR 712.

Pratten v. British Columbia (Attorney General), 2010 BCSC 1444, 325 DLR (4th) 79.

Pratten v. Attorney General of British Columbia, 2013 CanLII 30404 (SCC).

Processing and Distribution of Semen for Assisted Conception Regulations, SOR/96-254.

Rutherford v. Ontario (Deputy Registrar General) (2006), 81 OR (3d) 81, 270 DLR (4th) 90 (Sup Ct).

Quebec (Attorney General) v. A., 2013 SCC 5, 354 DLR (4th) 191.

Re Patrick, (2002) 28 Fam LR 579.

Reference re Assisted Human Reproduction Act, 2010 SCC 61, [2010] 3 SCR 457.

Reference re Same-Sex Marriage, 2004 SCC 79, [2004] 3 SCR 698.

S.G. c L.C., 2005 RJQ 1719 (available on CanLII).

S.G. c L.C. (26 November 2004), Montreal 500-09-014905-046, (CA).

S.G. c L.C. [2004] RJQ 1685 [*SG*].

Susan Doe v. Canada (Attorney General), 2007 ONCA 11, 84 OR (3d) 81.

Thomas S v. Robin Y, 618 NYS2d 356 (1994).

Thomas S v. Robin Y, 599 NYS2d 377 (1995).

X. v. Y. (2002) SLT (Sh Ct) 161.

Chapter 12

Dangerous Liaisons, a Tale of Two Cases: Constructing Women Accused of HIV/AIDS Nondisclosure as Threats to the (Inter)national Body Politic

Jennifer M. Kilty

The Evolution of Law in Cases of the Criminalization of HIV/AIDS Nondisclosure

In Canada, the criminalization of HIV-positive serostatus nondisclosure during sexual relations began in the late 1980s, and the number of people charged has risen consistently over the past two decades (Dej & Kilty, 2012; Mykhalovskiy & Betteridge, 2012). Interestingly, it was only after the HIV virus began to make its way from the most at-risk populations (i.e., gay men, men who have sex with men, and injection drug users) into the general population that two important socio-political transformations occurred in the fight against HIV/AIDS. First, public health initiatives began to target the wider population rather than only the aforementioned at-risk groups with new messages that proposed "AIDS was [now] everyone's concern" (Persson & Newman, 2008). Second, there was a shift in how the state came to respond to HIV/AIDS, where the invocation of criminal law began to encroach upon what was considered until that time to be a public health concern by prosecuting individuals who were thought to knowingly expose or transmit HIV to another person. These two facts mark a significant shift in the broader AIDS commentary and the evolution of the contemporary moral panic around HIV infection.

Someone can be found guilty of a criminal offence regardless of whether or not his or her sexual partner contracts HIV. Moreover, interpretations of "sexual partner" does not necessitate that penetration has occurred, as several cases have involved oral sex alone (*R. v. Edwards*, 2001; *R. v. Charron*, 2008). As of February 2011, approximately 115 people have faced charges for nondisclosure of HIV seropositivity during a sexual encounter and thus for knowingly exposing or transmitting the virus in Canada. Of these, Myhalovskiy and Betteridge (2012) found that 69 percent of known cases occurred between 2004 and 2010. While the majority of these cases involve HIV-positive men having unprotected sex with women, approximately 20 cases involve HIV-positive men having sexual relations with men, and there are at least 12 reported cases where an HIV-positive woman was charged as the result of a sexual encounter with a man (HIV/AIDS Legal Network, 2011). The majority of prosecutions come from Ontario, although there are cases throughout Canada.

Although some US states and some European and African countries have developed HIV/AIDS criminal offences, there is no specific charge for HIV/AIDS exposure or transmission in Canada, meaning Crown prosecutors must make their case using an existing *Criminal Code* charge. In the early 1990s, some of the first charges were for causing a nuisance and transmitting a noxious thing—again, regardless of whether or not actual HIV transmission occurred (Dej & Kilty, 2012). Since then, and while the crimes did not become any more severe, there has been a hardening of criminal charges to assault, aggravated assault, aggravated sexual assault, and, since the 2009 *Aziga* case, murder (Brown, 2009). The most common charge is aggravated sexual assault (Myhalovskiy & Betteridge, 2012). It is important to note that criminal charges in these cases became more severe at the same time as advancements in anti-retroviral therapy have allowed people living with HIV to lead longer and healthier lives, so much so that HIV/AIDS is no longer considered the death sentence it once was (Cameron, 2005).

Scholars have documented that the growing use of the criminal justice system as a mechanism to control the spread of HIV is not effectively reducing participation in risky activities that lead to HIV exposure (Adam, Elliott, Husbands, Murray, & Maxwell, 2008; Dodds, Bourne & Weait, 2009). It does, however, perpetuate discriminatory myths about individuals with HIV/AIDS that are rooted in an irrational fear of the virus and those who contract it; namely, that they are sexually promiscuous and even predatory. At the same time, as I have noted elsewhere (Dej & Kilty, 2012), the criminal law provides a false sense of security that suggests we are more protected from the HIV virus because of criminal justice measures that proclaim to deter nondisclosure. Subsequently, prosecuting people living with HIV for failing to disclose their seropositivity is counterproductive to HIV prevention efforts because it may deter some individuals from being tested out of fear of bearing the legal responsibility of disclosure should they find themselves testing positive. Criminalizing nondisclosure has also made previously confidential medical records the subject of legal and thus public scrutiny in the courtroom, which may inhibit individuals from getting tested or seeking counselling from public health and medical agents. Additionally, using the criminal justice system to manage a public health concern increases the stigma and discrimination that people living with HIV/AIDS already experience (Patton, 1990).

The Supreme Court of Canada set the initial precedent for the application of law regarding nondisclosure in 1998 with *R. v. Cuerrier*. Cuerrier had unprotected sex with two women without disclosing that he was HIV positive and while knowing the risks of unprotected sex. Both women asked Cuerrier about his HIV serostatus and he lied, claiming to be negative. The Supreme Court's decision in *Cuerrier* set the parameters by which to determine whether consent to sexual activity was given fraudulently and could thus be considered to have been vitiated because of nondisclosure. The accused must have knowledge of his/her HIV-positive status and of the ways HIV/AIDS can be transmitted and must then either deceive a sexual partner about their seropositivity or fail to disclose their HIV-positive status. Third, and most ambiguously defined, is that a "significant risk of serious bodily harm" must arise as a result of the dishonesty. Finally, the dishonesty on the part of the accused must be found to have "caused" the person to consent, meaning that the Crown must prove that the complainant would not have consented to sexual activity had he/she been aware of the accused's HIV-positive status.

Lower courts across the country have struggled to make sense of what "significant risk" means, whether from a legal, public health, or moral perspective, which has led to inconsistent application in common law.[1] The most inconsistent cases have differently interpreted risk in terms of condom use and viral load.[2] With reference to condoms, the majority ruling in the Cuerrier decision stated: "[T]he careful use of condoms might be found to so reduce the risk of harm that it could no longer be considered significant," while the minority judgment found that only "unprotected sex" without disclosure should be open to *Criminal Code* provisions. Because *R. v. Cuerrier* took place in 1998 when scientific evidence about HIV/AIDS was limited, the Supreme Court did not hear evidence concerning viral load and how it may alter the riskiness of different sexual activities. However, the Supreme Court rendered a decision in *R. v. Mabior*[3] in 2012 that stipulates that when a condom is used and the individual has an undetectable viral load, the "realistic possibility of transmission of HIV is negated." Otherwise, HIV carriers must still disclose their status to their partners.

The criminalization of HIV nondisclosure encroaches upon public health promotion and management via the transformation of the criminal law into a mechanism that persecutes people living with HIV/AIDS. While I do not deny that there are isolated cases of predatory sexual behaviour where an individual attempts to infect another person, current Canadian law provisions do not require proof of mens rea, or the intent to infect. Criminalizing nondisclosure constitutes all persons living with HIV as potential sexual offenders, which not only complicates established understandings of sexual offending, but has also resulted in a moralized AIDS commentary and a contemporary AIDS-related moral panic that calls for increasingly punitive responses to HIV exposure and transmission.

Moral Panic and the Continuity of Moralized AIDS Commentary

Since its inception, Cohen's (1973) theoretical construct of "moral panic" has been adopted predominantly in the disciplines of sociology, criminology, and communications and media studies, with scholars using it to examine a vast array of different subject matter. As Klocke and Muschert (2010: 298) document, topics have included: "witch hunts (Ben-Yehuda, 1986); AIDS (Watney, 1988; Weeks, 1989); drug scares (Armstrong, 2007; Baerveldt et al., 1998; Ben-Yehuda, 1986; Collin & Godfrey, 1998); street crime scares (Chambliss, 1995; Waddington, 1986); minority youth violence (Welch et al., 2004; Zatz, 1987); child abuse and pedophilia (Critcher, 2002; Jenkins, 1992, 1998; Parton, 1985); Satanism (Jenkins & Maier-Katkin, 1992; Victor, 1993); religious cults (Jenkins, 1992; Levine, 1992); crack mothers (Humphries, 1999); school shootings (Burns & Crawford, 1999); and day care ritual abuse (De Young, 2004), among others." The concept is also one of the few sociological terms that have penetrated lay discourse. For example, in his study of British news content, Altheide (2009: 83) found that since 1985 mass media news reporting has increasingly cited the concept, with more than two hundred articles in the United Kingdom's *Guardian* and the United States' *New York Times* referring to a moral panic between 2000 and 2007 alone. Cohen articulates moral panic in the following oft-cited passage:

> Societies appear to be subject, every now and then, to periods of moral panic. A condition, episode, person or group of persons emerges to become defined as a threat to societal values and interests; its nature is presented in a stylized and stereotypical fashion by the mass media; the moral barricades are manned by editors, bishops, politicians and other right-thinking people; socially accredited experts pronounce their diagnoses and solutions; ways of coping are evolved or (more often) resorted to; the condition then disappears, submerges or deteriorates and becomes more visible. Sometimes the object of the panic is quite novel and at other times it is something which has been in existence long enough, but suddenly appears in the limelight. Sometimes the panic passes over and is forgotten, except in folk-lore and collective memory; at other times it has more serious and long-lasting repercussions and might produce such changes as those in legal and social policy or even in the way the society conceives itself. (Cohen, 1973: 9)

Many scholars have examined how the HIV/AIDS virus has been conceptualized as "a condition" defined by many (and I would suggest this includes both politically right- and left-thinking people) as a threat to societal values and interests (Patton, 1990; Watney, 1996), and there are few who could deny that HIV/AIDS is frequently presented in a "stylized and stereotypical fashion" in mass media communications and news coverage. In fact, one of the most alarming results following the discovery of the AIDS virus was the social and political hysteria it caused, and, many would argue, continues to cause today. There have been instances where very public figures have denounced all those who contract the virus as "sinners" and as morally depraved threats to public health. Given the fact that AIDS hit the gay community hardest at its onset, some of the more hysterical discourses have problematically conceptualized and described homosexuality as the sinful cause and AIDS as the horrific consequence. For example, in the early days of the virus, American conservative columnist Pat Buchanan called the disease "nature's revenge on homosexuals," and Reverend Jerry Falwell described it as "proof of society's moral decay" (Wood, 1983). These are clearly extreme and hateful interpretations, yet they remain part of the public commentary and are linked to contemporary responses to the virus.

In his seminal book *Policing Desire: Pornography, AIDS and the Media* (1996/1987), Simon Watney discusses what I would term the survivalist nature of discourse, which he describes as a continuous and thus historically situated commentary about AIDS. Discourses or commentaries rarely disappear; instead, they transform, evolve, and adapt. However, in so doing, Watney argues against claims that media and public discourses on HIV/AIDS, particularly as they are related to homosexuality, constitute a moral panic according to Cohen's historic explanation. Instead, Watney suggests that the inflammatory, derogatory, misinformed, and misguided comments that are routinely peppered throughout contemporary mass media outlets and public, state, and other institutional discourses actually signify a broader and more deeply entrenched discourse or "commentary" about both AIDS and homosexuality. Watney's argument is important to those who wish to document the historic and ongoing efforts to "police desire" (in terms of both an individualized self-regulating ethic and a collectivized discourse involving structured regulatory and disciplinary technologies) and to remake homosexuality as unnatural. Watney contends that these discourses are born from the larger heteronormative ideological structure that morally condemns homosexuality. While he is hesitant to accept that these narratives constitute a moral panic, Watney acknowledges that they do make up distinct subjectivities regarding AIDS-related "folk devils"—although he avoids using the term "folk devil," likely to maintain his distance from traditional moral panic research.

> The successful policing of desire requires that we think of "the enemy" everywhere, and at all times. This is why there is such a marked conflict throughout the entire dimension of Aids commentary between the actual

> situation of people with Aids, and the model of contagion which they are made to embody.... We are not, in fact, living through a distinct, coherent and progressing "moral panic" about Aids.... There is a danger of identifying individual "moral panics" in a simple one-to-one relation to their ostensible targets. This is why I prefer to think in terms of Aids commentary, rather than assuming the existence of a unified and univocal "moral panic" over Aids. (Watney, 1996: 43–44)

Similarly, Critcher (2008, 2009) claims that health-related issues are rarely if ever fit to be declared moral panics. He specifically denotes that sexually transmitted infections, while highly moralized, "cannot in normal circumstances be perceived or constructed as threats to moral order," and thus it is "not feasible to use legal measures to secure compliance" (Critcher, 2009: 27, 29). Critcher does not specify what would constitute an abnormal circumstance that might give rise to the generation of a moral panic surrounding a sexually transmitted infection; however, his claim that some issues do not threaten public order as much as others is warranted. And while I agree that it is not "feasible" in the sense of practicality or effectiveness to use legal measures to secure compliance in matters of public health, particularly with respect to sexually transmitted infections, this fact does not preclude us from doing so. The extant literature on the state use of contagious and venereal diseases acts (Backhouse, 1985; Fordham, 2001; Klein, 2009; Mawani, 2002; Walkowitz, 1980) demonstrate how women's sexuality that falls outside heteronormative marital relations has historically been constructed as inherently threatening both to societal moral order and to the national body politic. The emerging and increasing use of criminal law to prosecute individuals for failing to disclose their HIV-positive serostatus (Dej & Kilty, 2012; Myhalovskiy & Betteridge, 2012) represents a contemporary reformulation and continuation of the goals set out by these earlier contagious diseases acts and are part of Watney's broader and ongoing AIDS commentary.

While I heed Watney's (1996) argument, I do situate this research in the moral panic literature, particularly the position advocated by Hier (2002, 2008, 2011; Hier, Lett, Walby, & Smith, 2011). There are several reasons for this. Most importantly, and as Hier (2002, 2008, 2011: 524; Hier et al., 2011) argues, moral panics exist as volatile and potentially episodic moments in a larger and longer-term moral regulation project. Hier's emphasis on situating moral panics within broader moral regulation discourses aligns with Watney's desire to locate narratives about HIV/AIDS within a larger and ongoing AIDS commentary. Starting from a position that there is a relatedness between and thus continuity of AIDS commentaries, Hier's position allows us to spotlight the criminalization of HIV/AIDS nondisclosure as a particular commentary or discourse resulting from a moral panic about people living with HIV as always already potential sexual predators.

Contemporary moral panic scholars suggest that moral regulation processes are increasingly expressed through the neoliberal language of risk, harm, and responsibility, and that moral panics are becoming routine features of everyday life (Hier, 2002, 2008, 2011; Hier et al., 2011; Rohloff, 2008; Rohloff & Wright, 2010). It is this shift that has encouraged scholars to begin to situate moral panics within the broader moral regulation literature. Moral regulation is typically conceptualized as a long-term effort to encourage citizens to internalize particular moral codes of conduct and to act in accordance with those codes; on the other hand, moral panics symbolize the need to control the immoral actions of dangerous and deviant "others." This suggests that moralization discourses function both on the individual (conceptualized as ethical self-formation) and collective (conceptualized as societal or cultural moral formation) levels, calling upon us to be prudent in our risk management and self-regulation. As Hier (2011: 528) states, "[T]he aim is to show how panics represent an extension rather than a subversion of routine moral regulation processes." Specifically, Hier et al. (2011: 263) write:

> Through the deployment of a set of sensational discourses that erupt suddenly, and subside quickly, the moral dialectic that situates individualized risk management against a collective dimension of harm is inverted. Discourses that call upon individuals to engage in responsible forms of self-conduct to manage risk are transposed into collectivizing discourses of risk management. The latter take the form of defensive group reactions against what is represented as an immediate dimension of harm posed by "irresponsible" others: those who fail to engage in individual risk management. As a volatile disturbance in the course of moral governance, "moral panics" are short-lived disturbances focused on limiting the agency of "folk devils."

When state agencies invoke regulatory legislations, the goal is to intervene directly upon the behaviours of those identified "folk devils" in order to prevent them from causing harm to others and to attempt to secure the public's "existential desires for phenomenal security" (Hier, 2002, 2011: 528). Like Watney's broader AIDS commentary, moralizing discourses are not temporally stable but rather shift and evolve over time. What remains stable is the call for personal responsibility and the dialectic of managing "harmful others" (Cohen's "folk devils") who fail to appropriately internalize accepted moral codes of conduct (Hier, 2011: 525, 528).

To construct public health concerns as "less morally evocative issues," as Critcher (2008, 2009: 26) does, is to minimize the felt effect of the threat they are seen to pose to the national body politic. Highly sensational language, so typical of moral panics, is increasingly used to describe public health concerns and outbreaks of contagious illnesses such as tuberculosis and SARS; for example, terms such as global "epidemic," "pandemic," and "threat" are regularly used to describe said outbreaks, despite the small number of cases and the success of treatment (Muzzatti, 2005). This suggests that public health concerns are conceptualized as threats to public order and can manifest moral panics about the danger of particular groups. For example, Muzzatti's (2005) work shows how the moral panic around SARS initiated a global public backlash toward Asian culture and bodies as potential threats to the (inter)national body politic. Specific to this chapter, when considering the moral demands for HIV serostatus disclosure during sexual relations, we can begin to unpack the dynamics of the moralization discourses that attempt to regulate or hail us into place, and the certain individual cases that evoke moral panics as "temporary manifestations, breakdowns, in some ongoing moral regulation processes" (Hier, 2011: 535). It is at this juncture that we increasingly see the use of criminal law to prosecute those "folk devils" that fail to modify their sexual behaviour in accordance with public health discourses advocating safe sex practices and the moral obligation to disclose. Legally speaking, for people living with HIV/AIDS, this means both disclosure of their HIV-positive serostatus to every sexual partner and always using barrier protection as the primary way to practice safe sex.[4]

While there are some moral panics that fit the ideal typologies set out by early theorists such as Goode and Ben-Yehuda (1994; Ben-Yehuda, 1986) and that appear to be exaggerated, irrational, and even delusional in their construction of the threats posed by particular "folk devils" (think here of panics associated with satanic worship and ritual daycare abuse) (Klocke & Muschert, 2010; Zajdow, 2008), this does not mean that more contemporary and/or public health issues do not manifest as moral panics. At least for the issue at hand, I suggest it is a matter of degree or scope rather than one of being or not being a moral panic. For example, as Garland (2008) contends, even moral panic scholars were initially hesitant to name fear of terrorism post-9/11 as generating a moral panic, certainly out of respect for victims and the very real harms terrorist actions pose, only to make claims of moral panic a year later.

The extant moral panic literature recognizes that some panics involve issues that pose real harms (e.g., terrorism, gun violence—Garland, 2008) while others do not (e.g., youth wearing hoodies—Hier et al., 2011); however, the real harms posed by public health concerns such as HIV transmission do not preclude them from evoking a moral panic. In the following sections I outline how, as public health initiatives to morally regulate the sex practices of people living with HIV are seen to fail, we have increasingly turned to using criminal law, itself a component of the manifestation of a moral panic surrounding HIV infection, to control those individuals whom we perceive as not self-governing appropriately. I examine the ways in which these individuals are constituted as contemporary HIV-positive "folk devils" by both the courts and media discourse, and how state responses to their nondisclosure contribute to the generation of a moral panic that is a part of Watney's broader AIDS commentary. In order to situate the analysis, I begin by providing a brief synopsis of the two cases (*R. v. J.M.*, 2005; *R. v. Iamkhong* 2007, 2009) under examination, followed by a description of the main finding—namely, that similar to the contagious and venereal diseases acts of days gone by, the women in these two cases are constructed as vectors of disease that threaten the (inter)national body politic.

A Brief Sketch of the Two Cases

J.M.

J.M. was raised in St. John's, Newfoundland, and has a documented history of both sexual abuse and alcohol dependency. J.M. was diagnosed as HIV-positive in 1994 at the age of 21; she was infected by her boyfriend, Harold Williams, who learned of his HIV-positive serostatus five months into their relationship but failed to disclose his serostatus to her for a year. In one of the earliest cases involving the criminalization of nondisclosure, Williams was tried and convicted of causing a nuisance and aggravated assault in 2000; upon appeal, the court upheld the nuisance conviction but reduced the charge to attempted assault because there was no proof that it was he who had exposed J.M. to the HIV virus. In 2003, the Supreme Court of Canada similarly ruled that Williams was guilty of aggravated assault, and he eventually served an additional five years in prison for failing to disclose his positive serostatus to two other women, although, unlike J.M., they did not become infected. That same year J.M. married a man who was in the military, and the couple relocated to the Canadian Forces Base (CFB) in Borden, Ontario. They separated after 10 months but stayed in contact and parted on amicable terms. During sentencing, her estranged husband was cited as a source of emotional support for her.

In February 2005, J.M. engaged in sexual relations with two men living at CFB Borden to whom she did not disclose her HIV-positive serostatus. At the time of her arrest, J.M. was a 32-year-old mother of an adolescent boy and had been living with HIV for almost 12 years. J.M. pled guilty to aggravated sexual assault on M.H., admitting that they had performed oral sex on one another, had sexual intercourse with a condom, and also had sexual intercourse without a condom. Both parties admitted that they were drinking at the time. M.H. claimed that he would not have had any sexual relations with J.M. had he known her HIV status; he was tested three times, and all of the tests found him to be negative for the HIV virus. J.M. also admitted to performing oral sex on and engaging in sexual intercourse with L.K., and while they used a condom during intercourse, it broke. Similar to her experience with M.H., both parties had been drinking at the time, and L.K. claimed he would not have had sexual contact with J.M. had he known her HIV status. L.K. was tested twice for HIV and both tests came back negative. J.M. served a conditional sentence—one year of house arrest at her mother's home, in large part due to her documented mental health problems being accepted by the court as a mitigating factor in her sentencing.[5]

In May 2007, the Crown dropped a new aggravated sexual assault charge against J.M. for allegedly failing to disclose her HIV-positive status to a man she had had sex with. The decision to charge J.M. despite the exculpatory evidence was presumably facilitated by the stigmatization arising from her first conviction. J.M. maintained that the man was fully aware of her health status and that a condom was used. She also identified two witnesses who were present when she disclosed her HIV status to the man, both of whom were prepared to testify on her behalf. In September 2011, J.M. was again charged with three new counts of aggravated sexual assault after allegedly failing to disclose her HIV-positive serostatus to three men. She walked away from a Barrie Elizabeth Fry Society transitional home in July 2012 and a warrant was issued for her arrest. To date, she has not been found.

Suwalee Iamkhong

Suwalee Iamkhong was born in 1969 and raised in a small village in Thailand. With only a fourth-grade-level education she moved to Hong Kong in 1994 to work as an exotic dancer. At trial, Iamkhong admitted to briefly engaging in sex work while she was living in Hong Kong; she tested positive for HIV during that time. Demonstrating that she understood the consequences of her diagnosis and the potential for and methods of transmission, Ms. Iamkhong claimed to then refrain from sexual activity. Iamkhong was issued her first work visa to enter Canada to work as an exotic dancer in 1995; speaking little English and no French, she moved to Toronto to work at Zanzibar Tavern. In 1996, Iamkhong met her future husband, Percy Whiteman, a patron of Zanzibar Tavern, while at work. They married in 1997, and Whiteman acted as Iamkhong's immigration sponsor. Prior to her marriage, Iamkhong underwent a blood test as part of the Immigration Canada health examination, which was required in order to secure the renewal of her work permit. Her manager at the Zanzibar Tavern told her that the results of the test were "okay" and that the test showed her to be "in the clear." She understood this to mean that the HIV test in Hong Kong had been incorrect and had presented a false positive; however, at the time the Immigration Canada health examination did not include an automatic test for HIV. Over the years, Iamkhong received a series of seven different Canadian work permits, between September 1995 and February 2002, before becoming a permanent resident of Canada on April 30, 2001.

At trial, Iamkhong submitted that she did not trust the Hong Kong medical establishment and indicated that she believed the Canadian system was inherently better, and she thus trusted that she was HIV-negative. It is important to note that Iamkhong attended the medical examination for Immigration Canada without an interpreter. In 2004, Iamkhong fell ill with cryptococcal meningitis, and given the severity of her symptoms and complications in treatment, underwent a series of medical tests, including one for HIV. It was only at this time that she claims to have learned of and thus disclosed her HIV status to her husband, who then also tested HIV-positive. The couple divorced in 2004, and Whiteman contacted police, who in May of that year laid charges against Iamkhong for criminal negligence causing bodily harm and aggravated assault. After a significant delay, Iamkhong's trial commenced in October 2007. Justice Todd Ducharme rejected her testimony and held that there was no evidence to support her claims that left him with a reasonable doubt about whether she believed she was HIV-negative. In Justice Ducharme's view, Iamkhong should have sought a second HIV test or at least medical counsel once she decided to resume sexual activity. On August 16, 2007, Iamkhong was sentenced to three years in prison. After serving two years in prison, and fighting the application for two years in court, Citizenship and Immigration Canada deported Iamkhong to her native Thailand in 2010.

J.M. and Suwalee Iamkhong: Threats to the (Inter)national Body Politic?

In different but related ways, both J.M. and Suwalee Iamkhong were constructed as threats to the (inter)national body politic as a result of their HIV infection and failure to disclose their HIV-positive serostatus to their sexual partners. Institutional discourses in both the media and legal forums relied on historical narratives that construct sexually active women as promiscuous vectors of disease that must be contained and, in a sense, quarantined. However, this notion of containment via sexual quarantine did not emerge in traditional public health forms, such as binding public health orders that mandate the individual to refrain from sexual activity. Instead, criminalization has increasingly become the state response to the moral panic about people who are living with HIV as hypersexual beings (in this case, the "loose" women) spreading the virus, by drawing a cordon sanitaire via incarceration around the individual seen as a threat. J.M. and Iamkhong were criminally charged with criminal negligence causing bodily harm, aggravated assault, and aggravated sexual assault. Punishment for these offences ranges from a period of imprisonment for a term not exceeding 10 years for criminal negligence causing bodily harm, to a period of imprisonment for a term not exceeding

14 years for aggravated assault, and up to imprisonment for life for aggravated sexual assault. J.M.'s documented mental ill-health and alcohol dependency were considered mitigating factors in her sentencing, and she received a one-year conditional sentence of house arrest at her mother's place of residence. Suwalee Iamkhong was detained for nearly two years pending her trial, following which she served a sentence of two years less a day in a provincial prison.

By criminalizing HIV nondisclosure, the state is attempting to protect the public by quarantining those individuals considered to be threats to the national body politic through a lengthy period of incarceration. It should be noted that HIV prevalence rates in Canadian federal prisons range between 4.5 percent for men and 7.9 percent for women;[6] these rates are estimated to be 7 to 10 times higher than rates in the general Canadian population (0.3 percent in those 15–49 years old) (UNAIDS, 2006; Zakaria, Thompson, Jarvis, & Smith, 2010). Moreover, this mechanism for preserving public health fails to acknowledge that prisoners are known to engage in sexual relations; in this way, prisoners are excluded from consideration as members of the national body politic, and their health and safety is thus secondary to that of free citizens. This constitutes prisoners as "sub-citizens," whom Aas describes as those who "find their citizenship status securitized or substantially depleted" (Aas, 2011: 340).

In J.M.'s case, the media emphasized that she solicited sex from male soldiers in the military barracks at CFB Borden, where she lived previously with her husband. The media was quick to secure man-on-the-street interview quotes from townsfolk and soldiers from CFB Borden in order to add to the scandalous tone in media commentaries.

> "They got her on trespassing because she'd been in the shacks," said a soldier at Borden, referring to the local name for singles' quarters. "During her time here she went through all the shacks," the soldier said, adding she'd seen [J.M.] wandering through the halls of one of the quarters, going from room to room dressed in only a pink G-string and knee-high boots. (Teotonio, 2005: A01)

This excerpt demonstrates the salacious nature of the news media coverage typical for these cases. By describing J.M.'s attire in such detail and referring specifically to her underwear as a "pink G-string" and to her "knee-high boots," this journalist was able to construct J.M. as a sexually promiscuous woman. Suggesting that J.M. was "wandering through the halls of one of the quarters, going from room to room" discursively implies and borders on outright naming her a prostitute. This commentary builds on historic discourses that paint sex workers and sexually active unmarried women as vectors of disease (Bruckert, 2012; Pheterson, 1993) and similar to the contagious diseases acts common in the first half of the twentieth century (Mawani, 2002), criminalization individualizes the threat of the larger moral panic, but in so doing allows the public to feel as though the threat is contained.

In response to this potential threat to the health of Canadian soldiers, military officials initially responded to J.M.'s charges by sending a statement, including J.M.'s photograph, to all staff and soldiers who lived or trained at CFB Borden at the time, imploring them to get tested if they had had sexual contact with her. This statement was later sent to all Canadian Forces, both in Canada and abroad. In reporting this fact, news articles noted the raw numbers of residents—both staff and soldiers—that inhabited CFB Borden. By referencing the military training base as a highly transitory space, "home to some 3,200 teaching and support staff," that "sees some 15,000 soldiers, sailors, and air personnel pass through annually for training" (Teotonio, 2005: A01), journalists were able to present the widest scope possible for the reader to interpret the potential risk of HIV infection.

> It's that transient traffic that has military investigators and health officials concerned. In an emergency message sent Thursday to Canadian Forces personnel worldwide, military investigators ask to speak to "anyone who believes they may have had sexual contact with this woman," and advise them to consult a doctor immediately. Giles characterized the warning as "an extra precaution." "I think we've captured everyone internally, but this is just an extra precaution," he said, pointing out that an earlier warning March 18 had already alerted public affairs officers in the region, and later at all *Canadian bases here and abroad.* (Teotonio, 2005: A01; emphasis added)

Sending out an accused's photograph to notify the public of a potential criminal threat is typically reserved for sexual offenders, and is a form of public shaming that can contribute to manifesting public belief in the guilt of the accused (Levenson, Brannon, Fortney, & Baker, 2007; Petrunik, 2003). In this case, it evidences the moral panic that emerged as a result of one woman's sexual relations with two men. In an even more sensationalized account, conservative columnist for the *Toronto Star* Rosie DiManno writes:

> She reportedly had casual sex with *multiple* partners on a return visit to CFB Borden earlier this year, she may have infected an *unknown number* of servicemen at the training base, military personnel now posted to all corners of the globe, *exponentially spreading* the virus that causes AIDS. (DiManno, 2005: A2; emphasis added)

DiManno's over-the-top comment that J.M. "may have infected an *unknown number* of serviceman" who are "military personnel now posted to all corners of the globe, *exponentially spreading* the virus that causes AIDS" is meant to incite shock and fear. In a culture that is pervasively constituted by risk narratives and discourses (Hier, 2008, 2011), these comments heighten the reader's feeling of uncertainty about where potential health-based risks may be hiding. If military servicemen, a cultural archetype of the preservation of national safety and security are at risk, then we are all at risk. DiManno writes in a matter-of-fact way, as though it were fact that "multiple" military servicemen had been infected, although neither of the *two* men J.M. had sexual contact with tested positive. Similarly, using the terms "multiple" and "exponentially" suggests the rate of infection may be rapidly growing, with Canadian soldiers spreading the virus worldwide. In this sense, DiManno implies that J.M. has not only threatened the national body politic, but is a vector of disease that has also threatened the international body politic. The irony is that the soldiers were not constructed as risky subjects, in spite of the fact that it would be they, if they proved HIV-positive, who would transmit the disease while abroad. The soldiers hold a respected and even honourable victim status, as having been harmed or exposed to harm while dedicating their lives to protecting others.

While the situation was somewhat different for Suwalee Iamkhong, her character construction in the media and legal discourses was similar to that of J.M. The media similarly painted an image of Iamkhong as a hypersexual woman. Given that Iamkhong worked as an exotic dancer for the duration of her time in Canada, and reportedly for a brief period as a sex worker during the short time she lived in Hong Kong just prior to immigrating to Canada, she proved easy fodder for sensational accounts of immigrant sex workers as diseased. The stigma associated with sex work (Bruckert, 2012; Pheterson, 1993) contributed to Iamkhong's construction as a dangerous woman and vector of disease. In fact, Iamkhong's main descriptors in the news coverage were threefold: her work identity as an exotic dancer or sex worker, her Thai nationality, and her HIV-positive status. Newspaper descriptions typically referred to her as "a stripper from Thailand" (Small, 2010a: GT3), "an HIV-positive exotic dancer" (Small, 2010a: GT3), "an HIV infected stripper" (Tibbetts, 2008: A8), "former prostitute in Asia then a stripper" (Small, 2010b: GT4), a "Thai stripper" (Nguyen, 2012: A11), and an "ex-stripper with AIDS" (Tyler, 2009: A3). While Iamkhong lived and worked in Canada for over a decade and became a permanent resident of Canada in April 2001, the constant references to her as a Thai foreign national easily distinguished and "othered" her different Asian body as a threatening prime character identifier.

In response to testing positive for HIV, Iamkhong's ex-husband sued her, along with Immigration Canada, a government doctor, and Zanzibar Tavern, alleging that their negligence led to him contracting the virus. While the case was later dismissed, Whiteman spoke openly with the media about his anger over having contracted HIV from his wife. In a *Toronto Sun* article titled "AIDS infected stripper deported to Thailand," Whiteman was quoted as saying:

> "I believe that she is still working in the sex trade in Thailand," Whiteman said on Monday. "It is the only job she knows and she has to support her family." Whiteman said there's a risk other men, like himself, will fall victim to the woman if she's working as a hooker in Bangkok. "I am actually shocked to hear she was finally deported," he said. "This woman will do anything to get what she wants—just look at me." (Godfrey, 2010)

Using sensationalist and provocative descriptors like "a hooker in Bangkok" situates Iamkhong's otherness at the intersection of her former participation in sex work and her foreign Thai nationality. It also intimates but cannot confirm that Iamkhong is engaging in sex work again despite her HIV-positive serostatus, which underlines her construction as a predatory repeat sexual offender who did not learn from her experience of criminalization and does not feel remorseful for having infected her ex-husband. This image runs contrary to the conclusions drawn by both the judge in her appeal (*R. v. Iamkhong*, 2009) and by Citizenship and Immigration officials (*Iamkhong v. The Minister of Safety and Emergency Preparedness*), who stated that they believed her to be sincerely remorseful. Indicative of the moral panic that emerged surrounding this case, Whiteman's narratives in particular made international news headlines. For example, a conservative Australian tabloid newspaper, *The Daily Telegraph* (2008), ran an article with the headline "If you slept with my wife, get a test," documenting Whiteman's public plea for men who have had sexual relations with Iamkhong to get an HIV test.

Following her prison sentence, itself a method for drawing a cordon sanitaire around the person seen to pose a public health risk, the Department of Citizenship and Immigration Canada ordered that Suwalee Iamkhong be deported to Thailand. This is a rare response reserved for those offenders who are seen to pose a continued risk or threat to the public; Iamkhong's conviction of criminal negligence causing bodily harm and aggravated assault was the basis for the deportation order. Judge Zinn refused to accept Iamkhong's appeal to stay in Canada on humanitarian and compassionate grounds, despite the fact that she would not have the same level of family support in Thailand, to which her sister, who also resides in Canada, testified. Moreover, health care and medications would be more difficult and costly to access in Thailand while Iamkhong would have fewer means of financially supporting herself. With this move, the Canadian government effectively stripped Iamkhong of her rights as a permanent resident of Canada and deported her, knowing that it would likely aggravate her illness and consequentially shorten her life.

The media coverage and the state decision to deport her constituted Iamkhong as unscrupulous and whose subjectivity was marked by interpretations of her failure to internalize the accepted moral codes of sexual conduct (that typically implicate the need for women to be chaste) or to act in accordance with those codes by disclosing her

HIV status. Instead of evoking sympathy for Iamkhong's lack of support and resources, Whiteman's public commentary suggesting that she would resort to sex work once deported to Thailand similarly teems with contempt and functions as a moralized discourse regarding appropriate sexual conduct. What was interpreted as a failure to morally regulate Iamkhong's sexual conduct created a moral panic rooted in historic fears of "loose" women and the dangerousness of different (Asian) bodies, and led to the invocation of the criminal law and deportation to control what were seen as the immoral actions of a sexually deviant and immoral foreign woman. These responses also marked her as a threat to the national body politic; however, the decision to deport her suggests that fears about her failure to act in accordance with accepted sexual moral codes of conduct do not extend to concern for the Thai body politic. Despite the fact that she would have had better access to health care, education, and support in Canada, arguably markers of the ability to successfully morally regulate her behaviour, immigration officials deported her.

Conclusion

Our knowledge about HIV has changed greatly since the dawn of the virus in the early 1980s. Consequentially, the broader AIDS commentary and our approaches to education, treatment, and prevention have also evolved. While infections continue to remain higher among gay men, it is now heterosexual women who make up the fastest growing subgroup of new infections (Grant, 2008; Myhalovskiy & Betteridge, 2012). Similarly, while there are few who call for the ritual quarantining, or permanent marking of the bodies of people living with HIV/AIDS with the scarlet letter "A" (Watney, 1996), efforts to publically "out" them continues in different forms. This chapter offers a brief case study of two women who were criminally convicted of a number of crimes for failing to disclose their HIV-positive serostatus to their respective sexual partners. Criminalization, now a component of the global AIDS commentary, is the contemporary manifestation of a moral panic around HIV exposure and transmission. A moral panic is a moment of disruption in the larger moral regulation and normalization project, and reflects the localization of cultural anxieties related to HIV/AIDS. As Hier (2002: 330) writes,

> Moral panics articulate a moment of problematization (i.e., the attribution of causality/blame) and a moment of solution (i.e., how to resolve the problem). That is, whilst moral regulation involves one set of persons acting on the conduct of others over a wide range of discursive sites with the ultimate goal of ethical reconstitution at some future point, panic narratives as political resources reduce the field of regulatory intervention

> to the extent that a tangible object is designated for immediate intervention, set in the context of a far more immediate moment of closure.

Criminalization has emerged as a way to attribute blame for exposure and transmission of the HIV virus and as a way to solve the potential problem of future exposure or transmission from individual "folk devils." In this way, criminalization creates a victim-centred discourse and designations of legitimate victim subjectivities associated with HIV, despite the fact that everyone who has HIV contracted it from someone else. This point resonates when you consider the fact that the criminalization of nondisclosure is imputed only when it takes place in the context of sexual relations; individuals who contract HIV through the sharing of needles or other drug paraphernalia are not afforded the same "worthiness" as victims (Hier, 2002: 331), largely because they do not evoke the same feelings of sympathy and because they are implicitly blamed for their HIV infection as a result of their failure to perform ethical self-regulation with respect to the preservation of their health and bodily integrity. In this sense, drug taking negates common-sense interpretations of and thus one's subjectivity as a moral or ethical innocent.

Criminalization, as part of the "panic narrative," significantly reduces the scope of public health education and intervention efforts that constitute the site of the moral regulation of ethical or safe sex conduct. Typical of moral panics, cases involving HIV nondisclosure and their adjunct "folk devils" erupt suddenly in the news media and are increasingly making national and international news headlines, which only further entrenches public fear of people living with HIV. Once a cordon sanitaire is drawn around the infected person via imprisonment so as to limit their sexual agency, these "folk devils" typically subside quickly from news coverage and our daily consciousness. In this way, the moral panic around HIV/AIDS nondisclosure is "a volatile disturbance in the course of [the] moral governance" (Hier et al., 2011: 263) of safe sex conduct for people living with HIV/AIDS. This is especially pertinent given that these two cases involved women who failed to disclose, when women have historically been and continue to be governed (more so than men) by moral discourses about appropriate sexual behaviour. The news coverage of these two cases focused on the danger posed by sexually active women who were fundamentally constructed as promiscuous and predatory, a gendered role reversal, as women are expected to be the passive recipients of the sexual advances of men. By ascribing increasing degrees of blame to people living with HIV in cases of nondisclosure, as evidenced by the increasingly severe criminal charges (Dej & Kilty, 2012), "the more innocent the victim is perceived to be, in turn making the mobilization of authoritative intervention that much more imminent" (Hier, 2002: 331). For J.M. and Suwalee Iamkhong, authoritative intervention took the form of public outing, naming and shaming, calls for other potential "victims" to be tested and to come forward, imprisonment, and—for Iamkhong—deportation after living in Canada for over 15 years, despite the fact that this action would undoubtedly aggravate her illness and shorten her life. The legal and media constructions of J.M. and Iamkhong established them as contemporary HIV-positive "folk devils" and lies, sex, and HIV as their weapons of choice; the assemblage of these subjectivities contributed to the broader AIDS commentary and moral panic that situates HIV-positive individuals as irresponsible, morally depraved, and potential sexual predators.

Notes

1 For a more detailed description of the evolution of Canadian case law in this regard, see Dej and Kilty (2012).

2 Viral load refers to the number of HIV copies in a millilitre of blood; a very low or undetectable viral load implies negligible risk of HIV transmission.

3 Relevant to the analysis presented in this chapter, Mabior was a foreign national who was deported back to South Sudan after he completed his prison sentence. This chapter aims to focus more exclusively on women constructed as threats to public health, but there is ample evidence to suggest that both race and class further aggravate this fact. See also Miller (2005) for a detailed discussion of Ugandan-born Charles Ssenyonga, one of the first cases (1993) involving the criminalization of nondisclosure in Canada.

4 While it is implied, it is not always stated that safe sex means using barrier protection such as condoms every time one engages in sexual activity, including but not limited to vaginal and anal penetration.

5 By late 2004, J.M. was found to be suffering from the mental condition Hypomania, which continued through 2005 including at the time of the offences. The results of a CT scan conducted while J.M. was in custody were consistent with some form of brain lesion. Forensic psychiatrist Stephen Hucker assessed and diagnosed J.M. as suffering from Mood Disorder due to HIV Infection with Hypomanic Features, at the time of the offence. He also found evidence of alcohol abuse, and of dependent, histrionic, and borderline personality traits. Hucker submitted to the court that an abnormally elevated mood could be responsible for episodes of extraordinarily poor judgment, especially of a sexual kind, and noted that alcohol—J.M. was drinking during her sexual encounters with both M.H. and L.K.—can trigger mood upswings.

6 The Correctional Service of Canada has found the prevalence rates to be exaggerated by race in addition to gender, where the rate of self-reported HIV infection among Aboriginal women (11.7 percent) was more than two times greater than the rate among non-Aboriginal women (5.5 percent) and all men (4.5 percent) (Zakaria et al., 2010).

References

Aas, K.F. (2011). "'Crimmigrant' bodies and bona fide travelers: Surveillance, citizenship and global governance." *Theoretical Criminology*, 15(3): 331–346.

Adam, B.D., Elliott, R., Husbands, W., Murray, J., & Maxwell, J. (2008). "Effects of the criminalization of HIV transmission in Cuerrier on men reporting unprotected sex with men." *Canadian Journal of Law and Society*, 23(1–2): 143–159.

Altheide, D.L. (2009). "Moral panic: From sociological concept to public discourse." *Crime, Media, Culture*, 5(1): 79–99.

Backhouse, C. (1985). "Nineteenth-century Canadian prostitution law reflection of a discriminatory society." *Social History/Histoire sociale*, 18(36): 387–423.

Ben-Yehuda, N. (1986). "The sociology of moral panics: Toward a new synthesis." *Sociological Quarterly*, 27(4): 495–513.

Brown, B. (2009, April 4). "Guilty verdict in Hamilton HIV murder case." *Toronto Star*. Retrieved from www.thestar.com/news/crime/2009/04/04/guilty_verdict_in_hamilton_hiv_murder_case.html

Bruckert, C. (2012). "The mark of 'disreputable' labour: Workin' it: Sex workers negotiate stigma." In S. Hannem & C. Bruckert, eds., *Stigma Revisited: Implications of the Mark* (pp. 48–67). Ottawa: University of Ottawa Press.

Cameron, E. (2005). *Witness to AIDS*. New York: I.B. Tauris.

Cohen, S. (1973). *Folk Devils and Moral Panics*. New York: Routledge.

Critcher, C. (2002). "Media, government and moral panic: The politics of paedophilia in Britain 2000–01." *Journalism Studies*, 3(4): 521–535.

Critcher, C. (2008). "Moral panic analysis: Past, present and future." *Sociology Compass*, 2(4): 1127–1124.

Critcher, C. (2009). "Widening the focus: Moral panics as moral regulation." *British Journal of Criminology*, 49(1): 17–34.

The Daily Telegraph. (2008, December 30). "If you slept with my wife, get a test." Retrieved from www.dailytelegraph.com.au/news/if-you-slept-with-my-wife-get-a-test/story-e6freuy9-1111118435218

Dej, E., & Kilty, J.M. (2012). "'Criminalization creep': A brief discussion of the criminalization of HIV/AIDS nondisclosure in Canada." *Canadian Journal of Law & Society*, 27(1): 55–66.

DiManno, R. (2005, March 30). "Stories about 'femme fatale' set us back to the dark old days." *Toronto Star*, p. A2.

Dodds, C., Bourne, A., & Weait, M. (2009). "Responses to criminal prosecutions for HIV transmission among gay men with HIV in England and Wales." *Reproductive Health Matters*, 17(34): 135–145.

Fordham, G. (2001). "Moral panic and the construction of national order: HIV/AIDS risk groups and moral boundaries in the creation of modern Thailand." *Critique of Anthropology*, 21(3): 259–316.

Garland, D. (2008). "On the concept of moral panic." *Crime, Media, Culture*, 4(1): 9–30.

Godfrey, T. (2010, August 30). "AIDS-infected stripper deported to Thailand." *Toronto Sun*. Retrieved from www.torontosun.com/news/torontoandgta/2010/08/30/15189991.html

Goode, E., & Ben-Yehuda, N. (1994). "Moral panics: Culture, politics, and social construction." *Annual Review of Sociology*, 20: 149–171.

Grant, I. (2008). "The boundaries of the criminal law: The criminalization of the nondisclosure of HIV." *Dalhousie Law Journal*, 31: 123–180.

Hier, S.P. (2002). "Raves, risks and the ecstasy panic: A case study in the subversive nature of moral regulation." *Canadian Journal of Sociology*, 27(1): 33–57.

Hier, S.P. (2008). "Thinking beyond moral panic: Risk, responsibility, and the politics of moralization." *Theoretical Criminology*, 12(2): 173–190.

Hier, S.P. (2011). "Tightening the focus: Moral panic, moral regulation and liberal government." *The British Journal of Sociology*, 62(3): 523–541.

Hier, S.P., Lett, D., Walby, K., & Smith, A. (2011). "Beyond folk devil resistance: Linking moral panic and moral regulation." *Criminology & Criminal Justice*, 11(3): 259–276.

HIV/AIDS Legal Network. (2011). *Criminal Law and HIV Nondisclosure in Canada*. Toronto: Canadian HIV/AIDS Legal Network.

Klein, A. (2009). "Criminal law, public health, and governance of HIV exposure and transmission." *The International Journal of Human Rights*, 13(2–3): 251–278.

Klocke, B.V., & Muschert, G.W. (2010). "A hybrid model of moral panics: Synthesizing the theory and practice of moral panic research." *Sociology Compass*, 4(5): 295–309.

Levenson, J.S., Brannon, Y.N., Fortney, T., & Baker, S. (2007). "Public perceptions about sex offenders and community protection policies." *Analyses of Social Issues and Public Policy*, 7(1): 137–161.

Mawani, R. (2002). "Regulating the 'respectable' classes: Venereal disease, gender and public health initiatives in Canada, 1914–35." In J. McLaren, R. Menzies, & D.E. Chunn, eds., *Regulating Lives: Historical Essays on the State, Society, The Individual, and the Law* (pp. 170–195). Vancouver: UBC Press.

Miller, J. (2005). "African Immigrant Damnation Syndrome: The case of Charles Ssenyonga." *Sexuality Research & Social Policy*, 2(2): 31–50.

Muzzatti, S.L. (2005). "Bits of falling sky and global pandemics: Moral panic and severe acute respiratory syndrome (SARS)." *Illness, Crisis & Loss*, 13(2): 117–128.

Mykhalovskiy, E., & Betteridge, G. (2012). "Who? What? Where? When? And with what consequences? An analysis of criminal cases of HIV nondisclosure in Canada." *Canadian Journal of Law & Society*, 27(1): 31–53.

Nguyen, L. (2012, February 1). "Toronto man sues over HIV infection." *Edmonton Journal*, p. A1.

Patton, C. (1990). *Inventing AIDS*. New York: Routledge.

Persson, A., & Newman, C. (2008). "Making monsters: Heterosexuality, crime and race in recent Western media coverage of HIV." *Sociology of Health & Illness*, 30(4): 632–646.

Petrunik, M.G. (2003). "The hare and the tortoise: Dangerousness and sex offender policy in the United States and Canada." *Canadian Journal of Criminology and Criminal Justice*, 45(1): 43–72.

Pheterson, G. (1993). "The whore stigma: Female dishonor and male unworthiness." *Social Text*, 37: 39–64.

Rohloff, A. (2008). "Moral panics as decivilizing processes: Towards an Eliasian approach." *New Zealand Sociology*, 23(1): 66–76.

Rohloff, A., & Wright, S. (2010). "Moral panic and social theory: Beyond the heuristic." *Current Sociology*, 58(3): 403–419.

Small, P. (2010a, January 5). "Husband's HIV case attacked by lawyers." *Toronto Star*, p. GT3.

Small, P. (2010b, March 12). "Federal government fails to get HIV suit dismissed." *Toronto Star*, p. GT4.

Teotonio, I. (2005, March 26). "Military warns all bases of HIV case; Canadian soldiers around the world to seek medical advice." *Toronto Star*. Retrieved from www.freerepublic.com/focus/f-news/1371553/posts

Tibbetts, J. (2008, December 17). "HIV infected stripper facing deportation." *National Post*, p. A8.

Tyler, T. (2009, February 19). "Ex-stripper with AIDS fights ouster." *Toronto Star*, p. A3.

UNAIDS. (2006). *2006 Report on the Global AIDS Epidemic*. Geneva: UNAIDS.

Walkowitz, J.R. (1980). *Prostitution and Victorian Society: Women, Class, and the State*. Cambridge: Cambridge University Press.

Watney, S. (1988). "AIDS, 'moral panic' theory and homophobia." In P. Aggleton & H. Homans, eds., *Social Aspects of AIDS* (pp. 52–64). Lewes: Palmer Press.

Watney, S. (1996). *Policing Desire: Pornography, AIDS and the Media* (3rd ed.). Minneapolis: University of Minnesota Press.

Wood, T. (1983, July 6). "Ministers debate AIDS and the politics of plague." *The Journal*. CBC. Retrieved from www.cbc.ca/archives/categories/health/public-health/the-early-years-of-the-aids-crisis/aids-and-the-politics-of-plague.html

Zajdow, G. (2008). "Moral panics: The old and the new." *Deviant Behavior*, 29: 640–664.

Zakaria, D., Thompson, J. M., Jarvis, A., & Smith, J. (2010). *Testing and Treatment for Human Immunodeficiency Virus and Hepatitis C Virus Infections among Canadian Federal Inmates*. Ottawa: Correctional Service of Canada.

Legal Cases and Statutes

R. v. Charron, Cour du Québec, District de Longueuil, Chambre criminelle, 706-01-010423-024, 1 May 2008, as cited in Claivaz-Loranger, S. (2010). "Panel—Criminalization of HIV Nondisclosure: New Developments and Community Responses." *HIV/AIDS Policy and Law Review*, 15(1).

R. v. Cuerrier, [1998] 2 SCR 371; [1996] BCJ No 2229 (QL), 83 BCAC 295; (1995), 26 WCB (2d) 378.

R. v. Edwards, [2001] NSJ No. 221, 2001 NSSC 80, 194 NSR (2d) 107, 50 WCB (2d) 255.

R. v. Iamkhong, [2009] O.J. No. 2446, 2009 ONCA 478; [2007] O.J. No. 3252, 74 W.C.B. (2d) 526.

Iamkhong v. The Minister of Public Safety and Emergency Preparedness (31 May 2010), IAD File No. TA9-13213 (Immigration and Refugee Board).

R. v. J.M., [2005] O.J. No. 5649.

R. v. Mabior, 2012 SCC 47; [2010] MJ No 308, 2010 MBCA 93; [2008] MBQB 201, 230 Man R (2d) 184.

Chapter 13

"Flattening Our Opposition": Neoliberal Governance and the (De)regulation of Adult Pornography in Canada

Camilla A. Sears

> If the scenes of fornication in "The Stewardesses" were "play acting," then if and when the smut wing of the movie industry holds an Oscar night the participants in "The Stewardesses," air hostesses, air crew, and passengers alike, have every right to anticipate a call from the stage to come forward to receive a deserving award. (*Daylight Theatre Company Limited v. The Queen*, [1973] S.J. No. 354)

It is unlikely that Judge Hughes anticipated that there would be an awards show for "the smut wing of the movie industry." However, just 11 years after the above case, the first *Adult Video News* (AVN) award ceremony was sponsored and presented by the American adult video industry trade magazine of the same name. The ceremony honours exceptional performance in various aspects of the creation and making of American pornographic movies, including awards for "best all-girl sex scene." In fact, they have been called the "Oscars of Porn." Such a development exemplifies dramatic shifts in society's tolerance of pornography over the last 50 years and suggests a growing acceptance of adult pornography, which has gained increased prominence in the public domain. New technologies have contributed to its rising production, distribution, and consumption. Imagery that was once "forbidden" or hidden from public view is now displayed frequently on television screens, in movie theatres, on the pages of magazines, and on billboards. In this way, adult pornography, or at least representations of sex, are not relegated to "dark corners": in the words of Nicola Simpson (2004: 635), "porn is no longer flirting with the mainstream; it *is* the mainstream" (emphasis added).

Consequent to this alteration in the socio-cultural landscape, social commentators have remarked on the modification to how adult pornography is talked about and researched. The emergent tolerance (and even normalization) of adult pornography reflects a larger paradigm shift evident in the academic and legal realms. Attention has gradually moved away from a consideration of the negative effects of pornography toward conceptualizing adult pornography as a cultural product subject to analysis, demonstrated by the development of a new field of porn studies (e.g., see Williams, 2004). Although this shift can be commended for providing insight and commentary on areas previously overlooked in research, it has not come without criticism. Feona Attwood (2002: 98) comments that these accounts and trends in research "flatten all our opposition to pornography." Further, Karen Boyle (2006: 2) strongly critiques this "re-mapping of porn studies," commenting that there is no sustained discussion of violent pornography in current research to the point where "violent pornography is largely ignored" (3). Consequently, she remarks that "to exclude such content sanitises the object of study and marginalises an extensive body of academic work" (3), which paid attention to "abusive production and consumption practices" (Boyle, 2008: 38). This has led to a subsequent decrease in our attention to the "problematic" place of adult pornography in society. The social changes and resulting moves in focus and concern point to the need to examine this field of study and consider the altered place of adult pornography in society and subsequent socio-legal reactions to it. In particular, it is vital to delineate how such modifications in social response impact on women.

Through a consideration of Canadian obscenity law from 1959 to 2009, this chapter contemplates these shifts and explores how the broader political rationality of neoliberalism relates to the regulation of adult pornography. It establishes that it is governance in a neoliberal era that has contributed to a reframing of the judicial response to adult pornography. The increasing pornographication of the mainstream (McNair, 2002) indicates the influence of the neoliberal political rationality, which acts as "a mode of governmentality that operates across a range of social spheres" (Gill, 2008b: 442–443). In this way, this chapter outlines a new regulatory regime that has reconfigured how adult pornography is responded to within the legal realm. Paying attention to judicial discourse, what becomes clear is that the harm-based approach that emerged in the 1980s and found prominence in cases such as *R. v. Butler* and *R. v. Labaye* has gradually contributed to a decline in adult pornography cases. Consequently, what has developed is a growing neoliberal model of law that creates conditions for citizens to govern themselves and make the "right" choices regarding sexual content instead of the state playing that role. Adult pornography is enabled to flourish as a commodity in a neoliberal age that is preoccupied with the individual. Utilizing case law examples, this chapter indicates the ways in which this trend has manifested through an adoption of neoliberal language and concepts such as "individual responsibility" and "freedom."

Furthermore, the chapter demonstrates the powerful connection between neoliberalism and post-feminism. In so doing, the gendered nature of neoliberalism is highlighted, queried, and considered in relation to how it plays out in the courtroom. Through the effects of neoliberalism and the resulting lack of prohibition, the courts have implicitly indicated that women no longer need to be "protected." Clearly, one of the goals of obscenity provisions was to protect women from degradation and dehumanization, which they no longer need if they are now *choosing* to consume and/or be involved in the production of pornography. In this way, the courts move away from legal paternalism and, instead, draw from ideas promoted by a post-feminist media culture that dispenses notions that women no longer need feminism and can "have it all." Such an idea is central to the post-feminist discourse, and it celebrates the fantasy that "women" have overcome gender inequalities and experiences of sexism, so much so that they can *all* have the lifestyle, the career, the relationship, and the sex life that they want. In fact, it suggests that "feminist struggles have ended" and "women today enjoy full equality and can 'have it all' if they put their minds to it.... [I]t is becoming a women's world, with a celebration of all things feminine" (Lazar, 2009: 371–372; see also Pomerantz, Raby, & Stafanik, 2013). In the legal context, this is illustrated through the concept of "the post-feminist porn star," where judges indicate that women have taken on a different role within the pornographic industry, one where they are viewed as making choices regarding their sexual subjecthood. Subsequently, this alters the judges' own response to the content, and their gradual refutation of the protectionist approach has contributed to the perception that we no longer need to be concerned with the production, distribution, and consumption of adult pornography. Citizens are constructed as "self-governing subjects" who have the ability to make their own choices regarding content, and therefore notions of violence and abuse are largely discarded within the legal realm. Such a transformation promotes ideas of equality and flattens existent differences among women and their varied experiences of the pornographic industry.

Governing through Discourse

The goal of this research is to consider the neoliberal global order and determine what it means for the individual Canadian citizen. Through an examination of judicial discourse, attention is paid to how this political rationality has been realized within the legal realm (a critical "sphere of governance") (Greene & Breshears, 2004: 214) and whether the courts have contributed to Canada's neoliberalization. In order to do this, I utilize Jäger's (2001: 47) notion of "discourse strands" to point to the numerous dominant and sub-themes within an overarching discourse. For example, Jäger (2001: 50) argues that "in a given society discourse strands form the overall societal discourse in a state of entanglement," and it is the role of the researcher to "untangle this net" and understand how the various discourse strands relate to each other. For the current research, neoliberalism is the general societal discourse (or as I maintain, "ideology") and comprises various discourse strands; this concept allows us to investigate the effects that the many discourse strands have on the construction and constitution of citizenship.

Furthermore, I employ Jäger's (2001: 49) concept of "discourse planes," which he maintains are "societal locations from which 'speaking' happens." In this way, the legal system was chosen as the site of interest and as a vital "sphere of governance" within Canadian society. I contemplate how this site acts as an effective tool in the regulation and monitoring of behaviour through the production of discourse. Through the review and analysis of legal cases before and after the emergence of a neoliberal political rationality, the hope was to draw attention to shifts in discourse within obscenity law and comment on how various "discourse strands" may operate to control or enable access to sexually explicit materials.

Key ideas were also adopted from feminist critical discourse analysis so as to challenge the gendered nature of discourse. Establishing a "feminist perspective in language and discourse studies" (Lazar, 2005) allows scholars to contest the social status quo "in favour of a feminist humanist vision of a just society, in which gender does not predetermine or mediate our relationships with others, and our sense of who we are or might become" (6). By critiquing discourses that serve to maintain and preserve the dominant social order, it can reveal ruling relations as they pertain to gender and other intersecting factors, such as sexuality, ethnicity, and social location.

Data collection involved a detailed analysis of obscenity cases within Canada legal history from 1959 to 2009. Utilizing three legal databases accessible in the public domain—Quicklaw, CanLII, and Westlaw Canada—I conducted two primary searches to retrieve all reported cases on obscenity and pornography. After extracting child pornography cases and those that did not relate to pornography or the research focus, the sample consisted of 218 cases. I used NVivo to assist in the generation of descriptive statistical data. Figure 13.1 shows the distribution of cases and demarcates their rise and fall across the 50-year time frame.

NVivo was also utilized to manage exemplary quotations from cases that demonstrated core ideas within judicial discourse around the production, distribution, and consumption of adult pornography.[1] Consequently, it was possible to provide an empirical basis for my conclusions that Canadian obscenity law has increasingly depicted a "neoliberal model of law" and has served to create concepts of normativity and "good" citizenship. Through a discourse analysis of the cases, it was possible to identify the dominant themes related to how the courts have viewed and dealt with adult pornography over the course of 50 years.

Figure 13.1: Distribution of Cases by Decade

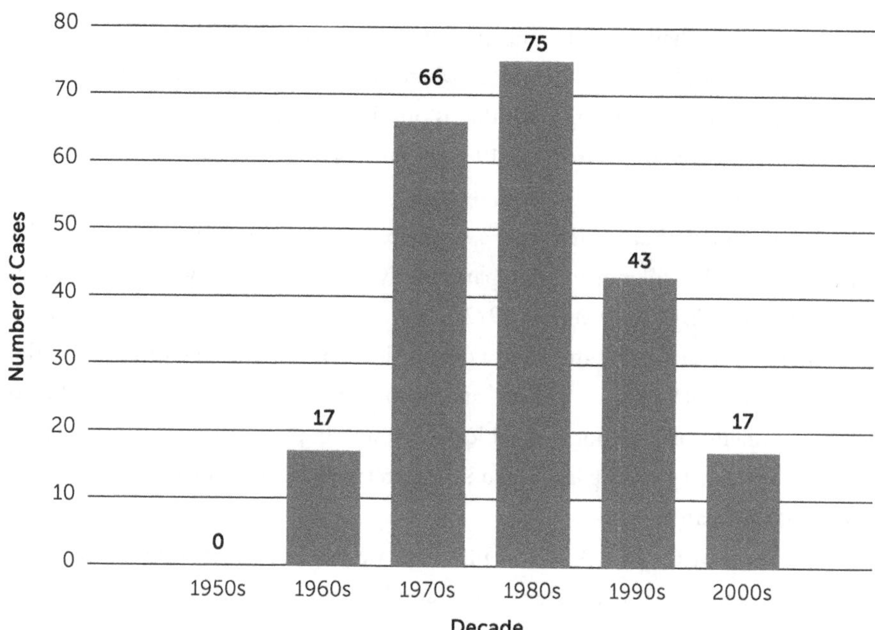

"Sexplosion": The Mainstreaming of Adult Pornography

Shifting attitudes and tolerance are evident in the case law. The judges in a number of cases comment on changing levels of acceptance and tolerance of sexually explicit material,[2] and we can see from the cases themselves that material that was classified as obscene in one year may well be, years later, considered a classic. We only have to look at the case of *R. v. Brodie* and its focus on *Lady Chatterley's Lover* to see that. In 1962, Justice Taschereau commented:

> Nobody would seriously think that this novel could be shown on television or that any respectable publisher would make available to the public in a newspaper or a magazine the complete story of "Lady Chatterley's Lover," without shocking the feelings of normal citizens. (*R. v. Brodie*, 1962, at para. 21)

However, as we know, the book has been made into a film a number of times. Justice Harper indicates this change in attitude, when he said:

> To those who have read the unexpurgated version of this D.H. Lawrence classic the book seems tame indeed when compared with the present-day explicit hard-core pornography that is prevalent in the modern video tapes. (*R. v. Neil's Ventures Ltd.*, 1985, at para. 14)[3]

To note that "things change" is hardly a surprise. In fact, Justice Riley contended that "it is trite to say that tolerance today, particularly regarding sex, is very different than in former years" (*Regina v. Johnson*, 1972, at para. 17). However, this does not change the explicit commentary by the judges on this issue and the implicit indicators that point to the gradual "sexing of society" and the broad sexualization of culture.[4] Judges include comments on "the pornographic progression in publications" (*R. v. Penthouse International Ltd.*, 1977, at para. 33), and "the relaxation of standards" (at para. 47) evident in Canadian society.

In fact, some of the judges commented that we live in an increasingly permissive society with rapidly changing values. For example, Justice Harper stated:

> I think it can safely be said that obscenity (especially as presented in the mode of video cassettes) is raging rampant across the nation with the producers gradually becoming each time more daring as more and more courts look to material which has previously been found to be within the "standard tolerated by the community" and then come to the conclusion—"well, that one was ajudged O.K. and this is only a little bit worse and those other ones were decided in 1984 and this is 1985 so—and the point at which no line can possibly be drawn is quickly reached." (*R. v. Lynnco Sound Ltd.*, 1985, at para. 34)[5]

His last line contends that there will be a point "at which no line can possibly be drawn," and it seems that through an analysis of the case law and consideration of what is currently available, this is a valid statement. The case of *R. v. Price* in 2004 helps us to come to such a conclusion. Price was charged with making, distributing, and circulating 11 obscene videos that portrayed bondage and discipline, dominance and submission, sadism and masochistic activities (BDSM). When reviewing the content of the various videos, the judge considered the types of fictional materials available to the public, such as the film based on the bestselling novel *American Psycho*. The court decided that because there is societal tolerance for explicit sexual activity coupled with graphic violence, Price must be acquitted.[6] This was not the case in 1959.

The growing acceptance of adult pornography and the mainstreaming of sex reflect this paradigm shift where academic and legal attention has gradually moved away from an analysis of adult pornography in the traditional legally paternalistic way. Academic attention has shifted from a consideration of the effects of pornography, and from being centred on the binary of the pro- and anti- arguments, to an analysis of pornography as cultural texts within a new field of porn studies. What we have seen is an increased role of pornography in the "academic marketplace" as courses are listed in university calendars and a subsequent decrease in our attention to the "problematic" place of pornography in society. Consequently, and as stated above, this shift has "flattened all our opposition to pornography" (Attwood, 2002: 98) to a point where violent pornography is largely ignored, and "abusive and consumption practices largely disappear from the agenda" (Boyle, 2008: 38). This indicates a fundamental change of focus and concern, which is also demonstrated in the legal realm and the case law analyzed in this research.

The underlying question to this is why has there been such a dramatic shift? As with most things, our values are ever-changing and technological innovations certainly contribute to this. But we may turn to the socio-political context to provide some answers to this question. Angela McRobbie (2009) points to the necessity of considering the dominance of a neoliberal ideology and articulates how it affects the (re)production of sex and sexuality. Therefore, it is essential to consider the rise of neoliberalism and how it has impacted our relationship with pornography. Further, we need to look at it in relation to the emergence of a harm-based approach and our shifting conceptions of risk and harm. The rise of neoliberal language and goals, demonstrated through a number of discourse strands, is evident in case law. The following discussion considers three discourse strands that emerge from the case law and display neoliberal ideals and a focus on "governing at a distance."

Calculating a Substantial Risk of Harm

The legal realm, particularly since the 1980s, acts as a "capillarylike" technology (Nadesan, 2008: 91) to assist people in governing themselves, particularly through its rejection of a community standards test of tolerance and its adoption of a harm-based approach. In 1992, the Supreme Court of Canada in *R. v. Butler* articulated a new legal framework for the determination of obscenity in which the notion of harm was central. This decision led to an explicit move away from harm merely being just one of the criteria in the assessment of obscenity to it playing a central role. As Justice Proulx noted,

> Since *Butler*, the degree of harm is no longer assessed separately from the community standard of tolerance, but rather according to this standard

> as an *underlying principle*. This is simply because it is impossible to apply standards of tolerance in an objective manner if there is no reliable way to take the pulse of society. (*Labaye v. R.*, 2004, at para. 49; emphasis added)

With this decision the Supreme Court was responding to the growing reference to degradation and dehumanization and consequently harm in the case law. The Court decided to formalize "harm" as central to the interpretation and meaning of the "undue exploitation of sex." To do this, the Court qualified the meaning of degradation and dehumanization by including the terminology of a "substantial risk of harm." This meant that not all materials that are degrading or dehumanizing would be considered obscene, but rather only those where it is proven to pose a substantial risk of harm to society. Justice Sopinka demonstrated this when he said:

> The courts must determine as best they can what the community would tolerate others being exposed to on the basis of the degree of harm that may flow from such exposure. Harm in this context means that it predisposes persons to act in an anti-social manner as, for example, the physical or mental mistreatment of women by men, or, what is perhaps debatable, the reverse. Anti-social conduct for this purpose is conduct which society formally recognizes as incompatible with its proper functioning. The stronger the inference of a risk of harm the lesser the likelihood of tolerance. The inference may be drawn from the material itself or from the material and other evidence. Similarly evidence as to the community standards is desirable but not essential. (*R. v. Butler*, 1992, at para. 59)

We can see from this quote that the Court intended there to be a focus on attitudinal harm, particularly as it pertained to the treatment of women. And Justice Sopinka contended that the Court is not only paying attention to harm, but rather to that which "rises to the level of being incompatible with the proper functioning of Canadian society" (Justice Binnie, *Little Sisters Book and Art Emporium v. Canada (Minister of Justice)*, 2000, at para. 59).

This was furthered in the case of *R. v. Labaye* (2005), when the Court set the obscenity provisions decisively within the context of harm, to the point where harm has to be *proven* if the material or conduct at issue is to be judged obscene or indecent.[7] The Supreme Court of Canada decision in *R. v. Labaye* provided a reconfiguration of the test of obscenity and indecency. In some ways, this case was the jurisprudential grand finale, as there have been few cases pertaining to adult obscenity and indecency since. What was at issue in the case was whether Jean-Paul Labaye could be found guilty of "keeping a common bawdy-house" contrary to s. 210.1 of the *Criminal Code*. The real question addressed was whether he, as a proprietor of a licensed establishment, could organize, for a fee, group sexual activities (or "swinging") for informed and consenting adults.[8] In their decision, the majority reconstituted the test of "undueness" through their theory of harm, which made harm the single most important factor for the courts to consider. One of the primary intentions was to increase the level of objectivity in such cases. In doing this, the majority used language in their harm-based approach from earlier decisions, such as *R. v. Butler* (1992), but went further in what the courts were required to consider when faced with an issue of obscenity or indecency. For example, Justice McLachlin stated, "[T]o ground criminal responsibility, the harm must be one which society *formally recognizes* as incompatible with its proper functioning" (*R. v. Labaye*, 2005, at para. 32; emphasis in original). It was this requisite that the majority felt would make the test objective, primarily because it is "not based on individual notions of harm nor on the teachings of a particular ideology, but on what society, through its fundamental laws, has recognized as essential" (at para. 33). It considered that this requirement would ensure that "people will not be convicted and imprisoned for transgressing the rules and beliefs of particular individuals or groups" (at para. 35).

The majority not only transformed how harm was to be considered but also what was required to prove its existence. This judgment demonstrated support for earlier murmurings that evidence should not only be admissible, but that it should be *essential* to an adjudication of harm.[9] For example, in her dissenting judgment in *R. v. Towne Cinema Theatres Ltd.*, Justice Wilson argued that it is necessary for the Crown to adduce evidence and stated, "[I]n my view it is naive to think that a judge, drawing on his own experience alone, can determine the objective standard against which impugned conduct is to be measured" (*R. v. Towne Cinema Theatres Ltd.*, 1985, at para. 84).[10] In doing so, she referred to the dissenting judgment in the case of *Regina v. Cameron*, where Justice Laskin held that "expert evidence to assist the Judge or Magistrate or Judge and jury is ... indispensable" (*Regina v. Cameron*, 1966, at para. 72). In such a way, the majority in *R. v. Labaye* held that

> these are matters that can and should be established by evidence, as a general rule. When the test was the community standard of tolerance, it could be argued that judges or jurors were in a position to gauge what the community would tolerate from their own experience in the community. But a test of harm or significant risk of harm incompatible with the proper functioning of society *demands more*. The judge and jurors are generally unlikely to be able to gauge the risk and impact of the harm, without assistance from expert witnesses. (*R. v. Labaye*, 2005, at para. 60; emphasis added)

Through a greater reliance on evidence, the majority contended that, not only will it assist in making the test more objective, but it will also be more likely that the Court will be able to determine real risk of harm, rather than relying on an assumption. Therefore, the Court held that "only if the impact of the acts in degree of harm poses a real risk of damaging the autonomy and liberty of members of the public, judged by contemporary standards, can indecency be established" (at para. 55).

In this way, the *R. v. Labaye* case was successful in delineating a stricter evidentiary test for proving harm and the consequent need for experts in this pursuit. This requirement of proof fits within the larger neoliberal trend of the importance of the expert and the "turn to the psychological" (Lunt, 2008: 537) that is evident in many areas of society. The idea that we can no longer simply have a "reasoned apprehension of harm" moves us closer to using the authority of experts on this issue. The courts have not always placed primacy on the use of experts; however, in this latter case, the requirements validate the wider reliance on experts trumpeted by neoliberalism. Expert knowledges and "the gaze of the expert" (Rose, 2001: 33) are central to governmentality and assist citizens in "correcting the self." "Experts" are viewed as capable of helping us delineate "healthy" and "risky" practices and determining the individuals who are to be conceived of as "failed" citizens due to their "harmful" consumption practices and choices. As Rose (1992: 151) contends, the mantra of the current age is, "[T]he self is to style its life through acts of choice and, when it cannot conduct its life according to this *norm of choice*, it is to seek expert assistance" (emphasis added; see also Lupton, 1999).

Governing at a Distance: The Emergence of A Responsible and Informed Citizenry

Consequently, the *R. v. Labaye* (1995) decision contributed to greater levels of individual freedom and responsibility afforded to Canadian citizens in regard to adult pornography, primarily due to the difficulties of proving harm in an age where sex and sexuality are increasingly accepted and displayed. The trend of relying on harm in the legal realm has gradually contributed to a decline in cases pertaining to adult pornography (as demonstrated in Figure 13.1). What emerges and becomes evident is a growing neoliberal model of law—and what David Garland (1996: 452) characterizes as "a *responsibilization* strategy" (emphasis in original). The legal realm creates conditions for citizens to *govern themselves* and make the "right" choices regarding sexual content, instead of the state playing that role. Subsequently, neoliberalism acts as a mode of governance that affects how the state, individual citizens, and social institutions interact regarding adult pornography. The role of the state is altered, and instead of being the one point of power, it now "appears as simply one element ... in multiple circuits of power, connecting a diversity of authorities and forces, within a whole variety of complex assemblages" (Rose, 1999: 5). Through such governing tactics, there is a greater emphasis on the individual to police and manage the self. Citizens are encouraged "to see themselves as individualized and active subjects responsible for enhancing their own well being" (Larner, 2000a: 11) and self-care.

Following a detailed analysis of cases, it is possible to demarcate this emergent reliance on the individual citizen to self-regulate and self-police. From the 1980s on, we see a trend toward personal choice and individual responsibility, which is demonstrated by the decline of adult pornography–related cases. It is supposed that Canadian citizens no longer need protection from adult pornographic content and are able to be "active citizens" (Larner, 2000b) who judge for themselves what to consume. Various cases talk about provincial film boards that are responsible for classifying and rating films to "enhance the public's ability to make informed viewing choices" (Justice Juriansz, *R. v. Glad Day Bookshops Inc.*, 2004, at para. 96).

As such, the larger societal movement toward a self-policing state has spilled over into our regulation of adult pornography. With the changes in technology and the rise of the Internet, it has become clear that prohibition of adult pornography does not work in a global culture. The Internet reflects the ultimate exchange of ideas and consumerism, which is difficult to regulate. As we see in the case law, between 1995 and 2009, there are only two Internet-related cases.[11] This seemingly demonstrates that it is almost impossible to regulate the creation and distribution of adult pornography on the Internet, to the point that it is left up to the consumer to take responsibility for the pornographic content they view. Pornographic material is subject to the regulations of a competitive marketplace, where consumers decide what will continue to (economically) thrive through their consumption habits. Case law demonstrates the growing trend of consumer sovereignty; for example, the obscenity provisions primarily target the creation and distribution of pornography, rather than the possession of it. However, this impacts on what is available to the consumer. In recent years, the consumer has been imparted with almost limitless access, due to the rarity of criminalizing or halting pornographic content. Thus, the consumer is viewed through a lens of individual responsibility, autonomy, and choice—key operating components of a neoliberal ideology. Therefore, citizens are considered free, autonomous subjects and come to be envisaged as "'empowered'—made free from debilitating state intervention—and encouraged to assemble their own lifestyles from among the array of commodified options available in the free market" (O'Malley, 2001: 16; see also Gill & Arthurs, 2006).

The cases that solidify this trend and the impact of the neoliberal ideology are *Kouri v. R.* (2004) and *R. v. Labaye* (2005). In the case of *Kouri v. R.*, Justice Otis contends that

> a pluralist and tolerant Canadian society does not condemn modes of sexual expression that vary from those of the majority, as long as they do not constitute a source of social harm and are not offensive. Outside these limits, individuals are *self-determining* and *make personal choices* regarding their mode of sexual expression for themselves, according to their own values and ethics. (at para. 51; emphasis added)

Further, the Supreme Court of Canada decision in *R. v. Labaye* places primacy on individual choice through its judgment on "swinging" (or partner swapping) and its realization of the harm-based approach. Justice McLachlin demonstrates this when she says in the conclusion of her judgment that "consensual conduct behind code-locked doors can hardly be supposed to jeopardize a society as vigorous and tolerant as Canadian society" (*R. v. Labaye*, 2005, at para. 71). Such a sentiment is also expressed in the dissenting judgment of Justice Proulx in the 2004 judgment in *Labaye v. R.* He comments:

> It seems to me difficult to speak of the abasement of a woman or her use as a sexual object for the gratification of others when she has entirely *preserved her autonomy* and considers swinging to be her *personal choice.* These women are not exploited; they participate in swinging activities as the others do or will. (at para. 74; emphasis added)

These cases highlight the importance placed on individual responsibility and choice. Through ultimately deciding that "swinging" is not indecent and is therefore tolerable, these cases signify the fundamental changes in terms of societal conventions toward pornography that we have witnessed and the impact of neoliberal ideals regarding the role of the state and sexual citizenship.[12] Further, the quote from Justice Proulx in the 2004 *Labaye v. R.* case presents a different perspective on women and *their* choices regarding sex and sexual expression, which veers away from the idea that women need to be protected. This is part of a larger trend within the case law.

The Post-Feminist Porn Star

Such ideas prompt us to think about how neoliberal discourse intersects and interplays with feminism and, consequently, the formation of sexual citizenship. It is vital to consider the consequences of such a political shift for women. Not only do we have to think about gender relations and women's place in the labour market (see Hannem & Bruckert, this volume; Jenson, 1996; Larner, 2000a), but also whether there are gender differences in what we consider "citizenship" and further, the ideal citizen, to be (James,

1992). Since the 1980s, we have seen significant shifts regarding the shape of feminism and how it is viewed within the social and cultural landscape. A number of scholars, such as Angela McRobbie, have pointed to the dismantling of feminism that has occurred in the last three decades. McRobbie (2009: 1) contends that the current milieu "is marked by a new kind of anti-feminist sentiment," where "there is no longer any place for feminism in contemporary political culture" (McRobbie, 2007: 721). As a result, it is wrongly assumed that women do not need "feminism" anymore and that women "are already empowered" (Aapola, Gonick, & Harris, 2005: 194). Further, there is a move to individualize problems, a key motif of neoliberalism. One result of this discourse strand is that we have witnessed the reshaping of both girlhood and womanhood "to fit with new or emerging (neo-liberalised) social and economic arrangements" (McRobbie, 2007: 721).

In this way, we have seen the emergence of post-feminism and the post-feminist female subject. As Tasker and Negra (2007: 2–3) maintain, post-feminism has emerged as "a dominating discursive system" that plays a role in (re)creating "the figure of woman as empowered consumer." Through the development of a post-feminist media culture, women and girls are continuously exposed to images of the "empowered" female imbued with agentive power; the "can-do girl" who is a "self-making, resilient, and flexible" subject (Harris, 2004: 6; see also Hasinoff, 2008). In her analysis of post-feminist media culture, Rosalind Gill (2007a) identifies a noticeable shift away from passivity/objectification toward "active" subjecthood, where women are constructed as "pleasing themselves" when they dress or act in a sexy manner" (Gill, 2007b: 91; see also Gill & Herdiecherhoff, 2006). For example, when girls wear T-shirts that display slogans such as, "One Sexy Bitch," "J'adore sex," or "F**K me, I'm legal!" it is because they want to, rather than as the result of a dominating male gaze. Gill (2008a) states that, in this vein, there is a dispersion of a particular image of womanhood, that of the, "young, attractive, heterosexual woman who knowingly and deliberately plays with her sexual power and is always 'up for it' (that is, sex)" (41). Gill (2008a) suggests that women are required to display a particular construction of self supported by post-feminist and neoliberal ideals and are therefore not "free" to construct their own sense of self. The prevalence of these post-feminist ideals therefore plays a significant role in the construction and "becoming" of self, and assists in the governance and regulation of female sexuality (Coleman, 2008). Thus, these constructed knowledges hold the potential to alter the relative possibility of women accessing full sexual citizenship.

The earlier quote from Justice Proulx in *Labaye v. R.* points to this widespread trend and demonstrates how it manifests in terms of women and adult pornography. What is evident is that there is "a profound relation between neoliberal ideologies and postfeminism" (Gill, 2008b: 442; see also Gill, 2010; Gill & Scharff, 2011), which is made explicit through an analysis of judicial discourse. In various judgments, there is commentary that points to this movement away from sexual objectification and toward sexual subjectification and sexual agency. Despite the courts setting the obscenity provisions decisively within the context of harm, there are clear examples of judicial reliance on notions of individual choice and autonomy when it comes to considering women's roles and involvement in the pornography industry. This fact points to a paradox: Canadian courts have indicated that harm is central to an analysis of obscenity while simultaneously moving away from interpreting adult pornography as harmful to women. Consistent with Gill's work, women are subsequently conceived of as *choosing* to be sexy, rather than doing so as a result of degradation and dehumanization by men. In this way, women in the pornography industry are "can-do" girls who are "active, desiring sexual subjects" (Gill, 2007a: 151).

From the case law, these ideas of freedom and choice, particularly as they pertain to women in the pornography industry, are implicitly established through the observations of the judges. They emerge through judicial comments on the rise of the pornography industry and the growing acceptance of it, and serve to contribute to the subsequent decline of the regulation of pornographic content within the legal realm. This particular discourse strand points to "the emergence of a new feminine subject … the 'sexual entrepreneur'" (Harvey & Gill, 2011: 1), or as I term it, the creation and emergence of the "post-feminist porn star." Instead of considering the harmful consequences of a pornographic industry, attention has shifted to contemplating women's *active* role in the films and their choice to be active and willing participants. In such a way, judicial discourse steps away from deliberating the possible abusive outcomes of such content and moves toward commentary that reveals the notion that women have supposedly achieved equality and no longer need legal protection from something that they are now *choosing* to be involved in. For example, this idea is evident in judicial comments made on the growth and success of the industry. The consequences of such success are highlighted by Justice Payne, who remarks on the rising fame and star quality of those involved in these films, along with the increasing "attractiveness" of its participants. He states:

> [T]here appears certainly to be an *upgrading* of the participants in such movies, in that both male and female persons who are involved are at least physically attractive. The women, in particular, are quite physically attractive and it may be some advancement in the industry, that these people now permit their names to be attached to these movies and they are described as starring, and the names of the director and the producer of this type of movie are shown with what appears to be a great deal of pride. As I recall, the old eight millimetre movies on this subject, they were all filmed in bad light, by a lot of scrawny individuals who didn't

> bother to identify themselves. (*R. v. Findlay*, 1987, at para. 11; emphasis added)

These observations are in direct contrast to earlier judicial rulings that were careful to comment on the violent and abusive nature of the pornographic films at issue. For example, prior to such rulings as *Labaye v. R.* (1994), Justice Borins contends that

> [i]n my opinion many of the films are exploitive of women, portraying them as passive victims who derive limitless pleasure from inflicted pain and from subjugation to acts of violence, humiliation and degradation. Women are depicted as sexual objects whose only redeeming features are their genital and erotic zones, which are prominently displayed in clinical detail. Whether deliberately or otherwise, most of the films portray degradation, humiliation, victimization and violence in human relationships as normal and acceptable behaviour. (*R. v. Doug Rankine Company Ltd. and Act III Video Productions Ltd.*, 1983, at para. 31)

The drastic difference in how these two cases adjudicated pornographic content and the depiction and representation of women illustrates the immense social changes that occurred in the 1980s. Although some judges maintained an earlier discursive mindset about harm, as demonstrated by Justice Borins, other judges, such as Justice Payne in *R. v. Findlay*, started to embrace notions of "equality" and "choice" in their rulings.

From the 1980s onward, this shift became increasingly evident. Judges began to identify a change in the tone of the films themselves, which is reflected in their analysis and subsequent judgments. For example, judges noticed women playing a more dominant and aggressive role in the films. As Justice Payne notes, "[I]t does appear as a general trend throughout all the movies that the women in the respective movies were the aggressors, and men, while they were active participants, seemed to be involved only for the use of the women in the particular scenes" (at para. 11). For Justice Misener, this seems to be indicative that women "at last are *asserting their equality*, if not their superiority. And not surprisingly, the male participants seem to be delighted with this new found assertation" (*R. v. Hawkins*, 1992, at para. 14; emphasis added). These statements reflect an alteration in the content of the films themselves, and subsequently in the type of comments made by the judges. The focus seemingly moves away from a consideration of degradation and dehumanization and toward a male appreciation of the "porn stars" and their physical appearance. Such a judicial discourse serves to diminish questions about harm and instead supports the idea of the "active, desiring sexual subject" within the pornographic industry.

This change in focus points to the growing assumption of equality that women now supposedly enjoy. The judges indicate that pornographic movies reflect this assumption of equality by having women take charge to be more sexually aggressive on camera. In this way, we have seen the entrance of the "post-feminist porn star," who chooses to be involved in the industry and enjoys it. The notion that we should be spending time considering the negative consequences and effects of the pornographic industry declines—even if we might question whether being the dominant sex in a pornographic movie really indicates that women have equality and are able to assert it. The lack of prohibition implicitly indicates that women no longer need to be protected. Clearly, one of the goals of the obscenity provisions, viewed through a harm perspective, was to protect women from degradation and dehumanization. This is indicated by Justice Anderson, who stated:

> If true equality between male and female persons is to be achieved it would be quite wrong in my opinion to ignore the threat to equality resulting from the exposure to male audiences of the violent and degrading material described above. As I have said, such material has a tendency to make men more tolerant of violence to women and creates a social climate encouraging men to act in a callous and discriminatory way towards women. (*R. v. Red Hot Video Ltd.*, 1985, at para. 32)

Justice Anderson supports the view that women need not be portrayed in such a way and should be protected from such depictions. Further, Justice Dickson commented that "it is not likely that at a given moment in a society's history, such publications will be tolerated" (*R. v. Towne Cinema Theatres Ltd.*, 1985, at para. 25). Despite such comments, which exemplify those decisions in the 1980s that continued to rely on the earlier discursive mindset about harm that sustained support for continued prohibition and regulation, the gradual inclination moved toward tolerance. The absence of cases in more recent years points to the rise of neoliberal discourses within judicial commentary and legal reasoning that emphasize the prudent and responsible citizen. However, as noted earlier, some feminist scholars suggest that this might not be an accurate set of assumptions about women's rights and equalities.

It remains challenging to critique post-feminism and its celebration of equality and female choice. It is difficult to argue that a move away from the strict legal paternalism that requires women to be protected is undesirable (see Hannem & Bruckert, this volume, for a discussion of this point in regard to prostitution laws). Still, there has to be some engagement and critique that recognizes that a level playing field does not exist for *all* women. The discourse evident in the case law errs toward a misplaced optimism that all women are able to "have it all" and make choices to be "sexy" in accordance with the traditional patriarchal notions of ideal femininity. It illustrates the perhaps gendered nature of neoliberalism, where, in this context, we can consider the ideas of Gill (2008b: 443) who argues that "it is *women* who are called on to self-manage, self-discipline" (emphasis in original). We see a clear example that, "to a much greater extent than men, women are required to work on and transform the self, to regulate every aspect of their conduct, and to present all their actions as freely chosen" (443).

Furthermore, such a perspective "erases real-life difference" (Heinecken, 2003: 154; see also Lazar, 2006) and creates "an equalitarian utopia in which sexual, racial, and ethnic differences among consumers recede" (Mizejewski, 2005: 123). Socio-economic inequalities are ignored and "emptied out of ... contemporary individualized notions of selfhood" (Ringrose & Walkerdine, 2008: 227), leaving a number of identities excluded and invisible from the public domain. This prevalence of "women's empowerment" in judicial discourse is representative of a larger assumption that women are "in full control of their sexuality" within post-feminist discourses. Such thinking serves to undermine difference between women and, subsequently, to mask "ongoing gender imbalances" and ignore socio-structural constraints (Burkett & Hamilton, 2012: 815). As a result, judicial notions of "equality" rely on visions of gender equality that mask intersectional oppressions. They are in line with the post-feminist media culture that celebrates "the idealized postfeminist subject" as a "white, Western, heterosexual wom[a]n" (Butler, 2013: 13), and rebuke the growing importance placed on intersectionality. As Kelly Hannah-Moffat (2010: 206) contends, intersectionality "refers to the interaction between gender, race, and other categories of difference in individual lives, social practices, institutional arrangements and the outcomes of these interactions." Hill Collins (1990) asserts the importance of embracing "a paradigm of race, class, and gender as interlocking systems of oppression" (at para. 3). Recognition of these intersecting factors reveals their power on women's lives and the complex nature of societal inequalities. However, a post-feminist narrative is exclusionary. Butler (2013: 47) highlights that post-feminism can work "to exclude women of color and reproduce racial inequality by reinstituting (Western) whiteness as a dominant cultural norm." In this way, differences are erased, and *all* women are delineated as "empowered" and expected to perform in certain acceptable and normative ways. In this sense, "successful femininity'" (Ringrose & Walkerdine, 2008: 228), as demonstrated by the concept of the "post-feminist porn star," is viewed as normal and universal, even though it is not likely to contribute to *all* (or even the majority of) women's notion of sexual citizenship.

Concluding Remarks

As indicated in the preceding discussion, the trend in obscenity law has been to follow the larger socio-political context and affirm a "neoliberal model of law." In such a way, there has been the promotion of *a new regulatory regime*. With the gradual decline of obscenity-related cases since the 1980s, adult pornography has been enabled to flourish in a neoliberal context without direct state control. This facilitates Canadian citizens' access to forms of sexual expression that they choose to consume, contributing to their sexual citizenship. Concepts of choice, responsibility, and autonomy have allowed adult pornography to thrive, as individual citizens are encouraged to self-regulate and self-police their own behaviours and consumption of pornographic materials.

This decline in the regulation of adult pornography is illustrative of the emergence of a bio-political conception of power, where the courts and judiciary delineate "tools for societal *self*-governance" (Nadesan, 2008: 3; emphasis in original). The legal realm creates conditions for citizens to govern themselves and make the "right" choices regarding sexual and pornographic content. Through their decisions, the courts demarcate ways to maximize individual well-being and minimize risk, particularly through its articulation of ideal notions of citizenship comprising "healthy" and "enterprising" selves.

The shifts in legal governance that this chapter highlights reveal the fundamental alteration in Canada's approach to the regulation of pornography.[13] Regardless of the economic and political challenges to neoliberalism, particularly evident in the most recent financial crisis, it seems to be thriving in the regulation of the "problematic" citizen. The courts are promoting a free-market mentality that constructs a framework in which individuals are encouraged to self-regulate and police their own behaviour and consumption. Further, this neoliberal mindset quickly perceives and defines risk in sexual content using a harm-based approach. Consequently, neoliberalism seems to be working when it comes to the regulation of adult pornography in Canada, and the reduction in cases demonstrates this trend.

Furthermore, although the obscenity provisions were often thought of in light of protecting women in society, with the emergence of neoliberal ideals and post-feminism, the protectionist approach has been discarded in favour of the notion of the post-feminist female subject or the "post-feminist porn star." Within this frame, women are constructed as having achieved equality, and are able to express it through choosing to be sexy and choosing to perform in pornographic films. However, we have to be careful of such an easy celebration of the notions of post-feminism and the post-feminist female subject. Assumptions of equality ignore the real differences and inequalities that exist for and between women that render problematic the idea that women can "have it all." Additionally, such rhetoric serves to flatten opposition to the growth of the pornographic industry and its burgeoning presence within mainstream culture.

Finally, it seems essential to comment on how feminists might respond to these conclusions of the gendered nature of neoliberalism. What stands out in this research is the gradual decline of regulatory measures, and the reliance on notions of post-feminist subjecthood and ideals of femininity within the legal realm as reasons for reducing regulation. Although it was suggested that within a neoliberal socio-political context it is difficult to maintain a system of legal regulation of adult pornography, it does seem important to query these shifts, the representations of women, and the assumptions made about "choice." Although a reduction of state intervention and legal prohibition can be celebrated, especially in the lives of women, it must also be subject to debate. This is obviously a complex discussion, but there is a substantial need to question the "neoliberal fantasy/imaginary of emancipation and empowerment for all" (Chen, 2010: 270), and to "problematize neoliberalist notions of the inherently free and hyper-responsible citizen" (Burkett & Hamilton, 2012: 815; see also Harvey & Gill, 2011).

There is a vast amount of literature on post-feminism; however, since the 1990s there has been "little direct political engagement" in relation to pornography (Dines & Jensen, 2008: 5). It is vital to encourage a revitalization of our engagement with the place of pornography in the socio-legal landscape. There is a demand to negotiate and critique these models of neoliberal subjectivity in order to disrupt and trouble the boundaries of the "ideal" self. There is potential for feminist action and resistance in the current Canadian context, and the need to create spaces for agency, resistance, and critique remains evident. Further, as noted, the paradigm shift witnessed within the academic and legal realm has served to "flatten all our opposition to pornography," but this does not mean that we should not draw attention to the varying definitions of harm and the political economy of pornography that can, at times, serve to exploit and marginalize women. These are issues that require attention and should be addressed inside and outside the academy.

Notes

1 It is important to note that this research paid attention to the *operation* of judicial discourse. Due to the nature of the research, it was not possible to comment on the *effects* of discourse.

2 For example, see *Re Application under Section 160 of the Criminal Code of Canada*, [1980] N.B.J. No. 106; *R. v. Arnold*, [1993] O.J. No. 471; *R. v. Cinema International Canada Ltd.*, [1981] M.J. No. 458; *Daylight Theatre Company Limited v. The Queen*, [1973] S.J. No. 354; *Dechow v. R.*, 1974 CanLII 45; *R. v. Emery*, [1991] O.J. No. 1433; *R. v. Findlay*, 1987 CarswellOnt 2565; *Regina v. McLeod and Georgia Straight Publishing Ltd.*, [1970] B.C.J. No. 581; *Little Sisters Book and Art Emporium v. Canada (Commissioner of Customs and Revenue)*, [2004] B.C.J. No. 1241; *Regina v. O'Reilly and four others*, [1970] O.J. No.

1553; *R. v. Pereira-Vasquez (B.C.C.A.)*, [1988] B.C.J. No. 799; *Priape Enrg. et al. c. Dep. M.N.R.*, [1979] Q.J. No. 199; *Regina v. Provincial News Co., Penthouse International Ltd. and Guccione*, [1974] A.J. No. 146; *R. v. Red Hot Video Ltd.*, 1983 CarswellBC 2076; *R. v. Universal News Ltd.*, [1972] S.J. No. 235; and *R. v. Yorke*, [1997] N.B.J. No. 24.

3 See also *Regina v. Mason*, [1981] O.J. No. 3263; and *R. v. Ronish*, [1993] O.J. No. 608.

4 An example of an implicit indicator is demonstrated in the judgment of Justice Isman in the *Georgia Straight Publishing* case. In relation to one of the counts, he stated the following: "I will deal first with count two which deals with the advertisement using the word 'muffdiving.' I have no evidence whatsoever as to the meaning of that word and it is not a word the meaning of which I can take judicial notice. I must confess that while I've heard a lot of words, particularly in these Courts and elsewhere, I do not think that I can take judicial notice of a word that I have not heard. Therefore, count two is dismissed" (*Regina v. Georgia Straight Publishing Ltd. and Mcleod*, [1969] B.C.J. No. 332, at para. 1). If such an issue were before the courts today, it is unlikely that a similar judgment would be made. Now, through a simple search on the Internet, you can get 807,000 hits on Google when you search the term—one example being a YouTube video on how to do muffdiving (an instructional video).

5 See also *Regina v. McLeod and Georgia Straight Publishing Ltd.*, [1970] B.C.J. No. 581; *R. v. Penthouse International Ltd.*, 1977 CarswellOnt 1268; and *R. v. Video World Ltd.*, [1985] M.J. No. 303.

6 *R. v. Price*, [2004] B.C.J. No. 814. This decision contrasts with earlier decisions, such as *R. v. Scythes*, [1993] O.J. No. 537, where displays of bondage were deemed harmful and, thus, intolerable.

7 See Jochelson & Kramar (2011) for a comprehensive discussion on obscenity and indecency law in Canada, with particular focus on the effect of the 2005 *R. v. Labaye* case. In particular, they argue that the case appropriated a "logic of pre-emption (or precautionary governance) into the heart of obscenity and indecency law" (283).

8 See also *Kouri v. R.*, [2004] J.Q. no 7724, which is another important case on this particular topic.

9 This requirement stems from that fact that "harm" is a very elusive concept, since it is very difficult to operationalize terms such as "degrading" or "dehumanizing."

10 See also *R. v. Penthouse International Ltd.*, 1977 CarswellOnt 1268; and *R. v. Scobey* (N.S. Co. Ct.), [1989] N.S.J. No. 330. *R. v. Butler*, [1989] M.J. No. 404 also includes an interesting argument on the difficulties posed if the court does not use evidence.

11 See *R. v. Price*, [2004] B.C.J. No. 814; and the case of *Smith*. There are a number of stages to this latter case that make the number of Internet-related cases look higher than it is. These are *R. v. Smith*, 2002 CarswellOnt 6152; *R. v. Smith*, [2002] O.J. No. 5018; *R. v. Smith*, 76 O.R. (3d) 435; *R. v. Smith*, [2007] O.J. No. 3074; *R. v. Smith*, [2007] O.J. No. 3075; *R. v. Smith*, [2007] O.J. No. 3076; and *R. v. Smith*, [2008] O.J. No. 740.

12 The notion of "sexual citizenship" can be conceptualized as the "varying degrees of access [a citizen has] to a set of rights to sexual expression and consumption" (Richardson, 2000: 107). It also raises the question: "[H]ow are we entitled to express ourselves sexually?" (Richardson, 2001: 153).

13 The focus of this chapter is Canada; however, there have been some interesting developments in the United Kingdom regarding the regulation of adult pornography that are worthy of mention and question the success of a neoliberal model of law. In 2008, the *Criminal Justice and Immigration Act* was enacted. The act introduced a new offence, "possession of extreme pornographic images." The act was created in response to concerns that the consumption of pornographic images, particularly via the Internet, leads to the normalization of perverted sexual pleasures and could result in actual sexual violence (Attwood & Smith, 2010). The act is an attempt to criminalize access and possession of such imagery, which is considered to be harmful. What is particularly interesting about this is that it marks a "shift from attempting to regulate media content to attempting to regulate the behaviour of *media users*" (Petley, 2009: 430; emphasis added). It authorizes the surveillance of individual users and their consumption habits, a legal trend in stark contrast to that witnessed in Canadian jurisprudence. Therefore, we cannot assume "a singular, uniform rise in neoliberalism" (Huey, 2009: 262). It is important to pay attention to modes of governance and how they manifest in varying locations.

References

Aapola, S., Gonick, M., & Harris, A. (2005). *Young Femininity: Girlhood, Power and Social Change*. New York: Palgrave Macmillan.

Attwood, F. (2002). "Reading porn: The paradigm shift in pornography research." *Sexualities*, 5(1): 91–105.

Attwood, F., & Smith, C. (2010). "Extreme concern: Regulating 'dangerous pictures' in the United Kingdom." *Journal of Law and Society*, 37(1): 171–188.

Boyle, K. (2006). "The boundaries of porn studies: On Linda Williams' Porn Studies." *New Review of Film and Television Studies*, 4(1): 1–16.

Boyle, K. (2008). "Courting consumers and legitimating exploitation: The representation of commercial sex in television documentaries." *Feminist Media Studies*, 8(1): 35–50.

Burkett, M., & Hamilton, K. (2012). "Postfeminist sexual agency: Young women's negotiations of sexual consent." *Sexualities*, 15(7): 815–833.

Butler, J. (2013). "For white girls only? Postfeminism and the politics of inclusion." *Feminist Formations*, 25(1): 35–58.

Chen, E.Y. (2010). "Neoliberal self-governance and popular postfeminism in contemporary anglo-American chick lit." *Concentric: Literary and Cultural Studies*, 36(1): 243–275.

Coleman, R. (2008). "The becoming of bodies: Girls, media effects, and body image." *Feminist Media Studies*, 8(2): 163–179.

Dines, G., & Jensen, R. (2008). "Pornography, feminist debates on." *The International Encyclopedia of Communication*. Retrieved from http://gaildines.com/2009/09/pornography-feminist-debates-on/

Garland, D. (1996). "The limits of the sovereign state: Strategies of crime control in contemporary society." *British Journal of Criminology*, 36(4): 445–471.

Gill, R. (2007a). "Post-feminist media culture: Elements of a sensibility. *European Journal of Cultural Studies*, 10(2): 147–166.

Gill, R. (2007b). *Gender and the Media*. Cambridge & Malden: Polity Press.

Gill, R. (2008a). "Empowerment/sexism: Figuring female sexual agency in contemporary advertising." *Feminism & Psychology*, 18(1): 35–60.

Gill, R. (2008b). "Culture and subjectivity in neoliberal and postfeminist times." *Subjectivity*, 25: 432–445.

Gill, R. (2010). "Mediated intimacy and postfeminism: A discourse analytic examination of sex and relationships advice in a woman's magazine." *Discourse and Communication*, 3: 345–369.

Gill, R., & Arthurs, J. (2006). "Editor's introduction: New femininities?" *Feminist Media Studies*, 6(4): 443–451.

Gill, R., & Herdieckerhoff, E. (2006). "Rewriting the romance: New femininities in chick lit?" *Feminist Media Studies*, 6(4): 487–503.

Gill, R., & Scharff, C. (2011). "Introduction." In R. Gill & C. Scharff, eds., *New Femininities: Postfeminism, Neoliberalism and Subjectivity* (pp. 1–20). Hampshire, UK: Palgrave Macmillan.

Greene, R.W., & Breshears, D. (2004). "Book review: *Foucault, Cultural Studies, and Governmentality* by Jack S. Bratich, Jeremy Packer & Cameron McCarthy (Eds.)." *Communication and Critical/Cultural Studies*, 1(2): 213–218.

Hannah-Moffat, K. (2010). "Sacrosanct or flawed: Risk, accountability and gender-responsive penal politics." *Current Issues in Criminal Justice*, 22(2): 193–215.

Harris, A. (2004). *Future Girl: Young Women in the Twenty-First Century*. New York & London: Routledge.

Harvey, L., & Gill, R. (2011). "Spicing it up: Sexual entrepreneurs and the sex inspectors." In R. Gill & C. Scharff, eds., *New Femininities: Postfeminism, Neoliberalism and Subjectivity* (pp. 52–67). Hampshire, UK: Palgrave Macmillan.

Hasinoff, A.A. (2008). "Fashioning race for the free market on *America's Top Model*." *Critical Studies in Media Communication*, 25(3): 324–343.

Heinecken, D. (2003). *The Warrior Women of Television: A Feminist Cultural Analysis of the New Female Body in Popular Media*. New York: Peter Lang Publishing.

Hill Collins, P. (1990). "Black feminist thought in the matrix of domination." In P. Hill Collins, *Black Feminist Thought: Knowledge, Consciousness, and the Politics of Empowerment* (pp. 221–238). Boston: Unwin Hyman. Retrieved from www.hartford-hwp.com/archives/45a/252.html

Huey, L. (2009). "Homelessness and the 'exclusive society' thesis: Why it is important to 'think local' to 'act local' on homelessness issues." *European Journal of Homelessness*, 3: 261–273.

Jäger, S. (2001). "Discourse and knowledge: Theoretical and methodological aspects of a critical discourse and dispositive analysis." In R. Wodak & M. Meyer, eds., *Methods of Critical Discourse Analysis* (pp. 32–62). London: Sage Publications.

James, S. (1992). "The good-enough citizen: Female citizenship and independence." In G. Bock & S. James, eds., *Beyond Equality and Difference: Citizenship, Feminist Politics and Female Subjectivity* (pp. 48–65). London & New York: Routledge.

Jenson, J. (1996). "Introduction: Some consequences of economic and political restructuring and readjustment." *Social Politics*, 3(1): 1–11.

Jochelson, R., & Kramar, K. (2011). "Governing through precaution to protect equality and freedom: Obscenity and indecency law in Canada after *R. v. Labaye* [2005]." *Canadian Journal of Sociology*, 36(4): 283–312.

Larner, W. (2000a). "Neo-liberalism: Politics, ideology, governmentality." *Studies in Political Economy*, 63: 5–25. Retrieved from www.newcastle.edu.au/centre/curs/downloads/2003/spe%20_revised_.pdf

Larner, W. (2000b). "Post-welfare state governance: Towards a code of social and family responsibility." *Social Politics*, 7(2): 244–265.

Lazar, M.M. (2005). "Politicizing gender in discourse: Feminist critical discourse analysis as political perspective and praxis." In M.M. Lazar, ed., *Feminist Critical Discourse Analysis: Gender, Power and Ideology in Discourse* (pp. 1–28). Basingstoke, Hampshire & New York: Palgrave Macmillan.

Lazar, M.M. (2006). "'Discover the power of femininity!' Analyzing global 'power femininity' in local advertising." *Feminist Media Studies*, 6(4): 505–517.

Lazar, M.M. (2009). "Entitled to consume: Postfeminist femininity and a culture of post-critique." *Discourse & Communication*, 3(4): 371–400.

Lunt, P. (2008). "*Little angels*: The mediation of parenting." *Continuum: Journal of Media & Cultural Studies*, 22(4): 537–546.

Lupton, D. (1999). "Risk and the ontology of pregnant embodiment." In D. Lupton, ed., *Risk and Sociocultural Theory: New Directions and Perspectives* (pp. 59–85). Cambridge: Cambridge University Press.

McNair, B. (2002). *Striptease Culture: Sex, Media and the Democratization of Desire*. London & New York: Routledge.

McRobbie, A. (2007). "TOP GIRLS? Young women and the post-feminist sexual contract." *Cultural Studies*, 21(4–5): 718–737.

McRobbie, A. (2009). *The Aftermath of Feminism: Gender, Culture and Social Change*. London: Sage Publications.

Mizejewski, L. (2005). "Dressed to kill: Post-feminist noir." *Cinema Journal*, 44(2): 121–127.

Nadesan, M.H. (2008). *Governmentality, Biopower, and Everyday Life*. New York & London: Routledge.

O'Malley, P. (2001). "Genealogy, systematisation and resistance in 'advanced liberalism.'" In G. Wickham & G. Pavlich, eds., *Rethinking Law, Society and Governance: Foucault's Bequest* (pp. 13–25). Oxford & Portland, Oregon: Hart Publishing.

Petley, J. (2009). "Pornography, panopticism and the *Criminal Justice and Immigration Act 2008*." *Sociology Compass*, 3(3): 417–432.

Pomerantz, S., Raby, R., & Stefanik, A. (2013). "Girls run the world? Caught between sexism and postfeminism in the school." *Gender & Society*, 27(2): 185–207.

Ringrose, J., & Walkerdine, V. (2008). "Regulating the abject: The TV make-over as site of neo-liberal reinvention toward bourgeois femininity." *Feminist Media Studies*, 8(3): 227–246.

Rose, N. (1992). "Governing the enterprising self." In P. Heelas & P. Morris, eds., *The Values of the Enterprise Culture* (pp. 141–164). London & New York: Routledge.

Rose, N. (1999). *Powers of Freedom: Reframing Political Thought*. Cambridge & New York: Cambridge University Press.

Rose, N. (2001). "Biopolitics in the twenty-first century—Notes for a research agenda." *Distinktion*, 3: 25–44.

Richardson, D. (2000). "Constructing sexual citizenship: Theorizing sexual rights." *Critical Social Policy*, 20(1): 105–135.

Richardson, D. (2001). "Extending citizenship: Cultural citizenship and sexuality." In N. Stevenson, ed., *Culture and Citizenship* (pp. 153–166). London: Sage Publications.

Simpson, N. (2004). "Coming attractions: A comparative history of the Hollywood studio system and the porn business. *Historical Journal of Film, Radio and Television*, 24(4): 635–652.

Tasker, Y., & Negra, D. (2007). "Introduction: Feminist politics and post-feminist culture." In Y. Tasker & D. Negra, eds., *Interrogating Post-feminism: Gender and the Politics of Popular Culture* (pp. 1–25). Durham & London: Duke University Press.

Williams, L. (Ed.). (2004). *Porn Studies*. Durham & London: Duke University Press.

Legal Cases and Statutes

Criminal Justice and Immigration Act 2008 (United Kingdom of Great Britain and Northern Ireland), Chapter 4, 8 May 2008.

Daylight Theatre Company Limited v. The Queen, [1973] S.J. No. 354.

Kouri v. R., [2004] J.Q. no 7724.

Labaye v. R., [2004] J.Q. no 7723.

Little Sisters Book and Art Emporium v. Canada (Minister of Justice), [2000] 2 S.C.R. 1120.

Regina v. Cameron, [1966] O.J. No. 1047.

Regina v. Johnson, [1972] A.J. No. 59.

R. v. Brodie, [1962] S.C.R. 681.

R. v. Butler, [1992] 1 S.C.R. 452.

R. v. Doug Rankine Company Ltd. and Act III Video Productions Ltd., [1983] O.J. No. 3339.

R. v. Findlay, 1987 CarswellOnt 2565 (Ontario Provincial Court, 1987).

R. v. Glad Day Bookshops Inc., [2004] O.J. No. 1766.

R. v. Hawkins, [1992] O.J. No. 1161.

R. v. Labaye, [2005] 3 S.C.R. 728.

R. v. Lynnco Sound Ltd., [1985] N.B.J. No. 157.

R. v. Neil's Ventures Ltd., [1985] N.B.J. No. 123.

R. v. Penthouse International Ltd., 1977 CarswellOnt 1268 (Ontario County Court, 1977).

R. v. Price, [2004] B.C.J. No. 814.

R. v. Red Hot Video Ltd., [1985] B.C.J. No. 2279.

R. v. Towne Cinema Theatres Ltd., [1985] 1 S.C.R. 494.

Chapter 14

Legal Moralism, Feminist Rhetoric, and the Criminalization of Consensual Sex in Canada

Stacey Hannem and Chris Bruckert

The sex industry is a large and varied commerce encompassing a wide range of labour practices and processes.[1] Some sex workers solicit clients on the street, others work out of brothels, dungeons, "massage parlours," or "holistic health centres," and still others work for escort agencies doing out-calls. Increasingly, sex workers are using the Internet to solicit clients as independents—these self-employed workers may provide services in the hotel rooms or homes of clients, or they may invite patrons into their place of residence/work. The services offered are similarly diverse. Some sex workers offer erotic massage with "happy endings" only, others, oral release, some provide domination or submission, some cater to fetishes, and others provide full sexual services. Workers are as diverse as any other population—they are male, female, and transgender; they come from different social, economic, and cultural backgrounds; some are Canadian nationals, others landed immigrants, and still others are undocumented migrants; they also vary in terms of family obligations, educational background, health status, and lifestyle. They have varied relationships to the work: some fully support themselves through sex work, others work part time, and for some it is an occasional income-generating activity.

For all their diversity, the workers in this occupational category share one significant characteristic—they labour in a criminalized and stigmatized occupation. While the exchange of sexual services for compensation is not, and has never been, illegal in Canada, *Criminal Code of Canada* sections 210 to 213 make it difficult for sex workers to labour without contravening the law.[2] This has significant implications for workers' lives—both professionally and personally. The enduring criminal condemnation of consensual commercial sex appears profoundly archaic in light of vast changes in Canadians' sexual mores and values over the last 50 years. We have gone from a time when women were expected to "save" themselves for marriage to a society where young women proudly claim their right to enjoy their sexuality and assert their right to be "sexy" in "slut walks."[3] Some of this battle has played out in the courts as women mobilize against paternalistic laws that deny them authority over their bodies, including the rights to abortion and birth control. We have also seen Pierre Elliott Trudeau's famous assertion that "the state has no business in the bedrooms of the nation" reflected in the 1969 decriminalization of homosexuality—an essential precondition for the 2005 *Civil Marriage Act* that recognized same-sex marriage.[4]

In the face of what appears to be a tidal wave of change around sexual mores in Canada, the continued criminalization of people labouring in sexual commerce begs the question—why? At the heart of this paradox are converging, albeit empirically questionable, stigmatic assumptions about sex workers. On the one hand, sex workers are constructed as a risk to the moral and physical health of communities. They are seen as "dirty," immoral, disruptive, and as vectors of disease (see, e.g., Hintonburg Community Association, 2006). This "contagion-risk" exists alongside assertions that "all prostituted women are at-risk"—of violence and/or exploitation at the hands of "pimps," "traffickers," or clients; of their own misguided decisions; of childhoods characterized by abuse; or of the intrinsic harm of prostitution itself (see, e.g., Farley & Kelly, 2000).[5] Emanating from different ideological and social locations,[6] these discourses appear to exist in tension and suggest that sex workers are both victim and victimizer. In this chapter we argue that stigmatic assumptions of sex workers as simultaneously at risk/risky legitimates legal moralism, justified by the need to manage risk and protect both (at-risk) sex workers and communities (at-risk from sex workers).[7] As we will see, these two seemingly bifurcated positions are really different sides of the same regulatory coin.

To this end, we begin by presenting the legal context in Canada and the recent constitutional challenge (*Bedford v. Canada (Attorney General)*, 2010) to these laws before drawing on the concepts of legal moralism, legal paternalism, and feminist maternalism to think critically about the competing discourses around sex work. This positions us to problematize the legitimacy afforded to second wave prohibitionist victim-feminist rhetoric. We then turn to an examination of what this criminal regulatory regime means to sex workers and how it conditions labour practices, increases their vulnerability to violence, and contributes to sex workers' social and civic exclusion. We conclude the chapter with a brief consideration of policy models, arguing that decriminalization is the only approach that would allow us to transcend the harms inherent in criminalization.

The Legal Context

There are three principal *Criminal Code of Canada* statutes that regulate sex work in Canada: section 210 criminalizes the owners/managers, workers, and clients of "bawdy houses";[8] section 212, a procuring law, targets third parties (mangers, pimps, bosses) and sex workers' partners; and section 213 makes it illegal to communicate in public for the purposes of prostitution.[9]

The oldest of these is the "bawdy house" provision. Section 210.1 criminalizes "keepers"—anyone who owns, manages, or provides assistance in the running of an in-call establishment. In real terms this means that, in addition to owners and managers, receptionists, bouncers, sex workers who help out with the phones, and workers who work out of their own homes are guilty of an indictable offence and liable to imprisonment for a term not exceeding two years. Workers without supervisory/managerial responsibilities and their clients are more likely to be convicted under section 210.2, a summary conviction offence,[10] that criminalizes "everyone who (a) is an inmate of a common bawdy-house, [or] (b) is found, without lawful excuse, in a common bawdy-house." In practice, the broad definition of "place"[11] prohibits sex workers from receiving clients in their own homes, hotel rooms, or even repeatedly taking clients to the same parking lot.

Section 212 of the *Criminal Code of Canada*, the wide-ranging "procuring" law, also affects sex workers:

> (1) Every one who
>
> (a) procures, attempts to procure or solicits a person to have illicit sexual intercourse with another person, whether in or out of Canada....
>
> (h) for the purposes of gain, exercises control, direction or influence over the movements of a person in such manner as to show that he is aiding, abetting or compelling that person to engage in or carry on prostitution with any person or generally....
>
> (j) lives wholly or in part on the avails of prostitution of another person,
>
> is guilty of an indictable offence and liable to imprisonment for a term not exceeding ten years.

This law is intended to protect sex workers from being exploited by "pimps," but in practice sanctions all professional relationships sex workers have with third parties (and some personal ones as well). Of particular note is the reverse onus offence,[12] s. 212(1)(j), which criminalizes living on the avails of the prostitution of another person.

Counterintuitively, case law has established that evidence of exploitation or unfairness is not required; anyone who is not in a cohabiting relationship but whose income is contingent on a sex worker's labour (receptionists, drivers, agents, website designers, managers, etc.)[13] is understood to *parasitically* live on the avails of another's prostitution, even when (s)he provides useful services[14] in exchange for reasonable compensation.[15] Justice Himel suggested that this situation "may actually serve to increase the vulnerability and exploitation of the very group it intends to protect" (*Bedford v. Canada (Attorney General)*, 2010, at para. 387).

Section 212(1)(j) also criminalizes some of the personal relationships sex workers have. Section 212(3) specifies that "evidence that a person lives or is habitually in the company of a prostitute ... is, in the absence of evidence to the contrary, proof that the person lives on the avails of prostitution." Although case law has refined the interpretation to exclude persons to whom the sex worker has a moral obligation (i.e., children, aging parents), partners and habitual companions of sex workers remain vulnerable to criminal sanctions since they are *presumed* to be living parasitically and are required to prove otherwise.

The most recently enacted statute, section 213, criminalizes "communication for the purpose of prostitution." Until 1972, the regulation of the street-based industry fell under the purview of the Vagrancy "C" provisions of the *Criminal Code of Canada*, section 175.1(c), according to which "a common prostitute or nightwalker found in a public place and who does not, when required, give a good account of herself" is guilty of vagrancy. Thus, prostitution was a gender-specific status offence.[16] In response to feminist mobilizing against this antiquated statute, the soliciting law (s. 195.1), which criminalized soliciting "in a public place for the purpose of prostitution," was enacted in 1972. The 1978 ruling by the Supreme Court of Canada in *Hutt v. R.* (1978) that the solicitation had to be "pressing and persistent" severely curtailed the ability of police to charge street-based sex workers, and coincided with the gentrification of the traditional "strolls" in urban centres including Vancouver, Edmonton, and Ottawa. The incoming middle-class residents, attracted by central locations and affordable real estate prices, mobilized to displace the erstwhile inhabitants, asserting that they were victimized by street-based sex work. They called for greater enforcement and harsher laws to rid their neighbourhoods of this "social nuisance," effectively leveraging their social, economic, and political capital (Lowman, 2000). Legislators responded by replacing the soliciting law with s. 213(1) of the *Criminal Code*:

> Every person who in a public place[17] or in any place open to public view
> (a) stops or attempts to stop any motor vehicle,
> (b) impedes the free flow of pedestrian or vehicular traffic or ingress to or egress from premises adjacent to that place, or

> (c) stops or attempts to stop any person or in any manner communicates or attempts to communicate with any person
> for the purpose of engaging in prostitution or of obtaining the sexual services of a prostitute is guilty of an offence punishable on summary conviction.

We see that although consensual sexual commerce is not illegal in Canada it is difficult to do sex work without contravening the law—especially for marginalized individuals who do not have the option of working as out-call escorts. This ambiguous situation has been the subject of much critique by Canadian parliamentarians (Parliament of Canada, 2006), lawyers (Pivot Legal Society, 2004, 2006), academics (Jeffrey & Sullivan, 2009; Lewis & Shaver, 2006; Lowman, 2000), and sex workers (POWER, 2011; Stella, 2005). It has also recently been the subject of a court challenge, to which we now turn.

Challenging the Law

In 2009, one current and two former sex workers, Amy Lebovitch, Terri-Jean Bedford, and Valerie Scott, launched a *Canadian Charter of Rights and Freedoms* (*Charter*) challenge[18] on the basis that sections of the prostitution laws[19] contravene their right to security of the person guaranteed under the *Charter*. On September 28, 2010, Justice Himel of the Ontario Superior Court concurred in a landmark ruling. She stated that the laws

> are not in accord with the principles of fundamental justice and must be struck down. These laws, individually and together, force prostitutes to choose between their liberty interest and their right to security of the person as protected under the *Canadian Charter of Rights and Freedoms* ... and that this infringement is not saved by section 1 as a reasonable limit demonstrably justified in a free and democratic society. (*Bedford v. Canada (Attorney General)*, 2010, at para. 3)

The ruling was only partially upheld by the Appeal Court of Ontario on March 26, 2012, which concurred that s. 210 ("bawdy-house") of the *Criminal Code* was unconstitutional, but that s. 212.1(j) ("living on the avails") could be saved by "reading in" the words "in circumstances of exploitation" (*Canada (Attorney General) v. Bedford*, 2012, at para. 327). The decision on the constitutionality of s. 213 was split 3–2, with the majority of the justices arguing that the law's infringement on the rights of sex workers is justified by the legislative objective of preventing nuisance to the community. The ruling was appealed to the Supreme Court of Canada, and the case was heard on June 13, 2013; on

December 20, 2013, the Supreme Court justice upheld the lower court's ruling holding that all three of the challenged provisions were unconstitutional (*Canada [Attorney General] v. Bedford,* 2013).

This legal challenge goes to the heart of the debates surrounding the regulation of sex work in Canada. The interveners for both sides of the case exemplify the competing discourses and perspectives on sexual commerce. For example, the by-and-for sex worker rights groups, POWER (Ottawa) and Maggie's (Toronto), were granted intervener status and presented to the Appeal Court justices. Although these two groups (in coalition with Stella, a sex worker rights organization from Montreal) were denied the right to speak to Canada's highest court on the issue, allied groups, such as the Pivot Legal Society and the Canadian HIV/AIDS Legal Network, were able to intervene at the Supreme Court hearings to support the arguments made by the three sex workers—Bedford, Libovitch, and Scott. At the same time, a number of groups that identify as "feminist,"[20] the Canadian Association of Sexual Assault Centres, the Native Women's Association of Canada, the Canadian Association of Elizabeth Fry Societies, and the Vancouver Rape Relief Society, and which are, on most issues, highly critical of state policies, took the opposing position. These groups formed a coalition (the Women's Coalition for the Abolition of Prostitution) that intervened on the same "side" as the Christian Legal Fellowship, the Catholic Civil Rights League, and REAL Women of Canada to retain the laws; strange bedfellows, indeed. The Women's Coalition for the Abolition of Prostitution is a group of prohibitionist victim-feminists who support the Swedish or "end-demand" model.[21] They argued before the courts that, while sex workers should not be sanctioned directly, laws criminalizing clients and managers are necessary to protect women because "prostitution itself is harmful to women" (Women's Coalition, 2010: 2). They maintain that eradicating the sex industry by ending the demand through prohibitionist laws is necessary to protect women from the harms of prostitution.[22] In light of the deep ideological crevices that exist between feminists and the conservative right, this alignment is counterintuitive. Equally surprising is that this "feminist" discourse is embraced by right-of-centre politicians who have a history of undermining women's rights.[23] Indeed, Joy Smith, a Conservative Member of Parliament, sponsored a private member's bill to criminalize the purchase (but not the sale) of sexual services, asserting that prostitution is "inherently harmful to women and youth as well as society" (Smith, 2011). More clearly, on October 28, 2013, the Conservative Party of Canada passed a resolution that coalesced neatly with the victim-feminist position:

> i) The Conservative Party rejects the concept of legalizing the purchase of sex;
> ii) The Conservative Party declares that human beings are not objects to be enslaved, bought or sold; and

> iii) The Conservative Party of Canada shall develop a Canada specific plan to target the purchasers of sex and human trafficking markets through criminalizing the purchase of sex as well as the acts of any third party attempting to profit from the purchase of sex. (Conservative Party of Canada, 2013)

In light of the proactive engagement of "feminist" groups in calling for legal sanctions, it seems doubtful that this is *only* an appropriation of (presumed) feminist orthodoxy by a conservative right. We argue that it speaks to a more fundamental convergence regarding the ways these groups conceptualize the agency of women in the sex industry and their own paternalistic/maternalistic advocacy roles. Beginning, on the one hand, from an assumption of the inherent immorality of non-monogamous sexual relations, and sex work, ergo, as degrading to women, and, on the other, from a position that sees sex work as inextricably mired in a patriarchy that prioritizes male sexuality and violently exploits women, the two groups come to the same conclusion. Their proposed "solution" supports repressive legal responses to a problem that is largely rooted in the moral stigma that relegates sex work to the margins of society. To theoretically position this argument, we turn now to a critical reflection on the intersections and interplay between legal moralism, legal paternalism, and feminist maternalism.

Legal Moralism, Legal Paternalism, and Feminist Maternalism

The principle of legal moralism suggests that it is a legitimate function of law in a civil society to prohibit and sanction behaviours that are commonly regarded as "immoral," even if these activities do not appear to cause harm and are practised in private by consenting adults (Devlin, 1965; Hart, 1963; Murphy, 1966). While acknowledging that standards of morality are often a site of disagreement among citizens, Devlin argued from a purely utilitarian standpoint that it was the purview of the state to enforce a common morality in order to ensure the security and order of that society. In contemporary Canadian society, the problem is that laws based on this notion of legal moralism contradict the rights of individual autonomy that are bestowed by the *Canadian Charter of Rights and Freedoms*. Specifically, the section 7 right to "life, liberty, and security of the person" suggests that the imposition of moral values in cases where harm to another person is not at stake would unduly restrict the individual freedom (or liberty) of action granted by the *Charter*. When laws based in legal moralism actually create conditions of harm, as is alleged by the *Charter* challenge of the laws surrounding prostitution, their legitimacy is further called into question. In the 2010 Ontario Superior Court ruling,

Justice Himel confirmed this interpretation, stating: "The prevention of 'dirt for dirt's sake' is not a legitimate objective which would justify the violation of one of the most fundamental freedoms enshrined in the Charter" (*Bedford v. Canada (Attorney General)*, 2010, at para. 223).

Casting further doubt on the validity of the principle of legal moralism, Hart pointed out that there is no empirical evidence to suggest that a divergence in moral values undermines the security or order of society; therefore, legal moralism is not required to protect society and poses an undue restriction on individual freedoms (Hart, 1963; see also Murphy, 1966). Murphy (1966) has taken the philosophical argument against legal moralism even further, arguing that Hart's challenge still relies on the application of a utilitarian principle that is unnecessary because the concept of legal moralism is itself based on an inaccurate understanding of the concept of "crime." Murphy argued that a "crime" must have a victim; ergo, the creation of a "victimless crime," based on the enforcement of a morality standard, is not a legitimate use of criminal law in that it makes criminals of consenting adults who do not believe themselves to be harmed or consider themselves "victims." Following this logic, sexual commerce would be victimless and therefore not a legitimate subject of criminal law. As we have already seen, two significant discourses emerged in the 1970s and 1980s that re-envisioned the sex industry and constituted new victims—communities and sex workers. The legal framing of sex work shifted in the mid-1980s, de-emphasizing the (im)morality of prostitution and instead focusing on perceptions of harm to communities, effectively repositioning neighbourhoods and citizens as the "victims" of this previously "victimless" social ill, and providing new justification for the criminal legislation surrounding bawdy houses (s. 210 of the *Criminal Code*) and a legal foundation for the "communicating in public" legislation (s. 213). More relevant to this chapter was the concurrent emergence of second wave and radical feminist rhetoric that frames the issue as one of violence against women—arbitrarily dismissing male workers, who comprise 20–25 percent of the industry (Parliament of Canada, 2006: 10), as "too few to count."[24] They maintain that sex workers are victims of individual men, of patriarchy, of their own histories of abuse, and, if they fail to recognize their victimization, of their own false consciousness. Moreover, this rhetoric suggests that all women are harmed when men can "purchase" one representative member.[25] This position moves away from an overt legal moralism toward what might better be characterized as legal paternalism/maternalism.

Gerald Dworkin (1972: 65) defined legal paternalism as "interference with a person's liberty of action justified by reasons referring exclusively to the welfare, good, happiness, needs, interests, or values of the person being coerced." In his analysis of this legal philosophy, Dworkin suggests that there is a "hypothetical consent" justification, whereby the state can legitimately impose limits on individual freedom as long as there is sufficient cause to believe that the harm being prevented is one that a "reasonable person" would not wish to be subjected to. Laws that regulate, for example, the wearing of helmets by motorcyclists, a minimum age for purchase of cigarettes, and mandatory automobile insurance are viewed as "reasonable" limitations on individual freedoms that protect citizens from harming themselves, reflecting legal paternalism.[26]

Neo-prohibitionist victim-feminists[27] engage maternalist rhetoric when they assert that women in the sex industry are in need of "saving" from the inherent exploitation of prostitution and assume that no "reasonable" person would choose to engage in sex work. Swedish activist Gunilla Ekberg[28] asserts:

> In prostitution, men use women's and girls' bodies, vaginas, anuses, mouths for their sexual pleasures and as vessels of ejaculation, over and over and over again. Prostitution is not sexual liberation; it is humiliation, it is torture, it is rape, it is sexual exploitation and should be named as such. Consequently, males who use women and girls in prostitution are sexual predators and rapists. (quoted in Wallace, 2011: 2)

The corollary to the rhetorical preoccupation with harm to sex workers and arguments that "prostituted women" (CLES, 2008: 2) must be supported and assisted to "escape" prostitution is the negation of agency, and the outright denial that people may choose to engage in sex work, having taken into account the material, social, and structural realities of their lives.[29] Indeed, in the following quote, we see that all sex workers who challenge this orthodoxy are first dismissed as a token "few" (apparently the many thousands of workers around the world who support decriminalization and assert their right to choose to do sex work are also "too few to count") before their ability to consent is simply negated:

> Most women in prostitution did not make a rational choice to enter prostitution.... Rather than consent, a prostituted woman more accurately complies to the only options available to her.... There is no doubt that a small number of women say they choose to be in prostitution, especially in public contexts orchestrated by the sex industry. In the same way, some people choose to take dangerous drugs such as heroin. However, even when some people choose to take dangerous drugs, we still recognize that this kind of drug use is harmful to them, and most people do not seek to legalize heroin. In this situation, *it is harm to the person, not the consent of the person that is the governing standard.* (Raymond, 2003; emphasis added)

The issue of choice and agency is another, albeit layered, point of convergence—not least because it becomes entangled in neoliberal narratives. We see this tension in the factums and oral submissions made to the Supreme Court of Canada in *Bedford*.[30] For example, while the lawyers for the Attorney General of Ontario implicitly negated structural constraints and simply responsibilized sex workers for making bad "risky" choices,[31] the Attorney General of the Government of Canada presented a somewhat more nuanced reading that recognized structural realities that push women toward sex work, but represented sex workers' ability to make the "right" choice (exit the industry) as evidence of agency that could transcend structural constraints—indeed the laws are lauded for their assumed deterrent effect (Attorney General of Canada, 2013, at para. 69). From this perspective, agency is presumed evident only in choices to desist from sex work, while the choice to engage in sex work is constructed as the result of personal misfortune and/or individual failing. At the same time, sex workers are made responsible for presumed moral failings such as drug use and addiction, promiscuity, and lack of education. Moreover, drawing on the victim-feminist trope, sex workers' agency is assumed to be limited to the extent that their personal histories and failings are construed as rendering them ready victims to exploitation:

> Many prostitutes share certain background factors that make them more vulnerable to being lured into prostitution. These "pre-existing vulnerabilities" include childhood physical and sexual abuse or emotional neglect, dissociation, isolation from family, lack of education or job skills. (Attorney General of Canada, 2013, at para. 12)

The Women's Coalition for the Abolition of Prostitution (2010, at para. 5) also attends to the characteristics that render some women vulnerable, mixing social and personal attributes: "many women are pushed into and remain in prostitution because of poverty, homelessness, low levels of education, and disability, including addictions." In their efforts to circumvent neoliberal rhetoric of choice, however, they come perilously close to a social deterministic argument that denies sex workers' agency: "the inequalities that shape and constrain women's entry into prostitution and their inability to exit" (at para. 22; emphasis added).

Feminist protectionism/maternalism segues into legal paternalism, and intersects with the interests of neoconservatives when repressive laws are embraced as an appropriate mechanism to redress social inequity—as when, for example, feminist prohibitionists push to criminalize clients and managers in what Bernstein (2010) calls "carceral feminism." Perhaps it is not surprising that this new legal moralism, cloaked in feminist sensibilities and grounded in rhetoric of harm to women, has crept into judicial reasoning. For example, the Attorney General of Ontario, citing Justice Lamer's assertion in the *Prostitution Reference* (1990) and reproduced in *R. v. Mara* (1996), argued that "the reason Parliament wants to eradicate prostitution is because it is harmful, a form of violence against women, related to men's historical dominance over women" (*Canada (Attorney General) v. Bedford*, 2012, at para. 159).[32] Though refusing to read into legislators' intent, the justices of the Appeal Court acknowledged the re-framing of sex work as violence against women when they left the door open for Parliament to "draft a bawdy-house provision that is consistent with the modern values of human dignity and equality" (*Canada (Attorney General) v. Bedford*, 2012, at para. 217).

The continued legitimation of prohibitive laws via maternalist discourse has significant implications for sex workers' lives: the laws perpetuate conditions that, rather than protecting workers from exploitation, further endanger their well-being and position them as marginal citizens. In the following sections we shift from discourse to practice and reflect on what criminalization means to sex workers in terms of occupational health and safety, social marginalization, and civic exclusion.

Criminalization and Occupational Health and Safety

Current and former sex workers (including the complainants in the *Charter* challenge), researchers, and workers' rights advocates point to the paradox of criminal laws, maintaining that these laws are directly implicated in the situational and predatory violence[33] that sex workers experience at the hands of aggressors and clients (Bruckert & Chabot, 2010; Jeffery & McDonald, 2006; Lewis & Shaver, 2006).[34] The risk of violence is not equally distributed among all sectors of the sex industry. It is generally acknowledged that in-call work, where sex workers receive clients in their homes or in establishments such as brothels, massage parlours, or holistic health centres, is the most secure and safest sector (Benoit & Millar, 2001; Jeffrey & MacDonald, 2006). Sex workers are not only familiar with the physical layout but are able to screen clients, restrict access, and implement emergency protocols. However, in-call sex workers are, as we have seen, vulnerable to being charged under the "bawdy-house" provisions (s. 210 of the *Criminal Code*). Accordingly, some sex workers make the decision to forego the greater security afforded by this labour site in order to minimize their risk of criminalization by working out-call—taking appointments and meeting in clients' hotel rooms or other locations. Here again, however, the ability to implement security protocols is restricted by workers' inability to legally hire, or work for, third parties (including drivers, agents, and managers) who may provide important security services (e.g., screening clients, safe calls, and physical protection) (Bruckert & Law, 2013). Section 212.1(j) ("living on the avails") prevents sex workers from legally engaging the services of these third parties, even for fair and agreed-upon compensation. Effectively, sections 210 and 212 "protect" sex workers by criminalizing and thereby limiting their options. At their root, these paternalistic and protectionist laws reflect and reinforce the construction of sex workers as incompetent neoliberal subjects who are incapable of making "good" choices. Unlike other participants in the labour market, sex workers are presumed to be incapable of weighing the costs and benefits of working independently, for someone else, or in collaboration with other workers.

Of course, not all sex workers are positioned to make free choices about the industry sector that they work in. Some workers are, in practice, excluded from the more lucrative and safer indoor sectors by virtue of their economic and social status. For example, working as an independent in-call worker is outside of the realm of possibility for someone who is homeless or precariously housed. These workers can choose to do sex work, but cannot choose *how* they work, defaulting to street-based sex work. As a result of these severe constraints, they are exponentially more likely to come to the attention of law enforcement; the communicating provision (s. 213) is the most regularly enforced of the statutes dealing with prostitution.[35] They also experience the highest levels of victimization.

The link between the laws and street-based sex workers' vulnerability to violence is captured well by Justice MacPherson, writing for the minority in the Ontario Appeal Court decision in *Canada (Attorney General) v. Bedford* (2012, at para. 364):

> The cumulative effect of these provisions was startling. The bawdy-house provision forbade prostitutes—practitioners of a legal occupation—from engaging in their occupation in relatively safe indoor locations, forcing them to work on the streets. Then, the communicating provision prohibited prostitutes from communicating with prospective clients, usually in idling cars, to assess clients' potential drunkenness, weirdness, or violence. The 1985 addition of the communicating provision to the existing bawdy-house and living on the avails provisions created an almost perfect storm of danger for prostitutes. Prostitutes were first driven to the streets, and then denied the one defense, communication, that allowed them to evaluate prospective clients in real time.

The "perfect storm of danger" is the direct outcome not only of workers' inability to legally communicate with clients in public, but also of their strategies to avoid (as best they can) coming to the attention of police. Workers will not "linger" beside a car and take time to assess the potential client. (Is he high or drunk? Is there a handle on the passenger side door? Is there someone in the back seat? Does he fit the description of someone on the "bad date" list?) They will solicit for clients in dark, less populated, more isolated, and unfamiliar areas, where there are few witnesses; therefore, it is unlikely that there will be help at hand if they are in distress. They will work alone and forego the deterrence strategy of collecting licence plate numbers from clients for each other.

They will communicate with clients in "code" language—a practice that can result in misunderstandings regarding, for example, services and fees.

In short, what we see are the "paradoxes they [sex workers] face in trying to maintain or maximize their safety while simultaneously minimizing their chances of being arrested" (Lewis & Shaver, 2006: 22). While violence is perhaps the most egregious by-product of the law, it is not by any means the only harmful one. We now turn to how criminalization plays out in the social and civic exclusion of sex workers.

Social Marginalization

Social exclusion and symbolic stigmatization on the basis of moral discredit plays out in the everyday lives of sex workers as they live and interact with those in their communities. They are stigmatized and excluded when their health care providers assume that they are drug addicts or lecture them about "safe sex," when children are taken from their custody because of the work that they do, when police "out" them in front of friends and family, when they are denied housing or work outside of the industry, and when they are asked to leave the coffee shop they have entered to warm themselves from the cold Canadian winter (Bruckert & Chabot, 2010).[36]

Police policies and tactics also work to exclude sex workers from public spaces and engagement in their communities. "Street sweeps" to rid neighbourhoods of sex workers, charging "known" sex workers who are seen in public while not working, and assigning prohibited "red zones,"[37] all limit sex workers' ability to live and work safely in their communities (see McGechie, 2011; see also Bruckert & Chabot, 2010). Some vocal citizens and community groups also contribute to the exclusion of sex workers, drawing on both the criminal law and its embedded stigmatic assumptions. For example, the Hintonburg Community Association (2006) in Ottawa lobbied for increased police response to prostitution in their neighbourhood on the premise that exposure to sex workers poses a danger to children, and that the sex industry leaves a dangerous physical residue of condoms and syringes on the streets of their community (under the somewhat questionable assumption that all condoms and needles originate from sex workers).[38] State regulation and criminalization provide formidable tools to those who would exclude, reducing complex issues of poverty, racialization, social inequality, and gender to criminal justice problematics. If sex workers are criminal, they, in the perception of at least some law-and-order-minded residents, inhabit a liminal space that exists outside of the general human and civil rights afforded to citizens—the rights to which such residents themselves lay such enthusiastic claim. This denial of rights also manifests in civic exclusion, to which we now turn.

Civic Exclusion

The laws around sex work, so often framed as a means of "saving" sex workers from themselves and others, not only play out in social exclusion but also undermine sex workers' ability to participate in economic life. Subsequently, the options of individuals (predominantly marginal street-based sex workers) who have been criminally convicted shrink. They also inhibit sex workers' ability to draw on the legal and civic protections available to other Canadians. Although being a sex worker is not against the law, sex workers may be hesitant to report victimization to the police because they fear that they and/or their employer may be charged with prostitution-related offences.[39] When sex workers take the risk of criminalization and public "outing" in order to report abuse, moral judgments, stigmatic assumptions about their (un)reliability, and the myth that "a hooker cannot be raped" are brought to bear; sex workers relate that when they report incidents of victimization to the police they are often disregarded, disbelieved, or dismissed as "just a whore" (Lewis & Shaver, 2006; see also Benoit & Millar, 2001; Jeffery & MacDonald, 2006; Pivot Legal Society, 2006).

Moreover, when sex workers are victims of assault that is unrelated to their work, such as domestic violence, they find that it is coded and responded to differently by police on the basis of their occupation. According to research by Currie and Gillies (2006), rather than charging the abusive partners of sex workers under assault legislation, police routinely lay charges under section 212.1(j) of the *Criminal Code* ("living on the avails"). The nature of this charge, resulting in the "outing" of their labour location, is a significant disincentive for a woman living in an abusive relationship to turn to the police, and one that detracts from the victimization she experienced: "Generic criminal laws [would] ... place the focus directly on the abusive activity itself; not on the woman's occupation or relationship" (Currie & Gillies, 2006: 55).

While legislators and lobbyists are often concerned about the potential "exploitation" of pimping or sex work management, they either fail to consider the economic exploitation and exclusion that results from the marginal status of sex work as a labour location or they simply dismiss it as inevitable. For example in the 2012 *Bedford* appeal, the Attorney General of Canada recognized this exclusion at the same time as it was normalized: "[P]rostitutes live on the fringes of society. They are isolated and therefore uniquely vulnerable to potential exploitation by others" (*Canada (Attorney General) v. Bedford*, 2012, at para. 244). This discourse renders the role of state and social policies in sex workers' exclusion invisible. The laws that protect other Canadian workers from exploitation, such as provincial labour laws and workers' compensation schemes, are not applicable to workers in the sex industry. Since, in the protectionist rhetoric of prohibitionist victim-feminists and many legislators, working in the sex industry is not considered a legitimate option and sex work is not considered legitimate work, the entire industry is outside labour protection, rendering these marginalized workers even further excluded. The legal "grey zone" in which they labour also renders their income ineligible for contribution to employment insurance, parental leave programs, and the Canada Pension Plan, further excluding workers from full citizenship. It is difficult to claim income from sex work on tax forms, resulting in difficulty demonstrating a legitimate source of income. This limits access to credit, and often prevents workers from obtaining a mortgage for a home or even from renting an apartment. It is clear that paternalistic/maternalistic and stigmatic assumptions about sex work directly perpetuate these conditions of marginality and civic exclusion.

Toward Sex Workers' Human, Social, and Civic Rights: Policy Alternatives

The current legal regime, pivoting on legal moralism/paternalism and reflecting and reinforcing archaic stigmatic assumptions, increases sex workers' vulnerability to violence and perpetuates social and civic exclusion. This begs the question of what policy model would safeguard the social and human rights of sex workers. In this final section of the chapter, we consider three alternatives to Canada's criminal-regulatory approach, drawing on international examples to illustrate the impact of partial criminalization (Sweden), legalization (Nevada, US), and decriminalization (New Zealand).

As we have already seen, the legal paternalism of the Canadian legal regime is echoed in the end-demand model promoted by prohibitionist victim-feminists who maintain, the wealth of empirical evidence to the contrary notwithstanding,[40] that "[t]he danger to women's security is a function not of the laws constraining prostitution, but of the actions of men who demand the sale of women's bodies" (Women's Coalition, 2010: 2). In Sweden we see how this carceral feminist "experiment in social engineering" (Jordon, 2012: 1) plays out.

In 1999, Sweden introduced the *Violence against Women Bill* (which introduced the *Sex Purchase Act*), which criminalizes clients, all third parties (including managers, protection, support staff), and anyone who profits from the sex work of another (landlords, partners), with the goal of abolishing the sex industry.[41] In principle, this bill posits the sellers of sexual services as victims who are therefore not criminalized; however, in practice, the sexual service providers who are, under the law, not committing a crime are nonetheless denied legal and labour rights and protections afforded to other workers (Jordan, 2012). In other words, civic exclusion is built into a model ostensibly intended to "help" or save sex workers by ensuring that they exit the industry. The law does not appear to have had the intended effect. According to independent research,[42] although the law may have displaced some workers, it has not had a noticeable impact on the number of sex workers operating in Sweden (Dodillet & Östergrem, 2011). However, the law has negatively affected sex workers. For example, sex workers are more vulnerable to violence as they "are forced to move to more hidden and thus potentially dangerous areas ... [and] to accept more risky clients who may turn out to be violent" (Jordan, 2012: 10). It has also undermined their ability to implement harm reduction strategies, not least because police interpretation of condoms as evidence of criminal activity is a significant disincentive to employing barrier protection (Dodillet & Östergrem, 2011). Workers also experience more police harassment and are (indirectly) criminalized; for example, those who refuse to testify against their clients are charged with contempt of court (Kulick, 2005). In addition, because landlords (who risk criminal sanction) "have the legal right to terminate leases and evict without notice individuals suspected of being sex workers—even when the selling of sex is not a crime" (NSWP, 2011: 6), sex workers' ability to retain housing is undermined. In short, sex workers in Sweden find themselves contending with similar challenges to their Canadian counterparts; clearly the end-demand model is not an appropriate response to sex work if one is committed to safeguarding the human rights of all citizens.

Unlike partial criminalization, legalization is much less paternalistically preoccupied with saving "at-risk" sex workers and more concerned with managing the risks that are assumed to accompany what is thought to be an unfortunate, albeit inevitable, social practice: organized crime, the nuisance of street-based work, and disease (Clamen, 2010). In principle, legalization gives sex workers access to criminal justice protection and redress, the security of labour laws, and a measure of legitimacy by virtue of licensing (Lewis & Maticka-Tyndale, 2000). In reality, however, stigmatic assumptions of sex workers as risky still permeate the regulatory systems, and the result is a hyper-regulatory approach that includes the layering of legislation (such as public health, federal or state law, and municipal regulation) that is far from the approach one would see with any other sort of employment.

For example in Nevada, US,[43] sex work is regulated under the *Nevada Revised Statutes* s. 244.345. This statute specifies that sex workers are able to work legally provided they obtain and pay for the appropriate municipal licence, undergo a police record check, are tested for STIs weekly, and always use barrier protection (failure to do so is a criminal offence). Similarly, there are labour restrictions on sex workers; they are prohibited (under criminal statute) from working as independents, soliciting on the street or in other public spaces (including casinos), or advertising on the Internet. Rather, they are obliged to work in one of the registered brothels—paying brothel fees of 40–60 percent of their earnings in addition to room and board. Tellingly, sex workers in Nevada, who are obliged to work under the control of third parties, are excluded from the protection afforded by labour laws because they are categorized as "independent contractors." In short, we see that Nevada's administrative laws, backed up by the potential for criminal sanctions, allow the state to regulate who can, and who cannot, be a sex worker and the conditions under which prostitution may occur (including where and when). As Sullivan (2010: 87) noted, this is a decidedly neoliberal approach in that it endeavours to realize "better practical governance of the sex industry."

Often conflated with legalization, the decriminalization of the sex industry relies on significantly different assumptions. Where hyper-regulatory legalized regimes assume a host of negative side effects (risks) that require management through legal restrictions and threatened sanctions, decriminalization, as it is practiced in New Zealand for instance, utilizes minimal regulatory requirements, comparable to any other service industry. The *New Zealand Prostitution Reform Act* of 2003, which decriminalized adult prostitution, permits sex workers to operate as individual service providers or in small worker-run collectives without a licence—individuals operating managed brothels that employ five or more sex workers must apply for an operator certificate and pay the associated fee. The locations of brothels and advertisements are determined by municipal bylaws, as with other businesses. There are no restrictions provided in the law for street prostitution. Both sex workers and clients are implicated in requirements for "safer sex" practices and are equally responsibilized for the use of barrier protection.

While New Zealand has certainly taken a large step forward in de-stigmatizing sex work and recognizing it as a legitimate form of labour, it is not a panacea. Laws against procuring remain as a last vestige of paternalistic/maternalistic protectionism in this decriminalized regime. Similarly, there are faint echoes of criminalization in the fact that violations of the "safer sex" provisions may result in criminal convictions for both sex workers and their clients, as opposed to the civil penalties appropriate to generic industry regulation. These issues notwithstanding, the New Zealand model of decriminalization is respectful of the agency of individuals who choose to labour in the sex industry and eschews reductionist or "saving" rhetoric.

Conclusion

The persistence of Victorian moralism, legal paternalism, and feminist maternalism have long stagnated the legal framework surrounding prostitution in Canada. The powerful convergence of these discourses has silenced the lived experiences of individuals working in the sex industry, effectively negating their assertions of agency and their resistance to oppressive legislation as "false consciousness" or industry "spin." The ideological commitment to legal paternalism and feminist maternalism continues despite the overwhelming empirical evidence presented in *Bedford* that the victimization of sex workers is, in large part, a product of the laws created to "save" them. Not only do the federal and provincial governments persist in appealing the rulings, but second wave feminist coalitions, fundamentalist Christian groups, and decidedly anti-feminist organizations such as REAL Women of Canada are intervening in support of a legal framework that, as we have seen in this chapter, harms sex workers.

The archaic rhetoric of conservatives, the Christian right, and prohibitionist victim-feminists notwithstanding, we are poised at a precipice of change. With the December 20, 2013, ruling in favour of the complainants (*Canada [Attorney General] v. Bedford*, 2013), the status quo is no longer acceptable and the laws will change. At the time of writing, Canada's new legal strategy to address prostitution has not yet been determined. Thus, we are turning to the experiences of other nations for direction. Careful analyses of international approaches to sex work suggest that although the models are diverse, paternalistic and moralistic rhetoric underlie many approaches and the consequences for workers in the industry are similar. As long as the approach to sex work is criminalized—regardless of whether criminalization comes in the form of the proverbial "stick" to ensure workers comply with the regulation (as in Nevada, US), or if laws outlaw the selling of sexual services or make it impossible to work within the confines of the law (as in Canada), or if they selectively criminalize clients and managers (as in Sweden)—sex workers will continue to confront the same challenges. Clearly we need to move beyond criminal law. While it is not a panacea for stigma nor for moralistic judgment, decriminalization, supported by appropriate labour rights and full civic inclusion, is the only model that can reduce violence against sex workers, protect their human and civil rights, and ensure their full inclusion in society.

Notes

1 In this article we focus our attention on what is legally referred to as prostitution. There is, of course, a range of sexual commerce, including pornography, phone sex, erotic dance, and webcam services, that operate in a "grey" zone.

2 Sex workers can only avoid contravening the laws if they work out-call, do not communicate in public about services, and do not use their own home or another location (such as a hotel room or client's home) on more than two occasions.

3 "Slut walks" call attention to the ongoing manifestations of rape culture. Occurring in cities around the world, the walks originated in protest of the victim-responsibilization/blaming "advice" offered by Constable Michael Sanguinetti, a Toronto Police officer, to students at York University on April 3, 2011, when he suggested that "women should avoid dressing like sluts" to decrease their risk of sexual assault.

4 It is important to appreciate that echoes remain even in 2012—the age of consent for anal intercourse is 18 (rather than 16 as it is for vaginal intercourse) unless partners are legally married (s. 159 of the *Criminal Code*); and anal sex involving more than two participants is prohibited under s. 159.3(a).

5 For more on this argument, see Bruckert and Chabot (2010); Bruckert and Hannem (2013).

6 The former discourse is associated with the police, neighbourhood associations, and the Christian right; the latter with radical (prohibitionist) feminists.

7 Hannem (2012) argues that when stigmatized attributes become linked to notions of "risk," which in turn justify intrusive interventions to reduce said risk, "structural stigma" becomes embedded in legal and institutional policy. We have previously examined the phenomenon of structural stigma in the context of Canada's prostitution laws (Bruckert & Hannem, 2013).

8 Section 211 of the *Criminal Code* also criminalizes those who transport individuals to bawdy houses.

9 The legal regulation of sex work is not restricted to sections 210–213 of the *Criminal Code*. For example, in addition to facing *Criminal Code* charges related to sex work, street-based sex workers are also regularly charged with a variety of other offences, including jay walking, loitering, mischief, vagrancy, and trespassing—municipal and provincial regulations that are rarely employed to police the general public. This hyper-regulation means that sex workers are penalized and fined for behaviours that are generally not criminalized, and thus, this marginal population faces the additional burden of economic sanctions (Bruckert & Chabot, 2010). In-door sex workers are also subject to municipal regulation in the form of licensing and zoning (van der Meulen & Durisin, 2008).

10 Summary conviction offences are punishable by "a fine of not more than two thousand dollars or to imprisonment for six months or to both," as stated in s. 785.1 of the *Criminal Code*. These offences can be tried in a lower court and with modified legal proceedings.

11 Section 197 of the *Criminal Code* specifies that a place "includes any place, whether or not (a) it is covered or enclosed, (b) it is used permanently or temporarily, or (c) any person has an exclusive right of user with respect to it."

12 There is a presumption of guilt in reverse-onus offences that necessitates that individuals charged under these provisions prove they are not guilty.

13 In other words, individuals who provide goods or services (grocers, clothing, car dealerships, child minders, etc.) not directly related to the sex worker's labour are outside the purview of the law.

14 Services provided by such third parties include screening clients, security, transportation, advertising, and transportation.

15 The justices of the Appeal Court of Canada in *Bedford* (*Canada (Attorney General) v. Bedford*, 2012, at paras. 232–235) relied on the Shaw principle of parasitism, which states that an individual is living parasitically on the avails of prostitution if "he was paid by prostitutes for goods or services supplied by him to them for the purpose of their prostitution which he would not supply but for the fact that they were prostitutes" (*Shaw v. Director of Public Prosecutions*, 1961, at para. 5). They noted that in *R. v. Barrow* (2001) the accused was convicted under s. 212.1(j) of the *Criminal Code* even though she, in exchange

for one-third of the fees, provided useful services and did not pressure the sex workers she hired for the escort agency she owned and operated. There are many cases where this legal principle has played out—see, for example, *R. v. Lukacko* (2002) and *R. v. Juneja* (2009).

16 The status of being a common prostitute was illegal, rather than the individual's actions.

17 In this section, "public place" includes "any place to which the public have access as of right or by invitation, express or implied, and any motor vehicle located in a public place or in any place open to public view" (R.S., 1985, c. C-46, s. 213; R.S., 1985, c. 51).

18 This is not the first time that the prostitution laws have been challenged on the basis of the *Charter*. In 1990 a freedom of expression challenge was rejected by the Supreme Court of Canada in the *Prostitution Reference*, [1990] 1 S.C.R. 1123.

19 The complainants are specifically challenging ss. 210, 212.1(j), and 213.1(c) of the *Criminal Code*.

20 While prohibitionists self-identify as feminists, the denial of women's right to choose what to do with their bodies in sexual commerce is certainly contrary to feminism's traditional commitment to women's choice in, for example, the right to have an abortion.

21 Laws that criminalize the purchase of sexual services and "living on the avails of another's prostitution" (pimping) are assumed to eradicate demand for prostitution. It is important to appreciate that in Canada we already have laws that serve this "end-demand" philosophy—clients are criminalized under ss. 210.2 and 213 of the *Criminal Code*. Moreover, "living on the avails" and other forms of procuring are criminalized under s. 212.

22 In some ways this alignment echoes of the pornography "sex wars" of the 1980s when radical feminists found themselves on the same side as conservatives in their support of censorship (Kahn, 2014).

23 Since coming to power in 2006, the Conservative government of Canada under Stephen Harper has introduced a number of measures that erode the fragile gains women have made toward equality. These include: (1) cutting the operating budget of Status of Women Canada by 38 percent, resulting in the closure of 12 of 16 offices, while removing "gender equality" from its mandate and restricting the organization's ability to fund programs or organizations that engage in advocacy for women's rights and equity, and lobbying for legal changes (which, not incidentally, resulted in cuts to funding for many women's shelters, which traditionally combine practical services with lobbying to end violence against women); (2) cancelling the Court Challenges Program, which provided funding to groups representing women and minorities to challenge legal rulings and legislation that violate equality rights under the *Charter of Rights and Freedoms* (for more detailed analyses, see Canadian Feminist Alliance for International Alliance & Canadian Labour Congress, 2010); (3) refusing to allow Canadian funds to pay for access to safe medical abortion for women in developing nations under the G8 Maternal Health funding scheme (Taber, 2010); and (4) failing to address the need for a national, affordable child care strategy.

24 The reference here is to feminist criminologists who argued that women offenders were ignored in criminology as simply "too few to count"—indeed, this is the title of a 1990 book by Ellen Adelberg and Claudia Currie.

25 See, for example, Barry (1979); Hoigard and Finstad (1992); James (1977); Jeffreys (1985, 1999); Millet (1973); O'Hara (1985); Wilson (1983); Wynter (1987).

26 de Marneffe (2010) has also argued, convincingly, that paternalism is at the root of the American criminal prohibition of prostitution. However, contrary to our point, he maintains that these paternalistic laws are justifiable, drawing on the radical victim-feminist discourse of sex work as harmful to women.

27 See, for example, CLES (2008); Farley (2004); Lakeman, Lee, and Joy (2004).

28 Ekberg is Special Advisor on issues of prostitution and trafficking in women at the Swedish Division for Gender Equality.

29 While there are certainly instances in which prostitution and/or the conditions of sex work are experienced by women as exploitative, the blanketing of all diverse experiences in the sex industry as gendered sexual violence obscures the realities of those women whose engagement in sexual commerce is neither coerced nor particularly unpleasant.

30 *Attorney General of Canada et al. v. Terri Jean Bedford et al.*

31 *Canada (Attorney General) v. Bedford,* [2013] SCC 72.

32 Justice Lamer was writing for himself, and his position was not accepted by the other judges of the Supreme Court.

33 Situational violence results from conflict between sex workers and their clients over, for example, disputes about services or costs. By contrast, predatory violence is premeditated. Aggressors may pose as clients, but the intent is not to purchase service but inflict harm. While other workers are also vulnerable to violence at work (i.e., nurses, teachers, convenience store clerks), sex workers are particularly vulnerable to predatory violence because of their marginal social location and the presumption that it will not be responded to by the authorities (which allows predators to go unpunished). See Lowman (2000) for more on this issue.

34 We unpack this relationship in some detail later in the chapter.

35 Although only 5 to 20 percent of the sex industry is street-based (Parliament of Canada, 2006: 5), it is this sector that is subject to the most vigorous policing and that experiences the most violence.

36 Many workers in the sex industry, in an effort to shield themselves from judgment, rejection, or salvation efforts, manage their public identity through nondisclosure, or what Goffman (1963) referred to as "passing." This strategy renders these individuals unable to discuss their occupation and its associated stresses with family or friends. The resulting emotional and social isolation (Blissbomb, 2010; Trautner & Collett, 2010) compounds feelings of exclusion.

37 "Red zones," also referred to as "boundary restrictions," are precisely delimited areas, defined by four streets, from which sex workers are excluded either as a probation condition (imposed by the courts) or as a "promise to appear" condition (imposed by the police). Failure to comply is considered a breach of probation and can result in criminal charges.

38 Another Ottawa area community group, Together for Vanier (n.d.), advises residents, "[A]lthough it is not illegal to stand on the street, if you suspect a prostitute is working in your neighbourhood you should report it."

39 This situation works in the interests of clients who can, and do, threaten to report the establishment to the police if they do not receive the services they desire.

40 See, for example, Bruckert and Chabot (2010); Jeffery and MacDonald (2006); Lewis and Shaver (2006); Lowman (2000).

41 Sweden is not the only country with this model—it has also been adopted by Norway.

42 A government of Sweden report that has been largely discredited, not only on the basis of methodological failings (Jordan, 2012) but also because of its predetermined agenda—"One starting point of our work has been that the purchase of sexual services is to remain criminalized" (Skarhed, 2010: 4)—takes a more careful position. Acknowledging that there is no evidence of a decrease, the authors "read" into the lack of increase, stating: "[I]t is reasonable to assume that prostitution would also have increased in Sweden if we had not had a ban on the purchase of sexual services" (Skarhed, 2010: 8).

43 Other countries that have legalized systems include Germany, the Netherlands, and a number of Australian states.

References

Attorney General of Canada. (2013). *Appellant Factum—Attorney General of Canada.* Retrieved from www.scc-csc.gc.ca/factums-memoires/34788/FM010_Appellant_Attorney-General-of-Canada.pdf

Barry, K. (1979). *Female Sexual Slavery.* New York: NYU Press.

Benoit, C., & Millar, A. (2001). *Dispelling Myths and Understanding Realities: Working Conditions, Health Status and Exiting Experiences of Sex Workers.* Vancouver: Prostitutes Empowerment, Education and Resource Society (PEERS).

Bernstein, E. (2010). "Militarized humanitarianism meets carceral feminism: The politics of sex, rights, and freedom in contemporary anti-trafficking campaigns." *Signs: Journal of Women in Culture and Society*, 36(1): 45–71.

Blissbomb, L. (2010). "Sex work for the soul: Negotiating stigma as a feminist activist and closeted sex worker." *Wagadu*, 8: 292–311.

Bruckert, C., & Chabot, F. (2010). *Challenges: Ottawa Area Sex Workers Speak Out.* Ottawa: POWER (Prostitutes of Ottawa/Gatineau Work, Educate and Resist).

Bruckert, C., & Hannem, S. (2012). "To serve and protect? Structural stigma, social profiling, and the abuse of police power in Ottawa." In E. van der Meulen, E. Durisin, & V. Love, eds., *Selling Sex: Canadian Academics, Advocates, and Sex Workers in Dialogue*. Vancouver: UBC Press.

Bruckert, C., & Hannem, S. (2013). "Rethinking the prostitution debates: Transcending structural stigma in systematic responses to sex work." *Canadian Journal of Law and Society*, 28(1): 43–63.

Bruckert, C., & Law, T. (2013). *Beyond Pimps, Procurers and Parasites: Third Parties in the Incall and Outcall Sex Industry*. Ottawa: Management Project.

Canadian Feminist Alliance for International Action & Canadian Labour Congress. (2010). *Reality Check: Women in Canada and the Beijing Declaration and Platform for Action*. Retrieved from www.canadianlabour.ca/sites/default/files/2010-02-22-Canada-Beijing15-NGO-Report-EN.pdf

Clamen, J. (2010). *Taking Action*. Ottawa: POWER.

CLES. (2008). *Keys to a World Free of Prostitution*. Montreal: Concertation des lutes contre l'exploitation sexuelle.

Conservative Party of Canada. (2013). *Policy Resolutions—2013 Conservative Convention*. Retrieved from www.scribd.com/doc/179616134/Policy-Resolutions-2013-Conservative-Convention

Currie, N., & Gillies, K. (2006). *Bound by the Law: How Canada's Protectionist Policies in the Areas of Both Rape and Prostitution Limit Women's Choices, Agency and Activities*. Unpublished Manuscript. Ottawa: Status of Women Canada.

de Marneffe, P. (2010). *Liberalism and Prostitution*. Oxford: Oxford University Press.

Devlin, P. (1965). *The Enforcement of Morals*. London: Oxford University Press.

Dodillet, S., & Östergren, P. (2011). *The Swedish Sex Purchase Act: Claimed Success and Documented Effects*. Retrieved from http://myweb.dal.ca/mgoodyea/Documents/CSWRP/CSWRPEUR/The%20Swedish%20Sex%20Purchase%20Act.%20Claimed%20Success%20and%20Documented%20Effects%20Dodillet%20&%20Ostagren%20May%202011.pdf

Dworkin, G. (1972). "Paternalism." *The Monist*, 56(1): 64–84.

Farley, M. (2004). "'Bad for the body, bad for the heart': Prostitution harms women even if legalized or decriminalized." *Violence Against Women*, 10(10): 1087–1125.

Farley, M., & Kelly, V. (2000). "Prostitution: A critical review of the medical and social sciences literature." *Women & Criminal Justice*, 11(4): 29–64.

Goffman, E. (1963). *Stigma: Notes on the Management of Spoiled Identity*. New York: Prentice-Hall.

Hannem, S. (2012). "Theorizing stigma and the politics of resistance: Symbolic and structural stigma in everyday life." In S. Hannem & C. Bruckert, eds., *Stigma Revisited: The Implications of the Mark* (pp. 10–28). Ottawa: University of Ottawa Press.

Hart, H.L.A. (1963). *Law, Liberty and Morality*. Stanford: Stanford University Press.

Hintonburg Community Association. (2006). *Dispelling the Myths: Street Level Prostitution*. Ottawa: HCA.

Hoigard, C., & Finstad, L. (1992). *Backstreets: Prostitution, Money and Love*. University Park: Pennsylvania University Press.

James, J. (1977). "The prostitute as victim." In J.R. Chapman & M.J. Gates, eds., *The Victimization of Women*. Beverly Hills: Sage.

Jeffrey, L.A., & MacDonald, G. (2006). *Sex Workers in the Maritimes Talk Back*. Vancouver: UBC Press.

Jeffrey, L.A., & Sullivan, G. (2009). "Canadian sex work policy for the 21st century: Enhancing rights and safety, lessons from Australia." *Canadian Political Science Review*, 3(1): 57–76.

Jeffreys, S. (1985). "Prostitution." In D. Rhodes & S. McNeil, eds., *Women Against Violence Against Women* (pp. 59–69). London: Onlywomen Press.

Jeffreys, S. (1999). "The sexual revolution was for men." In R.A. Nye, ed., *Sexuality*. Oxford: Oxford University Press.

Jordan, A. (2012). *The Swedish Law to Criminalize Clients: A Failed Experiment in Social Engineering*. Washington: Center for Human Rights and Humanitarian Law.

Khan, U. (2014). *Vicarious Kinks: Sadomasochism in the Socio-Legal Imaginary*. Toronto: University of Toronto Press.

Kulick, D. (2005). "Swedish Model." Paper presented at the United Nations Commission on the Status of Women Conference, Beijing. Retrieved from www.globalrights.org/site/DocServer/Don_Kulick_on_the_Swedish_Model.pdf

Lakeman, L., Lee, A., & Joy, S. (2004). "Resisting the promotion of prostitution in Canada: A view from Vancouver's Rape Relief and Women's Shelter." In C. Stark & R. Whisnant, eds., *Not for Sale: Feminists Resisting Prostitution and Pornography* (pp. 210–251). North Melbourne: Spifex.

Lewis, J., & Maticka-Tyndale, E. (2000). "Licensing sex work: Public policy and women's lives." *Canadian Public Policy*, 26: 437–449.

Lewis, J., & Shaver, F. (2006). *Safety, Security, and the Well-Being of Sex Workers: A Report Submitted to the House of Commons Subcommittee on Solicitation Laws*. Windsor: Sex Trade and Advocacy (STAR).

Lowman, J. (2000). "Violence and the outlaw status of (street) prostitution in Canada." *Violence Against Women*, 6(9): 987–1011.

McGechie, H. (2011). *The Impacts of Release Conditions on Criminalized Sex Workers in Ottawa*. Ottawa: Salvation Army.

Millet, K. (1973). *The Prostitution Papers: A Candid Dialogue*. New York: Avon.

Murphy, J.G. (1966). "Another look at legal moralism." *Ethics*, 77(1): 50–56.

NSWP (Global Network of Sex Work Projects). (2011). "The criminalization of clients." Briefing Paper #2. Retrieved from www.nswp.org/sites/nswp.org/files/Criminalisation%20of%20Clients-c.pdf

O'Hara, M. (1985). "Prostitution: Towards a feminist analysis and strategy." In D. Rhodes & S. McNeil, eds., *Women Against Violence Against Women*. London: Onlywomen Press.

Parliament of Canada. (2006). *Report of the Standing Committee on Justice and Human Rights—The Challenge of Change: A Study of Canada's Criminal Prostitution Laws*. Ottawa: Government of Canada.

Pivot Legal Society. (2004). *Voices for Dignity: A Call to End the Harms Caused by Canada's Sex Trade Laws*. Vancouver: Pivot.

Pivot Legal Society. (2006). *Beyond Decriminalization: Sex Work, Human Rights and a new Framework for Law Reform*. Vancouver: Pivot. Retrieved from www.pivotlegal.org/pivot-points/publications/beyond-decriminalization

POWER. (2011). *The Toolkit: Ottawa Area Sex Workers Speak Out*. Ottawa: POWER.

Raymond, J. (2003). "10 reasons not to legalize prostitution." *Coalition Against the Trafficking of Women (CATW)*. Retrieved from http://action.web.ca/home/catw/attach/Ten%20Reasons%20for%20Not%20Legalizing%20Prostitution.pdf

Skarhed, A. (2010). *Evaluation of the Ban on the Purchase of Sexual Services*. Stockholm: Government of Sweden.

Smith, J. (2011, October 22). "Swedish model offers a solution." Readers' Letters, *Toronto Star*. Retrieved from www.thestar.com/opinion/letters_to_the_editors/2011/10/22/swedish_model_offers_a_solution.html

STELLA. (2005). *Designing Our Future, A Sex Worker's Rendezvous*. eXXXpressions Forum XXX Proceedings: Designing Our Future, A Sex Worker's Rendezvous. Montreal: Public Health Agency of Canada.

Sullivan, B. (2010). "When (some) prostitution is legal: The impact of law reform on sex work in Australia." *Journal of Law and Society*, 37(1): 85–104.

Taber, J. (2010, May 11). "PM defends excluding abortion from G8 plan." *The Globe and Mail*. Retrieved from www.theglobeandmail.com/news/politics/ottawa-notebook/pm-defends-excluding-abortion-from-g8-plan/article4353033/

Together for Vanier. (n.d.). *Prostitution*. Retrieved from www.ensemblepourvanier.com/en/togetherforvanier/prostitution.php

Trautner, N., and Collett, J. (2010). "Students who strip: The benefits of alternate ideates for managing stigma." *Symbolic Interaction*, 33(2): 257–279.

van der Meulen, E., & Durisin, E.M. (2008). "Why decriminalize? How Canada's municipal and federal regulations increase sex workers' vulnerability." *Canadian Journal of Women and the Law*, 20: 289–311.

Wallace, B. (2011). *The Ban on Purchasing Sex in Sweden: The So-Called "Swedish Model" of Prostitution Licensing Authority*. Queensland, New Zealand: Office of the Prostitution Licensing Authority. Retrieved from www.traffickingpolicyresearchproject.org/PurchasingSexSweden.pdf

Wilson, E. (1983). *What Is to Be Done About Violence Against Women?* Harmondsworth: Penguin.

Women's Coalition for the Abolition of Prostitution. (2010). *Factum of the Interveners, Canadian Association of Sexual Assault Centres, Native Women's Association of Canada, Canadian Association of Elizabeth Fry Societies, Action Ontarienne contre la violence faite aux femmes, La concertation des luttes contre l'exploitation sexuelle, Le regroupement Quebecois des centres d'aide et du luttes contre les agressions á caractére sexuel, and Vancouver Rape Relief Society, Intervening as the Women's Coalition for the Abolition of Prostitution.* Retrieved from www.abolitionprostitution.ca/downloads/supreme-court-of-canada-factum-of-intervner.pdf

Wynter, S. (1987). "Whisper." In F. Delacoste & P. Alexander, eds., *Sex Work: Writings by Women in the Sex Industry* (pp. 266–270). Pittsburgh: Cleis Press.

Legal Cases and Statutes

Bedford v. Canada (Attorney General), [2010] ONSC 4264.

Canada (Attorney General) v. Bedford, [2012] ONCA 186.

Canada (Attorney General) v. Bedford, [2013] SCC 72.

Civil Marriage Act, S.C. 2005, c. 33.

Constitution Act, 1982 [en. by the Canada Act 1982 (U.K.), c. 11, s. 1], pt. 1 (Canadian Charter of Rights and Freedoms).

Criminal Code of Canada R.S.C., 1985, c.-46.

Hutt v. R., (1978) [SCC 82 D.L.R. (3d) 95].

Nevada Revised Statutes, NRS 244.345.

New Zealand Prostitution Reform Act, Public Act 2003 No. 28.

Prostitution Reference, [1990] 1 S.C.R. 1123.

R. v. Barrow (2001), 54 O.R. (3d) 417.

R. v. Downey, [1992] 2 S.C.R. 10.

R. v. Juneja, 2009 ABQB 243 (CanLII).

R. v. Lukacko, 2002 CanLII 451577 (ONCA).

R v. Mara, [1996] 27 O.R. (3d) 643 (C.A.), affirmed [1997] 2 S.C.R. 630.

Sex Purchase Act, Chapter 6 of the *Swedish Penal Code*, 1962, SFS 1962: 70.

Shaw v. Director of Public Prosecutions, (1961)[1962] A.C. 220 (H.L.).

Contributor Biographies

Gillian Balfour

Gillian Balfour is Associate Professor in the Department of Sociology at Trent University. Her main research interests include examining the practice of law as a social act that is constrained and enabled by socio-political interests of "law and order" and professional codes of conduct, and how identities of victims and offenders and the meaning of violence are encoded with stereotypes of Whiteness, Indianness, dangerousness, poverty, heterosexuality, femininity, and masculinity. She is particularly interested in law reforms in the areas of domestic and sexual violence, and Aboriginal peoples in the criminal justice system. She is the co-author of *The Power to Criminalize* and co-editor of *Criminalized Women,* both with Fernwood Press.

Chris Bruckert

Chris Bruckert is Full Professor in the Department of Criminology at the University of Ottawa. She has devoted herself to researching various sectors of the Canadian adult sex industry through the lens of feminist labour theory.

Angela Cameron

Angela Cameron is an Associate Professor at the Faculty of Law Common Law section at the University of Ottawa. Dr. Cameron's research is generally in the area of social justice, with a particular focus on the equality interests of women. Dr. Cameron's research areas include criminal law, restorative justice, property law, reproductive technologies law, family law, legal theory, sociological approaches to law, and human rights law.

Colleen Cardinal

Colleen Cardinal is Plains Cree from Saddle Lake Cree Nation, Treaty 6 territory (Alberta). As young girls, she and her sisters were "adopted out" into a non-Indigenous household in Ontario. She's currently producing a documentary about the "Sixties Scoop"–era of child welfare policy marked by forced removal of Indigenous children and disconnection from land, language, family, and traditions. Colleen is also involved in grassroots organizing to end violence against Indigenous communities, especially missing and murdered Indigenous women—having herself lost a sister and a sister-in-law to murder.

Vicki Chartrand

Vicki Chartrand is an Assistant Professor in the Department of Sociology at Bishop's University in Sherbrooke, Quebec. Her research interests include penal and colonial links; gendered, racialized, and institutional violence; and collaborative methodologies. Vicki has over 15 years' experience as a grassroots advocate in the anti-violence and anti-penal fields.

Emma Cunliffe

Emma Cunliffe is Associate Professor in the Faculty of Law at the University of British Columbia. Dr. Cunliffe's research focuses on scientific and behavioural evidence in child homicide trials, and more generally considers the interplay between expert (non-legal) knowledges, cultural knowledges, and legal reasoning. She is the author of *Murder, Medicine and Motherhood* (Hart Publishing, 2011), which examines the case of Kathleen Folbigg, a mother who was convicted of murdering her children based on misleading medical evidence.

Sheryl C. Fabian

Sheryl C. Fabian is Senior Lecturer in the School of Criminology at Simon Fraser University. Her main research interests include criminal harassment, intimate partner violence, research methods, policy analysis, and academic dishonesty. She is co-editor of the forthcoming book *Demarginalizing Voices: Commitment, Emotion, and Action in Qualitative Research* (UBC Press).

Kristen Gilchrist

Kristen Gilchrist self-identifies as a non-Indigenous woman with Scottish, Welsh, French-Canadian, and Ojibway relations, living on un-surrendered Algonquin lands. She's working on a doctorate in Sociology at Carleton University, is a survivor of sexual violence(s), co-founder of Families of Sisters in Spirit (FSIS), and ally in Ottawa's sex workers' rights movement.

Stacey Hannem

Stacey Hannem is Associate Professor in the Department of Criminology at the Brantford campus of Wilfrid Laurier University. She has published in the areas of release and re-integration for sexual offenders, restorative justice, and families affected by incarceration, and she is co-editor of *Stigma Revisited: Implications of the Mark* (University of Ottawa Press, 2010). Since 2008, she has acted as chair of the Policy Review Committee for the Canadian Criminal Justice Association.

Rebecca Jesseman

Rebecca Jesseman obtained her MA in Criminology from the University of Ottawa, and continues her affiliation as a sessional professor. Rebecca's interest in drug policy began with her role as a research assistant with the Senate Special Committee on Illicit Drugs in 2001. She has since worked at Health Canada and Public Safety Canada, and is currently a Research and Policy Analyst with the Canadian Centre on Substance Abuse.

Holly Johnson

Holly Johnson is Associate Professor of Criminology at the University of Ottawa. Her research on violence against women spans three decades. She has authored three texts and numerous peer-reviewed book chapters and articles on this topic, including *Violence Against Women in Canada: Research and Policy Perspectives* (Oxford, 2011) with Myrna Dawson, and the UN guidelines on statistical surveys on violence against women.

Florence Kellner

Florence Kellner is Professor Emeritus in the Department of Sociology at Carleton University. Her research interests include the epidemiology of substance use and abuse, with a special focus on alcohol; identification of Canadian trends in the use of psychoactive drugs; the phenomenology of addiction; and concepts of health and illness.

Amar Khoday

Amar Khoday is an Assistant Professor of Law at the University of Manitoba's Robson Hall Faculty of Law. He teaches and researches in the area of criminal law and procedure. His research also examines the intersections between law and resistance, as well as law and popular culture.

Jennifer M. Kilty

Jennifer M. Kilty is Associate Professor of Criminology and the Social Sciences of Health at the University of Ottawa. She adopts a feminist perspective to examine different topics that affect women at the intersection of health and law, including self-injurious behaviour in carceral settings, violence and victimization, drug use, medicalization, pregnancy and motherhood, and more recently, the criminalization of HIV/AIDS nondisclosure. She is the lead editor of the forthcoming book *Demarginalizing Voices: Commitment, Emotion, and Action in Qualitative Research* (UBC Press).

Kirsten Kramar

Kirsten Kramar is Associate Professor and Chair of the Department of Sociology at the University of Winnipeg. Her main research interests examine issues that affect women at the intersection of health and law, namely pregnancy, motherhood, and infanticide, and obscenity and pornography debates. She is the author and/or editor of five books, including *Unwilling Mothers, Unwanted Babies: Infanticide in Canada*, *Sex and the Supreme Court: Obscenity and Indecency Law in Canada*, *Undressing the Canadian State: The Politics of Porn from Hicklin to Butler*, and *Wife Assault and the Canadian Criminal Justice System*.

Ashley McConnell

Ashley McConnell recently graduated from the University of Ottawa with an MA in Criminology and a specialization in Women's Studies. Her main research interests include intimate partner violence and women offenders. She is currently working in the public service.

Emily K. Paradis

Emily K. Paradis is Senior Research Associate in the Faculty of Social Work at the University of Toronto. An activist, researcher, advocate, and front-line service provider with women facing homelessness for 25 years, Dr. Paradis's scholarly work focuses on homelessness among women and families, human rights dimensions of homelessness and housing, community-based research and action with marginalized groups, and participatory interventions to address socio-spatial inequalities between and within urban neighbourhoods. She takes up these problematics via a framework that is feminist, anti-racist, and decolonizing. Since 2008 she has collaborated on the National Film Board project HIGHRISE, a multi-media interventionist documentary project examining life in vertical communities of the global suburbs. She is currently Project Manager of the Neighbourhood Change Research Partnership, a seven-year study of neighbourhood inequality, diversity, and change in Vancouver, Calgary, Winnipeg, Toronto, Montreal, and Halifax. Dr. Paradis received her PhD in 2009 from the Ontario Institute for Studies in Education at the University of Toronto.

Mythili Rajiva

Mythili Rajiva is an Associate Professor in the Institute of Women's Studies at the University of Ottawa. Her research focuses on girlhood, the Canadian South Asian diaspora, and racialized identities, and has appeared in such journals as *Women's Studies International Forum*, *Girlhood Studies*, and *Feminist Media Studies*. She is also co-editor of *Reena Virk: Critical Perspectives on a Canadian Murder* (Women's Press, 2010).

Camilla A. Sears

Camilla A. Sears is an Assistant Professor in the Department of Sociology and Anthropology at Thompson Rivers University. She received her PhD from the School of Criminology at Simon Fraser University. Her doctoral work explored the impact of neoliberal policies on the regulation of sex and the body. Her other research interests include reality TV and post-feminist media culture. She has published articles in *Feminist Media Studies* and *Genders*.

Index

Page references ending in n refer to notes.